CAIAPHAS THE HIGH PRIEST

Studies on Personalities of the New Testament
D. Moody Smith, Series Editor

CAIAPHAS
THE HIGH PRIEST

Adele Reinhartz

Fortress Press
Minneapolis

CAIAPHAS THE HIGH PRIEST

First Fortress Press edition 2013
This book was originally published in hardcover by the University of South Carolina Press.

Copyright © 2011 University of South Carolina

All rights reserved. Except for brief quotations in critical articles or reviews, no part of this book may be reproduced in any manner without prior written permission from the publisher. Visit http://www.augsburgfortress.org/copyrights or write to Permissions, Augsburg Fortress, Box 1209, Minneapolis, MN 55440.

ISBN 978-0-8006-9940-6

Unless otherwise identified, scripture quotations are from the New Revised Standard Version Bible, copyright © 1989 by the Division of Christian Education of the National Council of the Churches of Christ in the USA. Used by permission. All rights reserved.

Cover art: *The Trial of Christ from Die Bile in Bildern (The Bible in Pictures)*, Julius Schnorr von Carolsfeld
Cover design: Justin Korhonen

The Library of Congress has catalogued the hardcover edition of this book as follows:

Reinhartz, Adele, 1953–
  Caiaphas the high priest / Adele Reinhartz.
    p. cm. — (Studies on personalities of the New Testament)
  "This project had its genesis in a paper delivered at a conference at the Institute for Advanced Studies at Hebrew University in March 2001"—Pref.
Includes bibliographical references and indexes.
  ISBN 978-1-57003-946-1 (cloth : alk. paper)
  1. Caiaphas, High priest, 1st cent. 1. Title.
BS2452.C34R45 2011
296.4'95092—DC22
[B]   2011000901

The paper used in this publication meets the minimum requirements of American National Standard for Information Sciences—Permanence of Paper for Printed Library Materials, ANSI Z329.48-1984.

Manufactured in the U.S.A.

For Barry, as always

מִזְמוֹר לְדָוִד יְהֹוָה מִי־יָגוּר בְּאׇהֳלֶךָ מִי־יִשְׁכֹּן בְּהַר קׇדְשֶׁךָ׃
הוֹלֵךְ תָּמִים וּפֹעֵל צֶדֶק וְדֹבֵר אֱמֶת בִּלְבָבוֹ׃
לֹא־רָגַל ׀ עַל־לְשֹׁנוֹ לֹא־עָשָׂה לְרֵעֵהוּ רָעָה וְחֶרְפָּה לֹא־נָשָׂא עַל־קְרֹבוֹ׃

Lord, who may dwell in your sanctuary? Who may live on your holy hill? He whose walk is blameless and who does what is righteous, who speaks the truth from his heart and has no slander on his tongue, who does his neighbor no wrong and casts no slur on others.

Psalm 15:1–3

CONTENTS

List of Illustrations *viii*
Preface *ix*

    Introduction: O Caiaphas, Where Art Thou? *1*
1. Caiaphas in Context *11*
2. Caiaphas in the New Testament *24*
3. Caiaphas in Early Christian Imagination *52*
4. Caiaphas in Literature *73*
5. Caiaphas on Stage *96*
6. Caiaphas on Screen *124*
7. Caiaphas in Historiography *144*
8. Caiaphas in History *165*
9. Face to Face with Caiaphas *180*
    Afterword *202*

Notes *207*
Bibliography *227*
Index of Ancient Sources *241*
Index of Modern Authors *247*
Subject Index *249*

ILLUSTRATIONS

Giotto di Bondone, *Christ before Caiaphas* 182
Duccio di Buoninsegna, *Christ before Caiaphas* 184
The Salvin Hours 185
Gerrit van Honthorst, *Christ before the High Priest* 186
At Oberammergau, pre-2000 188
The King of Kings, dir. Cecil B. DeMille 190
The Miracle Maker, dir. Derek W. Hayes 190
The Gospel According to Saint Matthew, dir. Pier Paolo Pasolini 192
At Oberammergau, 2010 198
Author with Anton Burkhart 200

PREFACE

This project had its genesis in a paper delivered at a conference at the Institute for Advanced Studies at Hebrew University in March 2001. The topic of the conference was "From Hellenistic Judaism to Christian Hellenism," and my particular contribution was to be a study of the role of Hellenism in recent historical Jesus research. What came to my attention were the ways in which some—though by no means all—recent scholarship construes Caiaphas the Jewish high priest as an instrument of Hellenism and an opponent of "pure" Judaism. So began my investigation of the numerous portraits of Caiaphas through the ages.

My pursuit of Caiaphas was greatly facilitated by the Institute of Advanced Studies in Jerusalem, where I was a fellow in 2000–2001; the Social Sciences and Humanities Research Council of Canada, through which I held a Standard Research Grant for this project in 2003–2007; the International Consortium for Research in the Humanities project on the Dynamics in the History of Religions, based at the Rühr-Universität Bochum; and Yale Divinity School, where I completed the manuscript in the spring of 2010. I also made extensive use of the libraries at the University of Ottawa (and RACER, the excellent Ontario system for interlibrary loans), the Hebrew University of Jerusalem, the Protestant and Catholic Theological Libraries at the Rühr-Universität Bochum, and the Yale University Library system. I wish also to express my appreciation to University of South Carolina Press, especially D. Moody Smith, who edits the series Studies on the Personalities of the New Testament.

I have enjoyed the opportunity to teach about Caiaphas at the University of Ottawa (2008) and Brite Divinity School (2009), where the enthusiasm and the insights of my students were a source of inspiration. The project was enhanced by the feedback from colleagues who heard Caiaphas-related papers at the meetings of the Society of Biblical Literature, the Association for Jewish Studies, and the Canadian Society of Biblical Literature. In addition I have benefited in many ways from numerous colleagues, among them Esther Chazon, Paula Fredriksen, Martin Goodman, Pierluigi Piovanelli, Amy-Jill Levine, Ed Sanders, James Shapiro, Fred Tauber, Jan Willem van Henten, and Reinhold Zwick. A special thank you goes out to Christian Stückl and Otto Huber, who shared their time so generously during my stay in Oberammergau in May 2010. My thanks also to Kyle Green for research assistance, Angela Springfield for assistance with the images of medieval and Renaissance art, to Simcha Walfish for his references to Dante and Oscar Wilde, to Shoshana Walfish for her beautiful drawings, and to Natalie Neill for preparing the indexes and proofreading. Thank you also to Maureen Price for accompanying me to the Church of Saint Peter in Gallicantu in December 2008 and taking such lovely photos.

My family as always has been a source of joy and stability throughout the lengthy process of researching and writing this book. The final stages were enlivened by the arrival of our grandson, Nehemia David, in 2009, and his sister, Adira Hana, in 2010, who have provided tremendous pleasure and a reminder of the miracles of the everyday life. And as always my love and thanks to Barry Walfish, for his unfailing love, his encouragement, and his editorial prowess.

Each page of this book will testify to my reliance on and appreciation of the work of my peers, past and present. Helen Bond's book *Caiaphas: Friend of Rome and Judge of Jesus?* aims to "piece together the story of his life from the fragments in the ancient sources . . . and [to] consider the way in which he was perceived afterwards by the earliest Christian Gospel writers."[1] The first nine chapters provide a detailed reconstruction of the life of the high priest at the time of Caiaphas, in the second and third decades of the first century C.E.; four additional chapters are devoted to the portrait of Caiaphas in each of the canonical Gospels. Although my views differ from Bond's on many points, her study is insightful and fascinating and has proven invaluable to my own musings about the high priest. A second book that I consulted almost daily was James VanderKam's masterful study of the postexilic high priests, *From Joshua to Caiaphas: High Priests after the Exile*. VanderKam's clear, detailed, and methodical approach made this book the essential reference for my own work. Finally I wish to mention Raymond E. Brown's *The Death of the Messiah*, which, like all of Brown's work, provides detailed exegetical and historical commentary along with open discussion of the difficult theological issues that are raised by any account of the events of Jesus' life and death.

The present study ranges over a long chronological period and examines a broad range of material, some it far removed from any subject in which I can claim expertise. This study does not by any means discuss all of the references to Caiaphas in all sources. Some have been omitted because of the limits of my knowledge, others as a result of limitations of length. I hope, however, that others will find this subject as interesting to read about as it has been to research.

INTRODUCTION

O Caiaphas, Where Art Thou?

Joseph Caiaphas served as high priest of Judaea from 18–36/37 C.E., during the governorship of Pontius Pilate. As high priest Caiaphas would have lived and worked in Jerusalem, not far from the Temple, the cultic activities of which he supervised. One December morning, I set out from my Jerusalem tourist apartment to find "The House of Caiaphas," whose location was marked in bold letters on my map. Following the narrow streets and alleyways of the Old City, past small shops, markets, schools, and tour buses, I came upon a magnificent church, situated on a slope overlooking the Hinnom, Kidron, and Tyropean valleys. How easy it was to imagine Caiaphas taking his morning meal on the terrace, then setting out for his daily duties at the Temple, some two hundred meters to the northwest. In the crisp stillness of that Jerusalem day, I could almost hear the high priest chide the council for their lack of political acumen: "You know nothing at all! You do not understand that it is better for you to have one man die for the people than to have the whole nation destroyed" (John 11:49–50).

The church on the site of the House of Caiaphas is dedicated not to the high priest but to Peter. The bronze entrance doors, designed by a Palestinian Christian and sculpted by an Israeli artist, depict a poignant scene that takes place during Jesus' last supper. When Peter declares passionately that he is ready to accompany his Lord "to prison and to death," Jesus responds: "I tell you, Peter, the cock will not crow this day, until you have denied three times that you know me" (Luke 22:33–34).[1] In the church's main courtyard stands a life-size bronze Peter vehemently denying Jesus in the presence of two servant girls and a Roman soldier. A crowing rooster perches on the top of the column against which Peter is leaning. Hence Saint Peter in Gallicantu—Saint Peter of the Crowing Rooster.

The Gospels state that Peter's denial took place in the courtyard of the high priest Caiaphas's dwelling.[2] But Caiaphas himself is present only in the caption of an outside mosaic (*Les Outrages de Caïphe*)[3] and at the margins of a crowded inside mosaic depicting Jesus' trial. My visit to the House of Caiaphas brought me face to face with Peter but kept hidden the high priest in whose courtyard Peter's failings were revealed (Matt. 26:70), in whose precincts Jesus may have been tried (Matt. 26:57), and in whose dungeon he may have been held in the hours before his execution (John 18:28).[4]

By the time I visited the Church of Saint Peter in Gallicantu in December 2008, the research for this book was nearly complete. The excursion crystallized for me the experience of searching for the historical Caiaphas, a figure who turned out to be much more elusive than I could have imagined.

THE DISAPPEARING HIGH PRIEST

Caiaphas looms large not only on tourist maps of Jerusalem's Old City but in the field of New Testament scholarship, especially in "life of Jesus" narratives and Gospel commentaries. For many scholars Caiaphas is the mastermind behind the plot to kill Jesus, the mediator between Judaea and Rome who aimed to defend his people against Roman aggression yet delivered one of his own into Roman hands. For some he is a bully who ran roughshod over the Jews in order to gain favor with Pilate. For others he is a pragmatic politician whose main concern was to maintain order in Judaea and thereby to keep the Roman legions away from the city and its holy temple.

Caiaphas's clear and distinct portrait in twentieth- and twenty-first-century scholarship made me optimistic that the historical Caiaphas could be found quite simply by first examining the primary sources, then evaluating scholars' interpretations of these sources, and finally taking a stand by agreeing with or modifying the consensus or, more dramatically, proposing a new reading altogether.

Alas, my hopes were quickly dashed. Certainly it did not take very long to gather the evidence: Caiaphas's name occurs twice in the works of the first-century Jewish historian Josephus, nine times in the New Testament, and twice on the sides of an ornate first-century ossuary that had been discovered in Jerusalem in 1990.[5] Upon closer examination, however, the powerful image drawn by histories and commentaries began to blur. That high priests were important in the biblical and Second Temple periods is abundantly clear from scriptural texts, as well as from extrabiblical and postbiblical sources. That Caiaphas was one of these high priests is also not in dispute. But beyond the fact of his high priesthood, Caiaphas's personality and activities were far more difficult to discern than the scholarship implied.

The ossuary is of little assistance; archaeologists and historians are divided as to the question of whether this is truly the ossuary of the high priest.[6] Furthermore Josephus, a normally loquacious writer, reveals the beginning and end of Caiaphas's tenure as high priest but is entirely silent about everything else, including Caiaphas's background, his life prior to the high priesthood, and the events of his high priestly career.[7]

The authors of the New Testament Gospels and Acts, in contrast to Josephus, are intensely interested in Jesus, and therefore also in Jesus' relationships to those in the halls of power. Yet the New Testament mentions Caiaphas by name only nine times. Five of these references occur in John's Gospel, in which Caiaphas articulates the need for Jesus to die (11:49–52) but does little to bring about that outcome. Matthew's Gospel, which names the high priest twice, states that it was in Caiaphas's house that the chief priests and elders met to decide Jesus' fate. It does not specify, however, whether Caiaphas himself was present at the time (Matt. 26:3–5). Matthew later has Caiaphas preside over the interrogation of Jesus and tear his garments when Jesus declares: "From now on you will see the Son of Man seated at the right hand of Power and coming on the clouds of heaven" (26:64). Caiaphas then disappears from the story. Mark's Gospel includes the interrogation scene but does not refer to the presiding high priest by name (14:43–15:1). Luke's Gospel has no dramatic role for Caiaphas at all; he merely includes his name in the verse that establishes the historical context for the ministry of John the Baptist (3:1–2). The Acts of the Apostles names Caiaphas as one of the authorities who interrogate the apostles Peter and John after Jesus' death but does not single him out in any way (4:14–15). Furthermore Luke and John pair Caiaphas with his father-in-law, Annas, to whom they also refer as high priest (Luke 3:2; John 18:19). No text explicitly places Caiaphas at Jesus' trial before Pilate or at his crucifixion.

The well-defined scholarly portrait of the high priest was disintegrating before my very eyes. Josephus's silence, the relatively sparse, fragmentary, and even contradictory nature of the New Testament references. and the tantalizing but inconclusive identification of the ossuary made me despair of finding Caiaphas anywhere at all.

Of course historians do not "find" historical figures so much as construct them. Intertwined, then, with the question of who Caiaphas was and what he did is another question: how and why were the few traces of Caiaphas in ancient sources shaped into the powerful, pragmatic, and ruthless high priest of modern scholarship?

As I sought the historical Caiaphas, it became evident that he was by no means confined to first-century sources or the tomes of modern scholarship. In fact this high priest pops up everywhere: at the art gallery and the library, in the theater and on television. Indeed Caiaphas has had a long career in virtually every genre of creative expression from the first century to the twenty-first. Paintings, woodcuts, sculptures, and manuscript illuminations portray the high priest at the moment he rends his robe upon hearing Jesus' "blasphemy" (Matt. 26:65; Mark 14:63). Novels, plays, and movies cast Caiaphas as the archenemy who whips up the Jewish crowd against Jesus, cajoles and threatens Pontius Pilate into ordering Jesus' crucifixion, and smirks with satisfaction when his plan succeeds.

These portraits of Caiaphas are interesting, and sometimes even amusing; Caiaphas is not only a heavy-handed figure but also at times a buffoon. Most striking, however, is their extraordinary similarity to the Caiaphas of New Testament scholarship. It is not merely that creative representations of Caiaphas use the same sources as do New Testament scholars. It is also that the roles, motivations, and character traits that one finds in the corpus of creative works on the Jesus story are remarkably similar to those found in the corpus of historical and exegetical scholarship.

IMAGINATION AND NARRATIVE

What the scholarly and artistic depictions of Caiaphas have in common is imagination. It is obvious, of course, that imagination is key in media such as art, fiction, drama, and film. But as philosophers of history have long noted, imagination is also a necessary requirement for historiography. One of the most compelling writers on this topic is R. G. Collingwood, whose book *The Idea of History* is an extended reflection on the historical imagination.[8] Collingwood points out that historical thought, by definition, is always about absence: "events which have finished happening, and conditions no longer in existence."[9] While the past feels substantial to those who have experienced or studied a particular set of events, the past as such does not exist as an object nor even as an event, but only as an idea. Historical thinking therefore is "that activity of the imagination by which we endeavour to provide [the idea of the past] with detailed content."[10] And because it is an idea, the past does not reside in real time and space but in the mind. For Collingwood, therefore, "historical knowledge is the knowledge of what the mind has done in the past."[11] This is not passive knowledge. The historian is part of the process that he or she is studying,[12] precisely because it can occur only through the active use of the imagination.

The historical imagination entails a reenactment and thereby a "perpetuation of past acts in the present."[13] Collingwood concludes: "If then the historian has no direct or empirical knowledge of his facts, and no transmitted or testimoniary knowledge of them, what kind of knowledge has he: in other words, what must the historian do in order that he may know them? My historical review of the idea of history has resulted in the emergence of an answer to this question: namely, that the historian must re-enact the past in his own mind."[14]

If we adopt Collingwood's perspective, the similarities across "fictional" genres, such as literature, art, drama, and cinema, and "historical" genres, such as life-of-Jesus research and New Testament exegesis, should not surprise us. Collingwood remarks that historians and novelists alike

> construct a picture which is partly a narrative of events, partly a description of situations, exhibition of motives, analysis of characters. Each aims at making his picture a coherent whole, where every character and every situation is so bound up with the rest that this character in this situation cannot but act in this way, and we cannot imagine him as acting otherwise. The novel and the history must both of them make sense; nothing is admissible in either except what is necessary, and the judge of this necessity is in both cases the imagination. Both the novel and the history are self-explanatory, self-justifying, the product of an autonomous or self-authorizing activity; and in both cases this activity is the *a priori* imagination.[15]

If the imagination is so important in historical work, on what basis is it possible to distinguish between history and fiction? According to Collingwood, "The novelist has a single task only: to construct a coherent picture, one that makes sense. The historian has a double task: he has both to do this, and to construct a picture of things as they really were and of events as they really happened."[16] In our own postmodern era, more than six decades after Collingwood wrote these words, many are less confident in the ability of historians to picture "things as they really were." I would venture, however, that life-of-Jesus research still aspires to tell a story that accords in its outline and even details with the events that actually transpired.

The similarities between history and fiction rest not only on the exercise of the imagination but on the use of narrative as the vehicle for self-expression. The influential critical theorist Hayden White specifically addressed the narrative imperative in an article titled "The Value of Narrativity in the Representation of Reality."[17] White points out that "it is not enough that a historical account deal in real, rather than merely imaginary, events; and it is not enough that the account in its order of discourse represent events according to the chronological sequence in which they originally occurred. The events must be not only registered within the chronological framework of their original occurrence but narrated as well, that is to say, revealed as possessing a structure, an order of meaning, which they do not possess as mere sequence."[18] This structure is what is commonly called plot, that is, "a structure of relationships by which the events contained in the account are endowed with a meaning by being identified as parts of an integrated whole."[19] Although we normally think of "plot" as a feature of fiction, drama, and film, it is characteristic of all narrative, including historiography.

RESURRECTING CAIAPHAS

Despite Collingwood's straightforward distinction between history and fiction, in practice it is not always easy or, indeed, possible to perceive clear boundaries between historiography and creative *Nachleben*. For example the New Testament Apocrypha contain numerous fanciful stories that sound completely fictitious to modern ears, yet it is possible, even likely, that their ancient audiences believed these events really happened.[20] In a more contemporary genre, Jesus movies contain fictional dialogue, characters, and scenes, yet are often judged according to their perceived historicity or absence thereof.[21] Even for Josephus and the New Testament, which are used as primary sources by later writers and artists, Caiaphas is an idea, a personage from the past who no longer exists but must be imagined. As such he can be molded and shaped to fit the stories into which they would place him: for Josephus the story of Jewish-Roman relations in the first century, and for the Evangelists the story of Jesus, the Christ, the son of God and agent of salvation for all humanity.

The imaginative depictions of Caiaphas are similar to the historiographical ones not only due to their narrative interests but also their shared contexts. Despite its self-referential tendencies, New Testament scholarship does not exist in a vacuum but is influenced by its political and religious contexts. The same is true of artistic expressions. An obvious factor across all genres has been changing societal views of the deicide charge. As public anti-Semitism has become less acceptable, especially after the Holocaust, the claim that (some or all) Jews killed Jesus is proclaimed much less vigorously than in earlier eras.[22] Furthermore there is both intentional and perhaps also inadvertent appropriation of concepts, portraits, and images across genre boundaries. Filmmakers and theater directors consult scholars; scholars use images found in art, drama, and film.

My search for Caiaphas began with history and moved to historiography and finally to representation; the narrative emerging from this search, however, will move in the opposite direction. The historical Caiaphas may ultimately elude any method of historical analysis, but there is another *histoire*—in the

INTRODUCTION 7

French sense of story—that can be told. This is the story of how less than a dozen references in first-century sources have been pieced together, embellished, amplified, and given new life in works of scholarship and imagination over the course of two millennia.

A NARRATIVE OF DEICIDE

This book contends that Caiaphas's migration from the margins of the primary sources to the center of subsequent retellings is shaped by the narrative imperative, that is, the need to select sources and fill in the gaps of the Gospel accounts in order to create a coherent story line. Sometimes these gaps are filled in with material from biblical and postbiblical sources, sometimes from other materials, and sometimes from pure imagination. The ways in which the gaps are filled are by no means neutral. Rather they frequently reflect an evaluation, whether implicit or overt, of Caiaphas's nature and behavior as a "good," "bad," "tragic," or "comic" figure. There is only one criterion that is used for this evaluation: the high priest's relationship and interactions with Jesus, which, however, must themselves be constructed on the basis of the same meager sources. The assessment of Caiaphas's moral status, in turn, is often closely related to the way in which the narrative construes the role of (some, many, or just a few) Jews in the death of Jesus. And this construction will depend at least in part on whether, to what degree, and in what ways anti-Semitic statements and behaviors are acceptable in the public sphere. If Collingwood is correct in his assertion that the historical imagination entails a reenactment and thereby the "perpetuation of past acts in the present,"[23] then portraits of Caiaphas are not mere imaginative explorations but can, and do, have implications in the real world.

The first two chapters look closely at the primary sources that are the foundation for both the historiographical and the nonhistorical representations of the high priest Caiaphas. Chapter 1 takes Josephus's references to Caiaphas as its starting point. Sparse though his treatment of the high priest may be, Josephus testifies to the historical and political framework within which Caiaphas operated. Other aspects of Caiaphas's lifestyle and his role in Jewish society can be pieced together from the array of biblical and postbiblical sources about the high priest and high priesthood more generally. In the Bible the high priest is first and foremost a cultic leader, responsible for overseeing the daily, weekly, and annual sacrifices. He, and only he, was allowed to enter the Temple's Holy of Holies, and then only on one day a year, Yom Kippur (the Day of Atonement), and for only one purpose: to atone for his sins and the sins of the people.

Although his cultic roles remained fundamentally the same, the status of the high priest and the high priesthood changed significantly over time. Such changes may have affected his depictions in first-century sources. Chapter 2 looks in detail at the references to Caiaphas in the New Testament Gospels and Acts of the Apostles. The Gospels were often used by ancient and premodern interpreters as straightforward historical evidence for Caiaphas and his role in Jesus' Passion. But New Testament scholars have long recognized that, while the Gospels and Acts include references to historical personages and to historical events, their narratives are profoundly shaped by the aims, experiences, and contexts of their authors. Although these narratives focus on the early decades of the first century, when the Temple was still standing, the texts themselves were written in the later part of the first century, after the Temple was destroyed.[24] This dual perspective may well have influenced the Evangelists' views of the high priest and his role in Jesus' life story. Chapter 2 assesses the historical value of these sources by inquiring into precisely what their authors knew about the "actual" Caiaphas and considering the role that the historical imagination played in the role they assign to the high priest in their narratives of Jesus.

As chapter 3 shows, the narrative development of Caiaphas that began in the New Testament continued on after the canonical Gospels and Acts were completed. Indeed some of the most thoughtful and imaginative reflections on Caiaphas appear in the writings of the church fathers and the New Testament Apocrypha. For the fathers of the church, Caiaphas represented all that was evil, and could therefore stand in for all groups and individuals whom the fathers saw as a threat to their own understanding of Christ. Just as the high priest plotted the death of Jesus, so did the "heretics" plot the death of the church. Origen, among others, wrestled with the question of how someone as wicked as Caiaphas could nonetheless utter a true prophecy. The New Testament Apocrypha tell fanciful tales about the high priest, almost always pairing him closely with Annas, his father-in-law. These narratives do not so much retell the Gospel story per se as fashion stories around it or address exegetical, theological, and conceptual issues raised by the Gospel accounts themselves. The apocryphal books as well as the writings of the church fathers reveal that already at this point the deicide charge was accepted without question, as was Caiaphas's role as the principal villain of the piece.

The following three chapters consider Caiaphas in literature, drama, and film. These chapters show that Caiaphas's reputation as a wicked deicide is both maintained and challenged, in the context of changing discourses about the role of the Jews in the life and death of Jesus and the acceptability, or lack thereof, of public expressions of anti-Jewish or anti-Semitic sentiments.[25] They also illustrate the high priest's usefulness as a figure through whom artists and writers could poke fun at ecclesiastical and political authorities in their own times.

Chapter 4 looks at literary portraits of Caiaphas. Although the high priest is mentioned in a number of famous poems, his principal literary career has been in fictional retellings of the Jesus story. Over the centuries literally hundreds of novels about Jesus have been written, in numerous languages. In this chapter I sample a few of these treatments and then compare and contrast the portraits of two twentieth-century works: *The Nazarene*, by the American Jewish writer Sholem Asch, published in 1939, and Dorothy Sayers's radio play cycle, *The Man Born to Be King* (1942–43), in which Caiaphas plays the oily, but occasionally thoughtful, ecclesiastical politician. Given that they were written in the Nazi era, these two works highlight the complex role of anti-Semitism in the representation of the high priest.

Chapter 5 looks at Caiaphas's stage career in English mystery cycles and in the European Passion play tradition. The Oberammergau Passion play is both famous and infamous. It is famous because of its popularity and longevity; it has been performed to sold-out audiences almost every decade from 1634 to the present. It is infamous, however, because of its connection to the Nazi regime. Hitler came to see the play twice, in 1930 and 1934, and praised it highly as a fine illustration of the perfidy of the Jews. Since the Second Vatican Ecumenical Council, the play has been revised several times, primarily in order to address issues of anti-Semitism. In this chapter I compare the portrait of Caiaphas in successive recent versions of the script used for the productions at Oberammergau.

Although the Passion play is still being performed in Oberammergau and other locations,[26] since the late nineteenth century it is cinema that has provided the broadest access to Caiaphas and the other players in the Jesus story. Chapter 6 examines the genre of Jesus films, which began as an attempt to bring Passion plays to a mass audience but quickly developed in its own directions. This chapter focuses on the ways in which the depictions of Caiaphas reflect the views of the filmmakers about the Jewish role in Jesus' death. In film, as in fiction and drama, the deicide charge and anti-Semitism come to the fore.

In chapter 7 the study turns from fiction to historiography. The differing historical narratives reflect diverse theories about the three-way relationship between the high priest, the Roman governor, and Jesus. While there are some who believe that the entire Jewish trial is a fabrication, most historical narratives assign to Caiaphas a significant role in devising and carrying out the plot against Jesus' life. Many historians argue that Caiaphas was responsible for maintaining order on behalf of Pilate, who spent most of his time in Caesarea. In this scenario Caiaphas was concerned that Jesus' actions, particularly in and around the Temple, would cause unrest, and therefore the high priest moved against him, using the means—intrigue and a rigged trial—at his disposal. The historiography also reflects different perspectives on and evaluations of the high priest. These differences, however, focus not so much on the events themselves but on the factors that led Caiaphas to take action against Jesus. Historical and exegetical discussions of Caiaphas are expressed in the modes of discourse that characterize historical-critical scholarship, including long discussions of New Testament passages and interactions with other scholars (a mode of discourse adopted by the present book as well). Nevertheless the similarities to the narratives told in literature, drama, and film will be obvious.

The mere fact that historical reconstructions make ample use of the imagination, are shaped by their contexts, and are subject to the narrative imperative does not mean, of course, that they are wrong about the personages and events that they attempt to bring to life. Chapter 8 engages in a detailed evaluation of some of the main points on which scholars agree: that Caiaphas was motivated at least in part by the requirement that high priests keep order on behalf of Rome and by Jesus' actions in the so-called Temple cleansing. Plausible as these points are in the context of narratives that require coherence and causality, close examination of the sources shows that they too, like the high priest himself, are difficult to pin down.

The final chapter argues that instead of lamenting the high priest's historical elusiveness, we simply accept that the only way to encounter Caiaphas is through his many representations. Novels, scripts, and screenplays are helpful, but perhaps the best way to come face to face with Caiaphas is through his visual representation. This chapter samples the visual Caiaphas, as portrayed in art, drama, and film, and considers some responses to "seeing" the high priest (or perhaps better, to seeing the "high priest") from the biblical period to the present.

The historical Caiaphas is entangled in the story of his emergence from obscurity to renown. Also embedded in the story are many other narratives. Each era, each genre, and each work of imagination and history has its own stories, from the struggle of emerging orthodox Christianity against those whom it labeled as heretics to the struggle of the directors of Oberammergau 2010 to overcome the anti-Semitism that pervades the script that they have inherited. Throughout this study I have remained fascinated by the interplay between presence and absence, the overt and the covert, and text and imagination, and the powerful force that narrative exerts on storytellers in all genres. At the same time, I have been dismayed at Caiaphas's lengthy reputation as a deicide, which raises serious questions about the role of narrative and representation in the perpetuation of anti-Jewish or anti-Semitic sentiments. It is my hope that the readers of this book will be drawn, as I have been, into both the pleasures and the challenges of seeking the historical, and the not-so-historical, Joseph Caiaphas, high priest of Judaea.

CAIAPHAS IN CONTEXT

The writings of Flavius Josephus (37 to c. 100 C.E.) are the principal literary sources of information about the high priesthood in the Second Temple period up to and including the first Jewish revolt against Rome. This is not to say that Josephus tells the whole truth and nothing but the truth. Indeed, with regard to the high priesthood, as with many other matters, the historian's own concerns are not difficult to discern. Of priestly heritage himself, Josephus has a generally positive view of the high priesthood.[1] For him the high priesthood and the Temple are the heart and soul of Judaism.[2] Aaron, the first high priest, is introduced with great fanfare (*Ant.* 3.151–92); he and his successors are charged with transmitting Moses' teachings intact from generation to generation.[3] Not all priests are revered, however. Onias II (*Ant.* 12.158) and the later Hasmonean high priests (*Ant.* 13.300–19, 431–32) serve as proof of the thesis of *The Antiquities of the Jews* that violation of Jewish law leads to disaster.[4] In some instances *The Jewish War* and the *Antiquities* give different evaluations of the same high priest. For example *The Jewish War* describes Ananus (Annas) II as a moderate and virtuous man (2.648–51; 4.15–17), whereas *Antiquities* 20.199 describes him as a rash and impetuous leader. These changes reflect the different literary and rhetorical aims of these works,[5] but also Josephus's effort to understand the role of the priesthood before and during the revolt, as well as to justify his own behavior.

Josephus provides a considerable amount of detail about some high priests, such as the aforementioned Ananus II, the youngest son of Annas (*Ant.* 20.197, 203; *War* 2.563, 648–53), and next to no detail about many, including Caiaphas. Nevertheless from his treatises it is easily possible to piece together a chronology of the high priesthood and to learn something of the political and social pressures upon that institution.[6]

Despite the fact that Josephus shaped his narratives according to his own literary and ideological concerns, there seems to be no basis on which to doubt the overall accuracy of his references to Caiaphas. Perhaps for Josephus, Caiaphas's career was unremarkable, or at least unrelated to the historian's intense interest in the Hasmonean era and in the period leading up to the revolt.[7] Nevertheless he provides an enormous service to those who seek the historical Caiaphas, by situating this high priest in a plausible chronology and historical context. Indeed Josephus provides what are perhaps the most important facts about Caiaphas: that he was appointed by the governor Gratus in 18 C.E., remained throughout Pilate's governorship (26–36), and was removed by Vitellius, the legate of Syria, in 36 or 37 C.E.

CAIAPHAS'S APPOINTMENT AS HIGH PRIEST

Josephus reports the following concerning Caiaphas's appointment to the office of high priest:

> Caesar's successor in authority was the third emperor, Tiberius Nero, the son of his wife Julia. He dispatched Valerius Gratus to succeed Annius Rufus as procurator over the Jews. Gratus deposed Ananus from his sacred office, and proclaimed Ishmael, the son of Phabi, high priest. Not long afterwards he removed him also and appointed in his stead Eleazar, the son of the high priest Ananus. A year later he deposed him also and entrusted the office of high priest to Simon, the son of Camith. The last-mentioned held this position for not more than a year and was succeeded by Joseph, who was called Caiaphas. After these acts Gratus retired to Rome, having stayed eleven years in Judaea. It was Pontius Pilate who came as his successor. (*Ant.* 18.33–35)

This report suggests a date of 18 C.E. for the appointment.[8]

RELATIONSHIP WITH PILATE

One of the puzzling aspects of Caiaphas's tenure is that Pilate did not replace him with his own appointee when he succeeded Gratus as governor in 26 C.E. Some have suggested that Annas, Caiaphas's father-in-law, offered Pilate financial inducements in order to keep Caiaphas in office until Annas's own son was ready for the high priesthood,[9] or that Caiaphas himself may have done so.[10] While it is not inconceivable that money may have changed hands in order to ensure Caiaphas's ongoing tenure under Pilate, there is no evidence for this conjecture.

Daniel Schwartz has a more detailed explanation for Caiaphas's long tenure. In Schwartz's view the narrative structure of *Antiquities* 18 suggests a gap between the end of Gratus's service and the timing of Pilate's arrival in Judaea.

Between the years 17 and 29, Vitellius Germanicus was touring the East in order to resolve a number of problems that had arisen in client kingdoms, such as the Syrian and Judaean complaints about oppressive taxes (Tacitus, *Ann.* 2.42.5). Schwartz argues that Vitellius sent Gratus back to Rome so that Tiberius could conduct a full review of the situation. If the result of this review was to appoint a new governor, there may have been a gap of several months between Gratus's departure and the arrival of his replacement. In support of this theory, Schwartz notes that while Tacitus records only complaints about taxes, it is possible that the residents of Judaea would also have objected to Gratus's high-handed practice of appointing and deposing high priests on an annual basis (*Ant.* 18.34–35). Schwartz suggests that either Vitellius or Tiberius attempted to assuage the Judaeans by removing Gratus and then denying his successor, Pontius Pilate, the right to appoint a new high priest. This scenario would account for the length of Caiaphas's appointment, in contrast with the short tenures of Gratus's four previous appointees.[11]

Most scholars, however, attribute Caiaphas's continuation throughout Pilate's governorship to the high priest's effectiveness.[12] In this view Caiaphas's long tenure reflects Pilate's satisfaction with him and his sense that Caiaphas was "a man who could be relied on to support Roman interests and who could command some respect among the people."[13] As Borg and Crossan put it, "We must presume that the Romans and Caiaphas worked well together. It is not necessary to demonize either Caiaphas or Pilate, but it would seem that, even from the viewpoint of Roman imperial rule, they collaborated not wisely but too well."[14] In the absence of any first-century sources that describe a direct encounter between the high priest and the Roman governor, this conclusion remains speculative.

REMOVAL FROM OFFICE

Josephus mentions Caiaphas again only when he is removed from his position. After a full discussion of the high-priestly vestments, the historian comments approvingly that

> Vitellius, on reaching Judaea, went up to Jerusalem, where the Jews were celebrating their traditional feast called the Passover. Having been received in magnificent fashion, Vitellius remitted to the inhabitants of the city all taxes on the sale of agricultural produce and agreed that the vestments of the high priest and all his ornaments should be kept in the temple in custody of the priests, as had been their privilege before.... After he had bestowed these benefits upon the nation, he removed from his sacred office the high priest Joseph surnamed Caiaphas, and appointed in his stead Jonathan, son of

Ananus the high priest. Then he set out on the journey back to Antioch. (*Ant.* 18.90–95)

There is some confusion as to whether Caiaphas was removed in 36 or 37 C.E. The problem arises because Josephus records that Vitellius made two visits to Jerusalem, one at Passover after he dismissed Pilate (*Ant.* 18.90–95) and another at a different, unnamed festival, during which time he stayed for three days and then deposed Caiaphas's successor, the high priest Jonathan (*Ant.* 18.120–24). Smallwood argues that Josephus confused two separate occasions. She agrees that Vitellius likely made two separate visits to Jerusalem, but that the first visit did not occur on a festival. On this first occasion, in late 36 or early 37, he heard the Jews' request for control of the high-priestly vestments, wrote to the emperor about this matter, and dismissed Caiaphas from his position. The second visit took place at the Passover, in April 37, during which he dismissed the high priest Jonathan and granted the request for the return of the vestments to the high priest's control. If Smallwood is correct, Caiaphas would have been deposed late in 36 or early in 37.[15]

CAIAPHAS'S CAREER AND PERSONAL LIFE

Virtually nothing is known about the private and professional life of Joseph son of Caiaphas.[16] An apocryphal text mentions a daughter, but there is no evidence to support this.[17] The ossuary on which his name is engraved contained not only the bones of an older man but also those of an adult woman, two infants, and two children. It is possible that these were family members, perhaps his wife, his unmarried daughter, and his children or grandchildren.[18] It has also been suggested that Caiaphas had a younger brother named Elionaeus son of Cantheras who, according to Mishnah Parah 3:5, was called "Elio'eynai the son of Qayaf" and nicknamed "HaQof," meaning, perhaps, "monkey" or "ape."[19] These conjectures remain speculative.[20]

If the evidence foils attempts at a detailed biography, the simple knowledge that Caiaphas was high priest can provide some insights into his lifestyle and daily activities. From the biblical period to the destruction of the second Jerusalem Temple in 70 C.E., the high priest's life was highly structured in accordance with precepts set forth in the Hebrew scriptures. The Hebrew Bible therefore can be used as a basis for imagining what Caiaphas would have done on a day-to-day basis, what sort of person he would have married, and how he would have dressed while performing his duties.

The High Priest and Covenant

Josephus's political interest notwithstanding, the primary role of the high priest was cultic and spiritual. The numerous and highly detailed rules governing the high priest's life make sense only in the context of Israel's self-understanding as a people in covenantal relationship with God and of the role of the high priest in maintaining that relationship. According to Hebrew scriptures, it was God who initiated this relationship by making a set of promises to Abram (renamed Abraham in Gen. 17:5) and commanding him to set out for an unknown land: "Now the LORD said to Abram, 'Go from your country and your kindred and your father's house to the land that I will show you. I will make of you a great nation, and I will bless you, and make your name great, so that you will be a blessing. I will bless those who bless you, and the one who curses you I will curse; and in you all the families of the earth shall be blessed'" (Gen. 12:1–3).

The covenantal relationship between God and Israel was a contract that required commitment and devotion from both parties. According to the terms of this contract, Israel was to obey and worship God, and God was to preserve and protect Israel. In the book of Exodus, God gives Moses the following message to convey to the Israelites: "Now therefore, if you obey my voice and keep my covenant, you shall be my treasured possession out of all the peoples. Indeed, the whole earth is mine, but you shall be for me a priestly kingdom and a holy nation" (19:5–6). In this context obedience meant living by the commandments that, according to the Exodus narrative, were given to Moses by God on Mount Sinai and recorded in the Pentateuch.

These laws included an elaborate system of animal and plant sacrifices, which were to be the means by which Israelites worshiped God. It should be noted that animal and plant sacrifice was a feature of religious worship throughout the ancient Near East, as well as in classical Greece and Rome. Strange as this mode of worship may seem now, Israel was by no means unique in this regard.[21]

The biblical books record the establishment of a priestly class, whose responsibility it was to administer and carry out this system, and at the head of this priestly class was the high priest. The sacrifices were performed in the portable tabernacle that the Israelites took with them as they wandered in the desert from Egypt to Israel.[22] After the Israelites were established in Canaan, sacrifices were carried out in temples specifically dedicated to this purpose. Over the course of time, the Hebrew Bible records, the sacrificial system became centered on a single, magnificent temple situated in Jerusalem, as befitted a single, all-powerful God.[23]

Although Israel's covenant with God bound her to obedience, it was recognized from the outset that, people being what they are, perfect compliance with the divine will was an ideal that could never be achieved. To accommodate human imperfection within the covenantal relationship with God, Israelite practice and belief provided processes of repentance and atonement that were enacted as required for individuals and on an annual basis for the entire people.

Lifestyle

His daily involvement in the activities of the Temple demanded of the high priest a higher level of ritual purity than of other priests, who in turn were subject to more stringent regulations than the general public. The high priest had to marry an Israelite. He was not to dishevel his hair or tear his vestments; approach a corpse, even that of his mother or father; or marry a nonvirgin, thereby ruling out marriage to a widow, divorced woman, or prostitute (Lev. 21:10–20). Nor could the high priest be blemished in any way (Lev. 21:17). Thus excluded was "one who is blind or lame, or one who has a mutilated face or a limb too long, or one who has a broken foot or a broken hand, or a hunchback, or a dwarf, or a man with a blemish in his eyes or an itching disease or scabs or crushed testicles" (21:18–20).

If these rules remained in place in the first century c.e., it is likely that Caiaphas adhered well enough to the purity laws to which his position bound him and generally lived his life as expected of a high priest. Had this not been the case, Josephus would probably have shown more interest in him, as he does those high priests who deviated from the proper path.[24] It is also likely that his physical appearance was unremarkable; at the very least, and contrary to his later visual portraits, Caiaphas probably had no visible blemishes or disabilities.[25] Nothing about Caiaphas's wife is known, except that she was the daughter of the former high priest Annas, who is identified in John 18:13 as Caiaphas's father-in-law. This pedigree identifies her as a woman of the right sort of background to be a high-priestly consort.

Cultic Responsibilities

The high priest had a broad range of duties related to the Temple and the sacrificial system, but by far the most important was his crucial role in the Yom Kippur (Day of Atonement) rituals, and particularly his entrance into the Holy of Holies. The exalted nature of this moment cannot be overstated, for the Holy of Holies was the one place from which all humans were forbidden at all times, except for the high priest on this one day each year. The high priest's role is described in Leviticus 16:1–30, in which God sets out the rules and regulations of Yom Kippur for Moses' brother, Aaron, the first high priest to carry out sacrifices in the Tabernacle. These rituals were later transferred to the Temple in Jerusalem.[26]

After carrying out a number of initial sacrifices of atonement on behalf of himself and his household, the high priest was to set two goats at the entrance of the "tent of meeting." He was then to cast lots on the two goats, one for the Lord and one for "Azazel." The goat dedicated to God was to be offered as a sin offering. The other was to be "presented alive before the LORD to make atonement over it, that it may be sent away into the wilderness to Azazel" (16:10). He was then to slaughter a bull, take a censer of coals of fire and two handfuls of incense, and bring them inside the Holy of Holies. He would put the incense on the fire "that the cloud of the incense may cover the mercy seat that is upon the covenant, or he will die. He shall take some of the blood of the bull, and sprinkle it with his finger on the front of the mercy seat, and before the mercy seat he shall sprinkle the blood with his finger seven times" (16:13–14).

The high priest then turned his attention to the goats that had earlier been set aside at the entrance to the Tabernacle or Temple. The goat "for the Lord," that is, the sin offering for the people, was slaughtered and its blood brought inside the curtain to be sprinkled upon the mercy seat. Some of the bull's blood and some of this goat's blood was then put on each of the horns of the altar. Afterward the high priest presented the "scape goat." He placed both of his hands on the goat's head and confessed the "iniquities of the people of Israel, and all their transgressions"; the goat was then sent away into the wilderness bearing the sins of the people (16:20–22). At the conclusion of this dramatic ceremony, the high priest removed the special linen vestments worn for the previous steps of the ritual, bathed in water, donned his usual vestments, and then offered some concluding sacrifices of atonement for himself and for the people (16:23–24).

In addition to atoning on behalf of the nation on Yom Kippur, the high priest officiated at the sacrifices that followed a priestly consecration, including his own (Lev. 9); he sacrificed a meal offering in the mornings and evenings, on behalf of himself and the entire priesthood (Lev. 6:14–15) and participated in the ceremony of the burning of the Red Heifer (used for purification after touching a corpse; see Num. 19:1–20). According to Josephus, the high priest customarily officiated on Sabbaths, feasts of the new moon, and at the three pilgrimage festivals of Passover, Pentecost, and Tabernacles (*Ant.* 15.408).[27] Absent evidence to the contrary, it is safe to assume that Caiaphas carried out his sacerdotal duties in a respectable and unremarkable way.

Political Responsibilities

In addition to his cultic functions, the high priest had a number of political and administrative responsibilities, such as collecting taxes, administering local affairs, and presiding over the council, or Sanhedrin, that governed Jewish civil affairs.[28] The nature, composition, and responsibilities of the Sanhedrin in the first century are extraordinarily difficult to determine. The Gospels refer to an assembly or council, *synedrion,* of chief priests, elders, and others (for example Mark 15:1 and parallels), but whether they understood its inner workings and legal jurisdiction is uncertain.[29] Josephus uses the term *synedrion* to refer to a council or court of law (*Ant.* 14.167, 15.173, 20.200; *Life* 62). Rabbinic literature contains numerous references to a large or superior court (*bet din hagadol;* Mishnah Sotah 1:4, 9:1; Mishnah Gittin 6:7; Mishnah Sanhedrin 11:2, 4; Mishnah Horayot 1:5), but it is not clear whether these rabbinic descriptions pertain to the first-century council.[30] One of the key problems pertinent to the life story of Jesus is the lack of clarity as to the council's jurisdiction in capital offenses. In John 18:31 the Jews tell Pilate: "We are not permitted to put anyone to death." Yet Acts 7:54–8:2 depicts the trial and execution, by stoning, of Stephen. No firm conclusion can be drawn, as evidence can be summoned in support of either position.[31] Nevertheless it is likely that Caiaphas had significant political roles, at least internal to the Jewish community.

High-Priestly Problems

By virtue of his position as the highest cultic official, the high priest held a considerable amount of power and prestige in the eyes of many, if not all, of those who were under his jurisdiction. By the time of Caiaphas, however, changing circumstances and politics had also changed the high priest's role, both in relationship to the people and in relationship to Rome. These changes were reflected in two issues: the process of choosing the high priest and control over the high-priestly vestments.

Choosing the high priest. In theory the high priesthood was a hereditary position. The Hebrew scriptures describe the biblical high priests as the descendants of Aaron (see, for example, 1 Chron. 6:3–15). This tradition cannot be verified historically, as there is evidence to suggest that in the period of the monarchy the high priest may have been a royal appointee.[32] In 586 B.C.E. the Babylonians, under Nebuchadrezzar, conquered the kingdom of Judah and destroyed Solomon's Temple. But with the return of the exiles some seventy years later, the building of a second Temple began in Jerusalem, and the sacrifices and related institutions were resumed.[33] In the absence of a monarchy, the Temple became the nation's most important institution, and the high priest took on the political role, and attendant honor, that had previously belonged to the king.[34]

The postexilic high priests traced their ancestry to Zadok, appointed as chief priest at Jerusalem by Solomon (1 Kings 2:35), who in turn was thought to be a descendant of Eleazar, the son of Aaron (1 Chron. 6:50–53). With the advent of the Hasmonean monarchy (143–37 B.C.E.), however, the prestige of the high priesthood began to dwindle. The fact that some of the Hasmonean kings also took on the role of high priest compromised the integrity of the high priesthood in the eyes of many; departure from the principle of dynastic succession tarnished its aura of sanctity and diminished its cultic authority. When Queen

Salome Alexandra died in 67 B.C.E., a bitter civil war broke out between her two sons, Aristobulus and Hyrcanus. As the elder son, Hyrcanus was the heir to the crown and the high priesthood. His removal from power by his brother, Aristobolus, provided an excuse for the Roman general Pompey to intervene and conquer Jerusalem, under the guise of restoring the kingdom to its rightful heir. Pompey, however, stripped Hyrcanus of the monarchy and left him solely as high priest.[35]

In 63 B.C.E. Judaea became a vassal state of Rome. For some decades thereafter, the Hasmonean rulers remained in place, but with the collapse of the Hasmonean kingdom and Rome's appointment of Herod as king in 40 B.C.E., the choice of high priest according to nonbiblical criteria continued unabated. From 37 to his death in 4 B.C.E., it was Herod who appointed the high priests; his son, Archelaus, took on this task for a decade or so. In 6 C.E. Rome created the province of Judaea, thereby subjecting Judaea to direct Roman rule rather than operating through a client king such as Herod. From 6 C.E. until 41 C.E., the high priest was a Roman appointee, chosen either by the legate of Syria or his subordinate, the governor of Judaea.[36]

Although the hereditary basis of the high priesthood was no longer in effect, family connections and influence were not irrelevant to the choice of high priest. Josephus suggests that the high priesthood was largely restricted to certain Sadducean families, those of Boethus and Annas; a number of other high priests came from the families of Phabi and Camithus.[37] After 41 the high priest was appointed by King Agrippa I and his successors, until the revolt, when the rebels symbolically elected Phannias son of Samuel as high priest. Whether he in fact served in the Temple is not known. The high priesthood came to an end with the Temple's destruction during the revolt of 66–73 C.E.[38]

The prestige of the high priesthood changed along with the political fortunes of Judaea and the manner of his appointment. The disruption of the dynastic line prompted concerns about the legitimacy of the Hasmonean and Roman-era high priests, perhaps including Caiaphas himself. The departure from the hereditary lineage may also have been a factor in the establishment of the Qumran community in the Hasmonean period, and its persistence until Rome quashed the Jewish revolt.[39] Nevertheless the fact that the high priest continued to oversee the sacrificial cult and to enter the Holy of Holies on the Day of Atonement spoke to his ongoing role in the cultic life of the people of Israel and in their covenantal relationship with the one God of Israel.

The high priest's vestments. Although the priests performed their ritual duties barefoot, they were required to wear special vestments when carrying out their official duties. These vestments comprised a tunic, a sash, head covering, and breeches (Exod. 28:40–42). In addition to these items, the high-priestly vestments included four garments: a robe, the "ephod," a breastplate, and a crown, whose appearance, colors, and materials are described in detail in Exodus 28:1–43 and again in Exodus 39:1–31. The vestments were colorful and elaborate. The sleeveless robe was purple and hemmed with blue, purple, and scarlet tassels shaped like pomegranates alternating with small bells that presumably chimed with every step. The ephod was a vest fastened with an onyx stone at each shoulder; these stones were engraved with the names of the twelve tribes of Israel. The breastplate was covered with twelve gems, each bearing the name of one of the twelve tribes. Fastened onto the breastplate was a pouch containing the Urim and Thummim (instruments of divination). The crown was a gold plate inscribed with the phrase "Holy unto God." The crown was attached to the head covering so that it rested on the high priest's forehead. These were the vestments that the high priest wore to carry out his special duties throughout the year; on the Day of Atonement, the high priest wore a special set of plain linen vestments (Lev. 16:4).[40] The vestments were not merely an adornment but an instrument essential to the high-priestly role. The names of the twelve tribes suggest the high priest's pan-Israel role; the Urim and Thummim symbolize his direct line to the divine, allowing him to mediate the covenantal relationship between God and Israel.

The central role of the vestments for the high priest's performance of his cultic obligations turned their control into an issue in the Herodian and Roman periods. Whoever controlled the vestments also subjugated the high priest, who could not perform his cultic role without these special garments. Here is Josephus's account of the vexed vestment issue:

> At that time the vestments were stored in Antonia—there is a stronghold of that name—for the following reason. One of the priests, Hyrcanus, the first of many by that name, had constructed a large house near the temple and lived there most of the time. As custodian of the vestments, for to him alone was conceded the right to put them on, he kept them laid away there, whenever he put on his ordinary clothes in order to go down to the city. His sons and their children also followed the same practice. When Herod became king, he made lavish repairs to this building, which was conveniently situated, and being a friend of Antony, he called it Antonia. He retained the vestments there just as he had found them, believing that for this reason the people would never rise in insurrection against him. Herod's successor as king, his son Archelaus, acted similarly. After him, when Romans took over the government, they retained control of the High Priest's vestments and kept them in a stone building, where they were under the seal both of the

priests and of the custodians of the treasury and where the warden of the guard lighted the lamp day by day. Seven days before each festival the vestments were delivered to the priests by the warden. After they had been purified, the High Priest wore them; then after the first day of the festival he put them back again in the building where they were laid away before. This was the procedure at the three festivals each year and on the fast day. (*Ant.* 18. 91–95)

Josephus wrote approvingly of the change wrought by Vitellius, commenting that the legate "was guided by our law in dealing with the vestments, and instructed the warden not to meddle with the question of where they were to be stored or when they should be used" (*Ant.* 18. 95).

The vestments remained under Jewish control until the death of Agrippa I in 44. The Roman procurator Fadus then demanded that the vestments be returned to Roman custody. The Jews petitioned the emperor Claudius, who granted their request and gave the authority over the vestments to Herod of Chalcis, the son of Agrippa I. With this also came the right to appoint the high priests. The vestments remained in Jewish hands until the revolt.[41]

It is unlikely that the Herodian and Roman leadership intended to impede the conduct of the sacrificial cult or to prevent the pilgrimage festivals from taking place. After all it was Roman policy to allow subjects to observe their ancestral customs. Paul Winter speculates that the vestments were worn by the high priest not only for religious purposes but also when the Sanhedrin met. If so, those who had custody of the vestments would necessarily have had prior warning and knowledge of when these meetings were to take place.[42] This is rather speculative, but whatever the specific reason, it appears that their symbolic significance was so great that control over the vestments also signified control over the high priest and, by extension, over the nation as a whole.

None of the first-century sources describe Caiaphas's garments; whether the robe that he tore during the council's interrogation of Jesus (according to the Passion narratives of Matthew and Mark) were his formal vestments is not known. Nevertheless it is reasonable to surmise that he wore the garments appropriate to his cultic duties. Josephus's account makes it clear that Caiaphas's vestments were under Roman lock and key and that he required Roman permission for their use. Whether he was irritated by this required gesture of subservience or simply accepted it is not known.

DEATH

Josephus does not reveal how or when Caiaphas's death took place. Apocryphal sources invent a gruesome death for him, as befitting their view of him as a deicide.[43] If the ossuary inscribed with his name did indeed contain the bones of the high priest and his family, and if all of them died at the same time, it is possible that their deaths were due to an infectious disease that swept through two or three generations of this family. Even the rich and powerful would have been powerless to defend themselves against such a disease. This is entirely speculative, however.

CONCLUSION

Josephus's lack of interest in Caiaphas is regrettable for historians and others interested in this high priest, but at least one may surmise that the information that he does provide cannot be dismissed on the grounds of tendentiousness. While uninformative about the details of Caiaphas's life, Josephus's comments are crucial for placing the high priest in his historical and political context. As high priest from 18 until 36 or 37, Caiaphas had a longer tenure by far than any other high priest in the Second Temple period. Ananias son of Nedebaeus comes a distant second, at eleven years (48–59 C.E.); most others were high priests for only a year or two. Caiaphas's long tenure is particularly noteworthy as it spanned the terms of two governors, Gratus and Pilate; a change in high priest normally accompanied a change in Roman governor, except in this one case. Second, and equally important, are Caiaphas's family connections. As a Roman appointee he clearly did not inherit the high-priestly mantle from his father, but it is worth noting that as the son-in-law of Annas, high priest in the period 6–15 C.E., Caiaphas belonged to a distinguished family that included five other high priests of his generation: his five brothers-in-law, the sons of Ananus (Eleazar, 16–17 C.E.; Jonathan, 36 or 37 C.E.; Theophilus, 36–41 C.E.; Matthias, 42–43 C.E.; Annas II, 62 C.E.). Being a member of a prominent high-priestly family likely did not hurt his position. It is also interesting to note that the vestments were under Roman jurisdiction during his tenure; this point emphasizes the power differential between Caiaphas and the Roman governor.

The information from the Hebrew Bible and Second Temple Jewish literature about the covenantal and cultic role of the high priest, his lifestyle, and his vestments helps us to imagine what Caiaphas's personal and professional life may have been like. By default it seems indisputable that he fulfilled the prerequisites of the high priesthood, that he presided over the council, that he entered the Holy of Holies annually on Yom Kippur, and that he enjoyed the respect of many, though not all, of the people of Israel by virtue of his office and perhaps also of his person.

Were Josephus and the ossuary the only sources on Caiaphas, this high priest would have disappeared into obscurity along with the rest of his colleagues. After all, how many people outside the guild of scholars of Second Temple Judaism have heard of Ishmael son of Phabi (15–16 C.E.; *Ant.* 18.34), or Jesus son of Damnaeus (62–63/4?; *Ant.* 20.203, 213)? Caiaphas's notoriety and the long history of his representation arise not from his role in Josephus's *Antiquities* but from the part he plays in the Gospels' dramatic accounts of Jesus' final days.

CAIAPHAS IN THE NEW TESTAMENT

From the second century c.e. to the present, all portraits of the high priest Caiaphas, in every genre, rely on the Gospels as their primary sources. The Gospels are historical sources in the sense that they set out to narrate a "real" story. The author of the Gospel of John insists that the testimony to the things written in his book are authoritative and true (21:24). The author of the Gospel of Luke declares that he has investigated "everything carefully from the very first" and decided "to write an orderly account" so that his audience "may know the truth concerning the things about which you have been instructed" (1:1–4).

Nevertheless, as scholars have long recognized, the Gospel accounts are shaped by numerous factors, including oral and written sources, theology, purpose, and the composition and history of the communities for which they were written.[1] Like the works of Josephus, the Gospels are retrospective works that tell a tale situated in Judaea during the first third of the first century from a vantage point that is both geographically and chronologically removed from that period. The Gospels are therefore not only sources of later representations of Caiaphas, they are themselves part of the high priest's *Nachleben*. To paraphrase Collingwood, the Evangelists, like modern historians, engaged in an activity of the imagination through which they reenacted a past that no longer existed, and which they did not themselves experience.[2] The major role that imagination played in their accounts is evident in the differences among them.

The name Caiaphas appears in the Gospels a total of eight times: once in Luke, twice in Matthew, five times in John, and not at all in Mark.[3] The title high priest appears a total of twenty-eight times, in twenty-five verses: seven in Matthew, eight in Mark, one in Luke, and nine in John.[4] Of these latter verses, all are relevant to our discussion except Mark 2:26, which recalls an incident involving the biblical King David during the time that Abiathar was high priest (see 1 Sam. 22:20).

With the exception of Luke 3:2, all Gospel references to Caiaphas, whether by name or by title, occur in the context of the Passion—the events that culminate in Jesus' death—or in the prelude to it. Whereas they differ to some degree on the content and chronology of Jesus' life and ministry, the Gospels' Passion narratives are remarkably similar in overall structure: Jesus is betrayed by Judas, arrested by a large crowd, interrogated by Jewish leaders, tried by Pilate, condemned, and crucified.[5] Within this common story line, however, there is considerable variety in detail, particularly with regard to the role of the high priest. A complicating factor is the major role played by the "chief priests" in this same sequence of events. The Greek term translated as "chief priests" in the New Revised Standard Version is *hoi archiereis,* which is simply the plural form of "high priest" (*ho archiereus*). The Gospels refer to the chief priests some fifty-four times, far more frequently than to Caiaphas by name or the singular high priest by function. In looking at how Caiaphas is constructed in each of the Gospels, it will be essential to look at the roles played by the chief priests, and at Caiaphas's relationship to this particular group.

THE GOSPEL OF MARK

Although Matthew's Gospel is first in the order of the New Testament canon, the present discussion will begin with the Gospel of Mark, which most scholars consider to be the earliest Gospel and a major source for the Gospels of Matthew and Luke.[6] Mark does not mention Caiaphas by name anywhere in his Gospel. But he does assign a significant role to the anonymous high priest in the events that lead up to Pilate's prosecution and sentencing of Jesus. The narrative divides easily into five sections: the plot (14:1–2), the betrayal and arrest of Jesus (14:43–14:52), the interrogation of Jesus by the council and high priest (14:53–65), Peter's denial of Jesus (14:66–72), and Jesus' delivery to Pilate (15:1). Although the high priest appears only in the second segment, it is important to look at the entire sequence in order to understand his role in Mark's literary structure.

The Plot (14:1–2)

> [1] It was two days before the Passover and the festival of Unleavened Bread. The chief priests and the scribes were looking for a way to arrest Jesus by stealth and kill him; [2] for they said, "Not during the festival, or there may be a riot among the people."

Jesus' death was not a random event but the result of a plot that got underway before the Passover. The Gospel of Mark attributes this plot to "the chief priests and scribes" rather than to an individual leader. Surely Mark's audiences would have caught the mocking and ironic point that despite the Jewish leaders' best intentions, Jesus' death occurred during the very period of time they hoped to avoid. This verse also recalls Jesus' prophecy in 8:31 "that the Son of Man must undergo great suffering, and be rejected by the elders, the chief priests, and the scribes, and be killed, and after three days rise again." That prophecy is about to be fulfilled.

The Betrayal and Arrest of Jesus (14:43–52)

> [43] Immediately, while he was still speaking, Judas, one of the twelve, arrived; and with him there was a crowd with swords and clubs, from the chief priests, the scribes, and the elders. [44] Now the betrayer had given them a sign, saying, "The one I will kiss is the man; arrest him and lead him away under guard." [45] So when he came, he went up to him at once and said, "Rabbi!" and kissed him. [46] Then they laid hands on him and arrested him.
>
> [47] But one of those who stood near drew his sword and struck the slave of the high priest, cutting off his ear. [48] Then Jesus said to them, "Have you come out with swords and clubs to arrest me as though I were a bandit? [49] Day after day I was with you in the temple teaching, and you did not arrest me. But let the scriptures be fulfilled." [50] All of them deserted him and fled. [51] A certain young man was following him, wearing nothing but a linen cloth. They caught hold of him, [52] but he left the linen cloth and ran off naked.

Not surprisingly the highest Roman and Jewish authorities, including the high priest, are absent from Jesus' arrest. But the presence of the high priest's slave implies that the high priest is at least aware of the plan to arrest Jesus, even if he had no apparent role in formulating the plan. The identities of the one who injured the slaves, the ones who left, and the young man who ran off naked are impossible to determine.[7]

The Interrogation of Jesus by the Council and the High Priest (14:53–65)

> [53] They took Jesus to the high priest; and all the chief priests, the elders, and the scribes were assembled. [54] Peter had followed him at a distance, right into the courtyard of the high priest; and he was sitting with the guards, warming himself at the fire.
>
> [55] Now the chief priests and the whole council were looking for testimony against Jesus to put him to death; but they found none. [56] For many gave false testimony against him, and their testimony did not agree. [57] Some stood up and gave false testimony against him, saying, [58] "We heard him say,

'I will destroy this temple that is made with hands, and in three days I will build another, not made with hands.'" ⁵⁹ But even on this point their testimony did not agree.

⁶⁰ Then the high priest stood up before them and asked Jesus, "Have you no answer? What is it that they testify against you?" ⁶¹ But he was silent and did not answer. Again the high priest asked him, "Are you the Messiah, the Son of the Blessed One?" ⁶² Jesus said, "I am; and 'you will see the Son of Man seated at the right hand of the Power,' and 'coming with the clouds of heaven.'"

⁶³ Then the high priest tore his clothes and said, "Why do we still need witnesses? ⁶⁴ You have heard his blasphemy! What is your decision?" All of them condemned him as deserving death. ⁶⁵ Some began to spit on him, to blindfold him, and to strike him, saying to him, "Prophesy!" The guards also took him over and beat him.

After his arrest Jesus is taken to the high priest, while Peter, who has followed him, waits in the high priest's courtyard. After hearing testimony that Jesus had made statements about the Temple, the high priest stands up and asks Jesus outright whether he is the Messiah. Jesus owns up to this identification and even expands upon it with an apocalyptic and eschatological prophecy that quotes from Daniel 7:13 and Psalm 110:1. Upon hearing this prophecy, the high priest tears his clothes, declares Jesus to have blasphemed, and asks those present for their verdict.

This passage suggests a negative answer to the question of whether the high priest was in on the plot to arrest Jesus by stealth and kill him. The false testimony drummed up by "the chief priests and the whole council" is intended to persuade the high priest of Jesus' guilt; he is the main audience for this testimony. Had the high priest been a party to the original plot, this interrogation would not have been necessary. For Mark the high priest, in contrast to the chief priests, is initially a neutral figure. While the presence of his slave at the arrest implies prior knowledge of Jesus, his behavior at the interrogation argues against an a priori view of Jesus as guilty and worthy of death.

The high priest does not seem overly concerned about Jesus' alleged utterances about the Temple. He does demand an answer to the accusations, but when Jesus fails to respond, his interrogation moves immediately to the all-important question that the Gospel as a whole intends to answer: is Jesus the Messiah?

Jesus' comment immediately escalates the tension and brings the scene to its climax. The high priest's question to Jesus not only supplies the impetus for the guilty verdict that propels the plot toward its inevitable conclusion, but also, and perhaps more important, provides Jesus with the occasion to declare explicitly his Christological identity—to the reader as well as to the high priest and council. Of course the verdict has been predetermined from the beginning, but the high priest, it seems, has genuinely reached it only now.

Whether and how Jesus' comments constituted blasphemy within the context of first-century Judaism are issues that are highly contested by historians, exegetes, and theologians.[8] The first part of Jesus' response to the high priest's question, "I am," affirms his identity as the Messiah and "Son of the Blessed One."[9] The second part of his response, concerning the son of man, quotes from Daniel and Psalms, as noted above, but the Old Testament prophecy does not explicitly name Jesus as the son of man. Whether or not Jesus is truly guilty of blasphemy under first-century Jewish law, it is clear that Mark portrays him as such, perhaps to sharpen the conflict between Jesus and the Jewish authorities and to focus the audience's attention on Jesus' Christological identity.[10]

Tearing one's clothes is a symbolic act expressing grief, most often in a response to hearing of the death of a loved one or of an important figure. For example Jacob tears his clothes when he hears that his son Joseph has died (Gen. 37:34);[11] David tears his clothes when he hears that the former king Saul and his son Jonathan have died (2 Sam. 1:11–12). Blasphemy or other offenses against God cause even greater grief, as in 2 Kings 18:30–19:1, in which King Hezekiah responds to hearing of Assyrian slights on the God of Israel by tearing his clothes and covering himself with sackcloth.

The high priest's behavior and the fact that he asks those present for a decision implies that this is a formal proceeding and that the death sentence is not his verdict alone but shared by those present. As Winter notes, regardless of what happened, or what could have happened historically, Mark 14:64b was meant to assert that a formal sentence of death had been passed by the entire Jewish Senate.[12] Marcus, on the other hand, argues that Mark's audience may have found the high priest's action itself blasphemous, for it signaled his failure to recognize Jesus' words and actions as God's saving activity. If so, the intended readers would have seen the high priest's protestations of concern for the honor of God as misguided and even hypocritical and the trial itself as a farce.[13]

The high priest's act foreshadows Jesus' imminent and necessary death, but also, for the purposes of Mark's narrative, focuses the nature of the conflict between them. This is not to say that the verse would really have been understood in this way by a Jewish high priest in the early decades of the first century. The passage as a whole, however, implies that Jesus has been unjustly tried and convicted formally by the Jewish council in a manner that demonstrates their complete rejection and also their utter misunderstanding of what he truly stood for and his relationship with God.[14] The very people—educated Jewish religious and spiritual leaders—who should have understood that Jesus was the fulfillment of scriptures, the son of God and the Messiah, have condemned God's son to death.

Peter's Denial of Jesus (14:66–72)

> 66 While Peter was below in the courtyard, one of the servant-girls of the high priest came by. 67 When she saw Peter warming himself, she stared at him and said, "You also were with Jesus, the man from Nazareth." 68 But he denied it, saying, "I do not know or understand what you are talking about." And he went out into the forecourt. Then the cock crowed.
>
> 69 And the servant-girl, on seeing him, began again to say to the bystanders, "This man is one of them." 70 But again he denied it. Then after a little while the bystanders again said to Peter, "Certainly you are one of them; for you are a Galilean." 71 But he began to curse, and he swore an oath, "I do not know this man you are talking about." 72 At that moment the cock crowed for the second time. Then Peter remembered that Jesus had said to him, "Before the cock crows twice, you will deny me three times." And he broke down and wept.

At the same time that Jesus is facing the formal interrogation of the high priest at the council, Peter is below, being questioned informally by the high priest's servant girl. If Jesus' words to the high priest constitute a confession of his messianic identity, Peter's response to the servant girl amounts to a denial of his identity as the disciple of this son of man.

Jesus' Delivery to Pilate (15:1)

> As soon as it was morning, the chief priests held a consultation with the elders and scribes and the whole council. They bound Jesus, led him away, and handed him over to Pilate.

The Jewish leadership meets again in the morning, though to what end is unknown. Afterward the prisoner is taken to Pilate, and the Jewish role in the legal proceedings is at an end. As in 14:1 the presence of the high priest is not noted.

Observations

This artful and compelling narrative interweaves the story of the high priest's interrogation of Jesus with that of his servant girl's interrogation of Peter; the juxtaposition suggests that these two encounters are occurring at the same time, in different parts of the high-priestly compound. This dramatic structure drives home the contrast between Jesus, who meets his fate with honesty and courage, and Peter, who evades his in cowardice. The passage also, more subtly, makes a second point: just as Jesus' prediction of Peter's denial comes to pass, so too will the prophecy that "the Son of Man must undergo great suffering, and be rejected by the elders, the chief priests, and the scribes, and be killed" (Mark 8:31; cf. 10:33) and, perhaps most important, that "you will see the Son of Man seated at the right hand of the Power,' and 'coming with the clouds of heaven" (Mark 14:62).

The high priest has a pivotal role in the plot. First he provides the occasion for Jesus' self-declaration and gets to what Mark sees as the heart of the matter. Far from dismissing Jesus' claims, the high priest takes them extremely seriously indeed; otherwise his dramatic gesture would be meaningless. Jesus' words are not frivolous claims but a rewriting of the covenantal relationship with God. If the high priest does not accept that this is God's will, he does at least understand the seriousness of the claim. This point is made much more powerful if we read Mark's high priest not as complicit with the plot from the outset but as the one whom the "prosecution's" (false) testimony is intended to persuade.

Second, in charging Jesus with blasphemy, tearing his own robes, and eliciting the guilty verdict from the council, the high priest sets the final phase of the plan into motion. From the perspective of Jesus' enemies, the chief priests, this is their plan that they will strive to see through to its conclusion: Jesus' death. From the point of view of the Evangelist, however, this is the divine plan, the working out of the events that Jesus prophesied before he even entered Jerusalem for his final Passover.

Despite his dramatic behavior, the high priest has a limited, almost negligible role in Mark's version of Jesus' last hours. Certainly he provides the venue for Jesus' first interrogation, presides over it, and elicits the verdict. But he does not display any animosity toward Jesus, and he is not implicated in the plot that results in his arrest and eventual conviction. In short it is not the high priest but the chief priests who seek Jesus' death in fulfillment of his Passion prophecies (Mark 8:31, 10:33).

Indeed throughout the Gospel it is the chief priests and scribes who are Jesus' archenemies. Mark 11:18 notes that "when the chief priests and the scribes heard it [that Jesus had made a scene in the Temple], they kept looking for a way to kill him; for they were afraid of him, because the whole crowd was spellbound by his teaching." The narrator notes their hostility as the events move toward the Passion: "It was two days before the Passover and the festival of Unleavened Bread. The chief priests and the scribes were looking for a way to arrest Jesus by stealth and kill him" (14: 1). The fact that it is the chief priests whom Judas seeks out when he decides to betray his master (14:10) implies that within Mark's story world, the chief priests' animosity toward Jesus was not a secret. Not only do they plot Jesus' death, but they also do their best to move the plot along even once they have delivered Jesus to Pilate. They accuse him of many things (15:3), incite the crowd to call for the release of Barabbas (15:11), and then mock him cruelly when he is on the cross: "He saved others; he cannot save himself" (15:31). Pilate, the narrator suggests, saw through their actions, "for he realized that it was out of jealousy that the chief priests had handed him over" (15:10).[15]

Finally we return to the fact of Mark's complete omission of the high priest's name. The most obvious explanation is that he simply did not know the high priest's name; this is Winter's view.[16] Fitzmyer suggests that Mark was aware of the tradition of an interrogation before a high priest but ignorant of its substance.[17] Others suggest that Mark knew the high priest's name but chose not to mention it. Brown, for example, views the omission of the name as consistent with the view that Mark wrote for a Gentile audience, to whom the name would not be meaningful.[18] Bond proposes that Mark omitted the name for theological reasons, namely to broaden responsibility from an individual to the Jewish leadership as a whole. In doing so Mark could convey to his readers that the trial was a "grand momentous drama in which, through their rejection of God's messiah, the Jewish leaders bring down destruction as a whole."[19] Bond may be right that Mark intended the proceedings to be seen as a farce, a kangaroo court, a travesty of justice.[20] But it is not clear whether the high priest was in on the travesty or whether he was manipulated by the others, a dupe himself. In the final analysis, it seems to me that ignorance is the simplest explanation of Mark's omission of Caiaphas's name. The burden of proof must rest on those who would see his silence as deliberate suppression.

THE GOSPEL OF MATTHEW

In contrast to Mark, for whom the high priest remains anonymous throughout, Matthew mentions Caiaphas by name twice. The first reference is in Matthew 26:1–5, which introduces the Passion sequence as a whole.

> [1] When Jesus had finished saying all these things, he said to his disciples, [2] "You know that after two days the Passover is coming, and the Son of Man will be handed over to be crucified." [3] Then the chief priests and the elders of the people gathered in the palace of the high priest, who was called Caiaphas, [4] and they conspired to arrest Jesus by stealth and kill him. [5] But they said, "Not during the festival, or there may be a riot among the people."

This passage sets the stage for the last events of Jesus' ministry: the dinner at the house of Simon the leper, Jesus' anointing by an unnamed woman, Judas Iscariot's decision to betray Jesus, the last supper, and the prayer at Gethsemane. Jesus' pronouncement in 26:2 has a formal quality that advises the disciples, and the readers, that the story is about to move into its final phase and that it will reach its climax—the crucifixion of the son of man—within two days. The next verses, 26:3–5, launch the chain of events that will fulfill Jesus' prophecy and introduce the dramatis personae that will hand Jesus over for crucifixion.

As in Mark the main actors are the chief priests and a second group, in this case the elders.[21] Although Matthew 26:3 identifies Caiaphas as the high priest, it does not directly attribute any particular activity or action to him. It merely states that a meeting of chief priests and elders took place in his palace. This comment solidifies the responsibility of the Jewish leaders as Jesus' enemies, formalizes their plot against him, and anticipates the place and context in which Jesus will soon be sentenced to death (26:57–58).[22] The verses do not implicate Caiaphas directly in the plot. By mentioning that the meeting took place in his house, however, the narrative introduces Caiaphas as a man of power and substance.

The Evangelist is not concerned to show cause and effect, that is, to explain why the chief priests and elders are against him or what event triggered their concern. Rather the aim is to show that the fulfillment of Jesus' prophecy began immediately after he uttered it. The prophecy in turn summarizes the Passion narrative, heightens the sense of suspense and tragedy, and allows the audience to discern the shape of the story to come.

Jesus' Delivery to Pilate (26:47–56)

> [47] While he was still speaking, Judas, one of the twelve, arrived; with him was a large crowd with swords and clubs, from the chief priests and the elders of the people. [48] Now the betrayer had given them a sign, saying, "The one I will kiss is the man; arrest him." [49] At once he came up to Jesus and said, "Greetings, Rabbi!" and kissed him. [50] Jesus said to him, "Friend, do what you are here to do." Then they came and laid hands on Jesus and arrested him.
>
> [51] Suddenly, one of those with Jesus put his hand on his sword, drew it, and struck the slave of the high priest, cutting off his ear. [52] Then Jesus said to him, "Put your sword back into its place; for all who take the sword will perish by the sword. [53] Do you think that I cannot appeal to my Father, and he will at once send me more than twelve legions of angels? [54] But how then would the scriptures be fulfilled, which say it must happen in this way?" [55] At that hour Jesus said to the crowds, "Have you come out with swords and clubs to arrest me as though I were a bandit? Day after day I sat in the temple teaching, and you did not arrest me. [56] But all this has taken place, so that the scriptures of the prophets may be fulfilled." Then all the disciples deserted him and fled.

This section includes a number of minor differences from the Marcan account, such as the identification of the slave's assailant as one of Jesus' followers.

Matthew 26:56 returns to the theme of prophecy by emphasizing that Jesus' arrest was the fulfillment of scripture. Like 26:1–5 this comment reminds the audience that the course of events is under the complete control of God and not Jesus' enemies, no matter what those enemies themselves might think.

The Interrogation of Jesus by the Council and High Priest (26:57–67)

57 Those who had arrested Jesus took him to Caiaphas the high priest, in whose house the scribes and the elders had gathered. 58 But Peter was following him at a distance, as far as the courtyard of the high priest; and going inside, he sat with the guards in order to see how this would end.

59 Now the chief priests and the whole council were looking for false testimony against Jesus so that they might put him to death, 60 but they found none, though many false witnesses came forward. At last two came forward 61 and said, "This fellow said, 'I am able to destroy the temple of God and to build it in three days.'"

62 The high priest stood up and said, "Have you no answer? What is it that they testify against you?" 63 But Jesus was silent. Then the high priest said to him, "I put you under oath before the living God, tell us if you are the Messiah, the Son of God." 64 Jesus said to him, "You have said so. But I tell you, From now on you will see the Son of Man seated at the right hand of Power and coming on the clouds of heaven."

65 Then the high priest tore his clothes and said, "He has blasphemed! Why do we still need witnesses? You have now heard his blasphemy. 66 What is your verdict?" They answered, "He deserves death." 67 Then they spat in his face and struck him; and some slapped him, 68 saying, "Prophesy to us, you Messiah! Who is it that struck you?"

In 26:57 the narrator reminds the reader that the plan to kill Jesus was hatched in the house of Caiaphas. Although this verse clearly refers back to the beginning of the chapter, here the parties to the decision are identified as the scribes and elders rather than the chief priests and elders, as in 26:3. Matthew seems less interested in precision than in implicating the broadest possible group of Jewish leaders in Jesus' death. The chief priests reappear, however, in 26:59 as the ones who, along with the council, seek false testimony to justify a death sentence. As in Mark the story of Jesus' interrogation is paralleled by that of Peter's denial, taking place in the courtyard outside.

One important difference between Matthew and Mark occurs in the climax to the interrogation. As in Mark the high priest stands up and demands Jesus' response to the accusations made against him. In the face of Jesus' silence, the high priest addresses him directly. Here this address is more emphatic, in that the high priest puts Jesus under oath. Jesus, in turn, is more evasive. Rather than clearly and openly accepting the identification as the Messiah, the son of God, Jesus is evasive, responding "You have said so" instead of "I am" (Mark 14:62).[23]

Second, some scholars attach significance to the fact that Matthew uses *himation* rather than Mark's term, *chiton,* to refer to the garment that the high priest tears upon hearing Jesus' declaration. Bond suggests that Matthew's term refers to the priestly vestments. By using this term, the Evangelist wants to show that the high priest is deliberately breaking the law, which forbids the tearing of the priestly garments, and thereby foreshadowing the end of the Temple and therefore the end of the importance of the high priest.[24] This variation in terminology may not be significant, however. Bond herself notes that Mark's term can also be used of high-priestly garments, and that another term, *stol* (meaning "stole" in English), is normally used by Josephus to refer to the vestments (*Ant.* 15.405–9, 18.90–95).[25] In any case it does not seem that Matthew is making more of this act than did Mark. The main focus remains on the high drama and symbolism of the high priest's response.

Also unconvincing is Bond's suggestion that Matthew has deliberately, if subtly, heightened the contrast between Jesus and Caiaphas in order to show that Jesus has usurped the high priest's role. Through his death, she argues, Jesus symbolically destroyed the old sanctuary and created a new temple: the community of believers in which God is uniquely present. Jesus is the high priest of this "temple." As high priest he has spiritual authority and saves his people from their sins (Matt. 1:21).[26] This is an overinterpretation, however. The verses cited to support this interpretation emphasize that God (1:23) or Jesus (18:20, 28:20) abides with those who believe, but there is nothing in these verses to imply that the Evangelist is specifically portraying the community as a new temple.[27]

Finally, and most striking for our purposes, Matthew's high priest, in contrast to Mark's, is named rather than anonymous. In Bond's view Matthew's use of the name accentuates the contrast between "Jesus, the hero, surrounded by his disciples," and "the high priest, the arch villain, surrounded by Jewish leaders."[28] Perhaps. But this too may be an overinterpretation. Although Caiaphas's name and title appear in the introduction to the scene (26:57), he is referred to only by his title throughout the interrogation itself. As in Mark it is the "high priest" rather than "Caiaphas" who tears his garment and elicits the guilty verdict from the council.

Nevertheless Matthew's use of the high priest's name raises the question of whether he had access to information to which Mark did not. In Fitzmyer's view Matthew filled in the information that Mark lacked at the time that he wrote. "At the time of Matthew's writing (A.D. 80–85), when Caiaphas has long since been deposed . . . the evangelist simply recalls that Caiaphas was the high priest of that year and inserts his name into his Marcan source."[29] Bond, on the other hand, believes that both Mark and Matthew knew the name of the high priest but that it suited Matthew's purpose—to heighten the drama—to insert it into Mark's account.

Peter's Denial of Jesus (26:69–75)

> 69 Now Peter was sitting outside in the courtyard. A servant-girl came to him and said, "You also were with Jesus the Galilean." 70 But he denied it before all of them, saying, "I do not know what you are talking about." 71 When he went out to the porch, another servant-girl saw him, and she said to the bystanders, "This man was with Jesus of Nazareth." 72 Again he denied it with an oath, "I do not know the man." 73 After a little while the bystanders came up and said to Peter, "Certainly you are also one of them, for your accent betrays you." 74 Then he began to curse, and he swore an oath, "I do not know the man!" At that moment the cock crowed. 75 Then Peter remembered what Jesus had said: "Before the cock crows, you will deny me three times." And he went out and wept bitterly.

As in Mark the story of Jesus' interrogation before the high priest and council is interwoven with that of Peter's denial, a dramatic and highly effective arrangement that contrasts the devotion and integrity of Jesus with Peter's lack of same.

Jesus' Delivery to Pilate (27:1–2)

> 1 When morning came, all the chief priests and the elders of the people conferred together against Jesus in order to bring about his death. 2 They bound him, led him away, and handed him over to Pilate the governor.

In contrast to Mark, Matthew assigns a specific purpose to this second consultation: to bring about Jesus' death. Note that there is no specific reference to the high priest, who is absent from the remainder of the Gospel account.

Observations

Matthew's Caiaphas, like Mark's high priest, is a neutral figure. Caiaphas expresses shock and dismay at his apocalyptic utterances but no animosity toward Jesus himself. It is the Jewish leadership as a whole—chief priests, elders, scribes, and council—who are hostile to Jesus and actively manipulate events to ensure his death.

As in Mark, Jesus' Passion predictions implicate the chief priests and other groups in his coming death. According to Matthew 16:21, "Jesus began to show his disciples that he must go to Jerusalem and undergo great suffering at the hands of the elders and chief priests and scribes, and be killed, and on the third day be raised"; as they go up to Jerusalem, Jesus reminds his disciples that there "the Son of Man will be handed over to the chief priests and scribes, and they will condemn him to death" (20:18). The chief priests and scribes became angry upon hearing reports of Jesus' amazing acts and of the children welcoming him in the Temple with the words "Hosanna to the Son of David" (21:15), and the chief priests and elders challenged him when he entered the Temple: "By what authority are you doing these things, and who gave you this authority?" (21:23). As in Mark, Judas approaches the chief priests when he plans to betray Jesus (26:14), and it is they who accuse him to Pilate (27:12), persuade the crowds to ask for Barabbas's freedom (27:20), shout for Jesus' crucifixion (27:62), and mock him (27:41).

It is difficult to say whether Matthew intended to include Caiaphas in this group or exclude him. It does seem clear, however, that there was no desire specifically to implicate the high priest. Furthermore if we accept that Matthew used Mark as a source, it would seem that Matthew largely accepted the Marcan version of events but made them more specific by drawing out the theme of the fulfillment of prophecy and adding some narrative details, of which the naming of Caiaphas is one.

THE GOSPEL OF LUKE

Caiaphas in Lucan Chronology (3:1–2)

In contrast to Matthew, Luke does not situate a cabal of Jewish leaders in the high priest's precinct, nor does he depict the high priest as presiding over a nocturnal interrogation. Indeed his sole reference to Caiaphas occurs in the introduction to his tale of Jesus' ministry, which places the activity of John the Baptist, when "the word of God came to John son of Zechariah in the wilderness," in its historical context "in the fifteenth year of the reign of Emperor Tiberius, when Pontius Pilate was governor of Judea, and Herod was ruler of Galilee, and his brother Philip ruler of the region of Ituraea and Trachonitis, and Lysanias ruler of Abilene, during the high-priesthood of Annas and Caiaphas."[30] This introduction grounds the story in the broad political history of Israel; Luke's narrative begins at a time when Israel was led by the high priesthood, which, though no longer hereditary and very much under Roman control, nevertheless retained considerable authority and prestige among Jews in Judaea and Galilee as well as in the Diaspora and concludes with a transfer of spiritual authority to a new leadership, the apostles who are led by the spirit.[31] Caiaphas does not appear as an actor or full-fledged character; rather, his name is included in a list of officials that is intended to locate Luke's narrative within a familiar historical and chronological context.

Luke adds some ambiguity by referring in the singular to the high priesthood of Annas and Caiaphas. This formulation implies that this position was held jointly by Caiaphas and his father-in-law. There is no evidence, however, that two men ever held this position at the same time. It would appear that Luke is simply imprecise on this point; the Evangelist may simply be referring to a period when Palestinian Jewry was dominated by two powerful figures.[32] Winter suggests that a textual problem underlies this confusing comment. In his view Luke originally had Annas as the high priest, and the verse was later corrected by someone who, on the basis of Matthew, wrote Caiaphas's name over that of Annas without erasing the latter. A later copyist noticed the problem but could not decide between them and simply included both names linked with an *and*.[33] There is no manuscript evidence, however, to support this conjecture. As Bond notes, the names of both presumably came down to Luke from his sources, whether written or oral. These traditions may have referred to each man as high priest, Annas because he was respected and Caiaphas because he was known to have been high priest at the time. In her view "Luke knew perfectly well that there was only one high priest, one mediator between God and humanity, and that the reference to the high priest had to be singular."[34] As with Mark, however, it is difficult to be certain that the Evangelist knew more than he wrote.

The Betrayal and Arrest of Jesus (22:47–54)

> 47 While he was still speaking, suddenly a crowd came, and the one called Judas, one of the twelve, was leading them. He approached Jesus to kiss him; 48 but Jesus said to him, "Judas, is it with a kiss that you are betraying the Son of Man?" 49 When those who were around him saw what was coming, they asked, "Lord, should we strike with the sword?" 50 Then one of them struck the slave of the high priest and cut off his right ear. 51 But Jesus said, "No more of this!" And he touched his ear and healed him. 52 Then Jesus said to the chief priests, the officers of the temple police, and the elders who had come for him, "Have you come out with swords and clubs as if I were a bandit? 53 When I was with you day after day in the temple, you did not lay hands on me. But this is your hour, and the power of darkness!" 54

Here, as in Matthew and Luke, the ear of the high priest's slave is severed by a sword. Luckily for the slave, Jesus heals his ear immediately. Jesus' followers are clearly at fault. Though they are anxious to defend their master, they also take care to ask whether they should strike with the sword. One of them does not wait for the answer and is sharply rebuked by Jesus for his hasty action.

Peter's Denial of Jesus (22:54–62)

> 54 Then they seized him and led him away, bringing him into the high priest's house. But Peter was following at a distance. 55 When they had kindled a fire in the middle of the courtyard and sat down together, Peter sat

among them. ⁵⁶ Then a servant-girl, seeing him in the firelight, stared at him and said, "This man also was with him." ⁵⁷ But he denied it, saying, "Woman, I do not know him." ⁵⁸ A little later someone else, on seeing him, said, "You also are one of them." But Peter said, "Man, I am not!" ⁵⁹ Then about an hour later still another kept insisting, "Surely this man also was with him; for he is a Galilean." ⁶⁰ But Peter said, "Man, I do not know what you are talking about!" At that moment, while he was still speaking, the cock crowed. ⁶¹ The Lord turned and looked at Peter. Then Peter remembered the word of the Lord, how he had said to him, "Before the cock crows today, you will deny me three times." ⁶² And he went out and wept bitterly.

The narrative tradition has firmly attached the story of Peter's denial to that of Jesus' interrogation. In contrast to Matthew and Mark, however, Luke does not interweave the two narratives but tells the Peter's story before recounting Jesus' experience with the council.

The Mocking and Beating of Jesus (22:63–65)

⁶³ Now the men who were holding Jesus began to mock him and beat him; ⁶⁴ they also blindfolded him and kept asking him, "Prophesy! Who is it that struck you?" ⁶⁵ They kept heaping many other insults on him.

Here Luke's account differs from that in Mark and Matthew, in which the abuse of Jesus takes place after the interrogation, not beforehand (Matt. 27:27–31; Mark 15:16–20).

The Interrogation of Jesus by the Council and Delivery to Pilate (22:66–23:1)

⁶⁶ When day came, the assembly of the elders of the people, both chief priests and scribes, gathered together, and they brought him to their council. ⁶⁷ They said, "If you are the Messiah, tell us." He replied, "If I tell you, you will not believe; ⁶⁸ and if I question you, you will not answer. ⁶⁹ But from now on the Son of Man will be seated at the right hand of the power of God." ⁷⁰ All of them asked, "Are you, then, the Son of God?" He said to them, "You say that I am." ⁷¹ Then they said, "What further testimony do we need? We have heard it ourselves from his own lips!" ²³:¹ Then the assembly rose as a body and brought Jesus before Pilate.

Like Mark and Matthew, Luke mentions the high priest's slave in his account of Jesus' arrest (22:50). In contrast to the other synoptic Gospels, however, there is no nocturnal interrogation; there is no confrontation between Jesus and Caiaphas, no charge of blasphemy, and no tearing of clothing. Indeed, despite the reference to Annas and Caiaphas in Luke 3:1–5, neither man appears as an actor within Luke's Gospel. But Luke, uniquely, gives a short account of the morning council meeting to which Mark and Matthew merely refer.

Brown suggests that Luke has edited Mark by moving material from the Passion narrative to the trial of Stephen in Acts 6:9–7:60.[35] This is certainly possible, as the Temple is a prominent motif in Stephen's trial. But it is also possible that Luke has simply created, or perhaps inherited, a pared-down version of the nocturnal investigation that is described by Matthew and Mark. While there is no reference to false testimony, the passage focuses on the same central issue: Jesus' identity as the Messiah. Jesus responds to the direct question with the same quotations from Daniel and Psalms. Whatever the composition history of this passage, it suggests that for Luke, at least, the high priest had no part in the proceedings against Jesus. Jesus' interlocutors are the chief priests and scribes who constitute the assembly of elders. In the view of this group, Jesus has condemned himself: They have heard it "from his own lips" (22:71).

Luke 3:1–2 indicates that the Third Evangelist knew of Caiaphas. That being the case, it is difficult to explain why the high priest's name was omitted in 22:54, which refers only to the house of the high priest. It is possible that as he does not have a lengthy trial narrative, Luke simply takes over his Marcan source at this point and does not identify the high priest by name (cf. Mark 14:53).

Bond suggests that Luke, like Mark, knew that Caiaphas presided over the interrogation, but simply chose not to say so. She posits three reasons for Luke's omission: to broaden responsibility for Jesus' death from the high priest to the entire assembly; to avoid detracting from the central Christological issue of the trial; and to postpone to a later stage in his narrative the theme of God's rejection of his people. Bond argues that Luke-Acts intends to show that although Israel has rejected her prophet Messiah, God does not turn from the Jews to the Gentiles until the trial of Stephen. This is the decisive point of the account in Luke-Acts. For this reason Luke delays the entrance of the high priest until the trials of the apostles in Acts 4–5, where he and his high-priestly family will act as a foil for ordinary Jews, who are repenting of their rejection of Jesus and turning to the new movement in droves. With the trial of Stephen and the subsequent high-priestly persecution of Christianity, Luke shows that the traditional leaders of Judaism have proven themselves to be no longer capable of guiding God's people, and that God's people will henceforth be composed of both Jews and Gentiles.[36] Luke, like Mark, is more interested in the high priest's symbolic function than in the man himself.[37]

No matter how one accounts for the brevity of Luke's account, the effect is to remove all responsibility for Jesus' death from the high priest. Like Mark and

Matthew, Luke focuses on the chief priests, the elders, and the scribes, who are not carefully distinguished from one another but rather arrayed together in opposition to Jesus.

THE GOSPEL OF JOHN

The Decision (11:47–53)

The majority of references to Caiaphas occur in the Fourth Gospel, and it is John who provides the most explicit rationale for the Jewish leaderships' plot against Jesus. In the aftermath of Lazarus's miraculous revivification, the chief priests and Pharisees fear Jesus' rapidly growing popularity.

> [47] So the chief priests and the Pharisees called a meeting of the council, and said, "What are we to do? This man is performing many signs. [48] If we let him go on like this, everyone will believe in him, and the Romans will come and destroy both our holy place and our nation." [49] But one of them, Caiaphas, who was high priest that year, said to them, "You know nothing at all! [50] You do not understand that it is better for you to have one man die for the people than to have the whole nation destroyed." [51] He did not say this on his own, but being high priest that year he prophesied that Jesus was about to die for the nation, [52] and not for the nation only, but to gather into one the dispersed children of God. [53] So from that day on they planned to put him to death.

As in the synoptic Gospels, the plot against Jesus is instigated by the chief priests and a second group, in this case, the Pharisees. Whereas the synoptic plot is prepared in the aftermath of Jesus' disruptive actions in the Temple, in John it is the raising of Lazarus and the people's overwhelming response to it that alarms the Jewish leadership. Their concern is that Jesus' behavior is attracting a large following and might therefore cause the Romans to destroy "our holy place" and the nation. Most commentators understand "our holy place" to be the Temple, though it is also possible that it refers to Jerusalem more generally.[38] The term *ethnos* in this context may refer to the population of Judaea or perhaps, as Winter suggests, "nationhood" or "national status."[39] The nation and the place, in the sense of Temple, occur together in 2 Maccabees 5:19–20:

> [19] But the Lord did not choose the nation for the sake of the holy place, but the place for the sake of the nation. [20] Therefore the place itself shared in the misfortunes that befell the nation and afterward participated in its benefits; and what was forsaken in the wrath of the Almighty was restored again in all its glory when the great Lord became reconciled.

This passage, like John 11:49–52, links the fate of the Temple with that of the nation. Why exactly the belief of the people, occasioned by Jesus' behavior, would result in such a strong Roman response is unclear. A number of different possibilities exist. One is that the Jewish leaders' concern reflects the view that Jews who believe in Jesus necessarily sever their covenantal relationship with God. That the Jewish leadership (in John's view) held this perspective is suggested by John 12:10–11, in which belief in Jesus is seen as desertion of Judaism. The fear is that this desertion might take place on a large scale, as intimated in John 12:19, in which the Johannine Pharisees express feelings of powerlessness in the face of the crowd's response to Jesus' miracles: "You see, you can do nothing. Look, the world has gone after him!" Such large-scale desertion in turn might prompt God to punish the Jews by sending the Romans to destroy the nation, just as in earlier days God sent the Assyrians and Babylonians to punish the Jews for turning away from the covenant. In the background may lie passages such as 2 Kings 21:12–15, in which God responds to Judaea's idolatry under King Manasseh with the following prophecy:

> 12 I am bringing upon Jerusalem and Judah such evil that the ears of everyone who hears of it will tingle. 13 I will stretch over Jerusalem the measuring line for Samaria, and the plummet for the house of Ahab; I will wipe Jerusalem as one wipes a dish, wiping it and turning it upside down. 14 I will cast off the remnant of my heritage, and give them into the hand of their enemies; they shall become a prey and a spoil to all their enemies, 15 because they have done what is evil in my sight and have provoked me to anger, since the day their ancestors came out of Egypt, even to this day.

The eventual destruction of Jerusalem and the Temple by the Babylonians was seen as the fulfillment of such prophecies. In the Maccabean era, a similar explanation was used for the ability of Antiochus IV to desecrate the Temple. 2 Maccabees 5:15–20 explains that "the Lord was angered for a little while because of the sins of those who lived in the city, and that this was the reason he was disregarding the holy place" (5:17). The Evangelist, who wrote his Gospel perhaps two decades after 70 C.E., may well have had in mind Rome's destruction of the Second Temple in Jerusalem. If so, however, it is an ironic reading, for from his perspective it was not the people's belief in Jesus that constituted desertion of God's covenant but the Jewish authorities' adamant resistance to such belief (cf. 9:41).

A second line of interpretation is political; the widespread belief of Jews in Jesus might make Rome fear rebellion and therefore prompt the empire to move against Judaea and the Temple. That the Romans behaved in just such a manner is implied in Acts 21:38, in which a Roman tribune asks Paul whether he is "the Egyptian who recently stirred up a revolt and led the four thousand assassins out into the wilderness." Josephus describes several situations in which Rome used military force against a group of Jewish followers of one would-be messiah or another (*Ant.* 20:97–99, 20:169–72, 20:188; *War* 2.258–63).[40] Given the multilayered nature of John's narrative and symbolism, both of these interpretations may be at play simultaneously.[41]

At this point Caiaphas speaks out. It is noteworthy that he is portrayed neither as the leader of the group nor as the one who presides over the meeting. He is described as "one of them," that is, one of the group that is meeting about this matter, and then as "high priest that year." This description does not draw particular attention to Caiaphas's authority; he is a peer among peers, chosen, it is implied, for that year. This statement may imply a (mistaken) belief on the part of the Evangelist that the high priest changed annually. It is also significant that Caiaphas does not explicitly address the concern for both temple and nation, emphasizing only the potential benefit that Jesus' death would have for the nation.

Although he is not described as the leader of the group, Caiaphas's words imply his authority. He chastises his colleagues for their failure to grasp the situation properly and articulates the need for Jesus to die on behalf of the nation and thereby avert the destruction of the nation as a whole. The narrator describes these words as a prophecy not only of Jesus' imminent death but also of its salvific and eschatological importance for all who believe.

Underlying Caiaphas's words here may be an allusion to the Day of Atonement and the practice of sending a goat out into the wilderness as a "scapegoat" that carries on its head the sins of the entire nation and, in dying, expiates those sins on the nation's behalf.[42] The sacrificial motif is present in the narrator's comment that Jesus dies not only for the nation but also for the scattered children of God (11:51–52).[43] The passage is also an expression of Johannine theology, in that Caiaphas becomes the spokesman for the idea that Jesus died a sacrificial death for the sake of the people (John 1:29).[44]

While this passage has no direct parallels in the synoptic Gospels, it does convey some of the same themes. One prominent motif is prophecy. In the synoptic Gospels, it is Jesus who prophecies his death; in John it is Caiaphas. A second theme, shared with Matthew, is the fear that Jesus' actions and his popularity threaten to disrupt the relationship between Judaea and Rome. Third is Caiaphas's lack of personal animosity toward Jesus. Although the high priest advocates and provides a rationale for Jesus' death, he is motivated not by fear or hatred of Jesus but national preservation, that is, the concern that his behavior might have dire consequences for the people as a whole.

A more cynical view of the high priest is also possible, however. Bond comments that while Caiaphas's words may simply express political expediency, she suspects that "what really matters to the high priest here is not simply the fate of the temple and the nation, but the maintenance of the status quo, his own supremacy, and that of his advisers. The pragmatic Jewish leader has no scruples in offering one man's life to safeguard his own position."[45] Yet the high priest's words are also ironic; here Jesus' archenemy articulates both the sacrificial nature and the salvific significance of Jesus' death.[46] Bond concludes that "in this scene, Caiaphas comes across as a hostile character, intent on self-preservation and callous in his disregard for human life. As high priest, he epitomizes Jewish opposition to Jesus and, like 'the Jews' generally in this Gospel, allies himself with the satanic forces of darkness and sin. Yet it is also apparent that John has some residual regard for the office of high priest; in that role, even a hostile character can unconsciously speak the words of God."[47]

One might suspect, however, that Bond is here reading into John the later interpretations of Caiaphas as unredeemably wicked. As a Jewish leader, the Johannine Caiaphas is clearly on the wrong side of the theological equation, but he is nowhere portrayed as directly hostile to Jesus as are "the Jews" or "the Pharisees." In John, as in the synoptic Gospels, the chief priests, along with other groups, remain active in their hostility against Jesus. In John 7:32 the chief priests and Pharisees send Temple police to arrest him after they hear the crowd muttering about him in the Temple at the Feast of Tabernacles, and then in 7:45 they question why this arrest did not take place. In the aftermath of Caiaphas's prophecy, the efforts to arrest Jesus intensify: "the chief priests and the Pharisees had given orders that anyone who knew where Jesus was should let them know, so that they might arrest him" (11:57). After Lazarus attracts their attention, "the chief priests planned to put Lazarus to death as well" (12:10). Caiaphas is absent from these accounts.

The Betrayal and Arrest of Jesus (18:1–11)

> [1] After Jesus had spoken these words, he went out with his disciples across the Kidron valley to a place where there was a garden, which he and his disciples entered. [2] Now Judas, who betrayed him, also knew the place, because Jesus often met there with his disciples. [3] So Judas brought a detachment of soldiers together with police from the chief priests and the Pharisees, and they came there with lanterns and torches and weapons. [4] Then Jesus, knowing all that was to happen to him, came forward and asked them, "For whom are you looking?" [5] They answered, "Jesus of Nazareth." Jesus replied, "I am he." Judas, who betrayed him, was standing with them. [6] When Jesus said to

them, "I am he," they stepped back and fell to the ground. ⁷ Again he asked them, "For whom are you looking?" And they said, "Jesus of Nazareth." ⁸ Jesus answered, "I told you that I am he. So if you are looking for me, let these men go." ⁹ This was to fulfil the word that he had spoken, "I did not lose a single one of those whom you gave me." ¹⁰ Then Simon Peter, who had a sword, drew it, struck the high priest's slave, and cut off his right ear. The slave's name was Malchus. ¹¹ Jesus said to Peter, "Put your sword back into its sheath. Am I not to drink the cup that the Father has given me?"

John's version of the betrayal and arrest is much more detailed than the Synoptic versions. This story also refers to the injury done to the slave of the high priest, but John specifies that it was not just any follower but Simon Peter who slices off the man's ear. The account includes a confession of Jesus' messianic identity, marked by the "I am" (*ego eimi*) formula so prevalent in the Fourth Gospel (see also 8:24, 8:28, 8:58, 13:19, 18:5, 18:6, 18:8).[48]

The Interrogation of Jesus by the High Priest, Part 1 (18:12–14)

> ¹² So the soldiers, their officer, and the Jewish police arrested Jesus and bound him. ¹³ First they took him to Annas, who was the father-in-law of Caiaphas, the high priest that year. ¹⁴ Caiaphas was the one who had advised the Jews that it was better to have one person die for the people.

The interrogation of Jesus by Annas marks a major departure from the synoptic accounts. The reader is reminded, however, of Caiaphas's role in the events by a reference back to 11:49–52. Josephus continues to use the high-priestly title in reference to men who formerly held the office (*War* 2.441; *Ant.* 20.205; *Life* 193). These passages suggest that former high priests retained the high-priestly title and may have continued to exert considerable influence in both secular and religious matters. More difficult is the question of how much authority was held by former high priests such as Annas.

The Interrogation of Jesus by the High Priest, Part 1 (18:12–14)

> ¹⁵ Simon Peter and another disciple followed Jesus. Since that disciple was known to the high priest, he went with Jesus into the courtyard of the high priest, ¹⁶ but Peter was standing outside at the gate. So the other disciple, who was known to the high priest, went out, spoke to the woman who guarded the gate, and brought Peter in. ¹⁷ The woman said to Peter, "You are not also one of this man's disciples, are you?" He said, "I am not." ¹⁸ Now the slaves and the police had made a charcoal fire because it was cold, and they were standing round it and warming themselves. Peter also was standing with them and warming himself.

In the Fourth Gospel, the interweaving of the two interrogations—of Jesus and of Peter—is more thorough and perhaps more artful than in Mark and Matthew, thus making the contrast between them stand out even more clearly.

The Interrogation of Jesus by the High Priest, Part 2 (18:19–24)

> [19] Then the high priest questioned Jesus about his disciples and about his teaching. [20] Jesus answered, "I have spoken openly to the world; I have always taught in synagogues and in the temple, where all the Jews come together. I have said nothing in secret. [21] Why do you ask me? Ask those who heard what I said to them; they know what I said." [22] When he had said this, one of the police standing nearby struck Jesus on the face, saying, "Is that how you answer the high priest?" [23] Jesus answered, "If I have spoken wrongly, testify to the wrong. But if I have spoken rightly, why do you strike me?" [24] Then Annas sent him bound to Caiaphas the high priest.

It is noteworthy that the narrator does not quote Annas directly but only Jesus. The former high priest, like numerous other interlocutors of Jesus in the Gospel of John, is a straw character whose main purpose is to act as a foil for Jesus and to give him an opportunity to speak his mind.[49] In any case this is hardly a formal trial. There are no witnesses called and no testimony given, false or otherwise. Annas's questioning is open-ended and concerns Jesus' disciples and his teaching and not, as in the synoptic Gospels, his messianic identity. Jesus' response is somewhat defensive and seems to be answering a more specific question, pertaining, perhaps, to secret teachings. Contrary to the synoptic accounts, here it is Jesus who takes the initiative by suggesting to Annas that he seek testimony to substantiate Jesus' account. Jesus is then taken off to Caiaphas, but the Evangelist offers no account of what happened during Jesus' hours in the high priest's precincts.

Peter's Denial of Jesus, Part 2 (18:25–27)

> [25] Now Simon Peter was standing and warming himself. They asked him, "You are not also one of his disciples, are you?" He denied it and said, "I am not." [26] One of the slaves of the high priest, a relative of the man whose ear Peter had cut off, asked, "Did I not see you in the garden with him?" [27] Again Peter denied it, and at that moment the cock crowed.

The interweaving of the two accounts suggests that Peter completes his denial of Jesus just as Jesus is being taken away to Caiaphas. Yet in contrast to the synoptic Gospels, the dramatic structure does not quite create a complete parallel between Jesus and Peter. This is because Jesus' encounter with Annas, in contrast to the synoptic stories of the interrogation before the high priest, does not focus on Jesus' messianic identity but on his teaching practices. Peter's denial is then primarily intended in John's hands to show the fulfillment of Jesus' prophecy in John 13:38. It affirms Jesus' prophetic abilities but not necessarily his Christological identity.[50]

Jesus' Delivery to Pilate (18:28)

> Then they took Jesus from Caiaphas to Pilate's headquarters. It was early in the morning. They themselves did not enter the headquarters, so as to avoid ritual defilement and to be able to eat the Passover.

The identity of those who take Jesus from place to place is not specified. *Pace* Bond, there is no basis on which to argue that "they" are Caiaphas and Annas.[51] The audience is here reminded of the timing; likely "they" would have realized the need for haste in order to complete this process before the beginning of Passover, when all Jews, including the chief priests and the high priest, would be eating the Passover lamb.[52]

John's version of the events leading up to Jesus' trial before Pilate differs considerably from the synoptic accounts both in content and in structure. The most significant difference pertains to the roles assigned to Annas and Caiaphas. As noted, in John's version Jesus is interrogated not by Caiaphas but by his father-in-law, Annas (cf. Luke's chronological reference in Luke 3:1–5). While some have tried to argue that in fact it is the high priest who interrogates Jesus in this passage, this reading cannot be supported from the Gospel narrative itself.

In Bond's view the interrogation before Annas is the climax of the Gospel's theme of the Jews' rejection of Jesus. She suggests that John, like Mark, is deliberately ambiguous here in order to contrast Jesus with the office of the high priest rather than with any individual holder of that office.[53] In doing so the Evangelist can assert that it is no longer the Jewish high priest but Jesus himself who mediates the covenantal relationship between God and Israel. This would be consistent with the self-representation of the Johannine Jesus in the farewell discourses as the one who goes before believers (13:16, 14:2–3, 16:22) and mediates for them in heaven (for example 16:23–24), as well as with his prayer in John 17.[54] Brant comments that the narrator demonstrates a consistent disregard for distinctions between Jewish leaders: for example in John 1:19–28, the Gospel blurs the difference between the Temple authorities and the Pharisees by treating John's interrogators first as representatives of the priests and Levites and then as those of the Pharisees. She notes that "by drawing attention to different interrogations by Annas and Caiaphas, the narrator makes clear that they are distinct individuals, but by using the title High Priest to identify both of them he seems to deny the power of a title to determine a person's identity."[55]

These interpretations are possible but not compelling. Perhaps the simplest conclusion is that Caiaphas himself was no longer important once he had articulated the desirability of arranging for the troublemaker's death in order to spare the people as a whole.

ACTS OF THE APOSTLES

Outside the Gospels Caiaphas's name appears only in the Acts of the Apostles, written by the author of Luke's gospel.[56] Caiaphas is mentioned alongside Annas in Acts 4:6. According to Acts 4:1–15, Peter and John were arrested by the priests, the captain of the Temple, and the Sadducees after healing a man from illness in the name of the resurrected Jesus. The next day Annas "the high priest," Caiaphas, and others of the high-priestly family interrogated the prisoners, but when they "saw the man who had been cured standing beside them, they had nothing to say in opposition. So they ordered them to leave the council while they discussed the matter with one another" (14–15). The apostles continued their preaching and healing and gained a large following (5:16). Noteworthy here is that, at least as written, it is Annas and not Caiaphas who is identified as high priest. This may be carelessness or simply lack of knowledge; this is consistent with the ambiguous reference to the high priesthood of Annas and Caiaphas in Luke 3:1–2.

This episode is followed by a long story (5:17–42) in which the high priest—apparently Annas, on the basis of 4:6—arrests the apostles and has them imprisoned overnight. In the middle of the night they are freed by an angel who tells them to go and preach in the Temple (17–20). The Temple police are shocked to discover the empty prison and even more surprised to hear that the apostles are preaching in the Temple (21–25). The captain retrieves them, and the apostles stand for cross examination before the council, led by the high priest (26–33). The apostles' remarks enrage the Jewish authorities, but they are defended by the Pharisee Gamaliel, who reminds the council of the incident involving Theudas, who "rose up, claiming to be somebody, and a number of men, about four hundred, joined him; but he was killed, and all who followed him were dispersed and disappeared. After him Judas the Galilean rose up at the time of the census and got people to follow him; he also perished, and all who followed him were scattered. So in the present case, I tell you, keep away from these men and let them alone; because if this plan or this undertaking is of human origin, it will fail; but if it is of God, you will not be able to overthrow them—in that case you may even be found fighting against God!" (34–39).

The council heeds Gamaliel, has the apostles flogged, and releases them on condition that they cease to preach in Jesus' name. This is an order the apostles promptly violate (40–42).

In contrast to the Gospels' trial narratives, the high priest in this passage is actively engaged in hostilities against Jesus' followers. He and his fellow leaders flounder around and look like fools. The point is to show that God abandoned his support of the Jewish religious and political leadership and is now on the side of Jesus' followers. Several other stories in Acts similarly recount an interrogation conducted by an unnamed high priest, though not all end as peacefully as the one in Acts 5 (cf. the arrest and trial of Stephen in Acts 6:7–7:2).

These stories in Acts are dramatic, but they add little to the New Testament portrait of the high priest Caiaphas. What they do emphasize, however, is the absolute opposition of the Jewish leadership to the apostles' activities. This view is adumbrated in John 16:2, in which the Johannine Jesus warns his disciples that "they will put you out of the synagogues. Indeed, an hour is coming when those who kill you will think that by doing so they are offering worship to God. And they will do this because they have not known the Father or me."[57] The narratives in Acts also anticipate the type of scene that becomes typical in postcanonical literature depicting disputations between Jewish and Christian leaders.

CONCLUSION

Although Caiaphas appears by name and/or by title in all four canonical Gospels, his role varies in each case, and he is a major player in none. For Mark and Matthew, the high priest is a leader among the Jewish authorities who presides over an interrogation at the end of which he tears his robes and charges Jesus with blasphemy, but he is apparently not involved in the plot that led to Jesus' arrest in the first place. In John the high priest is the one who formulates the plot to have Jesus killed and articulates the rationale for doing so, but he apparently does not interrogate Jesus, let alone tear his robe or charge him with blasphemy.[58] In Luke he has no place at all except as a chronological marker. Neither is there a consensus on who interrogated Jesus: for Mark it is the high priest, for Matthew it is Caiaphas, for Luke it is the assembly, and for John it is Annas. It is tempting to harmonize these separate traditions, but doing so ignores the substantial narrative and theological differences among them.

Alongside these significant contradictions, the Gospels' accounts exhibit a disconcerting vagueness on a number of key points. One is the role of Annas. The references to Annas as high priest may be confusing, but as we have already seen, Josephus's writings confirm that the title of "high priest" could be used to refer to a former high priest after he has left office (*War* 2.243). Schürer comments that "with the High Priests constantly changing, there was always a considerable number of them no longer in office. These too nevertheless occupied an important and influential position, as may be demonstrated in respect of at least some of them. It is clear from the New Testament that the elder Annas enjoyed great esteem even as a deposed High Priest."[59] The references to Annas may thereby simply be a sign of respect for a former pontiff who remained active in affairs of state. One cannot rule out, however, that the Evangelists, whose Gospels reached final form outside Judaea in the decades after the Temple's destruction, did not have precise information about the high priests and their tenure or an accurate understanding of the high priesthood as an institution.

This view is not shared by Bond, who is convinced that all four Evangelists knew that Caiaphas was the high priest. If so, omissions of his name from the Passion accounts must be explained on literary and/or theological grounds.[60] Winter, on the other hand, argues that both Luke and John may have conflated the elder Annas with his youngest son, also named Annas, who was high priest in 62 C.E. and who, according to Josephus, was responsible for the stoning of Jesus' brother James.[61] In a similar vein, Borg and Crossan point out that Jesus and all the first-century Christians whose deaths are known to history were executed under high priests from the family of Annas, namely, Stephen in Acts 6–7, whose execution may have taken place during Caiaphas's tenure; James, brother of John in Acts 12:2; and James brother of Jesus in *Antiquities* 20.197–203.[62] This suggestion is intriguing but difficult to substantiate, as the author of Acts does not focus on the role of the high priests in these events, and we learn of the death of James the brother of Jesus only from Josephus. Yet one cannot discount the possibility that the Evangelists were more familiar with the events that occurred closer to their own time and then attributed to Annas I and his son-in-law the same hostility toward Jesus that his son may have done toward Jesus' family and followers. It is important to remember, however, that the portrayal of Caiaphas is rather mild in this regard, at least when compared with the hostility attributed to the "chief priests" as a group.

Even if we cannot show that specific later details were read back into the time of Jesus, it is reasonable to consider the impact that their post-70 context may have had on the Gospels' representations of Judaean society in the era before the revolt, including Jesus' own actions in relation to the Temple and its authorities. Bond suggests, for example, that after 70 "Johannine Christians began to realize that they could do without the temple. As far as they were concerned, Jesus had fulfilled and superseded everything they once held sacred: they had their own spiritual temple and their own high priest, true worship was no longer to be found in a sacred place, but among those who chose to abide in the body of Jesus Christ."[63] In Bond's view this shift is symbolized by the seamless robe that Jesus wore to the cross, which represents the high-priestly garb.[64] Also relevant may be the early Christian belief that the Temple was destroyed on account of the Jews' refusal to believe Jesus to be the Messiah (Matt. 22:7, 23:38).

The second major area of ambiguity pertains to whether Caiaphas is included among the "chief priests." Placing Caiaphas among the chief priests would greatly amplify the high priest's presence and activity in the Passion by including him in the group that paid Judas to betray Jesus (Matt. 26:14–15), accused Jesus before Pilate (Matt. 27:12), persuaded the crowd to ask for Barabbas's release, and clamored for Jesus' crucifixion (John 19:6). The Gospels, however, are frustratingly vague on this point. John 11:49 refers to Caiaphas as "one of them," but whether "they" are the chief priests, the Pharisees, the council, or all three (11:47) is impossible to tell. Matthew and Mark have the chief priests present false testimony to the high priest, thereby distinguishing Caiaphas from their ranks. Perhaps it is the narrative imperative that has pushed some of the Gospels to name the high priest in lieu of the chief priests. It may not be a big step, narratively speaking, to move from the collective of "high priests" (as the Greek reads) to the singular high priest, a figure of some power who is a worthy but ultimately inferior opponent to the messianic protagonist.

The contradictions and ambiguities strongly suggest that the Evangelists did not know exactly what role, if any, Caiaphas played in the events leading to Jesus' death.[65] The differences among the works of the Evangelists with regard to the high priest Caiaphas's role in Jesus' death, while frustrating to historians, provide excellent opportunities for those who create imaginary narratives to fill in the gaps and piece events together, linked with newly created ones, in a way that makes for a dramatic and satisfying story.

It may well be that the Gospels themselves are already evidence of that type of imaginative construction at work. Indeed it would seem that the process of adding flesh to the dry bones of Caiaphas began with the Evangelists who sought to create a coherent narrative on the basis of their own literary and oral sources. In the Gospel of John, Caiaphas moves the plot forward considerably by articulating the need to eliminate Jesus and the rationale for doing so. As the narrator notes, "from that day on they planned to put him to death" (11:53). In Matthew, Mark, and John, the interrogation before the high priest (Mark), Caiaphas (Matthew), or Annas (John) coheres with the theme of antagonism between Jesus and the Jewish leadership that these Gospels develop throughout their accounts of Jesus' mission.

It is significant, however, that even where he is identified as Jesus' interlocutor, Caiaphas is not explicitly singled out as the representative of the hostile forces arrayed against Jesus, which are still collective in nature. It is the chief priests as a group, and not the high priest as an individual, who are responsible for plotting against Jesus and relentlessly pursuing his elimination.[66] For the Evangelists, then, Caiaphas the high priest is by no means a hero, but neither is he the wicked archvillain, the deicide, the Christ-killer, which he becomes in Christian tradition, history, and culture.

CAIAPHAS IN EARLY CHRISTIAN IMAGINATION

Sometime between the completion of the New Testament Gospels and the appearance of the earliest Christian writings, Caiaphas's reputation underwent a drastic and permanent change.[1] No longer the neutral, if strategic and dramatic, high priest, he was now the wicked Christ-killer, the enemy of all Christians everywhere. Of course he was not alone in his wickedness; his father-in-law, Annas, usually stood by his side, and these two in turn were often aided and abetted by Pilate, Herod, and the Jews in general. Although the precise process by which Caiaphas's transformation occurred cannot be tracked, it involves one simple exegetical move: the assumption that all of the "chief priest" passages refer directly and specifically to the high priest, even if they also designate the chief priests as a group. For those who are looking to scapegoat the high priest, this is an obvious and easy move, for in Greek, as we have seen, "chief priests" is simply the plural of "high priest."

PATRISTIC LITERATURE

Although it is customary to speak of patristic literature in general, the fathers of the church are far from a homogeneous group. They lived in different locales, spoke different languages, and had different concerns, friends, and enemies. The so-called Ante-Nicene fathers lived and wrote before the Council of Nicaea (325 C.E.), and those who lived and wrote after the council are designated Nicene and Post-Nicene. Most wrote in either Greek (for example Origen, Justin Martyr, John Chrysostom) or Latin (for example Tertullian, Jerome, Augustine of Hippo). Furthermore they had very different personalities and dispositions. As Boniface Ramsey puts it, the church fathers are "variously, scintillating, tedious, sober, vulgar, profound and superficial, compassionate and prejudiced (they are notorious for being anti-Jewish), and often a single Father, because he is human, will manifest each one of these qualities."[2]

The earliest patristic writings were apologies, intended to defend the church and its teachings from pagan and Jewish attacks. In later centuries theological matters, such as the mystery of the Trinity, the relationship of the divine persons to one another, and the nature of Christ, predominated. The integration of "barbarians" into Christian civilization was an important issue in the West, while the Eastern fathers were often preoccupied with Christological disputes.[3]

Despite the differences among their writings, patristic references to Caiaphas offer a rather uniform understanding of the story, which for the church fathers was also history: Caiaphas was the mastermind of the plot against Jesus, he and/or Annas interrogated Jesus and elicited a guilty verdict on the charge of blasphemy, and he arranged for Pilate to try Jesus and condemn him to death.

Caiaphas the Christ-Killer

The underlying premise of all patristic treatments of Caiaphas is the high priest's adamant and absolute opposition to Jesus. This antagonism is shared by Annas, Pilate, Herod, and the Jewish people as a whole, all of whom, for the church fathers, are intimated in the words of Psalm 2. As Tertullian proclaims in his homily *On the Resurrection of the Flesh:* "For in the person of Pilate 'the heathen raged,' and in the person of Israel 'the people imagined vain things'; 'the kings of the earth' in Herod, and the rulers in Annas and Caiaphas, 'were gathered together against the Lord, and against His anointed'" (chap. 20).[4] In his own *Exposition of Psalm 2*, Hippolytus (ca. 170–ca. 236) writes:

> When he came into the world, He was manifested as God and man. And it is easy to perceive the man in Him, when He hungers and shows exhaustion, and is weary and athirst, and withdraws in fear, and is in prayer and in grief, and sleeps on a boat's pillow, and entreats the removal of the cup of suffering, and sweats in an agony, and is strengthened by an angel, and betrayed by a Judas, and mocked by Caiaphas, and set at nought by Herod, and scourged by Pilate, and derided by the soldiers, and nailed to the tree by the Jews, and with a cry commits His spirit to His Father, and drops His head and gives up the ghost, and has His side pierced with a spear, and is wrapped in linen and laid in a tomb, and is raised by the Father on the third day.[5]

As in Acts of the Apostles, the Caiaphas of patristic literature is hostile not only to Jesus but also to Jesus' followers. For example in praising martyrdom, the *Apostolic Constitutions* (late fourth century) states: "And if any one who accompanies with them is caught, and falls into misfortune, he is blessed, because he is partaker with the martyr, and is one that imitates the sufferings of Christ; for we ourselves also, when we oftentimes received stripes from Caiaphas, and Alexander, and Annas, for Christ's sake, 'went out rejoicing that we were counted worthy to suffer such things for our Saviour.' Do you also rejoice when ye suffer such things, for ye shall be blessed in that day."[6]

Caiaphas's reputation as a deicide was so strong that he served as a symbol of all opponents to the "true" Christianity that the church fathers were in the process of constructing. In *On the Opinion of Dionysius,* Athanasius (ca. 293–373) writes that "the Arians appeal to Dionysius as the Jews did to Abraham: but with equally little reason. They emulate this characteristic of Caiaphas and his party, just as they have learned from them to deny Christ."[7] In his *Encyclical Epistle to the Bishops throughout the World,* Athanasius describes Gregory, a leader of "the impious Arians," as exhibiting "the disposition of a Caiaphas" in that he "furiously raged against the pious worshippers of Christ."[8] In the third of his *Four Discourses against the Arians,* Athanasius mocks the Arians as "scholars of Caiaphas and Herod" and declares that to refer to Arianism as religious faith "is to call even Caiaphas a Christian, and to reckon the traitor Judas still among the Apostles."[9] In his letter *To Adelphius, Bishop and Confessor: Against the Arians,* he describes the Arians as "those who have imitated the behavior of Judas, and deserted the Lord to join Caiaphas."[10]

"High Priest That Year"

The church fathers read scripture carefully and pondered the same exegetical cruxes as did later commentators.[11] Like modern exegetes the church fathers were perturbed by the Johannine references to Caiaphas as the high priest "that year" (11:49, 51; 18:13). In book 1, chapter 10 of his *Church History,* Eusebius (ca. 260–ca. 337) provides a lengthy explanation. On the basis of Luke 3:1–2, he dates Jesus' baptism and the beginning of his ministry to "the fifteenth year of the reign of Tiberius, according to the evangelist, and in the fourth year of the governorship of Pontius Pilate, while Herod and Lysanias and Philip were ruling the rest of Judea." From Luke's reference to the high priesthood of Annas and Caiaphas, Eusebius deduces that since Jesus "began his work during the high priesthood of Annas and taught until Caiaphas held the office, the entire time does not comprise quite four years." This deduction takes into account Josephus's chronology, according to which Annas left the high priesthood in 15 C.E. and Caiaphas came into office in 18 C.E. Eusebius explains that "the rites of the law having been already abolished since that time, the customary usages in connection with the worship of God, according to which the high priest acquired his office by hereditary descent and held it for life, were also annulled and there were appointed to the high priesthood by the Roman governors now one and now another person who continued in office not more than one year."[12] In this way he resolves the issue of why Luke refers to Annas as high priest when it was well known that Caiaphas held this office during Pilate's governorship. This solution is based on the Johannine chronology of Jesus' ministry, which extends over three Passover seasons, rather than the synoptic chronology, in which Jesus is engaged in his ministry for one year or less.

In *Homily 79* on Matthew 25:31–41, John Chrysostom (347–407) has a different explanation of "that year": "And how many high priests were there? For the law wills there should be one, but then there were many. Whence it is manifest, that the Jewish constitution had begun to dissolve. For Moses, as I said, commanded there should be one, and that when he was dead, there should be another, and by the life of this person He measured the banishment of them that had involuntarily committed manslaughter. How then were there at times many high priests? They were afterward made for a year."[13]

Augustine (354–430) also attributes the multiple high priesthood to the breakdown in Jewish law. In tractate 49 of his *Lectures or Tractates on the Gospel According to St. John*, Augustine writes:

> It may, however, be a question in what way he is called the high priest of that year, seeing that God appointed one person to be high priest, who was to be succeeded only at his death by another. But we are to understand that ambitious schemes and contentions among the Jews led to the appointment afterward of more than one, and to their annual turn of service. For it is said also of Zacharias [Zecharaiah]: "And it came to pass that, while he executed the priest's office before God in the order of his course, according to the custom of the priest's office, his lot was to burn incense when he went into the temple of the Lord" [Luke 1:8–9]. From which it is evident that there were more than one, and that each had his turn: for it was lawful for the high priest alone to place the incense on the altar [Exodus 30:7]. (11:27)[14]

In tractate 113, however, Augustine resolves the problem by offering a more detailed explanation of the arrangement:

> But let us return to what follows in the Gospel narrative. "And Annas sent Him bound unto Caiaphas the high priest." To him, according to Matthew's account, He was led at the outset, because he was the high priest that year. For both the pontiffs are to be understood as in the habit of acting year by year alternately, that is, as chief priests; and these were at that time Annas and Caiaphas, as recorded by the evangelist Luke, when telling of the time when John, the Lord's forerunner, began to preach the kingdom of heaven and to gather disciples. For he speaks thus: "Under the high priests Annas

and Caiaphas, the word of the Lord came upon John, the son of Zacharias, in the wilderness," etc. [Luke 3:2]. Accordingly these two pontiffs fulfilled their years in turn: and it was the year of Caiaphas when Christ suffered. And so, according to Matthew, when He was apprehended, He was taken to him; but first, according to John, they came with Him to Annas; not because he was his colleague, but his father-in-law. And we must suppose that it was by Caiaphas' wish that it was so done; or that their houses were so situated, that Annas could not properly be overlooked by them as they passed on their way (18:5).[15]

Here Augustine explicitly harmonizes what he finds in Luke 3:2 with the account of Jesus' trial before the high priest in Matthew and the Johannine narrative of Jesus' interrogation by Annas, by suggesting that Caiaphas acted out of filial respect for Annas.

The Trial(s) of Jesus before Caiaphas and/or Annas

By harmonizing all four gospel accounts, one could posit two trials, one presided over by Annas and one by Caiaphas.[16] But in which order did these trials occur? According to the *Apostolic Constitutions*, Caiaphas presided over a nocturnal interrogation, as in Matthew, and Annas presided over the second meeting the following morning (Matt. 27:1; Mark 15:1): "They led Him to the house of Caiaphas the high priest, wherein were assembled many . . . who did many things against Him, and left no kind of injury untried, spitting upon Him, cavilling at Him, beating Him, smiting Him on the face, reviling Him, tempting Him . . . calling Him a deceiver, a blasphemer, a transgressor of Moses, a destroyer of the temple . . . till it was very early in the morning, and then they lead Him away to Annas, who was father-in-law to Caiaphas; and when they had done the like things to Him there . . . they delivered Him to Pilate."[17] By contrast, Augustine, in his Harmony of the Gospels, 3.6.24, relies on John to argue that the trial before Annas preceded the one before Caiaphas: "In the line of Matthew's narrative we come next upon this statement: And they that laid hold on Jesus led Him away to Caiaphas the high priest, where the scribes and the elders were assembled. We learn, however, from John that He was conducted first to Annas, the father-in-law of Caiaphas. On the other hand, Mark and Luke omit all mention of the name of the high priest."[18]

So who was actually the high priest at the time? For Augustine the answer must be Annas:

> The high priest asked Jesus of His disciples, and of His doctrine. . . . Annas sent Him bound to Caiaphas the high priest [John 18:19–24]. This certainly shows us that Annas was high priest. For Jesus had not been sent to Caiaphas

as yet, when the question was thus put to Him, Do you answer the high priest so? Mention is also made of Annas and Caiaphas as high priests by Luke at the beginning of his Gospel. After these statements, John reverts to the account which he had previously begun of Peter's denial. Thus he brings us back to the house in which the incidents took place which he has recorded, and from which Jesus was sent away to Caiaphas, to whom He was being conducted at the commencement of this scene, as Matthew has informed us (*Harmony of the Gospels*, 3.6.24).[19]

Why, then, does John not provide details of the interrogation before Caiaphas, nor indicate that Caiaphas was present when Jesus was questioned by Annas?

In like manner John, after recording what was done with the Lord as fully as he deemed requisite, and after telling also the whole story of Peter's denial, continues his narrative in these terms: Then lead they Jesus to Caiaphas, unto the hall of judgment. And it was early. Here we might suppose either that there had been something imperatively requiring Caiaphas' presence in the hall of judgment, and that he was absent on the occasion when the other chief priests held an inquiry on the Lord; or else that the hall of judgment was in his house; and that yet from the beginning of this scene they had thus only been leading Jesus away to the personage in whose presence He was at last actually conducted. But as they brought the accused person in the character of one already convicted, and as it had previously approved itself to Caiaphas' judgment that Jesus should die, there was no further delay in delivering Him over to Pilate, with a view to His being put to death. And thus it is that Matthew here relates what took place between Pilate and the Lord (*Harmony of the Gospels*, 3.7.28).[20]

These extracts show how attentive Augustine was to the discrepancies among the Gospels' accounts of Jesus' encounters with the high priest(s). Although he attempts to resolve them when commenting on specific passages, he does not notice, or perhaps does not care, that his own resolutions contradict one another.

Caiaphas's House

Although Augustine confirms Annas's status as high priest in *Harmony of the Gospels* 3.6.19, he does not hesitate to refer to Caiaphas as high priest in other writings, such as *Lectures or Tractates on the Gospel According to St. John*, tractate 114, in which he addresses a different exegetical problem: where did Caiaphas's interrogation of Jesus take place?

Let us now consider, so far as indicated by the evangelist John, what was done with, or in regard to, our Lord Jesus Christ, when brought before Pontius Pilate the governor. For he returns to the place of his narrative where he had left it, to explain the denial of Peter. He had already, you know, said, "And Annas sent Him bound unto Caiaphas the high priest" [John 18:24]: and having returned from where he had dismissed Peter as he was warming himself at the fire in the hall, after completing the whole of his denial, which was thrice repeated, he says, "Then they bring Jesus unto Caiaphas into the hall of judgment (pretorium)" [John 18:28]; for he had said that He was sent to Caiaphas by his colleague and father-in-law Annas.

Here Augustine, contrary to most other commentators, reads *ad Caipham*, "to Caiaphas," rather than *a Caipha*, "from Caiaphas."[21] This reading, however, creates a contradiction: "But if to Caiaphas, why into the hall of judgment?" Augustine explains this contradiction by suggesting that the pretorium was also Pilate's home, which, in turn, was situated in the house of Caiaphas: "Nothing else is thereby meant to be understood than the place where Pilate the governor dwelt. And therefore, either for some urgent reason Caiaphas had proceeded from the house of Annas, where both had met to give Jesus a hearing, to the governor's pretorium, and had left the hearing of Jesus to his father-in-law; for Pilate had made his pretorium in the house of Caiaphas, which was so large as to contain separate apartments for its own master, and the like for the judge" (28:28–32:1).[22] This passage illustrates the convoluted lengths to which Augustine could go to harmonize scripture, to the point of turning Caiaphas and Pilate into housemates.

The Prophet Caiaphas

For the church fathers, the most problematic aspect of the Gospels' portrayal of Caiaphas did not pertain to the discrepancies among their accounts but rather to his prophecy in John 11:49–52. How could the Jewish high priest have uttered a prophecy? What was the origin and status of this prophecy? In his tractate 49 on the Gospel according to John, Augustine comments:

"And one of them, [named] Caiaphas, being the high priest that same year, said unto them, Ye know nothing at all, nor consider that it is expedient for us that one man should die for the people, and that the whole nation perish not. And this spake he not of himself; but being high priest that year, he prophesied." We are here taught that the Spirit of prophecy used the agency even of wicked men to foretell what was future; which, however, the evangelist attributes to the divine sacramental fact that he was pontiff, which is to say, the high priest (Tractate 49:27).[23]

In his *Reply to Faustus the Manichaean,* Augustine explains:

> the words of Caiaphas had a different meaning from what he intended, when, in his hostility to Christ, he said that it was expedient that one man should die for the people, and that the whole nation should not perish, where the Evangelist added that he said this not of himself, but, since he was high priest, he prophesied. . . . When Moses said to the Hebrew people, "Thou shalt see thy life hanging, and shalt not believe thy life," he not only spoke of Christ, as he certainly did, even though he spoke without knowing the meaning of what he said, but he knew that he spoke of Christ. For he was a most faithful steward of the prophetic mystery, that is, of the priestly unction which gives the knowledge of the name of Christ; and in this mystery even Caiaphas, wicked as he was, was able to prophesy without knowing it. The prophetic unction enabled him to prophesy, though his wicked life prevented him from knowing it.[24]

As Augustine notes in *On the Holy Trinity,* book 4: "Many things, too, are foretold by a kind of instinct and inward impulse of such as know them not: as Caiaphas did not know what he said, but being the high priest, he prophesied."[25] For Augustine, then, it was conceivable that even a wicked person like Caiaphas could be a vehicle for the Holy Spirit.

For Origen (185–254), however, this point did not come quite so easily. Over the course of a lengthy discussion in book 28 of his commentary on the Gospel of John, Origen works his way through this problem to an inconclusive resolution.[26] For Origen, like other church fathers, the wickedness of Caiaphas and his despicable status as a deicide were indisputable. He takes heart, however, from his conviction that Caiaphas and the chief priests who plotted against Jesus merely represented the physical high priesthood; it is Christ who is the true high priest. If the chief priests destroyed Jesus' body, Jesus and his spiritual teachings destroyed the chief priests and other opponents (95–96).

Origen begins his examination of Caiaphas's prophetic ability by stating categorically that "the fact that someone prophesies does not make that person a prophet. Caiaphas, indeed, being high priest of that year, prophesied that Jesus was to die for the nation, and not only for the nation, but also to gather together into one the scattered children of God. He was by no means also a prophet" (98). This statement is supported by analogy to another wicked prophet of the Bible, Balaam: "although Balaam prophesied the things recorded in Numbers. . . . it is clear that he was not a prophet, for it is recorded that he was a seer," that is, one who practiced divination, and therefore was not a prophet in the divinely inspired sense of the term (99; cf. Josh. 13:22). This is followed by a restatement of the general principle, which also makes an important logical distinction: "If, therefore, someone is a prophet, he no doubt prophesies, but if someone prophesies he is not necessarily a prophet" (100). Origen supports this distinction exegetically, observing that when the Gospels refer to biblical prophets, such as Jeremiah, they specify their title, saying, for example, "Jeremias the prophet said" (Matt. 6:2).

Later, however, Origen does entertain the possibility that even a wicked soul is capable of prophesying, at least on occasion. He refers again to Caiaphas's wickedness, this time by appealing to Matthew 26:47, which describes the wickedness of the chief priests in hiring Judas to betray Jesus (107) and numerous other examples involving the chief priests (107–118), among whom Origen counts Caiaphas, the high priest "that year." Recognizing that he has gone on at some length, Origen concludes this discussion as follows: "We have set these words out more fully to prove the abundance of Caiaphas' evil through the numerous testimonies of all the gospels, and to show that although he contended against Jesus, none the less he prophesied. John has clearly taught us, therefore, that he prophesied" (120).

Origen then shifts the discussion to prophesy's inspiration: "You will ask, no doubt, whether if someone prophesies he prophesies by the Holy Spirit" (121a). In case someone might think that this issue has no pertinence to the investigation (121b), Origen gives the example of David, who sinned against Uriah, the husband of Bathsheba, and then feared that the Holy Spirit would leave him (Wisdom 1:5). In 122–126 Origen therefore considers whether it is possible for someone who has sinned after obtaining the Holy Spirit to regain the Holy Spirit. At the same time, however, he is adamant that Caiaphas did not possess the Holy Spirit, despite the fact that he prophesied. Because these events occurred before Jesus' glorification, no one, except for Jesus, had the Spirit (John 7:39). He bolsters this point with an *a fortiori* argument: "And if indeed the Spirit was not even in the apostles before Jesus was glorified, how much less was he in Caiaphas?" (128). Apparently realizing that according to this reasoning, no personalities from the Hebrew scriptures could have possessed the Holy Spirit, Origen then expounds at length (129–38) on Balaam and the messengers of Saul who prophesied to David (1 Kings 22:20).

Now Origen comes to the theological heart of the matter. If prophecy is by definition of the Holy Spirit, how can an evil person prophesy of the Holy Spirit? Are there evil spirits or demons who also provide prophecies? Perhaps, suggests Origen, it is not a matter of whether or not the prophecy comes true but of the goal or intentionality of the one who is prophesying, "for the goal of [Caiaphas's] power was not to make the hearers believe, but to provoke the chief priests and Pharisees in the council against Jesus, that they might kill him. This was not to act in accordance with the Holy Spirit" (151). Caiaphas's evil intentions are evident in his words: "You neither know, nor do you consider that it is expedient for us that one man should die for the people, and the whole nation not perish" (John 11:49–52).

The crux of the matter is the clause "it is expedient for us." Is this Caiaphas's reason, or is it just an excuse for some other incentive (152–53)? Here the question revolves around the frame of reference for this expediency. One possibility is that Caiaphas is referring to salvation: "If he is telling the truth, then Caiaphas and those who struggled against Jesus in the council are saved, since Jesus died for the people." Origen rejects this possibility: "But if it is absurd to declare that Caiaphas and those in the council against Jesus are saved, and that they obtained that which was expedient when Jesus died, it is clear that it was not the Holy Spirit which inspired these words to be spoken, for the Holy Spirit does not lie" (153).

But perhaps there is a deeper meaning. Origen expounds on the meaning of Jesus' death, through which Jesus "took away our sins and infirmities, since he was able, by taking up all the sin of the whole world into himself, to bring it to nought, and destroy and obliterate it" (160). Origen concludes: "This man died, then, for the people, and for this reason the whole nation did not perish." He then suggests that the term *people* be taken to refer to the Jews ("those of the circumcision") and *nation* to refer to the Gentiles. In that sense Caiaphas's prophecy came to pass.

The challenge, then, is to reconcile two seemingly contradictory points: Caiaphas was evil and therefore cannot be said to possess the Holy Spirit (if indeed the Spirit could be possessed at this time); at the same time, his prophecy was true. John 11:51 provides a way out of the exegetical impasse by pointing out that "he did not say this of himself" (John 11:51). In 171–72 Origen appeals to human nature and everyday experience: we all sometimes "say some things of ourselves, there being no power that inspires us to speak, but there are other things that we say when some power prompts us, as it were, and dictates what we say, even if we do not fall completely into a trance and lose full possession of our own faculties, but seem to understand what we say."[27] That is what happened to Caiaphas (172). Origen suggests that the high priest of a given year also may have had the ability to prophesy despite himself, as the examples of Saul's messengers and Balaam show (175–77).

Given that Caiaphas's words ignited a plot to kill Jesus, what sort of spirit could have caused such a prophecy? Those who say that the prophecy nevertheless came from the Holy Spirit would appeal to Jesus' own worthiness, which caused unbelievers to be blind. But it is also possible that while the intention of the prophecy was in accordance with the Holy Spirit, it was misinterpreted by the Pharisees and chief priests, who "did not understand correctly the prophecy about our Savior that Caiaphas spoke—a prophecy that is true in that it is better for us that one man die for the people and the whole nation not perish—but thought the meaning and intention of his counsel was something else" (190).

In the final analysis, Origen appears to opt for the position that Caiaphas's prophecy, while unintentional and involuntary, was nevertheless true and for that reason originated with the Holy Spirit. Yet in the last paragraph of this section, Origen retreats from this conclusion: "Now I say these things in conformity with the interpretation that it was the Holy Spirit who prophesied through Caiaphas. I do not in the least maintain that this was the case, but leave it to readers to decide what one must recognize as correct concerning Caiaphas, and the fact that he has been moved by the Spirit" (191).[28]

Conclusion

The treatment of Caiaphas in the writings of the church fathers focuses on both the narrative and the theological imperatives of the high priest's role. Because they uphold the historical value of all of the Gospel accounts, the church fathers resolve the narrative discrepancies through harmonization. These resolutions testify to a considerable quotient of imaginative energy as they sometimes lead to the creation of new "facts" such as the quarters shared by Pilate and Caiaphas. Underlying all treatments is the deicide charge, on the basis of which Caiaphas is an unequivocally evil character. It is this charge that prompts the question concerning his prophetic ability that so vexes Origen. The deicide charge also lays the foundation for the use of Caiaphas as a figure symbolizing any and all "heretical" groups that would undermine the developing patristic views of what constituted orthodox Christian doctrine.

THE NEW TESTAMENT APOCRYPHA

The terms *New Testament Apocrypha*, *Christian Apocrypha*, and *Apocryphal New Testament* refer to an amorphous and diverse group of Christian writings, dating from the second century to the fourth century or even later.[29] The terms *apocrypha* and *apocryphal* themselves refer to something hidden or secret and were applied to texts that were thought to be esoteric writings meant for a restricted audience or that were considered to be spurious on historical and theological grounds. Despite their noncanonical status, apocryphal texts had a large popular audience,[30] and by the early Middle Ages were an important influence on Christian narrative and art of all genres, including church mosaics.[31]

Many of the Christian apocryphal writings imitate the principal genres of New Testament literature, such as Gospels, acts, apocalypses, and letters.[32] The texts are pseudepigraphic, in that they are attributed to New Testament figures such as Paul and the apostles and many minor characters as well, such as

Thomas, Nicodemus, and Joseph of Arimathea. As J. K. Elliott notes, "The Apocryphal New Testament is the body of writings that includes the Infancy Gospel of Thomas, when Jesus behaves like an enfant terrible, killing those who vex him, or, to change our language, a wunderkind confounding his teachers, stretching planks, or causing clay birds to fly. This is the body of literature that has Peter in the Acts of Peter revive a dead tunny fish; that has John rebuke bedbugs which disturb his sleep in the Acts of John; that has a parricide who castrates himself, and a protracted story that ends in an attempted necrophiliac rape, both also from the Acts of John; that has Paul baptize a lion in the Acts of Paul."[33]

In this body of literature, Caiaphas too comes in for his share of strange treatment. *The Arabic Gospel of the Infancy of the Saviour*, for example, identifies Caiaphas with another Joseph, or is it the historian Josephus?[34]

> With the help and favour of the Most High we begin to write a book of the miracles of our Lord and Master and Saviour Jesus Christ, which is called the Gospel of the Infancy: in the peace of the Lord. Amen. We find what follows in the book of Joseph the high priest, who lived in the time of Christ. Some say that he is Caiaphas. He has said that Jesus spoke, and, indeed, when He was lying in His cradle said to Mary His mother: I am Jesus, the Son of God, the Logos, whom thou hast brought forth, as the Angel Gabriel announced to thee; and my Father has sent me for the salvation of the world.[35]

The author clearly knows nothing about Caiaphas except his name and the fact, though not the nature, of his association with Jesus.

Many apocryphal texts are examples of rewritten Bible, making use of canonical texts as well as legendary materials.[36] This use did not take place in a mechanistic, cut-and-paste manner but involved a skillful weaving together of canonical and legendary material for dramatic effect.[37] These processes can be seen at work in the apocryphal representations of Caiaphas the high priest.

Caiaphas among the Christ-killers

Caiaphas's role in extracanonical narratives is straightforward and unequivocal: he is the one who, along with a few others such as Judas, Herod, and Pilate, bears responsibility for Jesus' death. As in Acts 4:5–6, his name often appears alongside that of Annas in a list of Jewish authorities that collectively constitutes the implacable enemy of Jesus and his followers. A typical example is found in the *Acts of Pilate*:[38] "Having called a council, the high priests and scribes Annas and Caiaphas and Semes and Dathaes, and Gamaliel, Judas, Levi and Nephthalim, Alexander and Jaïrus, and the rest of the Jews, came to Pilate accusing Jesus about many things."[39] Later in the story, Nicodemus makes a great feast, to which he invites "Annas and Caiaphas, and the elders, and the priests, and the Levites to his house" (chap. 15).[40] Most references to Caiaphas in the New Testament Apocrypha occur in a list of this type.[41]

Throughout the literature Caiaphas and Annas are grouped together. Indeed in the view of some they shared living quarters as well as the high-priestly role. For example the *Gospel of the Nazaraeans,* as cited in the *Historia passionis Domini,* states that John son of Zebedee, the son of a Galilean fisherman, "often brought fish to the palace of the high priests Annas and Caiaphas."[42] In this way the text explains how it could be that Jesus' "beloved disciple," traditionally identified as John son of Zebedee, could have been known to the high priest in Jerusalem (cf. John 18:16).[43]

Other texts differentiate slightly among the various villains, usually in order to exult in their ultimate fates. In the *Letter of Tiberius to Pilate,* the Emperor Tiberius castigates Pilate for condemning Jesus and refers to Archelaus, Philip, Annas, and Caiaphas as Pilate's accomplices. To prove his master wrong, Pilate arranges their arrest and transport to Rome. All, however, die in painful and demeaning ways: Caiaphas died in Crete, but the earth would not receive his body, and he was covered with a cairn of stones; Annas was sewn into a fresh bull's hide, which contracted as it dried and squeezed him to death. The other chiefs of the Jews were beheaded; Archelaus and Philip were crucified. Pilate does not fare well himself; one day the emperor went out to hunt and chased a hind to the door of Pilate's prison. Pilate looked out the window, but at that moment the emperor shot an arrow at the hind, which went in through the window and killed Pilate instead.[44]

Caiaphas in the Narrative of Joseph of Arimathea

In most apocryphal treatments, Caiaphas is a minor figure, simply one among many enemies of Jesus. There are two narratives, however, in which Caiaphas plays a major role. In the *Narrative of Joseph of Arimathea,*[45] Joseph of Arimathea—known from the Gospels as the one who buries Jesus (Matt. 27:59, 60; Mark 15:46; Luke 23:53; John 19:38–42)—tells a tale about the robbers who were crucified on either side of Jesus. One, named Gestas, was a cold-blooded murderer of travelers. The other, Demas, was a Galilean innkeeper who played the role of Robin Hood, attacking the rich and benefiting the poor. In addition to robbing the multitude of the Jews, Demas stole "the law" itself in Jerusalem, stripped naked the daughter of Caiaphas, who was priestess of the sanctuary, and removed some mysterious objects placed there by King Solomon himself.

The story is farfetched, to say the least. Whether Caiaphas had a daughter is not known (though the ossuary evidence may point in that direction);[46] in any case the Temple in Jerusalem did not have cultic priestesses. The purpose of the story is to show the humiliation of Caiaphas's family and undermine the validity of the Temple ritual. But this is not the end of the matter. Somehow this event becomes woven into the elaborate plan by which Caiaphas entraps Jesus: "The day that this man was captured was the same day that Jesus was taken. The high priest and all the Jews were in mourning because the sanctuary had been plundered by the robber, and they called on Judas, who was Caiaphas's nephew, whom they had planted in Jesus' groups of disciples 'not that he might be obedient to the miracles done by Him, nor that he might confess Him, but that he might betray Him to them,' which he did, for two years."

Here we learn about yet another one of Caiaphas's family members: his nephew Judas. The story emphasizes that Caiaphas's plan to kill Jesus was carefully prepared; in becoming a disciple and then betraying Jesus, Judas was not acting on his own but rather carrying out his uncle's orders. Here is Joseph of Arimathea's version of the plan. On the third day, before Jesus was taken,

> Judas says to the Jews: "Come, let us hold a council; for perhaps it was not the robber that stole the law, but Jesus himself, and I accuse him." And when these words had been spoken, Nicodemus, who kept the keys of the sanctuary, came in to us [the council], and said to all: "Do not do such a deed. For Nicodemus was true, more than all the multitude of the Jews." And the daughter of Caiaphas, Sarah by name, cried out, and said: "He himself said before all against this holy place, I am able to destroy this temple, and in three days to raise it." The Jews say to her: "Thou hast credit with all of us." For they regarded her as a prophetess. And assuredly, after the council had been held, Jesus was laid hold of.

The two young people accuse Jesus of theft (stealing the law, perhaps referring to the Torah scroll) and terrorism (plotting to destroy the Temple), and Jesus is arrested. Annas and Caiaphas interrogate him, but he does not answer. Finally the multitude seeks to burn Caiaphas's daughter, "on account of the loss of the law; for they did not know how they were to keep the passover." But she deflects them:

> "Wait, my children, and let us destroy this Jesus, and the law will be found, and the holy feast will be fully accomplished." And secretly Annas and Caiaphas gave considerable money to Judas Iscariot, saying: "Say as thou saidst to us before, I know that the law has been stolen by Jesus, that the accusation may be turned against him, and not against this maiden, who is free from blame." And Judas having received this command, said to them:

"Let not all the multitude know that I have been instructed by you to do this against Jesus; but release Jesus, and I will persuade the multitude that it is so." And craftily they released Jesus.

The plot, then, is to arrest Jesus, not for prophesying against the Temple but for theft of the law. This story accentuates the perfidy of the Jews by making the plot to kill Jesus extremely elaborate and accusing them of other crimes such as the humiliation of Caiaphas's daughter and the removal of sacred items from the Temple. The blame is shared by the Jewish leadership, principally Annas and Caiaphas, and his family members Sarra and Judas.

In this fanciful tale, one can readily detect the narrative imperative at work. The story uses the basic narrative structure of the canonical Passion narrative, in which Jesus is arrested, interrogated, and condemned. Its whimsical elements notwithstanding, the story adds coherence to the biblical narrative by explaining how it was that Judas became a disciple (at his uncle Caiaphas's instigation) and describing a plot that did not arise suddenly at the end of Jesus' ministry but was planned out and prepared with some patience over a lengthy period of time. In doing so it enhances the villainy of the high-priestly duo and draws on (incomplete and incorrect) information, such as the role of priestesses in temples and the role of the Law in the celebration of Passover, which may or may not reflect what was taken to be common knowledge at the time of writing.

Caiaphas in the Acts of Pilate

An even more detailed consideration of Caiaphas occurs in the *Acts of Pilate* (*Acta Pilati*), which is preserved in the *Gospel of Nicodemus*.[47] This text was originally composed in Greek and exists in two main versions, with various sub-versions as well and numerous manuscripts.[48] The dating is uncertain. Epiphanius mentions the *Acts of Pilate* in his writings against the Quartodecimans (Haer. 50:1), in 375 or 376.[49] The texts may have been known earlier, however. In his *First Apology* 35, Justin Martyr refers to the Passion and crucifixion of Jesus and states: "And that these things happened you can ascertain from the Acts of Pontius Pilate." A similar statement appears in chapter 48. Tertullian also mentions a report made by Pilate to Tiberius, in which Pontius Pilate informs the emperor that he has pronounced an unjust sentence of death against an innocent and divine person. The emperor in turn is so moved by the report of the miracles of Christ and his resurrection that he proposes that Christ be received among the gods of Rome; this request is refused by the Roman Senate (*Apologeticum* 5). Later Tertullian says that the "whole story of Christ was reported to Caesar (Tiberius) by Pilate, who was already a secret Christian" (*Apol.* 21, 24). On this basis some have concluded that the *Acts of Pilate* was already available in the second century.[50]

Other scholars, however, prefer a fifth-century dating for the current version, on the basis of the manuscript evidence. John Quasten writes, "The whole work, which in a later Latin manuscript is called the *Evangelium Nicodemi*, must have been composed at the beginning of the fifth century, but it seems to be more or less a compilation of older material."[51] It is possible that the material in the *Gospel of Nicodemus* was written to refute the pagan *Acts of Pilate* created in 311, mentioned by Eusebius: "Having therefore forged Acts of Pilate and our Saviour full of every kind of blasphemy against Christ, they sent them with the emperor's approval to the whole of the empire subject to him, with written commands that they should be openly posted to the view of all in every place, both in country and city, and that the schoolmasters should give them to their scholars, instead of their customary lessons, to be studied and learned by heart" (*Church History* 9.5.1).[52]

Although its original date is uncertain, the *Acts of Pilate* was translated into Latin before the sixth century. By the end of the medieval period, the Latin version was one of the most influential religious texts outside of the Christian canon.

According to its prologue, the *Acts of Pilate* was written by one Ananias, who describes himself as one who was learned in the law, knew Jesus from the scriptures, came to faith, and became baptized. Ananias claims to have discovered a Hebrew manuscript, which he translated into Greek. The manuscript contained "memorials" which, he insists, were written by Nicodemus shortly after Jesus' death "in the fifteenth year of the government of Tiberius Caesar, emperor of the Romans, and Herod being king of Galilee, in the nineteenth year of his rule, on the eighth day before the Kalends of April, which is the twenty-fifth of March, in the consulship of Rufus and Rubellio, in the fourth year of the two hundred and second Olympiad, Joseph Caiaphas being high priest of the Jews, that is, in 29 C.E." In this introduction, as in Luke 3:1–2, the reference to Caiaphas is intended to situate the story in a familiar history and chronology.

The story begins with an embassy of "the high priests and scribes Annas and Caiaphas and Seines and Dathaes, and Gamaliel, Judas, Levi and Nephthalim, Alexander and Jairus, and the rest of the Jews" to Pilate (chap. 1). The Jewish leaders claim that Jesus declared himself the son of God, crowned himself king, profaned the Sabbath, and sought to abolish Jewish law. The Jews insist that Pilate put Jesus on trial. The procurator protests—"Tell me how I, being a procurator, can try a king?"—but eventually relents. Annas and Caiaphas head up the prosecution; numerous people, as well as inanimate objects—Roman standards, for example—testify in Jesus' defense. To Pilate's dismay, Jesus is crucified. He granted permission to Joseph, "a councillor from the city of Arimathea, who also waited for the kingdom of God," to bury Jesus. "And he took it down, and wrapped it in clean linen, and placed it in a tomb hewn out of the rock, in which no one had ever lain" (chap. 11).

Joseph's actions are an affront to the Jews, who lock him up until the first day of the week, when they plan to expose him to the "birds of the air," that is, kill him and yet deny him a burial as punishment for giving Jesus a decent burial (chap. 12). The room has no window and its entrance is both sealed and guarded.

> And on the Sabbath, the rulers of the synagogue, and the priests and the Levites, made a decree that all should be found in the synagogue on the first day of the week. And rising up early, all the multitude in the synagogue consulted by what death they should slay him. And when the Sanhedrin was sitting, they ordered him to be brought with much indignity. And having opened the door, they found him not. And all the people were surprised, and struck with dismay, because they found the seals unbroken, and because Caiaphas had the key. And they no longer dared to lay hands upon those who had spoken before Pilate in Jesus' behalf. (chap. 12)

The story then continues with confrontations between the Jews and Jesus' supporters and followers.[53]

Meanwhile, shortly after Jesus' burial, a priest, a teacher, and a Levite come from Galilee to Jerusalem and testify before the "rulers of the synagogue, and the priests and the Levites" that they saw Jesus and his disciples on the mountain and heard Jesus give the "great commission" (Matt. 28:18–20) to his disciples. They then saw Jesus being taken up into heaven. The elders and the priests and Levites make these three men swear to the truth of their testimony but still do not believe them, referring to their account as "idle tales." The Jewish leaders then "came together into the synagogue, and locked the door, and lamented with a great lamentation, saying: Is this a miracle that has happened in Israel?" To this lamentation Annas and Caiaphas respond: "Why are you so much moved? Why do you weep? Do you not know that his disciples have given a sum of gold to the guards of the tomb, and have instructed them to say that an angel came down and rolled away the stone from the door of the tomb?" (chap. 14). The priests and the elders counter that if so, how could it be that the men said they saw him going about in the Galilee? Annas and Caiaphas cannot not respond but simply say "after great hesitation: It is not lawful for us to believe the uncircumcised."

As chapter 15 opens, the Jews finally get hold of Joseph of Arimathea. After consultation their leaders write to him apologizing for their earlier actions against him. Joseph returns and is greeted courteously. Nicodemus hosts a great feast, attended by Annas and Caiaphas, and the elders, priests, and Levites. They all "rejoiced, eating and drinking with Joseph; and after singing hymns, each proceeded to his own house. But Joseph remained in the house of Nicodemus."

The next day there is a meeting of the Sanhedrin. Joseph sits down between Annas and Caiaphas, who make him swear on the law to tell them exactly what happened, including the manner of his escape. Joseph recounts how he remained locked up all Sabbath, and at midnight he saw a light before his eyes. It was Jesus, who showed him the empty grave and then took him home, kissed him, and warned him not to leave the house for forty days, for Jesus was going to Galilee. The Jewish leaders, including Annas and Caiaphas, are so overwhelmed by this report that they "became as dead, and fell to the ground, and fasted until the ninth hour. And Nicodemus, along with Joseph, exhorted Annas and Caiaphas, the priests and the Levites, saying: 'Rise up and stand upon your feet, and taste bread, and strengthen your souls, because to-morrow is the Sabbath of the Lord'" (chap. 16). At the conclusion of the book, "all the people praised the Lord" with numerous biblical verses, after which they disperse, "each man to his own house, glorifying God; for His is the glory for ever and ever. Amen."

The triumphalist tone and the reference to the idea that "all" went away glorifying God leave open the possibility that Caiaphas, Annas, and the other leaders were finally convinced of the truth of the claims that Joseph and others were making about Jesus. But it is also possible that the reference is not to all who are present, including Caiaphas and Annas, but to "all the people" who witness the dialogue between Joseph and the Jewish leadership. If so, then Caiaphas and Annas remain fixed in their stereotypical roles as the implacable enemies of Jesus and, by extension, of "all the people" who believed in him.

Caiaphas in the Pseudo-Clementines

The *Acts of Pilate* is not the only text to imply Caiaphas's interest in Jesus and the possibility that he may have converted.[54] The Pseudo-Clementine *Recognitions*, book 1, chapters 44–71,[55] portray Caiaphas as having a long-standing desire to engage Christians in a disputation. Despite Caiaphas's repeated requests, the apostles "often put it off, always seeking for a more convenient time," until they were persuaded that "this very question, whether He is the Christ, is of great importance for the establishment of the faith; otherwise the high priest would not so frequently ask that he might either learn or teach concerning the Christ."

The high priest's interest, and the apostles' acquiescence to his request for a debate, does not, however, signify rapprochement. This is the fault of the Jews, for all the unbelieving Jews are stirred up with boundless rage against us, fearing lest haply He against whom they have sinned [Christ] should be He [the messiah]. And their fear grows all the greater, because they know that, as soon as they fixed Him on the cross, the whole world showed sympathy with Him; and that His body, although they guarded it with strict care, could nowhere be found; and that innumerable multitudes are attaching themselves to His faith. Whence they, together with the high priest Caiaphas, were compelled to send to us again and again, that an inquiry might be instituted concerning the truth of His name. (chap. 53)

Over several chapters Caiaphas and the Christians carry on a disputation, with arguments and counterarguments put forth by each side. Chapter 62 reports Caiaphas's attempts at intimidation: "Therefore Caiaphas, again looking at me ["Clement"], and sometimes in the way of warning and sometimes in that of accusation, said that I ought for the future to refrain from preaching Christ Jesus, lest I should do it to my own destruction, and lest, being deceived myself, I should also deceive others. Then, moreover, he charged me with presumption, because, though I was unlearned, a fisherman, and a rustic, I dared to assume the office of a teacher."

Caiaphas's unrelenting persecution of the believers culminates in his commissioning of Saul (later known as Paul the apostle) to persecute the Christians. This information was conveyed by a delegation from Gamaliel, "bringing to us secret tidings that that enemy [Saul] had received a commission from Caiaphas, the chief priest, that he should arrest all who believed in Jesus, and should go to Damascus with his letters, and that there also, employing the help of the unbelievers, he should make havoc among the faithful; and that he was hastening to Damascus chiefly on this account, because he believed that Peter had fled thither."

Here Caiaphas remains intransigent. In other texts, however, he softens and, indeed, becomes a secret believer, a plot development perhaps inspired by the Gospel of John, which states that "many, even of the authorities, believed in him. But because of the Pharisees they did not confess it, for fear that they would be put out of the synagogue; for they loved human glory more than the glory that comes from God" (John 12:42–43).

One such account can be found in a Syriac text called *Didache: The Teaching of the Apostles,* which recounts:

> The disciples, moreover, after they had appointed these Ordinances and Laws, ceased not from the preaching of the Gospel, or from the wonderful mighty-works which our Lord did by their hands. For much people was

gathered about them every day, who believed in Christ; and they came to them from other cities, and heard their words and received them. Nicodemus also, and Gamaliel, chiefs of the synagogue of the Jews, used to come to the apostles in secret, agreeing with their teaching. Judas, moreover, and Levi, and Peri, and Joseph, and Justus, sons of Hananias, and Caiaphas and Alexander the priests—they too used to come to the apostles by night, confessing Christ that He is the Son of God; but they were afraid of the people of their own nation, so that they did not disclose their mind toward the disciples (para. 3).[56]

In none of these texts is Caiaphas an object of interest in and of himself. In addition to epitomizing the Jewish opposition to Jesus, Caiaphas's interrogation of witnesses to Jesus' marvelous deeds and words provides the opportunity for the anonymous authors of these apocryphal texts to testify to the truth as they see it. Generally he is depicted alongside Annas and other leaders as Jesus' persecutor and prosecutor. This is in keeping with the anti-Jewish tone of much of the apocryphal literature. As Elliott notes,

> Anti-Jewish sentiment may be nascent in the New Testament proper, where it can be seen that the blame for Jesus' arrest and crucifixion is increasingly pinned on the Jews *en bloc*, thereby exonerating the Romans, despite the reluctant constitutional role they were obliged to play. But in the apocryphal literature that theme is dominant. In the Gospel of Peter the motive for not proceeding with the plan to expedite Jesus' crucifixion by breaking his legs is Jewish malevolence—they want his death to be prolonged and painful. The Jews are responsible for the crucifixion in the Gospel of Peter 3 and in the Descensus (Gospel of Nicodemus part 2). In the Letter of Pilate to Claudius, found, among other places, in the Gospel of Nicodemus, the Jews are reported as plotting the crucifixion "out of envy." In the story of Mary's dormition her coffin is desecrated, significantly by a Jew, during her funeral procession. Again, we detect that a minor theme in the New Testament becomes exaggerated in the later, non-canonical writings. Doubtless, it was literature like this that fueled medieval anti-Semitism and justified it.[57]

Although the role of Caiaphas as deicide predominates, it is not the only important element in the portrayal of the high priest in the New Testament Apocrypha. Caiaphas is also the representative par excellence of the Jews and, as such, a fitting target for evangelization. The apocryphal Caiaphas persecutes Jesus and his followers, but he also, perhaps despite himself, is interested in what they have to say. For the most part, he is not won over, a failure that is due to the high priest's extreme intransigence. But once in awhile, he does indeed bend. Imagine how powerful Christ must be if even his staunchest enemy is won over!

CONCLUSION

Early readers of the Gospels were by no means oblivious to the fragmentary and contradictory nature of the Gospels when it came to the role of the high priest in the events leading to Jesus' death. The approach of the church fathers was to harmonize the Gospel accounts and fill in the blanks just enough to smooth out the contradictions, whether narrative—how could Annas and Caiaphas be high priests at the same time?—or theological: how could a wicked man prophesy the truth? The New Testament Apocrypha, by contrast, weave new narratives around the figures from the Gospels, including Caiaphas the high priest. These narratives draw freely from the Gospels as well as Acts, but also from other traditions and, no doubt, the fertile imaginations of their creators.

In both the patristic and apocryphal sources, however, it is possible to recognize a phenomenon that will appear in other eras and genres, namely, the plasticity of Caiaphas. Caiaphas is useful in polemical situations as a symbol of the enemy, whoever that enemy happens to be. Thus the misguided wickedness of the Arians is compared to Caiaphas's death-dealing behavior; just as Caiaphas plotted Jesus' death, so will the "heretics" mortally harm those who believe in Jesus. Any reader who does not want to be as wicked as Caiaphas must stay well away from the Arians. On the other hand, Caiaphas can also stand in for the unbeliever who can be educated and enlightened by those who believe sincerely in Jesus as God's Son; thus his case illustrates the tremendous power and forcefulness of the Christian message.

CAIAPHAS IN LITERATURE

Caiaphas's reputation as a wicked Christ-killer accompanied him from patristic and apocryphal literature into poetry and fictional Jesus narratives from the medieval period to the mid–twentieth century, after which the Holocaust contributed to a growing reluctance to depict Jewish figures as deicides. So large is the literary corpus in which Caiaphas plays a part that this chapter will touch on only a few examples. After a brief overview, this chapter examines in more detail two examples from the period of Nazi domination in Europe, Sholem Asch's *The Nazarene* (1939) and Dorothy Sayers's radio play, *The Man Born to Be King* (1942). Although Sayers's work is a drama, originally written to be performed, this examination will focus on the written text of that work, which includes her witty introductions to each play.

CAIAPHAS IN POETRY

Dante's Inferno

Caiaphas first enters the Western canon of imaginative literature via the *Inferno*, the first part of Dante's three-part epic poem, *The Divine Comedy* (1308–21). *The Divine Comedy*, written in the first person, describes Dante's journey through the three realms of the dead. This journey begins the night before Good Friday and ends the Wednesday after Easter in the year 1300. Dante is guided through Hell and Purgatory by the Roman poet Virgil and through Heaven by the beautiful Beatrice.

In the *Inferno* (Hell), Dante is thirty-five years old, lost in a dark forest, in deep despair. He is rescued by Virgil, who takes him on a journey through the nine circles of the Underworld. Here they have exhilarating adventures and encounter numerous sinners, among them Caiaphas and Annas. The two high priests are located in the sixth subcircle of the eighth circle of hell, a canyon reserved for hypocrites. In this canyon the souls of the hypocrites are weighted down with cloaks that are gold on the outside but lead on the inside. These are the Jewish leaders who are the target of Jesus' diatribe in Matthew 23:27–28: "Woe to you, scribes and Pharisees, hypocrites! For you are like whitewashed tombs, which on the outside look beautiful, but inside they are full of the bones of the dead and of all kinds of filth. So you also on the outside look righteous to others, but inside you are full of hypocrisy and lawlessness." In canto 23 Virgil describes the fate of Caiaphas and Annas:

> I began: "O friars, your evil . . ." but I said no more,
> for into my view came one crucified to the earth with
> three stakes.
> When he saw me, he twisted himself all over,
> puffing into his beard with sighs; and Brother
> Catalano, who perceived it,
> told me: "That one staked there at whom you are
> looking counseled the Pharisees that it was
> expedient to put one man to death for the people.
> He is stretched naked out across the road, as you
> See, so that whoever passes, he must feel his weight first.
> And his father-in-law is laid out in the same way
> In this detch, and the others of the council that sowed
> So ill for the Jews."
> Then I saw Virgil marveling over him who was
> so basely stretched cross-wise in eternal exile. (109–24)[1]

Whereas Jesus' crucifixion exalted him, lifting him above the earth, the crucifixion of Annas and Caiaphas debases them, requiring all who pass to tread over them. Whereas Jesus was resurrected to eternal life, Annas and Caiaphas are condemned to the sixth circle of hell for all eternity. Their relegation to the realm of the hypocrites reflects their association with the scribes and Pharisees. Corporate responsibility, however, is also maintained, by referring to the council and to the Jews as a whole. Dante here accepts and reinforces the notion of the deicide charge and implies that all Jews suffer the punishment exacted upon Caiaphas, his father-in-law, and all others who led Jesus to his death.

To be sure Caiaphas and Annas are not the only hypocrites; the canyon is full of them. But so evil are these two Jews that even other hypocrites step upon them. Durling notes that for Dante, "the hypocrites who voted to kill Jesus must feel the weight of the hypocrisy of all the others. This is a parodic parallel to the traditional idea that Christ on the Cross bore the weight of all men's sins."[2] Dante's views did not disappear but continued to be spread by at least some later commentators. John Carroll, for example, comments in his 1903 exposition:

> It is no wonder that good men should scorn the crucifiers of Christ, and, as it were, trample them under foot; but it is at first glance strange that hypocrites should do so. Yet it is the simple truth. In every age since the crucifixion the hypocrites of the Christian religion have trampled in contempt on Caiaphas and his companions in this crime, not knowing that they themselves are partakers of the self-same spirit. Dante wishes to mark the last limit of scorn: the very hypocrites despise them and tread them underfoot. That these arch-hypocrites have no mantles may mean that as they crucified Christ naked, in like nakedness they are themselves crucified; and perhaps also it has some reference to our Lord's own words on the eve of His death: "If I had not come and spoken unto them, they had not had sin: but now they have no cloke for their sin." Probably it is this which constitutes the special heinousness of the hypocrisy of Caiaphas and his accomplices—it was hypocrisy naked and undisguised.[3]

Carroll uses Caiaphas and Annas as vehicles to castigate the hypocrites who consider themselves superior to these high priests, similar to the way in which the church fathers used Caiaphas in their polemical writings as a symbol of those with whom they differed.

Oscar Wilde, The Ballad of Reading Gaol

Caiaphas makes only rare appearances in modern poetry. Perhaps the best-known example is in Oscar Wilde's poem *The Ballad of Reading Gaol*.[4] The reference occurs in the last stanza of the first section. Referring to an unnamed prisoner—perhaps himself—the poet writes:

> He does not stare upon the air
> Through a little roof of glass;
> He does not pray with lips of clay
> For his agony to pass;
> Nor feel upon his shuddering cheek
> The kiss of Caiaphas.

Wilde here substitutes Caiaphas for Judas in the role of Jesus' betrayer. This creates the alliterative effect of the final line quoted above, but perhaps also draws upon a well-established practice of using Caiaphas to represent any and all opponents to what is good and right.

CAIAPHAS IN FICTION

Caiaphas the Christ-killer

Most, but not all, literary retellings of the Jesus story find a place for Caiaphas in the events leading up to Jesus' death. Novelists use Caiaphas as a vehicle for expressing their views on the Jewish role in Jesus' death and, by extension, on Jews and Judaism more generally. In many novels Annas is his son-in-law's sidekick and indispensable partner in crime. As the narrator of Robert Graves's novel *King Jesus* puts it: "The Sadducee leader was old Annas, who had been High Priest for nine years beginning with the year in which Archelaus the Ethnarch was deposed, and without consulting whom Caiaphas, who had now held the office for eleven years, took no important decision."[5]

Due to their explicitly imaginative context, fictional portrayals of Caiaphas are more varied than those in extracanonical Christian literature. Nevertheless in fiction too, Caiaphas is perceived primarily as a wicked deicide, and here too he can stand in for evil individuals or groups within the author's own context. Some novels do not hesitate to depict Caiaphas as the main mover behind Jesus' death. In Nikos Kazantzakis's novel *The Last Temptation of Christ*, Pilate tells Jesus that Caiaphas wants his death and refers to the Jews as the "disgraceful Hebrew race."[6] Nevertheless, in accord with the Gospels, Kazantzakis does not place Caiaphas among the crowd that shouts "Crucify him."[7] Others try to avoid blaming Caiaphas exclusively for Jesus' death. In Morley Callaghan's novel *A Time for Judas*, as in the Gospels of Luke and John, Caiaphas is absent from the interrogation; some other priests are there but "Caiaphas wasn't with them."[8] Some novels, such as Nino Ricci's *Testament*, portray Pilate and not Caiaphas as the principal villain.

Caiaphas and Pilate

One of the most frustrating gaps in the accounts of the Gospels and Josephus concerns the relationship between Caiaphas and Pilate. Neither Josephus nor the Gospels depict an encounter between the two men. Nevertheless, in most Jesus novels, the high priest and the governor collude in order to keep the peace. Norman Mailer's *The Gospel According to the Son* describes the arrangement as follows: "Pontius Pilate allowed his solders to commit no insolence against the Great Temple, and Caiaphas tolerated no orthodox burial for those Jews who died in attacks upon Roman soldiers. Thereby they maintained order.... Caiaphas had been High Priest for more than ten years. The sum of his agreement with Pontius Pilate was that he also abhorred an uprising."[9]

In *King Jesus* Graves suggests that the governor felt contempt for the high priest. Graves's Pilate "called him 'the perfect valet,' because of his obsequiousness to his masters, his haughtiness to his inferiors, his adroitness, his correctness, and his fundamental falsity."[10] Later the narrator provides the high priest's perspective: "Caiaphas had known Pilate long enough and been humiliated by him often enough to be frightened by his jocose manner. He [Pilate] must have hit on a new and profitable scheme, in which Jesus somehow figured, for blackmailing the Sanhedrin; but precisely what the scheme was remained obscure."[11] This particular Caiaphas has the measure of his devious and antagonistic boss.

In Jose Saramago's *The Gospel According to Jesus Christ*, Pilate and Caiaphas are also at loggerheads. Caiaphas tells the governor: "You see, Pilate, he confesses, and you cannot spare the life of one who publicly declares his hatred of you and Caesar." The narrator then comments: "Sighing with exasperation, Pilate rebuked the priest, 'Be quiet.'" Later: "Roused from his complacency, the high priest suddenly realized what was happening and protested, 'You mustn't write King of the Jews but Jesus of Nazareth who claimed to be king of the Jews.'" Pilate's response: "Stop interfering."[12]

Whereas Saramago's Caiaphas is silenced by his Roman superior, Mikhail Bulgakov's acclaimed *The Master and Margarita* portrays an assertive high priest and an even more volatile governor. The main character, "The Master," has written a novel about Pontius Pilate and Jesus that has been rejected for publication. In the Master's novel Caiaphas insists on the release of Bar-Rabban (Barabbas), but before this is announced, Pilate has a private word with the high priest in an attempt to change his mind. A highly antagonistic confrontation takes place. Caiaphas declares to Pilate: "The Jewish people know that you hate them with a cruel hatred, and will cause them much suffering, but you will not destroy them utterly! God will protect them! He will hear us, the almighty Caesar will hear, he will protect us from Pilate the destroyer!" To this Pilate responds with threats: "Oh no! ... You have complained about me too much to Caesar, and now my hour has come, Kaifa! Now the message will fly from me, and not to the governor in Antioch, and not to Rome, but directly to Capreae, to the emperor himself, the message of how you in Yershalaim are sheltering known criminals from death ... you will regret having sent to his death a philosopher [Jesus] with his peaceful preaching!"

The narrator then notes:

The high priest's face had become covered with blotches, his eyes burned. Like the procurator, he smiled, baring his teeth, and replied, "Procurator, do you yourself believe what you just said? No, you do not! It was not peace that that rabble-rouser brought to Yershalaim, and you, Knight, know that very well. You wanted to release him so that he would stir the people up, do violence to their religion, and subject them to Roman swords! But I, High Priest of Judea, shall not, so long as I live, allow the faith to be profaned, and I shall protect the people! Do you hear, Pilate?" And here Kaifa raised his hand threateningly, "Take heed, procurator!"[13]

The high priest and Pilate are archrivals and Jesus a mere pawn in the power struggle between them. Although Pilate, as Rome's representative in Judaea, theoretically has the upper hand, Caiaphas is not deterred by his threats.

These novels illustrate just a few of the fictional representations of Caiaphas the high priest. Like the Gospels these works are not interested in Caiaphas per se but only in the role he plays in Jesus' life story; Caiaphas proves both necessary and useful not only because of his presence in the source texts but also because he so readily fills the role of the villain, which is essential to the plot of any narrative. The fictional constructions of this role tend to reproduce the largely negative evaluation of his character and behavior that are found in the writings of the church fathers and New Testament Apocrypha, but they often nuance this evaluation by developing the complexities of the relationship between a Roman overlord and his Jewish underling. A more detailed discussion of some of these novels will fill out this picture.

Sampling the Fictional Caiaphas

Robert Graves, *King Jesus*

Some novels avoid casting strong and overt blame onto the high priest, but nevertheless conclude that he is a deicide, even if not the only one. An extended treatment of Caiaphas that falls into this category can be found in Graves's *King Jesus*. In this novel Caiaphas is disinclined initially to act against Jesus. Indeed he has him under his personal protection. The presidents of the high court send their eloquent secretary, Joseph of Arimathea, to Caiaphas to discuss Jesus' case with him. Joseph urges Caiaphas to leave Jesus alone: "He is a simple, and, I think, pious man."[14] Caiaphas responds:

> In general, I incline to agree with you. If we leave him alone, the mob will tire of his rantings, and the synagogue elders when they find out what sort of company he keeps will soon close their doors to him. Inform your learned and pious Presidents with my compliments that I shall refrain from any disciplinary action against this miracle-monger until he forgets himself one day and bawls out some anti-Imperial nonsense of which I am forced to take cognizance. By the way, do you not think that he has a touch of insanity? Does he perhaps believe himself to be the Messiah? I ask because of the cry with which he interrupted last year's solemnities on the Day of Willows.[15]

Joseph agrees but says that Jesus probably does not nurse any grandiose delusions.

Caiaphas grows increasingly troubled by Jesus' popularity and removes his personal protection. He still hopes to keep Jesus from harm, however, and to this end instructs the captain of the Temple: "Let your Levites throw no stones at the miracle-worker from Nazareth; I have promised the High Court not to molest him." Yet the captain understands the instructions implicit in this message and reports to his Levite sergeants that "Jesus of Nazareth is no longer under the High Priest's protection. If stones fly at the Fish Gate this evening and he is driven out of the City, none of our people will be there to make arrests. Nevertheless, let no murder be done."[16]

Later, however, Caiaphas finds himself presiding over a private trial and sending Jesus off to Pilate. By this point he is anxious to be rid of Jesus, yet the question remains: how? One elder explains that normally it would be advisable to transfer the case to the high court, which is empowered to inflict the death penalty for blasphemy. In this case, however, the high court would be unlikely to convict Jesus, as his utterances did not fulfill the technical requirements of blasphemy: he did not recite the divine name. Annas is the one who provides the solution: to refer the case to the "Governor-General," that is, Pilate. The case may be tenuous, but given that Pilate is less scrupulous than the Jewish high court, the evidence that Jesus had earlier caused a riot and that he claimed to be Messiah would be enough for Pilate to convict him. Annas further advises that "we should ask the Governor-General's permission to have him stoned to death outside the City as an act of popular justice. His Excellency will doubtless accede to our wishes, the prisoner being a proved trouble-maker, and I will let him know privately, through his Oriental Secretary, that we are setting aside certain Pharisaic legal rulings in the interests of peace and the original Law."[17]

Graves's Caiaphas is no saint, but neither is he the wicked high priest of patristic and apocryphal literature. He is personally indifferent to Jesus, even somewhat disdainful, but hardly inclined to act against him. In the end, however, as in many other versions of the story, he and Annas together manipulate the events to ensure that Pilate will sentence Jesus to death by crucifixion.

Norman Mailer, *The Gospel According to the Son*

In Mailer's *The Gospel According to the Son,* Caiaphas prefers to avoid Jesus altogether. An old Pharisee tells Jesus:

> "I know you have a noble heart. It speaks from your eyes. I mean only to warn you. Already a few say that you are the Son of God." And he lowered his eyes before so blasphemous a remark. Only then could he speak again: "Some claim that you say it yourself. I pray no harm will come to you from this. If you meet the high Priest Caiaphas, do not say anything of this nature to him.

For if he should hear such words from your mouth, the sacrilege would be beyond measure. Yet for so long as he [Caiaphas] does not hear it from your mouth but only from others, he will prefer not to listen. For then he will not have to declare that a mortal sacrilege exists. Of such is your safety."[18]

In the end, of course, Caiaphas condemns Jesus. Mailer's Jesus interprets the rending of the clothes thus: "With deliberation, the High Priest tore his robes and said, 'We need no witnesses. All of you have heard this blasphemy.' And in ripping his garment Caiaphas had declared to all that I had no claim to be the Son of the Father; no, I was a son of the Jews. This son had committed so great a sacrilege that he, the High Priest, had had to rend his clothes. By the common bond of our people's blood, I was his offspring. Condemned by him, I was to be mourned as dead."[19]

Mailer's Caiaphas behaves like his counterparts in the Gospels and most later narratives, but his reasons and emotional stance resemble those of a pained father more than a smug or indifferent opponent.

James Martin, *The Letters of Caiaphas, the High Priest*

The only fictional work that has Caiaphas as a main character is James Martin's 1960 novella, *The Letters of Caiaphas, the High Priest*. The book consists of twenty-three letters that "purport to have been written by Caiaphas, the ruling High Priest of the Jews at the time of the crucifixion of Jesus of Nazareth, to Annas, his predecessor in that office." The "editor," however, does not thereby claim they are authentic:

> Frankly, I am personally most doubtful of that. They were revealed to me as I pondered the happenings of the first Easter, and each of them, I noticed, bore the signature of Caiaphas. I noticed at the same time, however, that they contain many anachronisms of thought and of phrase, a feature which may suggest that they are, after all, no more than the creation of my own mind. Nevertheless, they seem to demand the conclusion that, if not actual letters of Caiaphas, they are in the main such letters as Caiaphas might well have penned. And so I have decided that others than myself may care to read them through.[20]

These fictional letters trace the sequence of events from the trial of Jesus to his death, the crucifixion, finding of the empty tomb, Pentecost, the stoning of Stephen, and the conversion of Paul. They are written from the perspective of Caiaphas and addressed to Annas, who is away from Jerusalem taking the cure at a spa near the Dead Sea.

In his first letter, Caiaphas gloats over the success of the plan to have Jesus put to death by Pilate. The high priest endures a tense and competitive relationship with Pilate, whom he calls a "stubborn fool" who needs to be put in his place. Caiaphas also expresses contempt for the "weak" members of the Sanhedrin, Joseph of Arimathea and Nicodemus, who bury the body, and for Rabbi Gamaliel, who, regrettably, is somewhat sympathetic to the dead man.[21]

Caiaphas's exultation does not last long; the second letter already reveals his concern about the disappearance of Jesus' body. From Caiaphas's missives it becomes clear that Annas espouses what the two men come to call the "swoon theory": that Jesus did not really die on the cross but was comatose at the time of his deposition and burial. Jesus must have been awakened by the cold air, suggests Annas, and somehow managed to extricate himself from the tomb. Caiaphas, on the other hand, believes that the disciples stole the body (cf. Matt. 28:13–15). But the facts do not easily support either of these theories. It is hard to imagine that a person weakened by an attempted crucifixion could have unshrouded himself, rolled the heavy stone away from the inside of the tomb, and gone unnoticed. The stolen body theory also poses problems, however: Why has not the body been found? And why are the disciples so happy? For there is in fact a third theory, put forth by the disciples themselves: that Jesus was resurrected. According to the "editor" of these letters, Caiaphas finds this belief astounding, though one might parenthetically observe that a Sadducee who did not believe in bodily resurrection would nevertheless be familiar with Pharisees who did hold this belief and therefore not find this claim for Jesus so strange as all that.[22] In letter 9 Caiaphas concludes that they are no closer to solution or resolution of the swoon theory as opposed to the theft theory, but perhaps it does not matter much: "The Nazarenes will do little harm by clinging to their foolish notions so long as they are not bothering anyone else with them."[23]

The tide against Caiaphas seems to turn when he meets the young Saul of Tarsus, who has volunteered his services for putting down the Nazarenes. "He will be a tremendous asset to us and his assistance should enable us to exterminate them even more quickly than I had been anticipating." Caiaphas has not encountered anyone with "such a violent and uncompromising hostility toward the followers of Jesus and their resurrection doctrine. His hatred of them is even fiercer than my own," and the high priest is thrilled: "How I am going to enjoy seeing these obnoxious people get what they deserve!"[24] But in letter 21 he conveys to Annas the alarming report that Saul "has gone over to the enemy." Caiaphas has trouble believing this rumor, for Saul's "is not a foolish mind that might be easily ensnared by any false doctrine."[25]

Caiaphas sinks again into despair: "This seems to me the last straw, the climax of a vexatious series of disappointments and frustrations, and, if the matter were not so important, I think I would throw the whole thing up and leave these hateful Nazarenes to their own devices."[26] As the correspondence draws to a close, he summarizes the whole affair and acknowledges defeat: "I feel as if I am living in a nightmare from which I cannot wake up. I simply cannot make head or tail of the sequence of events. They seem to be beyond explanation—unless, of course, unless . . . but that does not bear contemplating, for it simply cannot be true. I must close. Greetings, Caiaphas."[27]

Martin's novella is unique in presenting the events strictly from the perspective of the high priest. In doing so he creates some initial sympathy for Caiaphas and also illustrates that from the point of view of the figures within the Jesus narrative there were several possible interpretations of the empty tomb, of which resurrection may have been the most difficult to defend. Nevertheless Caiaphas's determination to be rid of the troublemaker, and his dismay at the subsequent turn of events, including Saul/Paul's own "defection" from the fold, show that this work, like many others, accepts Caiaphas's status as a deicide. And while the narrative voice is that of the high priest, the true subject of the book, of course, is Jesus.

Complicating Caiaphas

Perhaps the most masterful fictional treatments of Caiaphas are to be found in two very different works: the radio play cycle *The Man Born to be King*, by the British author Dorothy Sayers, and the epic novel *The Nazarene*, by the Jewish American author Sholem Asch.

These books have several things in common. First, they are roughly contemporary. Sayers's play cycle was first broadcast on the BBC in 1941–42; Asch's novel appeared in English translation in 1939 and in the original Yiddish in 1943. Second, both Sayers and Asch were already acclaimed both in their own countries and internationally, primarily though not exclusively for their works of fiction. Third, both works were highly controversial at the time of publication. By examining their respective portraits of Caiaphas, it will be possible, first, to discern these authors' attitudes toward Jews and Judaism in an era when the role of Jews as a minority group in modern democratic societies was a fraught issue for Jews and non-Jews alike; second, to examine how Sayers and Asch address, and make the most of, the gaps in the Gospel narrative.

Dorothy Sayers, *The Man Born To Be King*

Dorothy Leigh Sayers was a British author well-known for her mysteries and short stories featuring amateur sleuth Lord Peter Wimsey, her translations of

Dante's *Divine Comedy*, and her plays and essays on Christian themes.[28] *The Man Born to Be King* is a cycle of twelve radio plays written for broadcast on the BBC, one play per month, beginning on Sunday, December 21, 1941.[29] The play cycle makes for entertaining reading even for those who have never heard it performed. This enjoyment is due not only to the wit and drama of the plays themselves, but also to the detailed notes that precede each play. While originally intended to guide the producer and director, these notes convey Sayers's distinctive narrative voice and provide insight into her views of each character.[30] Her main focus throughout the cycle is on the complex relationship between Judas and Jesus.[31] Caiaphas, however, has a major supporting role as the leader of the council. In this capacity the high priest plots Jesus' death, hires Judas to betray him, persuades Pilate to have him crucified, exults at the success of his own scheming, and is ultimately defeated, spiritually if not physically.

For Sayers, Caiaphas is "the complete ecclesiastical politician—a plausible and nasty piece of work,"[32] "a smooth and supple politician, and completely unscrupulous. The timid decency of Nicodemus and the passionate insults of Judas slide off him like water off a duck's back." But he has a long memory for those who slight him: "One feels that he keeps a sinister little dossier, in which the names of disaffected or rash persons are carefully noted down for future reference," though he does have "one moment of sincerity": "when he pays homage to the politician's household god of 'expediency.'"[33]

Caiaphas's devious nature comes to the fore in his first interview with Judas, whom he hopes to manipulate into betraying Jesus:

CAIAPHAS: The Sanhedrim[34] have been disquieted by rumours—no doubt quite unfounded—that your Master is engaged in political activities of a rather indiscreet kind, such as might provoke reprisals from the Government. We are very unwilling to believe that this is the case.

JUDAS: You may take my word for it, the story is quite untrue.

CAIAPHAS: Good. We are glad to hear it. It would be a pity that your charitable work among the . . . the poor, and so on should be interfered with. But as you know, Rome does not look with favor on group activities which might have a subversive tendency.[35]

Judas explodes with rage:

JUDAS: . . . You think my Master belongs to the Nationalist party. You think he might encourage Jewry to shake off the Roman yoke. Little you know him! And how little you know of this nation! Rome is the punishment that this people must bear for their sins. Jewry is corrupt, and Rome is God's judgment on her. The Roman rod is laid on the sinner's back, and the Roman axe to the root of the rotten tree.... Does that gall you, my Lord Caiaphas?... There was a time when the Lord High Priest could give orders in Israel. Today you must cringe to Caesar. That is the measure of your humiliation, and of your sin.

Annas, who is almost always at Caiaphas's side, upbraids Judas for his insolence, but the high priest ignores Judas's insults, notes his views on Jewish culpability, and articulates his own approach to the political realities of his time: "Your own views on the subject of national regeneration are most important and interesting. I think myself that a policy of reconstruction and collaboration with Rome is in the best interest of Jewry."[36]

Caiaphas's words to Judas can be read as a fairly straightforward elaboration upon his "prophecy" to the council in John 11. Underlying the notion that it is expedient to sacrifice one man for the good of the nation is a policy of "reconstruction and collaboration" according to which the Jewish leadership aims to avoid unrest and to remain in Rome's good graces. But it is likely that Sayers is also reflecting Josephus's account of the events preceding the Jewish revolt against Rome. The words she ascribes to Caiaphas echo the speech that Josephus places in the mouth of King Agrippa I, in which he expresses the conviction that armed revolt against Rome is folly. Only a collaborative and constructive approach will preserve Jewish lives and at least some measure of autonomy in Judaea. Agrippa urges the people to submit to Rome rather than rebel: if other, larger groups such as the Parthians saw fit to "bend to the yoke" and thereby to maintain a truce with Rome, how much more so should the tiny population of Judaea (*War* 2.379, 389)? He entreats his people: "Spare the temple and preserve for yourselves the sanctuary with its holy places; for the Romans, once masters of these, will refrain their hands no more, seeing that their forbearance in the past met only with ingratitude.... if you decide aright, you will enjoy with me the blessings of peace, but, if you let yourselves be carried away by your passion, you will face, without me, this tremendous peril" (*War* 2.401).[37]

Sayers acknowledges that her portrait of Caiaphas owes much to the events of her own time. The high priest, she writes, is the consummate politician, "appointed, like one of Hitler's bishops, by a heathen government, expressly that he might collaborate with the New Order and see that the Church toed the line drawn by the State."[38]

Yet the views that Caiaphas expresses to Judas also call to mind the prewar British policy of appeasement toward Hitler and Nazi Germany. Under Prime Minister Neville Chamberlain, England, along with Italy and France, signed the so-called Munich Pact with Germany on September 29, 1938. The pact determined the conditions under which the German-speaking Sudetenland area of Czechoslovakia would be ceded to Germany on October 1, in exchange for a promise that Hitler would not claim any additional European territory.[39] That Sayers was very concerned about this issue is evident from her presidential address to the Modern Language Association on January 5, 1939, in which she criticized the role of propaganda in making possible Germany's bloodless conquest in Austria and the Sudetenland.[40]

Sayers's Caiaphas does not merely manipulate and deceive Judas, but as is evident in the seventh play, he also bullies those members of his council who dare to defend Jesus against the high priest's accusations.

CAIAPHAS: Brother Joseph, and Brother Nicodemus. Do I understand that you admit the claim of Jesus of Nazareth to be the Messiah? Because that is what he does claim. He does not say he is a prophet: he says he is the Christ. If you propose to support that claim publicly, you may. Of course, there *is* a penalty attached. A person was excommunicated the other day for the same offence. Only a pauper, certainly, but God forbid that the Sanhedrim should be any respecter of persons, however wealthy they may be, Joseph of Arimathea. If anybody takes the view that Jesus bar-Joseph is the promised Messiah and the King of Israel, he had better say so at once, and then we shall know where we are.

NICODEMUS after a pause: I have no wish to defy the Sanhedrim.

JOSEPH: I am only anxious that an innocent person shall not be victimized.

CAIAPHAS: The word "victim" always arouses feeling. But I said before, and I say again, that it is better to sacrifice one man, rather than the whole nation. That is not persecution. It is policy.[41]

It is in the tenth play, "The Princes of This World," that Sayers's antipathy toward Caiaphas emerges most explicitly. In the introductory notes to this play, Sayers insists that "there is in this politician nothing of the priest, as we understand the word. The sight of a soul in torment is to him merely another irritating interruption, wasting precious minutes when he wants to hurry off to Pilate. Nothing of what Judas is saying means anything to him—how should it? since he is totally destitute of any sense of sin."[42]

Yet Sayers is not entirely without empathy for the high priest. A slight softening is apparent in the introductory notes to the eleventh play, "The King of Sorrows," which she calls Caiaphas's apologia: "For once, he is completely sincere, and speaks as a true prophet. He puts his finger on the central weakness of Jewry, and his speech is that of a man who clearly foresees the failure of his own lifework.... At this point, and at this point only, we ought to feel sympathy with Caiaphas."[43]

As the eleventh play draws to a close, Caiaphas shares with his two worrisome council members some reflections on the larger political questions at stake in the current situation:

CAIAPHAS: Joseph and Nicodemus, let me tell you something. Jewry has gone for ever. The day of small nations is past. This is the age of empire. Consider. All through our history we have tried to slam that door. Jewry was to be a garden enclosed—a chosen race, a peculiar people. But the door was opened. By whom?

NICODEMUS: In the strife between the sons of Alexander, when Hyrcanus appealed to Rome.

CAIAPHAS: True. That strife brought us Herod the Great—the creature of Rome, who for 30 years held Jewry together in his gauntlet of iron. And when he died, what? New strife—and the partition of Israel, with Pilate the Roman made Governor of Judaea. Under Herod a tributary nation; after Herod, three tributary provinces. With every Jewish quarrel, Rome takes another stride. One stride—two strides—the third will be the last. . . . I have killed this Jesus, who would have made one more faction; but for one pretender crucified, fifty will arise. . . . One day, the Zealots will revolt and the sword will be drawn against Caesar. Then the ring of fire and steel will close about Jerusalem; then the dead will lie thick in the streets, and the tramp of the Legions will be heard in the inner Sanctuary of the Temple. I, Caiaphas, prophesy.

JOSEPH: What would you have us do?

CAIAPHAS: Accept the inevitable. Adapt yourselves to Rome. It is the curse of our people that we cannot learn to live as citizens of a larger unit. We can neither rule nor be ruled; for such the new order has no place. Make terms with the future while you may, lest in all the world there be found no place where a Jew may set foot.

JOSEPH: Strange. You echo the prophecies of Jesus. But he, I think, would have enlarged the boundaries of Israel to take in all the world. . . . Is it possible that he saw what you see, and would have chosen to fling the door wide open? Not to exclude, but to include? Not to lose Israel in Rome, but to bring Rome into the fold of Israel? . . .

CAIAPHAS (drily): Quite mad. It is the duty of statesmen to destroy the madness which we call imagination. It is dangerous. It breeds dissension. Peace, order, security—that is Rome's offer—at Rome's price.

JOSEPH: We have rejected the way of Jesus. I suppose we must now take yours.

CAIAPHAS: You will reject me too, I think. . . . Be content, Jesus, my enemy. Caiaphas also will have lived in vain.[44]

To the end Caiaphas asserts that he had only the best interests of his country at heart. When it is all over, Joseph asks him:

JOSEPH: Caiaphas, as man to man, what do you think you have done?
CAIAPHAS: The best I could for Israel.[45]

Beneath the standard, derogatory contrast between narrow, exclusivistic Judaism and expansive, universal Christianity, can we detect at least some faint sympathy for a man who did what he could, albeit in his own misguided, manipulative, and hostile way?

The Man Born to Be King created a huge stir during its first broadcast season, from late 1942 through 1943. As a nonvisual medium, the radio play was not subject to the prohibition against portraying Jesus in a film or play (a prohibition not lifted until 1968).[46] The liveliness of Sayers's Jesus, however, raised serious concerns for some segments of the BBC's audience. Imagine a son of God who joked and laughed, and in colloquial English, no less. Some irate listeners held Sayers's plays responsible for the fall of Singapore and implored the BBC to remove them from the air before Australia was lost as well. Others, by contrast, credited the plays with British victories in Libya and Russia.[47]

Within the media and in the church, the debate eventually blew over. The play cycle was broadcast in its entirety numerous times, to great acclaim. Certainly Sayers's depiction of Caiaphas is to some extent allegorical, pointing to the attitudes of certain British politicians and ecclesiastical leaders in her own era. But the use of a Jewish leader to make these points and, more generally, the criticisms of Jewry that emerge throughout the play cycle make it difficult to avoid the question of Sayers's own attitudes to Jews and Judaism during this critical period.[48]

British anti-Semitism in this period has been well-documented.[49] In his 1945 essay "Anti-Semitism in Britain," George Orwell noted: "The Jews are not numerous or powerful enough, and it is only in what are loosely called 'intellectual circles' that they have any noticeable influence. Yet it is generally admitted that anti-Semitism is on the increase, that it has been greatly exacerbated by the war, and that humane and enlightened people are not immune to it. It does not take violent forms (English people are almost invariably gentle and law-abiding), but it is ill-natured enough, and in favourable circumstances it could have political results."[50]

Sayers's novels contain a number of Jewish characters whose ethnic identities are mentioned but not dwelt upon.[51] *The Man Born to Be King*, by contrast, conveys a sense of discomfort not so much with respect to individual Jews but with the role of the Jewish people in society. Sayers addressed this question directly in her wartime correspondence. In a letter to Sir Wyndham Deedes, dated April 16, 1943, Sayers was critical of what she perceived as the unwillingness of Jews to adhere to British social norms and mores:

> The British Jewesses in 1939 dashing to the bank and announcing in loud tones: "of course, we're sending all our money to America"; the children who

cannot learn the common school code of honour; the Jewish evacuee offering his landlady double the rent she asked in order to secure the rooms and then informing against her to the billeting authorities; the inhabitants of a London street complaining bitterly that everybody, from the high-class publishers' staff at one end to the little rookery of prostitutes at the other, eagerly did their turn of fire-watching—all except the houseful of Jews in the middle. They word it in different ways; but it all really boils down to the same thing: "bad citizens."[52]

The most important factor shaping Sayers's attitude to Jews was their rejection of Christ. As she wrote to a Mr. Lynx in 1943: "I cannot, you see, bring myself to approach the question as though Christ had made no difference to history. I think, you see, that He was the turning-point of history, and the Jewish people, whose religion and nation are closely bound up with the course of history, missed that turning-point and got stranded: so that all the subsequent course of their history has to be looked upon in the light of that frustration."[53]

After resisting Mr. Lynx's persistent requests for some time, Sayers finally produced an article for a symposium titled "The Future of the Jews." The article amounted to a complex theological treatise arguing that Jewish misfortune must be seen as "the sad but inevitable consequence of their failure to recognize their Messiah when he came."[54] This article, being both too long and too dense for public consumption, was never published, perhaps the outcome that Sayers had intended all along.

Sayers's letters make explicit the attitudes that lurk just beneath the surface of her play cycle. Caiaphas is made out to be the spokesman for Jewish otherness and parochialism, and the beleaguered Pilate, who tried so hard to have Jesus set free, articulates the perspective that may have been closest to Sayers's own: "I don't trust Jews."[55] Nevertheless Sayers does not blame only the Jewish high priest and, by extension, the Jewish people for Jesus' death. Rather she sees humankind as complicit both in that ancient crime and in the catastrophe of World War II. Not only is Caiaphas like one of Hitler's bishops, but the elders of the synagogue, she suggests, "are to be found on every Parish Council—always highly respectable, often quarrelsome, and sometimes in a crucifying mood." Sayers insists, however, that the elders represent us all:

> Tear off the disguise of the Jacobean idiom, go back to the homely and vigorous Greek of Mark or John, translate it into its current English counterpart, and there every man may see his own face. *We* played the parts in that tragedy, nineteen and a half centuries since, and perhaps are playing them to-day, in the same good faith and in the same ironic ignorance. But to-day we cannot see the irony, for we the audience are now the actors and do not

know the end of the play. But it may assist us to know what we are doing if the original drama is shown to us again, with ourselves in the original parts.[56]

These remarks suggest that despite Sayers's obvious ambivalence toward Jews, her portrayal of Caiaphas is intended not only to attribute some measure of responsibility to him for the chain of events leading to Jesus' death, but also to mount a critique of the political leadership of her own country in the prewar period and to comment on the experience of the British people in the early war years.

Sholem Asch, *The Nazarene*

Sholem Asch was a Polish-born, Jewish American novelist, playwright, and essayist in the Yiddish language. *The Nazarene* is the first and best-known of a trilogy of "Christian novels" that includes *The Apostle* (1943) and *Mary* (1949). *The Nazarene* presents the life and death of Jesus from the perspectives of three characters: Cornelius, a Roman centurion who had the ear of Pilate; Jochanan, a disciple of the Pharisaic rabbi Nicodemon; and Jesus' betrayer, Judas. Their three stories are framed by a narrative, set in 1930s Poland, that features an elderly Pole, Pan Viadomsky, who hires an impoverished Jewish student to help him translate the long lost "Gospel of Judas."[57] Viadomsky is a virulent anti-Semite who collaborates with a priest on a treatise designed to prove that Jews made use of Christian blood to prepare their Passover matzot. Yet he develops a love/hate dependency on his young Jewish assistant, to whom he reveals his shocking secret: Viadomsky is himself the Roman centurion named Cornelius. Furthermore the student too was alive in the early first century, when he was the young disciple Jochanan, who became a follower of Jesus.

Although it is very long—close to seven hundred pages in English translation—*The Nazarene* is one of Asch's most accessible novels. The improbability of the frame narrative contrasts with the vivid detail and realism of the three intersecting stories set in Jesus' era. The book is rich in content, texture, and suspense, a real page-turner even now, almost seven decades after its publication.

In contrast to Sayers's work, *The Nazarene* pays attention to both the religious and the political aspects of the high-priestly role. Nevertheless it sets the high priest apart from the people and emphasizes the Jews' dislike for the office: "The High Priest . . . was the highest religious functionary, and, at the same time, the uncrowned king. He could send out his messengers to arrest Jews even beyond the frontiers of Judaea. And the Priesthood was like a leech, sucking the blood and marrow out of the people. The High Priests were bloated with wealth; for apart from the tithes and the first-fruits, payable in kind, they imposed additional taxes on the people."[58]

The Jews' antipathy toward their high priest was set aside on the annual Day of Atonement, when he entered the Holy of Holies. As Cornelius narrates, "During these festivals of theirs the Jews were even capable of wild ecstasies of joy. What a sight they were, for instance, on the night of the ending of their most solemn sacred day, the Day of Atonement, when their High Priest issued from the mysterious Holy of Holies unharmed by his contact with supreme sanctity! The bitterness which they felt throughout the whole year against the High Priest and his acolytes was forgotten and forgiven on that day."[59]

As members of the higher aristocracy, the high priests were Rome's natural allies, but the relationship was tense nonetheless.[60] At their first meeting, Caiaphas's attempts to assure Pilate of his loyalty met with an equivocal response:

> Pilate's fleshy nose sank downward; he glanced at the [high priest's] party furtively from under his heavy eyelids and said, briefly:
> "That we shall see. It depends on good will."
> "On one side at least that good will always exists," answered the High Priest.
> "That will have to be proved by deeds," said Pilate.[61]

Indeed from the moment of his arrival in Jerusalem, Pilate's disdain for and even hatred of Jews was evident, at least to Cornelius. After Pilate's first confrontation with the high priest, Cornelius teases him:

> "Procurator," I said, "the first thing you will have to do on reaching the Antonia, is to send for leeches, to have the bad blood drawn from your veins."
> "I am thinking of very different methods for ridding myself of my bad blood."
> "I know it, Procurator. By drawing the blood of the Jews."[62]

In addition to highlighting the tension between the Jewish high priest and the Roman governor, Asch creates a subplot that involves jealousies and intrigues within Caiaphas's own family. Most troublesome to Caiaphas's peace of mind are the former high priest Hanan (Annas) and Hanan's youngest son, also named Hanan. Cornelius writes:

> Hanan ben Hanan was a born fighter, and there was occasion enough for fighting. It was no light thing either for us Romans or for the Jewish Priesthood to retain power in Jerusalem, and the boy was hungry for power. Hunger for power shouted from his person, as it did, for that matter, from the person of his father. But while the old man had learned, from long experience, to go about its satisfaction with infinite cunning and patience, contenting himself with the outward show of the civil authority delegated to him by his son-in-law, Hanan ben Hanan was too young, too impetuous, and too inexperienced to conceal his envy of the regnant High Priest.[63]

The various conflicts and tensions—within the high-priestly family, between the Romans and the Jews, and between Pilate and Caiaphas—come to a head in the events leading to Jesus' death. In Asch's novel, however, neither the high priest nor the Roman governor bears the weight of responsibility for his arrest. That role belongs to Cornelius. On his deathbed Viadomsky confesses to his Jewish assistant that it was he, in his role as Cornelius, who, in the aftermath of the "cleansing of the Temple," initiated the events leading to Jesus' death:

> I am he, the man who laid the first hand on your Rabbi, when our frightened little servants of the High Priest thought that if they but touched him they would be consumed by the fire of his mouth. . . . The fact is that your frightened little Jews did not dare to place a hand on the Rabbi. I have good grounds for believing that even your foxy old Hanan was infected by the terror; he took your Rabbi for a fiery angel direct from heaven. They were frightened out of their wits before I brought the man to them, a prisoner; and even afterwards, in the very court of Hanan, they shied away from him. The fact is that the High Priests gave me a great deal of trouble in connection with your Rabbi, particularly after you [Jesus' followers] proclaimed him the Jewish King and brought him in procession to Jerusalem.[64]

In Cornelius's version of the story, Caiaphas, far from desiring and plotting Jesus' death, does what he can to forestall Jesus' arrest. His first tactic is to downplay Jesus' importance: "Kaifa pretended to be very phlegmatic. 'Why,' he said, 'Every year our Jews proclaim a new King-Messiah, and no harm is done; the Roman Government still stands where it did, and Herod's authority is not diminished by a hair. Let them have their little joke.'"[65]

The high priest insists that Jesus' behavior in the Temple was just an internal matter, but Cornelius disagrees and threatens Caiaphas with reprisals.

> "What happened in the Temple court," I replied, firmly, "was not directed solely against the Temple administration. It was an assault on the whole system of laws and a threat against all order in the Province of Judaea. Considering the harm which the man did to your prestige, we cannot but wonder that you extend your protection to him. How can we help suspecting that you have your own reasons? We have neither the time nor the means to untangle all the details of your mystical, complicated religious affairs, which so easily take on the aspect of rebellion. Our straightforward Roman commonsense tells us that if the supreme religious authority extends its protection to a man who has delivered such a blow against its prestige, then this same highest religious authority must find it to its interest to make common cause with a rebel and a disturber of the peace. That interest cannot be in consonance with the well-being of the constituted order."[66]

Caiaphas asks fearfully: "Hegemon, do you dare to doubt our loyalty to Rome?" Cornelius presses the point: "It is not a question of doubting or of not doubting. Can such an attitude on the part of the High Priesthood seem otherwise than suspicious to the legate and the Procurator?"[67]

Cornelius demands that Caiaphas produce Jesus immediately. Despite the Roman's threats, however, the high priest remains evasive: "But we assure you that we do not know where the man is; and we promise we shall take immediate steps to discover his whereabouts. The moment we ourselves know, we shall transmit the information to you."[68]

Here ensues a debate within the high-priestly family; old Hanan is willing to hand Jesus over, and the younger Hanan insists upon it, but Caiaphas refuses. Eventually Jesus is found and brought to the council for investigation, a process that is nearly scuttled by the fierce arguments between the Sadducean and Pharisaic members with regard to interpretation of the law. Finally Jesus utters the words that even Caiaphas considers to be blasphemous, and he tears his robe as a sign of mourning.

Still the question remains: should Jesus be turned over to Pilate as the Hegemon had demanded? Predictably both Hanan senior and his youngest son argue vigorously that the council must comply with Cornelius's demands: "If not, it would mean that we believe [Jesus' claims] to be true, and we would have to prostrate ourselves at his feet and proclaim him the King-Messiah." Others object: "If this man has transgressed against us, against the Jewish faith, then we will be the judges. Since when does Israel admit strangers into his garden, to do the weeding for him?"[69] Old Hanan prevails, however. Jesus is handed over, and the story ends as it always does: with Jesus dying on the cross.

The length of this novel affords Asch the time and space fully to develop the setting, the characters, and the plot. But as a Jewish immigrant to the United States from Eastern Europe, writing in the Nazi era for a primarily Jewish audience, Asch is also motivated to provide a more complex view. He draws a three-dimensional high priest who is not without his faults but also not blinded by hatred or political ambition. Most important, he attributes to Caiaphas the same sort of conflict—between tradition and modernity, adherence to religion and adopting secular ways—that was central to the Jewish experience in Europe in the modern era, and to the experience of immigration to the United States from the late nineteenth century onward.[70]

This inter-Jewish cultural debate is adumbrated in the novel by the contrast between the high-priestly family and Joseph of Arimathea, who became one of Jesus' followers. Like the high-priestly family, Joseph was "a man of great wealth, steeped in Hellenistic culture and in company of Roman officials and circle of Greek philosophers."[71] Whereas the high priests kowtow to Rome, Joseph is engaged in a fierce internal conflict: "The unhappy struggle between the Greek and Jewish worlds found its echo in Joseph's heart. His strict adherence to the tradition of his people had by no means killed in him the inclination toward the brilliant world of the gentiles. He carried on a perpetual if secret war within himself; he dreamed of finding reconciliation with the temptations of Hellenism without at the same time destroying the barriers which the Jewish sages had put up against its spiritual barrenness."[72]

Whether Joseph's struggle would have rung true to Hellenized Jews like Philo of Alexandria is difficult to say. But Asch's description accurately reflects the dilemma faced by Jews in the transition between a closed and intense religious life in Eastern Europe and the openness of Western culture.[73] The emotional tenor of these struggles was heightened by the experience of anti-Semitism, which had a long European history but was intensified in the Nazi context. At the time Asch was writing, the war had not yet begun, yet in Jewish circles the state of alarm was already extremely high due to the Nazi persecution of the Jews that had begun with Hitler's rise to power.[74]

The Nazarene quickly became a national best seller, ranking ninth in national sales in 1939 and fifth in 1940, and was praised by prominent Jewish book reviewers such as Clifton Fadiman in the *New Yorker* and Alfred Kazin in the *New Republic*.[75] But in Yiddish literary circles, the novel's highly favorable portrayal of Jesus and his followers created a major storm and precipitated Asch's fall from his position as the most popular and respected Yiddish writer of twentieth-century America. Asch's longtime editor, Abraham Cahan, refused to serialize the novel in the *Forverts* [the *Forward*], the foremost Yiddish newspaper of the era. Cahan accused Asch of currying favor with non-Jews and even of proselytizing; he went so far as to attack Asch's knowledge of history, his mastery of Hebrew, and even his use of Yiddish in previously published works.[76] The original Yiddish version of *The Nazarene* was finally published in 1943 by a Jewish communist paper, *Di Frayhayt*.[77] The communist connection did nothing to endear Asch to his Yiddish readership, but at least it meant that they could read the novel.

The sympathetic use of Christian subject matter was certainly not new to Jewish culture or to Yiddish literature.[78] Asch himself had written previous works about Christianity, and other Jewish writers, scholars, and artists had portrayed Jesus in sympathetic terms.[79] One thinks, for example, of Joseph Klausner's 1922 book, *Jesus of Nazareth*, and the paintings of Marc Chagall such as *White Crucifixion*.[80] The turn to Christological themes has been described as an "expression of the hybrid culture in which modern Americans lived, a turn to a figure whose historical significance in shaping Western culture could not be ignored."[81] In early-twentieth-century Europe and America, Jesus could be seen as a Jewish brother, and the language of crucifixion and Christian martyrdom could be used to describe the Jewish experience of anti-Semitism and persecution. Theologically some Jews were ready to reclaim Jesus as a Jew, by emphasizing that Christianity as such was a later development.[82] In the immediate prewar and war period, however, concerns about the role of Christianity in anti-Semitism predominated and, parenthetically, continue to run high among some segments of the Jewish population today. In writing so positively about Jesus on the eve of the Holocaust, and publishing his novel first in English rather than in Yiddish, Asch, some felt, had betrayed his primary Yiddish audience.[83]

The focus on Asch's favorable depiction of Jesus distracted his Jewish audience's attention from the important ways in which *The Nazarene* differed from most other retellings of the Jesus story. For Asch, Caiaphas is not an unscrupulous politician intent on ridding the world of Jesus but a complex individual with the unenviable task of mediating between an oppressed and unruly populace and the empire that would keep them in check. Neither is first-century Judaea a society divided between the poor who long for a savior to deliver them from Roman rule and the authority figures—priests, scribes, Pharisees—who collaborate with Rome in oppressing their people. Asch allows readers to imagine their way into the midst of Jewish society, its rivalries, and its tensions, as well as the seriousness with which it took Jewish belief and practice, in all its solemnity and joy. In doing so he provides a rich medium with which Jews in the twentieth century—and, I might add, in the twenty-first century as well—could think through the push and pull between Jewish identity and practice on the one hand and participation in a free and open society on the other.

CONCLUSION

Caiaphas comes to life fully in *The Man Born to Be King* and *The Nazarene*. Both Sayers and Asch use Caiaphas's prophecy in John 11 as the starting point for their depictions of the high priest as a political figure caught between his Jewish compatriots and the Roman imperial machine. Both authors exploit the gaps within the Gospel accounts and use Josephus as well as other ancient sources to amplify their depictions of Judaea under Roman rule and the role of the high priest in the decades prior to the first Jewish revolt against Rome. Both also acknowledge the ambiguity of the Gospels with regard to the roles and responsibilities of Annas the former high priest during the tenure of his son-in-law Caiaphas. In Sayers's play cycle, Annas is at Caiaphas's side throughout the play cycle. Asch, by contrast, casts the former high priest as the central figure in a complex subplot involving jealousy and intrigue in the highest quarters. While the details are his own, Asch uses Josephus's accounts of the tenures of Annas,

Caiaphas, and the younger Annas as the framework for this subplot.[84] For neither Asch nor Sayers is Caiaphas a likable figure. Yet both authors acknowledge the difficult situation in which a first-century Jewish high priest would find himself vis-à-vis the Judaean population on the one hand and the Roman governor on the other.

Finally both authors place the story of Jesus, and the role of Caiaphas within that story, in the broader context of the history of Jewish relations, beginning with the first century down to their own difficult days. Despite their different ethnic identities and personal experiences, Sayers and Asch both lament the parting of the ways between Judaism and Christianity.[85] Their laments, however, reflect opposing perspectives. Asch argued that Judaism and Christianity were a single culture and civilization;[86] in his view anti-Semitism was caused by the decision of Jesus' followers to separate from Judaism.[87] Sayers, on the other hand, believed that the Jews were tragically mistaken to reject the Christian message and justified anti-Semitism as the inevitable consequence of the Jews' ongoing insistence on being different.

In fiction Caiaphas is a deicide who is important not only for his role in the story but as a metaphor through which a critique of contemporary institutions and society can be mounted. What makes Caiaphas so real in the best of these fictional accounts, however, is his complexity. Caiaphas remains the high priest deeply implicated in Jesus' crucifixion. But in his fictional guise, he does not always rejoice in this role and occasionally displays his ambivalence. In the hands of Sayers and Asch, and to a lesser extent in Graves and Mailer, Caiaphas remains the high priest under whom Jesus was crucified but also a man who was subject a variety of forces and powers beyond his control.

CAIAPHAS ON STAGE

The dramatic nature of Jesus' story is already apparent in the Gospel accounts, which may indeed have been intended for oral presentation or dramatization.[1] From the medieval period to the present day, the story has been amplified and developed in numerous dramas, ranging from informal children's productions, such as Christmas or Easter pageants, to major professional productions. This chapter begins with a brief examination of the medieval English mystery play cycles and then focuses in more detail on the Passion play genre, specifically on the Passion play at Oberammergau, the most famous and enduring of the European Passion plays. In both the mystery and Passion plays, Caiaphas has a major role that is exploited not only for its dramatic but also for its comic and satirical potential. The discussion in this chapter focuses entirely on the scripts or textbooks for these plays; the visual elements, including costuming and staging, will be considered alongside other visual representations in chapter 9.

MYSTERY CYCLES

Mystery plays were among the earliest formal plays in Europe. The earliest evidence of these plays is from the tenth century, after which the genre underwent a lengthy period of development that lasted until the sixteenth century. Although numerous mystery plays were in existence, four major cycles survive: the York cycle, the Chester cycle, the Towneley/Wakefield plays, and the N Town Plays, also known as the Ludus Coventriae cycle or Hegge cycle. Some cycles are still being performed on occasion; the York and Chester plays were performed in 1951 as part of the Festival of Britain; the Lichfield Mysteries were revived in 1994; and the N Town cycle has been revived as the Lincoln mystery plays. The York cycle was performed in Toronto in 1998, and in 2001 and 2009 an African version of the Chester plays was performed in London by the Isango Portobello Theater of South Africa.[2]

The York Cycle

The York cycle is a prime example of drama as sacramental theater and is widely considered the most lavish, long-lasting, and complex form of collective theatrical enterprise in English theater history. The cycle has direct links to the feast of Corpus Christi.[3] Even after the abolition of the feast in 1548, the citizens of York continued to mount performances on that day. The plays present biblical narratives through living tableaux with accompanying antiphonal song. Although the mystery play cycles were initially performed in churches, the York plays were written and produced by the trade guilds and mounted on "pageant waggons" that moved slowly through the city and played sequentially at somewhere between ten and sixteen different stations appointed and approved by the city.[4]

In the mystery plays, biblical characters and events are drawn into analogy with contemporary events and social realities.[5] As in the other postcanonical texts examined thus far, Caiaphas, Annas, and Pilate constitute an unholy triumvirate; the two high priests are ecclesiastical tyrants, and Pilate is slightly more sympathetic. As Laut notes, such depictions "would appeal to an audience familiar with the legal and ecclesiastical abuses which brought on the Peasants' Revolt. Court procedure and methods of inquiry in this and the following plays are based on medieval interrogations of the Inquisition, for Christ is treated as a heretic and there is incessant questioning and the threat of torture."[6] Humor is characteristic of the plays, in which Caiaphas and Annas are useful not only for portraying the events leading to Jesus' death but also for satirizing the clergy.[7] A brief discussion will give the flavor of the portrayal of Caiaphas in this genre of material.[8]

Pageant 29: Christ before Annas and Caiaphas

Caiaphas appears throughout the York cycle, but most prominently in pageant 29, sponsored by the Bowers' Guild and the Fletchers' Guild.[9] Pageant 29 opens with a speech by Caiaphas in which he boasts of his own mastery of the law, for which, he avers, he is highly deserving of praise. Caiaphas later disdainfully dismisses the reports of Jesus' ability to heal the sick and give sight to the blind as "false and lucky blundering." He is irked to distraction by Jesus' evident desire to do nothing other than to break the law. Particularly irritating are Jesus' transgressions of the Sabbath laws and his defamation of God. He must, Caiaphas proclaims, be brought to justice for his false teachings.

Caiaphas's father-in-law, Annas, too has heard of Jesus and even knows his parentage. When Annas marvels at Jesus' deeds, however, Caiaphas cuts him off sharply: "With witch-craft he fares with all / Sir, that you shall see full soon." Caiaphas sends his knights off to find Jesus, leaving him with time for a little refreshment and relaxation. Annas suggests that Caiaphas slake his thirst with some wine—"T'will do you well, I dare warrant"—and rest while they wait for news. Caiaphas takes well to this idea and is assisted by one of the soldiers, who promises that the wine "will make you wink." Sure enough, Caiaphas is soon ready for a nap; he orders his servant to tuck him in well and keep the others from bothering him.

Eventually the soldiers return with Jesus. Caiaphas sends for Annas, and the two get ready for some sport, during which Annas plays "bad cop" to Caiaphas's "good cop." Annas gets angry at Jesus' refusal to bow down to him, but Caiaphas restrains his colleague, reminding him that "it's not sporting to beat beasts who are bound." Caiaphas asks Jesus to "truthfully, tell us some tales we can trust." Annas continues to mock Jesus: he is "an empty old round" whose brain is "in a twist."

Caiaphas then seeks the testimony of the soldiers, who play the "false witnesses" of Matthew 26. The soldiers testify to Jesus' transgression of the Sabbath and to his popularity among the populace. Finally they describe in detail Jesus' predictions about the Temple, which, if destroyed, "this ribald has bragged that he'd rapidly raise!" Caiaphas instructs the soldiers to leave him and Annas alone with the prisoner for a private interrogation. Caiaphas orders Jesus to name his henchmen, but Jesus' "language is lorn"; to the displeasure of his tormentors, he remains silent. Caiaphas is aghast. Annas recommends using force—"Now, by Belial's blood and his bones, / The best thing to do is go beat him"—but Caiaphas restrains him yet again and asks Jesus outright: "By great God that is living, and last shall for aye / If you are Christ and God's son, say it is so." Finally Jesus responds: "Sir, you said it yourself: now truly I say / That I came from my Father; to him I shall go, / And worthily with Him in wealth dwell always."

Caiaphas explodes in anger: "Why, shame on you, trickster untrue! / Your father you've foully defamed!" Jesus has condemned himself. Annas chimes in and declares that there is no need for further witnesses; Jesus has blasphemed and deserves to die. Caiaphas demands that Jesus answer these charges, but Jesus calmly refuses. The soldiers eagerly jump in to mock him. One exclaims: "My Lord, will you hear? By Mahound,[10] / To go further now, there's no need." Caiaphas is fed up and orders the soldiers to kill Jesus. But Annas intervenes and proposes a more cunning plan: to send Jesus to Pilate, the "doomsman" who is "next to the King." Let Pilate hear the whole story and see whether he helps Jesus or hangs him. Caiaphas agrees but orders the soldiers to "teach yonder boy better to bend and to bow." The soldiers are only too happy to oblige. The soldiers beat—"buffet"[11]—him throughout the night. Caiaphas then orders them to take Jesus off to Pilate and report that the prisoner is striving to destroy their laws and must be dealt with that day, before the Sabbath that "comes in the morn."[12] As the pageant concludes, Caiaphas tells his soldiers: "Sir, your fair fellowship we betake to the fiend! / Go on now, and dance forth in the devil's way."[13] This may be a reference to actual dancing in the pageant, which was used as a way to clear the scene and ease the transition to the next pageant.

Although Caiaphas and Annas are united in their animosity toward Jesus, the cycle distinguishes between them for dramatic and comic effect. Caiaphas is blustering, pompous, and hotheaded, while Annas, occasionally at least, comes across as suave and circumspect. Each is intent on Jesus' destruction and more than pleased when he is beaten to a pulp.[14]

Staging the Mystery Plays

The negative portrayal of Caiaphas and Annas appears not only in the scripts of the various mystery cycles but also in the staging. In writing about the Wakefield cycle, Robinson notes that during the interrogation and sentencing, Jesus is standing on the "Place"—an open field or amphitheater ground where the main action takes place—while Annas and Caiaphas are seated on a scaffold above.[15] At the end of the play, Caiaphas leans over the edge of the scaffold to take a swipe at Jesus, but he just misses him and exclaims: "Say, why standys he so far?" (line 299). Caiaphas, who had risen from his throne, must be told to sit down again. The slapstick farce is based on a literal but playful reading of Job 5:12, which states that God "frustrates the devices of the crafty, so that their hands achieve no success."[16] Robinson refers to this as the "most imaginative and intelligent uses of the Place and Scaffold in the whole of medieval drama."[17]

Observations

While the humor of these plays is beguiling, the plays themselves simply adopt the view of Caiaphas as a wicked deicide.[18] As Robinson notes, "Annas, Caiaphas and their knights are sinners and enemies of God. . . . Annas and Caiaphas form the "council of the malignant" of Psalm 21 (21.17)"[19] Pilate too is condemned, though his sympathy toward Jesus is also noted. Like some of the writings of the church fathers, the mystery plays use Caiaphas as a vehicle for exploring issues of concern to medieval society, in this case, the rule of law. Beckwith comments:

> In the sequence of Trial plays [including also the trial before Pilate], the law is examined as the very machinery of injustice, perverted by the protection of power, the display of wills that have entirely lost the good of intellect. Implicit in these dramas is the claim that any regime that administers law in this way and that converts truth to power will be a regime that crucifies

Christ again. Through the figure of Pilate and the relationship of Pilate with Annas and Caiaphas, the difference between sheer brutality and law, between authority and tyranny, is explored. Pilate in the Conspiracy and in the two plays of the judgement before Pilate seems to be able to see quite clearly that Annas and Caiaphas suffer from a rawness of emotion, an anger and a hatred that are not simply unseemly in the episcopacy but that are directly generated out of the perversion of their will rather than any relation to truth or justice.... These bishops are "overcruell"; they even want to strike Jesus themselves rather than delegating the job. There is nothing legally admissible in the desire of Annas and Caiaphas to crucify Jesus, Pilate keeps declaring, and hence it is the nasty specificity of that desire that is exposed.... but as soon as his own interests are closely touched, his own power addressed, and his own will interpellated, Pilate's high-minded defenses of the law evaporate rapidly.[20]

As in other genres, Caiaphas appears in these plays as a Jewish ecclesiastical leader who views Jesus not only as a threat to his own power and to the people under his leadership, but also as a personal irritation. Although the representations of Caiaphas in the medieval productions poke fun at local ecclesiastical authorities, this satirical element does not replace or disarm the anti-Jewish elements of these plays, which loudly proclaim the deicide charge against Caiaphas and the Jews.

PASSION PLAYS

The most prominent dramatic form in which Caiaphas appears is the Passion play. In the medieval era, Passion plays were commonly performed throughout Europe during the week immediately preceding Good Friday, sometimes over a period of several days. The origins of the Passion play tradition are not entirely clear, due to the scarcity of early texts. In the latter part of the nineteenth century, it was thought that the Passion play developed from the *planctus,* a lyrical expression of grief and lament usually voiced by Mary at the foot of the cross, often in dialogue with the apostle John. Early-twentieth-century scholars argued that this genre developed out of the dramatic recitals of Gospel accounts of the Passion, or perhaps as a prelude to the Easter play, which dramatizes the resurrection. More recently scholars have resisted the attempt to find a single originating factor. Instead they suggest that the play was the product of a broader environment, with many contributing elements, arising as a natural consequence of the artistic, aesthetic, and religious climate of the twelfth century, which saw a growing interest in Christocentric piety, a more humanistic treatment of Christ, and a perception of the Passion as a dramatic human episode.²¹ Some argue that the plays do not arise directly from liturgy but from additions called tropes. Tropes are additions to, amplifications of, or interpolations in the authorized liturgy.²² At some point in the Middle Ages, perhaps as early as the tenth century, these may have developed into larger dramas in order to edify and instruct the masses. Why or how the trope functions in this role is unclear; it is possible that the practice of doing brief dramatizations at certain points in the Easter service was known long before the Middle Ages.²³

Early Passion Plays

The earliest known Western Passion play is the twelfth-century Montecassino text, first published in 1936.²⁴ This play opens with the meeting between Judas and the chief priests and thereafter follows the Gospel accounts closely, with particular emphasis on Matthew's Passion narrative.²⁵ The extant fourteenth-century manuscript, in contrast to the mystery plays and most other Passion plays, omits Annas completely. This manuscript places Caiaphas explicitly at the foot of the cross as one of those who mocks Jesus and provides detailed stage directions, for example, instructing Caiaphas to rise when he rends his garment and indicating that some lines are to be spoken "alta voce."²⁶

The earliest available Passion play written in the vernacular is the Saint Gall play. The extant manuscript dates from the fourteenth century, but the original dating of the play itself is not known.²⁷ The Saint Gall play injects notes of humor and sarcasm into the pious drama that later became a hallmark of the genre and required the removal of these pious dramas from the church to the marketplace.²⁸ The Saint Gall play is also unusual in that it features a fictional character, Rufus, a venomous, redheaded Jew who takes the lead in inciting other Jews, cajoling Pilate, and paying soldiers to scorn and beat Jesus.²⁹ As in the mystery cycles, however, Caiaphas and Annas have major roles. The two men almost always appear together and divide between them the dialogue assigned to Caiaphas and to other Jewish leaders in the canonical Gospels. The two leaders take turns cross-examining the man born blind (John 9),³⁰ and it is in response to Annas, not the high priests as a group, that Caiaphas articulates the need to eliminate Jesus (John 11:49–52).³¹ In the cross-examination of Jesus at the trial, it is Annas who takes the lead, asking the Jews, "Does no one among you know of a crime which this man has committed? Let him tell us now, that we might bring charges against him," and then continuing, as in Matthew, by putting Jesus under oath and demanding: "Tell me the honest truth: are you the son of the true God to whom Heaven and earth are subject?" It is Annas, not Caiaphas, who tears his clothes and declares that "this man reviles God; therefore, he shall suffer death, as the Law of Moses commands." And it is Annas who refuses to take back the blood money when Judas regrets betraying his master.

Caiaphas is by no means absent, however. He charges the evil Jew Rufus with the task of complaining to Pilate about Jesus, thereby moving forward the priests' diabolical plan.[32] After Jesus is led to the crucifixion field, Caiaphas gives voice to the ongoing unbelief of the Jews:

> Now all the world shall see:
> he helped other people
> in many divers ways,
> but now his power is gone.
> If he were God, as he said,
> he would not suffer this pain.
> If he would now come down from the cross,
> we would believe in him;
> however, he must grant us our disbelief.[33]

Caiaphas at Oberammergau

The most famous Passion play of all is still performed regularly in Oberammergau, a picturesque village in the Bavarian Alps, ninety kilometers (fifty-six miles) southwest of Munich. Legend has it that in the midst of the Thirty Years War between Catholics and Protestants in Germany, the bubonic plague hit Germany. Oberammergau, a Catholic village, remained relatively unscathed until 1632, when a day laborer, Kaspar Schisler, brought the plague with him from a neighboring village. Over the next month, it is said, eighty-two villagers died. In an attempt to cut the outbreak short, the villagers marched to the parish church. Before the altar they solemnly vowed that if God would rid them of this plague, they would enact a Passion play in perpetuity.[34] From that day forth, no one died of the plague in Oberammergau, and the villagers have continued to fulfill their vow. The first play was staged in 1634, the next in 1644. In 1680 the village moved to scheduling the plays in every year ending in 0, as well as on the centennials and half-century anniversaries of the 1634 production.

Yet one should probably not set much historical store by this account. It is likely that the Oberammergau play performed in the seventeenth century was the continuation of an early Passion play tradition. Evidence for this theory is the fact that the earliest text of the Oberammergau Passion play is itself an amalgam of a late-fifteenth-century Catholic play and a Protestant "tragedy," *The Passion and Resurrection of Christ,* dated to 1566. As James Shapiro points out, it is hard to understand why the first production of the play would have been based on a set of scripts that were antiquated already in 1633, unless the tradition of producing the play, perhaps sporadically, was already in existence at that time.[35] Yet the legend itself has exerted a powerful force over the village, as indicated by the extraordinary length to which villagers have gone to preserve their tradition over a period of centuries and their often passionate resistance to revising its script. Nevertheless changes have occurred over time, often in response to external pressures.

In 1770 the Bavarian government banned all Passion plays, on the grounds that "the great mystery of our holy religion should not be displayed on a public stage."[36] After vigorous efforts and some revisions, the village of Oberammergau managed to have its own play declared an exception, and the play was performed again in 1780 and 1790. In order to avoid later bans, a new play, based more directly on biblical texts, was written in 1811 by Otmar Weis, a monk residing at the Ettal monastery a few kilometers from Oberammergau. In 1860 the text was substantially rewritten by Joseph Alois Daisenberger, the Oberammergau parish priest from 1845 until 1883, and it was this text that became the basis for subsequent productions as well as for other Passion plays in Europe.[37] The Weis and Daisenberger versions are still described as sources for the 2010 production, although the extensive revisions undertaken by Christian Stückl and Otto Huber are also acknowledged.[38]

An overview of the scripts over the last century reveals three broad phases. Until 1970 the Passion play script was based fundamentally on the Daisenberger version, with only minor changes and revisions. The 1970 and 1980 versions and the 350th anniversary production in 1984 represent a transitional period of controversy as the village attempted to respond to Catholic critique in the wake of Second Vatican Council and to serious concerns raised by American Jewish organizations such as the Anti-Defamation League of the B'nai B'rith as well as the American Jewish Committee. Significant changes, however, occurred only with the appointment of Christian Stückl and Otto Huber as director and assistant director in 1990; Stückl and Huber continued on for the productions of 2000 and 2010. Despite these numerous and far-reaching changes, villagers still associate even the most recent productions with the Daisenberger version, a perception that the directors are content to maintain.[39]

The Daisenberger Play

The Plot

The Daisenberger script drew elements from the four canonical Gospels but also made numerous additions that included new characters, dialogue, and entire scenes. The playbooks prior to 1960 describe the play as a "religious festival play [*ein geistliches festspiel*] in three sections with twenty-four tableaux vivants"; by 1960 the number of these tableaux was reduced to twenty.[40] The tableaux vivants are "frozen arrangements of costumed performers" used in Christian drama to reproduce biblical scenes that were seen as foreshadowing or otherwise pertinent to scenes in the life of Jesus.[41] Each act and scene opens with a prologue and a tableau, and the play as a whole concludes with a final hymn of praise.

The opening scene combines the triumphal entry and the "cleansing" of the Temple. A number of traders who are ousted from the Temple precincts denounce Jesus to the council, over which the high priest Caiaphas is presiding. One of them, named Dathan, offers to recruit someone to betray Jesus, a friend who has become a disciple and become disenchanted. Caiaphas is overjoyed; now he will finally have the ammunition to triumph over Jesus. The scene now switches to Bethany, where Christ is having dinner with Simon, Lazarus, Thaddeus, Peter, and others. Mary Magdalene enters and anoints Christ's feet with precious ointment against Judas's objections. Mary, the mother of Jesus, comes to see her son before he sets off for his fateful journey to Jerusalem. Christ and his followers then journey to Jerusalem, where Christ bids his disciples to prepare the lamb for the Passover festival. Meanwhile Dathan and his friends find Judas, who has become disgruntled with Jesus and is easily persuaded to betray him for a substantial reward.

By this time the disciples have prepared the Passover meal, and the twelve eat with Jesus, who washes their feet, as per the Gospel of John, institutes the Eucharist, as per the synoptic Gospels, and identifies Judas as his betrayer, as per all four Gospels. Dathan introduces Judas to the council and is interviewed by Caiaphas, who wants to be assured that Judas truly does intend to betray Jesus to them. Caiaphas pays Judas his thirty pieces of silver, and the erstwhile disciple promises to give Jesus into their hands that evening. When Judas leaves, Caiaphas articulates the plan to kill Jesus. "Is it not better that one man die than that the whole nation perish?" They resolve to sit in formal judgment on Jesus and then take him off to Pilate.

As Judas leads the soldiers to the garden of Gethsemane, Jesus is praying and warning his followers of the events that are to come. Just then Judas approaches, Jesus is arrested, and Dathan prepares to take him to the high priest. Judas and others report their success to Annas, but when the former high priest announces that "his [Jesus'] death is decided," Judas panics; he is now tormented by his decision to cooperate with the Jewish authorities.

In the early morning, Jesus is brought to Caiaphas and the council for formal questioning; they convict him of blasphemy and send him off the Pilate. Pilate and Caiaphas, supported by Annas, confront one another, Pilate seeking to exonerate Jesus and Caiaphas to condemn him. The Jewish priests are resolute in their determination that Jesus must die. Pilate tries to avoid responsibility by sending Jesus off to Herod Antipas, while Caiaphas attempts to persuade Herod that Jesus must be condemned to death. Jesus is returned to Pilate, who again is subjected to incessant lobbying, including threats, on the part of the high priest and the council. Pilate offers to release one prisoner; the crowds, heavily incited by the high priest and council, choose Barabbas and cry out for Jesus' crucifixion. Jesus is sentenced to death on the cross and dies, with his mother, Mary Magdalene, and two supporters, Nicodemus and Joseph, looking on. Joseph offers to bury Jesus in his own new tomb. The play concludes with a finale celebrating the triumph and glorification of Christ.

Dialogue

The dialogue assigned to Caiaphas accentuates his animosity toward Jesus and his determination to do away with him. A persistent theme in this version is Caiaphas's hatred of Jesus, which is portrayed as the complete opposite to the love that Jesus preached. Caiaphas and Annas are overjoyed when the traders who had been expelled from the Temple precincts come to Caiaphas to lodge a complaint against Jesus and one of them, Dathan, offers to find them an informant. Caiaphas exclaims: "Praise be to the God of our Fathers! I live again. Now with such men as these we can accomplish our purpose. Now we shall see who will triumph! He with his followers, to whom he preaches without ceasing, of love—a love that includeth publicans and sinners, and even Gentiles or we with this multitude, filled with hate and revenge, that we are letting loose against him." Annas chimes in: "This victory will be vouchsafed us by the God of our fathers! How joy will rejuvenate me in my old days."[42]

Caiaphas's actions are motivated by his rabid hatred for Jesus. Annas claims that he will die a happy man if only Jesus is killed. In act 12, part 2, scene 1, he insists that Jesus' death will save his religion: "Shall I now in my old age see the Synagogue overthrown? No! With this stammering tongue will I cry for the life and blood of this malefactor and then descend into the tomb of my fathers when I have seen this evil-doer die upon the cross."[43]

For the plan to work, however, there must be both a formal trial before the high council and a condemnation by Pilate. In act 6, scene 4, Caiaphas impresses upon his colleagues the necessity of sitting "in formal judgment upon this man, to examine Him and bring witness against Him, so that the people may not be confirmed in the opinion that we only persecute him through hate and envy..... For the rest, it would be the safest for us, if we could carry it out through the Governor of the Province and have him condemn this Man to death. Thus would all the responsibility be taken from us."[44] While Caiaphas and his entourage acknowledge among themselves that they are motivated by hatred, they want to maintain their moral and religious stance and authority before the people. For this reason they must at least go through the motions of due process. Having Jesus condemned by Pilate will absolve them of direct responsibility, at least publicly. Privately they are quite happy to take the credit.

The high priest's motivation is ostensibly religious. But he also has an eye on his posterity: "So this day will see the religion of our Fathers saved, and the honour of the Synagogue heightened, so that the echo of our fame reach to our latest descendants" (act 9, scene 4).[45] The Caiaphas of Oberammergau views his conflict with Jesus as a battle between the synagogue and the church, thereby effacing Jesus' Jewish identity entirely. The death of Jesus will remove the threat that the church poses to the synagogue. Yet the statement is ironic. For in killing Jesus, Caiaphas has indeed ensured that his fame, or rather, his notoriety, will persist for centuries.

Caiaphas uses Pilate to his own ends, though his straightforward plan is nearly foiled by Pilate's inexplicable reluctance to condemn Jesus. Pilate is willing to scourge and wound Jesus, but no more than that. When Caiaphas insists, Pilate comments: "Is your hate against this man so deep and bitter that he cannot satisfy by the blood from his wounds! Ye compel me to tell you openly what I think. Urged by ignoble passions, you persecute him, because the people give more heed to him than to you" (act 12, scene 2).[46]

In order to convince Pilate to condemn Jesus, Caiaphas urges his followers, including the traders and members of the council, to "go into the streets of Jerusalem, summon your friends, our trusted followers, to come here. Gather them together in great crowds, kindle in them the most glowing hate against the enemy of Moses" (act 12, scene 4).[47]

Finally Caiaphas succeeds in persuading the crowd to call for Barabbas's release. Yet Pilate's reluctance to crucify Jesus to death mystifies the high priest: "Am I allowed a question? Why art thou so anxious about the condemnation of this man, thou who a little while ago, for a seditious cry, caused hundreds to be put to death, without trial and without sentence, by thy soldiers?"[48] Pilate does not respond, but rather, asks for water.

CAIAPHAS: The people will not move from here until thou hast pronounced sentence upon this enemy of Caesar's.

PEOPLE: Yes! We will not move from this place till the sentence is pronounced.

PILATE: I am compelled by your violence to yield to your desire. Take him and crucify him. But see! I wash my hands. I am innocent of the blood of this just man. It will rest upon you.

PRIESTS AND PEOPLE: We take it upon us, His blood be upon us and upon our children. (act 13, scene 2)[49]

The hate that originated with a high priest obsessed with a plain-speaking Galilean has now spread to the entire people, who willingly take full responsibility upon themselves and their descendants. The responsibility of the entire Jewish people is made even more explicit in the death sentence, which reads: "I, Pontius Pilate, viceroy of the mighty Claudius Tiberius Casesar, in Judea, at the desire of the High Priests, the Sanhedrim, and the whole Jewish people, pronounce the sentence of death upon a certain Jesus of Nazareth, who is accused of having incited the people to revolt and forbidden them to pay tribute to Caesar and of having proclaimed himself King of the Jews." The people rejoice: "O joyful day! The enemy of Moses is thrown down! . . . Happiest Passover! Now is peace returned to Israel! It is finished with the Galilean!" (act 13, scene 2).

Caiaphas's hate persists even after Jesus' death, for he cannot rest until "I have seen that his bones are broken, and his body thrown in to the pit of the malefactors." Annas is of the same mind: "It would delight mine eyes to see his body torn by wild beasts" (act 15, scene 2).[50]

Anti-Judaism

These excerpts from the Daisenberger script show that while the Passion play draws directly upon the canonical Gospels, it greatly expands the role of Caiaphas, Annas, and the other Jews. It also shows that the play has strong potential not only for theological anti-Judaism, but also for its racial analogue, anti-Semitism. This potential was felt by at least one spectator, Rabbi Joseph Krauskopf, a Prussian-born American rabbi who saw the play in 1900. Krauskopf reports that

> up to the commencement of the Prelude I felt the keenest enjoyment in having come, in the strange sights I had seen, in the quaint and interesting people I had met. But from the moment the play began, the enjoyment ceased. I had resolved to look at the play as a sightseer, not as a critic. I had thought I could deceive myself, but I soon found I could not. I had made myself believe that I had come as a tourist, to look at the *Passion Play* as I might look at any other spectacular performance, as I might look at the *William Tell* play in Switzerland, or at the *Hiawatha* play in Canada. But I could not. The moment the play began, and the opening hymn was sung, and the opening lines were spoken, the tourist turned critic; the traveller, theologian; the cosmopolitan, Jew. The moment the Prelude began to tell us that we are under the curse and wrath of God, and that atonement and salvation can be found only in the blood of His incarnate Son; the moment the tableau of the expulsion of Adam and Eve was presented, to teach that Paradisian happiness will be forever barred to us if we do not open our obdurate hearts to

the belief in the only Saviour; the moment we were told of the sweet airs of peace that breathe through the world since God's only begotten Son was sent to earth, commissioned, by his own pre-ordained death, to take upon himself the sins of human kind,—that same moment the unyielding Jew within me rose to his full height, to assert anew his deathless allegiance to that pure form of monotheism from which our fathers never departed, not even in darkest ages and under direst cruelties.[51]

Now Krauskopf could finally understand what he had heard before coming to Oberammergau concerning "the emotional and hysterical outbreaks on the part of some of the spectators at the sight of the outrages perpetrated against the Jesus of the Passion Play." He could now see the connection between the Passion play and the anti-Semitic pogroms of the Middle Ages and later, based on "feelings against Jews that hundreds and thousands of these spectators would take home with them to all parts of Europe, and to distant lands across the seas, as a souvenir of Oberammergau."[52]

Krauskopf describes his responses to the portrayal of the Jewish characters in the 1900 production:

The very opening of the afternoon part represented one of the High Priests [Annas] on the balcony of his house, in the midnight hour, thirsting for the blood of the patriot of Nazareth, unable to sleep until he shall have feasted his eyes on the sight of that miscreant in chains. His feverish craving is soon satisfied. The victim of his hatred is led before him,—not led, but crowded, pushed, jostled by an infuriated mob of Jews.... Insolent questions are put by the High Priest to Jesus. He disdains to answer them, excepting the one in which he is asked to give an account of the pernicious doctrines he had taught: "I have spoken openly," replies he, "men have heard me; let them tell thee what I have taught." For this dignified answer, he is cruelly smitten in the face, to which Jesus righteously answers: "If I have taught wrong, tell it; if not, why smitest thou me?" This is more than the High Priest Annas, whose name might more worthily have been Haman, can endure. He bids them take the culprit out of his sight, and to afford that delectable treat, of seeing Christ in chains, also to Caiaphas, the other High Priest.[53]

Finally "the unfortunate prisoner" is dragged to Caiaphas and the assembled Sanhedrin. Krauskopf continues:

Caiaphas is the younger High Priest of the two, very cleverly acted by the village beadle of Oberammergau; but not a whit inferior is he to Annas, in hatred against the unoffending son of his race, faith, nation.... [Jesus] is accused of still greater crimes, of the greatest of all conceivable crimes, of having arrogated to himself the right of God in forgiving sin, of having committed blasphemy in calling himself the Messiah of Israel, the Son of God.

As in the Gospels, the high priest is horror-stricken and rends his clothes "as a sign of the nation's humiliation and contrition at the blasphemy of one of its sons." He and the mob shout out Jesus' guilt as Jesus is turned over to the guard for safe-keeping till morning, when he will be tried by Pilate and crucified.[54]

Krauskopf is eloquent in his description of the anti-Semitic outbreaks to which the previous performances of the Passion play may have contributed:

> It is the month of the greatest martyrdoms in Israel. Turn the pages of Jewish history, and read, if you have the heart, the martyrology crowded annually, for centuries, between the days of Good Friday and Easter Monday, days which the Jew might well name *Black Friday* and *Easter Moanday,*—here a hundred tortured, there twice and thrice that number burnt and massacred; here a thousand driven out, there twice and thrice that number mobbed and pillaged; here a whole settlement wiped out, there helpless little ones torn from their parents and dragged to the baptismal font. Verily, the Christian's Easter worship of the Resurrected Prince of Peace has, throughout the Dark and Middle Ages, meant, for the Jew, riot and ruin, pillage and plunder, outrage and atrocity, torture and death.[55]

He expresses his good fortune to live in modern times, when

> there is no fear . . . in the Jewish quarter, as there was then, of insult or assault; there is no placing of special guards at ghetto gates; there is no barricading of doors and windows; there is no burying of special valuables in fear of plunder; there is no concealing of women behind mounds and tombstones of cemeteries; there is no hiding of helpless little ones and of helpless aged; our men are not assembled for an all-day service of fasting and mourning in the synagogue, attired in their funeral-shrouds, tremblingly awaiting the Christian's rushing from his church—tremblingly awaiting his merciless onslaught with club and pike and torch. There is no longer a compulsory Jewish quarter at all. Torn down are the ghetto walls. Destroyed are the external dividing lines between the Christian and the Jew. Yea, thanks to the spirit of the Reformation, to the work of the printing press, to the popularization of knowledge, to the teaching of science, thanks to the layman's throwing off the yoke of priests and monarchs, here, under Columbia's protective wing, we fear no Easter onslaught on Jews, have had no fear of it in the past, and shall have no fear of it in the future.[56]

The rabbi's reflections read ironically in light of the Holocaust, which postdated Krauskopf's Oberammergau experience by some forty years and which he could not have anticipated, though he acknowledged that anti-Semitism still existed in many parts of Europe.[57]

Hitler at Oberammergau

The play's anti-Jewish content rendered it highly compatible with Nazi ideology. Adolf Hitler and Joseph Goebbels were in the audience in the 1930 season, and Hitler returned in 1934. That year marked the tercentenary of the first performance. The preface to the jubilee text included the following statement: "Is there any other time more favorable than these days of the suppression of the anti-Christian powers in our fatherland to remember the price the Son of God himself paid for his people, the people who adhere to him and to his banner?"[58] Although the anti-Semitism expressed in the Passion play fell short of Nazi standards, Hitler professed to be pleased. As he later said during a dinner party on July 5, 1942:

> One of our most important tasks will be to save future generations from a similar political fate [to that of Britain] and to maintain forever watchful in them a knowledge of the menace of Jewry. For this reason alone it is vital that the Passion Play be continued at Oberammergau; for never has the menace of Jewry been so convincingly portrayed as in this presentation of what happened in the times of the Romans. There one sees in Pontius Pilate a Roman racially and intellectually so superior, that he stands out like a firm, clean rock in the middle of the whole muck and mire of Jewry. If nowadays we do not find the same splendid pride of race which distinguished the Grecian and Roman eras, it is because in the fourth century these Jewish-Christians systematically destroyed all the monuments of these ancient civilizations.[59]

The Nazis intended to commission an entirely new script for the 1940 season, but this plan did not eventuate: the 1940 production was abandoned due to the war.

The Transitional Years: 1970–1984

The 1950 and 1960 productions substantially preserved the Daisenberger script and production, despite the claim on the title page of the 1960 textbook that it is "revised and newly published." In the years leading up to the 1970 production, however, Oberammergau was gripped by serious conflict and controversy engendered by developments within the Catholic Church and pressure by Jewish groups. In 1965 the Second Vatican Council, under Pope Paul VI, issued the groundbreaking document *Nostra Aetate*, which rejected the deicide charge.

True, the Jewish authorities and those who followed their lead pressed for the death of Christ; still, what happened in His passion cannot be charged against all the Jews, without distinction, then alive, nor against the Jews of today. Although the Church is the new people of God, the Jews should not be presented as rejected or accursed by God, as if this followed from the Holy Scriptures. All should see to it, then, that in catechetical work or in the preaching of the word of God they do not teach anything that does not conform to the truth of the Gospel and the spirit of Christ.

Furthermore, in her rejection of every persecution against any man, the Church, mindful of the patrimony she shares with the Jews and moved not by political reasons but by the Gospel's spiritual love, decries hatred, persecutions, and displays of anti-Semitism, directed against Jews at any time and by anyone.[60]

Oberammergau's refusal to revise its script in conformity with *Nostra Aetate* resulted in the withholding of the *missio canonica*, the official church blessing. At the same time, Jewish organizations, such as the American Jewish Congress, the Anti-Defamation League of B'nai B'rith, and the American Jewish Committee, whose mandate is to combat anti-Semitism and the teaching of contempt and hatred of Jews, spearheaded a boycott of the 1970 production. Pressures from the Catholic Church and from these Jewish groups resulted in blocks of empty seats for the first time in many decades.[61]

The Oberammergau script underwent revision in May 1983 in preparation for the 350th anniversary production of 1984; this revision was approved by deputation of the ecumenical committee of the German Bishops' Conference, thereby restoring the *missio canonica*. The overall structure of the plot remained, including the opposition between Jesus and Caiaphas as the driving force and the role of Annas as supporting actor. The motif of Caiaphas's irrational and extreme hatred for Jesus, however, was removed, and the scenes where it was emphasized were shortened or eliminated. Caiaphas was now portrayed in slightly more sympathetic terms as a leader motivated not only by overtly political concerns but also by concern for the good of the people.

In act 1, scene 4, Caiaphas recounts that "when he came into the city, the Galilean had himself proclaimed as the Son of David, which means the Messiah, and soon they will extol him as the King of Israel. Then discord will arise among the people, there will be a revolt against the Romans and they will come with their armies and bring ruin to the land and people. Woe to the children of Israel! Woe to the holy city! Woe to the temple of the Lord! The last moment has come to avert the destruction of Israel. Friends and brothers, the responsibility is ours, the guardians of Zion. We must decide today what has to be done."

Caiaphas now poses a question to his colleagues: "What shall be done with this man when he is in our power?" One priest, Zadok, suggests that Jesus be thrown into the deepest dungeon. But for Caiaphas this is not enough: "Which of you will guarantee that his supporters do not cause an Insurrection among the people to free him? None of you, I see! Therefore, as High Priest, I say it is better that one man should die than that the whole nation should perish" (cf. John 11:49–52). The council agrees, and arrangements are made for a "trial" involving false witnesses. The last piece of the plot involves Pilate. This too has been thought through carefully by the high priest: "So far as carrying out the sentence is concerned, the safest thing for us would be if we could arrange for the Governor to condemn him to death" (act 5, scene 3).[62]

After the interrogation Caiaphas announces: "He has been condemned to death by the High Council. But it is not I, not the High Council,—God's law itself pronounces the judgment on him." The council pronounces Jesus "guilty of disobeying the law, profaning the Sabbath and blasphemy, and accordingly deserves to die" (act 8, scene 3).[63]

Caiaphas promises to receive back those who had followed Jesus. "Yes, you are still the true descendants of your father Abraham. Thank God that you have escaped from the indescribable doom which this deceiver wishes to bring on you and your children." The words that Pilate utters before washing his hands are somewhat less inflammatory than in earlier versions; the reference to Jewish violence is gone: "Bring me some water. So you put pressure on me to comply with your wishes. (To Aurelius.) Have the death sentence written out immediately. See, I wash my hands of it, I am innocent of the blood of this just man. All of you, see!" The blood curse remains, however. Caiaphas calls for Pilate to "put this blasphemer to death," and the people shout: "We take His blood upon us and our children." This outcry is repeated by the priests and the people, after which Caiaphas proclaims: "Victory is ours! Rejoice, our faith is saved! . . . Let our triumphant procession now go through the middle of Jerusalem" (act 11, scene 2).[64]

Although the motif of Caiaphas's hatred of Jesus has been softened, the 1984 script continued to lay blame on the Jewish authorities and all the Jews. This collective blame is emphasized in the Roman governor's formal decree that, as in the 1960 script, refers to the entreaty of "the High Priests, High Council and people of Jerusalem" (act 11, scene 2).[65]

The introduction to the 1984 playbook, written by Josef Forstmayer, ecclesiastical counselor and the priest of Oberammergau, denied that the play is anti-Semitic in any way. "When the text was revised in past years particular attention was given to avoiding any expression which could hurt the feelings of the Jewish people. In a world in which peoples, races and religions strive for understanding the Passion Play must also show consideration. The Play is not concerned to seek a guilty party. Holy Scripture includes the whole of mankind and its representatives in the guilt for Jesus's death."[66]

But at least some who viewed the 1984 production were not convinced. Saul Friedman wrote that "the worst malefactor is the aged high priest Annas, who is portrayed sharing authority with his son-in-law Joseph Caiaphas.... Daisenberger's original text contained a lengthy scene showing Annas wringing his hands as he awaited news of Jesus's arrest. No fewer than thirty-four lines were given to express Annas's anxiety and contempt.... Yet even today, in an abbreviated scene, Annas's delight knows no bound when runners inform him that Jesus has been apprehended. It is all invention. It is a performance worthy of nineteenth-century melodrama, and would be laughable if it were not so pathetic."[67]

The Stückl-Huber Productions

In advance of the 1990 production, Christian Stückl and Otto Huber became the new director and assistant director. Not only was Stückl a veteran of several Passion plays, but he was also a professional theater director who had developed a strong vision of what the Oberammergau play could and should be. Stückl envisioned major and radical changes in both the script and the staging of the play, which he has introduced over the course of the 1990, 2000, and 2010 productions, though not without controversy and opposition.[68] For the 1990 production, Stückl's hands were tied by Rudolph Pesch, the head of the Oberammergau committee that had the final say on any changes to the text of the play.[69] The discussion focused in great measure on the "blood curse" (Matt. 27:25), which numerous critics, both Jewish and Christian, wanted to excise as a major step toward toning down the anti-Semitic potential of the Passion play. In 1990 the blood curse remained, but other changes were incorporated. Although in this version Caiaphas is still a major force in the plot against Jesus, the role of Pilate is accentuated to some degree, and the blood curse, while present, is no longer repeated several times. Pilate asks for some water and says to Aurelius: "They shall have the death sentence written out immediately. See, I wash my hands of it, I am innocent of the blood of this man. All of you, see!" This contrasts with the earlier versions (and with Matthew 27:25), in which Pilate orders the Jews to "see to it yourselves." Several in the crowd shout out "Blood be on us and on our children," but the curse is not repeated (act 11, scene 2).[70] Nevertheless Caiaphas is still implicated, if not directly by name, in Pilate's official decree: "I, Pontius Pilate, governor of Judaea under mighty Caesar,

Claudius Tiberius, on entreaty by the high priests and high council; hereby pronounce the sentence of death on Jesus of Nazareth...."[71]

A more substantial revision was undertaken for the 2000 production. For his second production of the play, Stückl emphasized more explicitly the situation of Roman domination and developed the theme of political motivation while omitting overt references to Caiaphas's hatred for Jesus. This version stresses the Romans' hatred for the Jews, which in turn makes Caiaphas's concern for the safety and existence of his people more plausible. Nevertheless Caiaphas's determination to do away with the troublemaker is as prominent as in the earlier versions, and it is this persistence that is a major driver of the plot.

These elements are all in view in act 1, "Jesus enters Jerusalem." The 2000 version omits the role of the Temple traders, who in the earlier versions complain about Jesus to the high priest and then offer to bring Judas. Nor does Caiaphas overtly articulate his hatred for Jesus. Nevertheless his final speech of the opening act expresses his animosity clearly enough: "This man has too many followers. This could cause a dangerous battle and provide the blood-thirsty Romans with an excuse to put an end to the uprising with their swords. Trust me! Let me take charge! If you do that, the blasphemer will receive the punishment he deserves."[72]

As in earlier versions, Caiaphas argues that Jesus poses a major threat to both Torah and Temple. In words only lightly revised from the 1960 and 1984 versions, he tells the priests:

> To our shame we had to watch how the Galilean with his followers walked through the gates and streets of our holy city. You heard the deluded crowd shout hosanna. We were eye witnesses to his false pride when he arrogated to himself the office of the high priest and had the impudence to give orders in the Temple of God. What is lacking before we have a total overthrow of divine and secular order? Only one more step, and the Law, given to us by God through Moses, will collapse, the teachings of our fathers will be despised, the priests will be defrocked and dishonored, and the holy sacrifice will come to an end. (act 3, scene 1)[73]

Later Caiaphas predicts that, "encouraged by his success, this man will proclaim himself king of Israel. This will cause division in the land and insurrection against the Romans who will arrive with their mighty armies and destroy the land and the people. If we wish to silence the Galilean, we must now immediately act as we should have acted long ago" (act 3, scene 1).[74]

The 2000 play also makes some changes to the trial scene and the words by which Caiaphas condemns Jesus. In contrast to earlier versions, Caiaphas no longer calls upon God to condemn Jesus. Rather it is Jesus who has condemned himself (act 7, scene 1). The words with which he is sent off to Pilate are less specific than in earlier versions: "But no one shall accuse us of an act of injustice. He has not only violated our Law but has also broken Roman law in various ways. Take the prisoner before the judgment seat of Pontius Pilate. We will not be the ones to pronounce the sentence of death. This will be done by the procurator himself" (act 7, scene 1).[75] In this way Caiaphas creates at least some justification, or excuse, for sending Jesus to Pilate to be judged.

Caiaphas and Pilate hate each other as much in 2000 as they did in the earlier versions, but Caiaphas has developed a more confrontational stance toward the governor. Why is Pilate so determined to set Jesus free when he has summarily sent so many others to the cross?

> Pilate, you wish to set Jesus of Nazareth free for only one reason: to have him incite the people to riot, to have him blaspheme our faith, and to have him lead the people under the Roman swords. The people of Judea know that you persecute them with vicious hatred and wish to add to their torments, but you cannot corrupt them. God will protect them. He will hear us, and even the mighty Caesar will hear us and protect us from Pilate the destroyer. Do you hear me, Pilate?! (act 8, scene 3)

Pilate responds with derision: "I have heard—heard your voice, the croaking voice of a man whom I have elevated to the position of High Priest not very long ago.[76] Caiaphas, here in Jerusalem, the only voice is the voice of the governor" (act 8, scene 3).[77] The scene is a dramatic showdown between Pilate and Caiaphas and affords a glimpse, if only fleeting, of the limits to Caiaphas's power, his devotion to his people, and his difficult position vis-à-vis Rome.

In the 2000 version, the blood curse and Pilate's formal declaration had finally been modified so as to soften the portrayal of Caiaphas and the Jews as a whole. The calls for Jesus' crucifixion come from various people in the crowd, and the crowd as a whole, not specifically the high priest or other priests. At the moment that Pilate relents, he cries out: "Water! I give in to your urging in order to prevent greater evil. The death sentence on Jesus of Nazareth will be prepared in writing and proclaimed in public."[78] The blood curse of Matthew 27:25 is omitted completely. But Annas and Caiaphas are overjoyed here, as in earlier versions. Annas cries out: "We will bless this day and repeat the name Pontius Pilate with grateful joy." Caiaphas gloats: "Triumph! The victory is ours! The enemy of the High Council is destroyed!" (act 8). Pilate's final proclamation omits all reference to the role of the high priest and Jewish leadership in Jesus' condemnation by using the passive rather than active voice: "I, Pontius Pilate, governor of Judaea, under Caesar, Claudius Tiberius, hereby pronounce the sentence of death on Jesus of Nazareth, who is accused of having incited the people to riot, forbidden them to pay taxes to Caesar, and proclaimed himself King of the Jews" (act 8).[79]

These changes toned down the play's excesses to some degree.[80] Yet the 2000 script did not entirely allay all concerns. Franklin Sherman comments that while the written text was a major improvement, sometimes its good intentions were undone by the visual appearance of the actors.

> In the text the high priest, Caiaphas, is depicted as a self-serving sycophant, while Pontius Pilate, true to what we know of him from history, is a ruthless tyrant. But in the performance Caiaphas was played by a tall, burly actor of such verbal and psychological force that he completely overshadowed Pilate, who seemed like a mild-mannered bureaucrat. (At least this was true in the version I saw; two actors are assigned to each major role and play on alternate days.) The result is that the blame for the death of Jesus—as in the New Testament itself—attaches disproportionately to the Jews. The other problem is that the part of the crowd that shouts in Jesus' defense manages only a weak and disorganized outcry, compared to the thunderous roar of those who shout condemnation. It was hard to remember that, historically, only a small number of Jews would have been involved in these outcries.[81]

After watching a rehearsal of the 2000 version, Shapiro commented:

> I had badly wanted the text to be better than this. I knew that there were elements introduced to counterbalance the effect, small groups onstage who would indicate to the audience that not all the Jews were bloodthirsty or sought Jesus's death. Maybe the problem was that the actors sharing the roles of Caiaphas and Annas were so overpowering; this left the indelible impression that the Jewish leaders were the implacable foes of Jesus, relentlessly pressing for his death. All the assurances that Pilate would be a far darker character, one more deeply implicated in the sentencing of Jesus, made little difference. This was between the Jewish leaders and Jesus. The blood curse was gone, and no death decree was issued by the Sanhedrin. Yet these omissions hardly mattered. Daisenberger was a runaway train: all the brakes, all the safeguards, all the changes made to prevent anti-Judaism from taking over, had barely slowed it down.
>
> The [revised] play certainly did not insist on universal Jewish guilt in perpetuity, and that was a major step forward. I could readily imagine how much more inflammatory the old text must have been in performance. I knew it wasn't fair to judge on the basis of this read-through, which didn't have the ameliorative effect of the tableaux paying tribute to Moses and other figures from Jewish history. Nonetheless, the scaled-down version

had the advantage of isolating and magnifying the ways in which the anti-Jewish structure of the gospel story on which it was based was too powerful for even the best-intentioned revisers to neutralize.[82]

The 2010 production provided yet another opportunity for Stückl and his codirector, Otto Huber, to develop the themes that had begun to emerge in their earlier productions and thereby also to continue to address their own and others' ongoing concerns about the play's anti-Semitic potential. In preparation for the new production, the cast not only rehearsed their lines and took measures to ensure their "authenticity" (including, for those in the Jewish crowds or Jewish leadership, growing their hair and beards), but they also listened to lectures on the historical Jesus and the characters in the Gospels[83] and traveled to Israel. Representatives of Jewish groups and Jewish-Christian dialogue organizations were consulted.[84]

The 2010 script emphasized Jesus' Jewishness even further, including not only the Hebrew blessings that had been featured in 2000, but also a moving scene in which a choir comprising the crowds as well as the Jewish authorities joins Jesus and his disciples in a beautiful Hebrew rendition of the "Shema" ("Hear O Israel," the central prayer of Jewish liturgy) facing the open Torah scroll (a facsimile rather than an authentic scroll) that Jesus is holding aloft. Also modified were the tableaux vivants, which now carefully avoided supersessionist claims. In addition to ensuring that Jesus was portrayed unequivocally as a Jew, the script accentuated the role of Pilate as the dictatorial representative of the Roman Empire. Stückl and Huber created an analogy between the situation in first-century Judaea and that of Vichy France and asked the actors to imagine Pilate as a Goebbels-like figure, with Caiaphas akin to Marshal Pétain, much as Dorothy Sayers had done. This captured the directors' sense that Caiaphas was caught between the needs and demands of his own people, including other leaders who put pressure on him, and the Roman governor, to whom he owed his position, livelihood, and perhaps his very life. Both emphases—Jesus' Jewishness and the colonial situation—created a new narrative framework in which the conflict between Caiaphas and Jesus was an inter-Jewish matter, not one between Judaism and Christianity that had to be understood in the context of Roman domination.[85]

In the script Caiaphas's difficult position comes through quite clearly. In act 2, scene 2, it is Pilate who expresses both knowledge of and concern about Jesus' activities. Jesus has already come to Caiaphas's attention, but he feigns disinterest and downplays Jesus' potential to sow dissatisfaction and create disorder. To Caiaphas's confident declaration that Jesus "is only an insignificant itinerant preacher," Pilate exclaims: "Insignificant? The entire city flows toward him.... Your mouth has apparently been sealed by admiration. Caiaphas, do I need to remind you: it is always such insignificant itinerant preachers who instigate revolt and rioting under the guise of divine mission and bring people to religious fanaticism." Pilate then threatens Caiaphas:

> What was your people before I took over? An unruly mob—without obedience, without leadership. And there was no peace in this god-damned land until I crucified all those rebels and had all their collaborators executed as well.... I let [you] remain in the position of High Priest; I put you in charge of watching over peace and order in this city.... If order is not restored in the city I will take everything from you I have given you.... If there is conflict in the land and rebellion against Rome I will come with the army's might and plunge you, your land, and your people, into ruin and perdition. Now leave! I don't ever want to hear anything of this Jesus again. (Act 2, scene 2)[86]

The image of Pilate as an authoritarian leader is reinforced by the prologue to act 8:

> The prisoner is led before the Roman judge.
> Confronting a ruler of the world stands Jesus,
> he who ushers in the Reign of God
> and throughout the land has proclaimed the kingdom of the Father.
> But Pilate, intoxicated by his own power,
> Remains deaf to the voice of truth.[87]

Caiaphas views Pilate's behavior as a threat on many levels: "Woe to the children of Israel. Woe to the Holy City! Woe to the temple of the Lord! And woe to me, if I put up with his provocative demeanor and his presumptuous manner of speech! Curses and disgrace on all pagans" (act 3, scene 3). [88]

In 2010, as in all earlier versions of the Passion play, Caiaphas's machinations result in Jesus' arraignment before Pilate, contrary to Pilate's explicit instructions (act 8, scene 1). Pilate screams at the high priest: "Caiaphas, I have told you that I never again wanted to hear anything of this Jesus. Caiaphas—look at me—you dare bring him before me, the Governor of the Emperor, and to disregard my orders. How dare you drag a stray dog into my palace? If this Jesus has violated your laws, take him and judge him according to your law."[89]

From this point forward, however, the clear image of the tyrannical Pilate and the subordinate Caiaphas begins to blur. Despite the concern that Pilate expressed in the first half of the play about the possibility that Jesus will foster insurrection, he refuses to condemn him once Jesus has been brought before him and strongly advocates Jesus' release. As the second half unfolds, it is, as always, Caiaphas who clamors for Jesus' condemnation, incites the crowd to ask for Barabbas's release, and rejoices when Pilate relents. In contrast to the 2000 version, in which Pilate does not proclaim his innocence, the 2010 play restores this line from Matthew 27:24–26, but omits the blood curse and reinterprets Pilate's declaration, so that he is not innocent of Jesus' death so much as of the havoc that he declares will attend the release of Barabbas, a known murderer and insurrectionist: "Water!—It's muggy, we will have a thunder storm.—And Julius, bring Barabbas and the other two insurgents and murderers here out of prison. Barabbas will be released at your demand. Take him away—out the city gate, that he never again set foot in this land! But know, High Priest, henceforth you shall never again know peace. Too often, have you threatened me. Concerning everything that is about to happen, Caiaphas, I want you to know,—I wash my hands in innocence. Later today a message will be sent to Rome that you, Caiaphas, shield rebels against Rome from the death penalty" (act 9, scene 1).[90]

By this point in the play, Pilate's attention has shifted completely from Jesus, whose significance he now seems to have dismissed entirely, to Barabbas. He even takes on a prophetic, if still threatening, role, implying, perhaps, that Caiaphas will be to blame for the unrest sown by Barabbas and will suffer for it. There is an implicit suggestion here that it is the release of Barabbas, for which Caiaphas bears responsibility, that leads inexorably to the Jewish revolt against Rome some four decades hence, along with the destruction of the Temple and the end of the high priesthood. Pilate's formal condemnation of Jesus, however, provides a rationale for his death as a threat to Roman hegemony in Judaea as articulated in the official decree, which, as in 2000, convicts Jesus "of having incited the people to riot, forbidden them to pay taxes to Caesar, and proclaimed himself King of the Jews" (act 9, scene 1).[91]

Yet the focus on the tension between Pilate and Caiaphas does not entirely account for Caiaphas's determination to see Jesus dead. The first scene in the play illustrates Jesus' moral superiority over Caiaphas, when Caiaphas brings an adulterous woman to Jesus in order to entrap him but then must walk away when Jesus declares that only one without sin can cast the first stone (act 1, scene 1).[92] This message is reinforced by the play's reinterpretation of Matthew 23. In the context of Matthew's Gospel, this chapter is a lengthy and passionate condemnation of the Pharisees and scribes as hypocrites who love nothing better than to show off in public and boast about their deeds. In the 2010 Oberammergau script, Jesus omits all references to the Pharisees and addresses these words directly to the priests: "Woe to you, hypocrites who lock the kingdom of heaven to the people. . . . You blind leaders who strain out gnats but swallow camels?" (act 3, scene 1).[93] This reorientation and considerable shortening of Matthew 23 are intended to deflect attention from the Pharisees, whom Christian tradition has despised as hypocrites based on this Matthean chapter. For the 2010 Oberammergau production, it is Caiaphas who epitomizes hypocrisy.

Caiaphas's hypocrisy and deceitfulness emerge very clearly in his dealings with Judas, who comes to the high priest as a naive but frustrated disciple who wishes to arrange a meeting of reconciliation between Jesus and Caiaphas. Caiaphas initially greets Judas with suspicion, but once he realizes what the disciple is offering, he offers empathy and encourages the young man to confide his worries and fears. The high priest then tells Judas: "Don't be afraid. Like you, I think highly of your rabbi. I yearn to speak to him for that reason, and it is only for that purpose that I am searching for him. I want to search for him the way a shepherd searches for his sheep if they have strayed from the flock. You know where he withdraws in the evening, would you be prepared to show us the place? Judas, trust us. In the silence and seclusion of the night they will bring him to me and no one shall know of it" (act 3, scene 4).[94]

Caiaphas offers Judas thirty pieces of silver. Of course the arrest is anything but quiet. Rather it is accomplished amid considerable noise and confusion, in the presence of Roman soldiers and Temple guards. Judas gradually begins to realize that he has been deceived, but when he confronts Caiaphas, the high priest just laughs him off and refuses to have anything further to do with him. If Judas has inadvertently—or better, naively—betrayed his master, he himself has been betrayed by the high priest, deliberately and cruelly.

And if Pilate is manipulating Caiaphas, the high priest is nevertheless a hypocritical, deceitful, self-serving, and even paranoid leader who is hardly worthy of the respect that should be due to someone in his position. Like Pilate he can brook no dissent in the ranks. He is well aware that some among the council are attracted to Jesus and his message and believe that Caiaphas is behaving unjustly toward him. As in earlier versions, Caiaphas defends himself against this charge: "No one, Nicodemus, no one shall accuse us of injustice. He has not only violated our law but has violated Roman law in a variety of ways. Not we but the procurator shall pronounce the death sentence over him" (act 6, scene 2).[95] Yet the idea of delivering a fellow Jew to the Roman authorities does not sit well with some council members. Joseph of Arimathea exclaims: "What have our fellow-believers not already had to suffer! How many death sentences have been pronounced and most cruelly executed? How can you, Caiaphas, deliver a son of Israel to the cruel Roman?" But Caiaphas will not bend. He cuts off further discussion by saying: "You do not understand these things. Joseph, I owe you no account for my actions. Now, silence, you apostates!" (act 6, scene 2).[96]

Also telling is a conversation between Caiaphas and Annas in act 3, scene 3. Caiaphas confesses to Annas: "I will not deny that I am annoyed by a Galilean mocking the priests." Annas replies, somewhat astonished: "You are annoyed? And that is all you have to say? To our shame we had to watch how the Galilean and his entourage paraded through the gates and streets of our sacred city . . . this man arrogantly assumed the dignity of the High Priest and dared act as lord in the temple of God. What is still missing before all secular and divine order is overturned?"[97]

Observations

Even the most recent versions of the script assign to Caiaphas a much more prominent role than he plays in the scriptural accounts. Indeed Caiaphas is the prime mover of the plot against Jesus, supported, to be sure, by Annas, the high council, and, less directly, by the Jewish crowds. The plot structure as a whole emphasizes the strong opposition between Caiaphas and Jesus; Caiaphas is the antithesis of all that Jesus stands for, and Caiaphas will not rest until Jesus has been apprehended, tried, and killed. It is Caiaphas's determination to be rid of Jesus that drives the plot against Jesus and that leads directly and inexorably to his death. Where the versions differ is in the motivations attributed to the high priest and his minions, the reasons behind his insistence that Jesus be condemned and executed by Pilate, and the question of corporate responsibility. All of these elements pertain directly to the deicide charge. In all cases Annas is also present and very important to the drama as Caiaphas's main adviser.

It is widely acknowledged that the negative portrayal of the high priest and the other Jewish figures could have an impact on Christian behavior toward Jews in real life.[98] At the same time, these plays did not "create" European anti-Semitism. As Martin notes the Oberammergau Passion play did not evolve in some mysterious fashion into "a play that depicted the vengefulness and hatefulness of the Jews as innate, racially determined characteristics. Rather, it was developed into such a play by persons motivated to create such a depiction of Jews."[99]

While outside agencies express qualified appreciation for the successive revisions to the play, the changes have created significant tensions in the village.[100] There are many who regret the deviations from the traditional script and performance style, which they see as essential to the play and even to their identity as a village preserved by an eternally binding vow to God. On the other hand, there are others, including the current directors and many of the actors, who applaud the removal of anti-Jewish elements and the high aesthetic standards of the staging, lighting, music, and acting.

Underlying this tension is a fundamental question of genre: is the Passion play theater or religious experience? For Stückl and Huber, the answer seems to be the former, though they acknowledge that for many the play is also a religious experience. Indeed marketing for the play emphasizes its potential as a spiritual experience. An advertisement from a tour agency for the 2010 production describes Oberammergau as follows: "Passion Plays recount the life and ministry of Jesus Christ from the four gospels in a dramatic form. This tradition began in the Middle Ages and [Passion plays] are often performed in churches during Easter week. By watching a Passion Play we have a chance to reflect on the events most central to our faith, that Jesus died, was buried and rose again from the dead." The tour includes devotional time on the morning of the performance, for "the Passion Play is the moving story of our Lord and we want to prepare our hearts."[101] As a Jewish visitor to Oberammergau in May 2010, I did not sense any anti-Semitism in my strolls through the village. But of course there is not a single Jewish resident of Oberammergau, and only a handful of Jewish theatergoers throughout the entire season.[102]

CONCLUSION

The plots of the mystery and Passion plays reveal similar trends to those of literary narratives. As in most retellings from the early Christian period to the present, Caiaphas and Annas are partners in crime; Pilate also comes in for his share of the blame, but even in the most recent versions of the Oberammergau play, which emphasize the context of Roman domination in which the high priest functioned, the Roman governor is a more sympathetic character than Caiaphas, at least in his wish to release Jesus rather than Barabbas. In contrast to fiction, however, these plays do not portray Caiaphas as a complex figure who might have had some ambivalence about handing a fellow Jew over to the Romans for execution. Caiaphas remains a deicide.

In creating a role for Caiaphas, these plays go beyond the Gospel passages that refer specifically to the high priest, whether by name or by title, by drawing upon the references to the chief priests in the plural and attributing the chief priests' actions to the high priest alone. In taking this route, these plays can intensify Caiaphas's villainy far beyond the Gospel accounts and thereby heighten the drama of their productions.

Even more than fiction, dramatic presentations of the Passion story raise the specter of anti-Semitism. This response may be related to the impact of dramatization itself, which makes the story come alive in the present in a way that fiction cannot always do. It is also, however, related to historical situations, in which audiences of these plays all too readily saw a direct connection between the Jewish deicides on the stage and the Jewish residents of their own towns and villages.

To be sure, some of these plays use Caiaphas to represent not only the impious and murderous Jews but also the ecclesiastical establishment that exercised its oppressive authority over ordinary people. Nevertheless the high priest's symbolic association with Christian bishops does not serve to elevate the Jewish high priest but rather to take the Christian clerics down many notches to the deicide's own level.

CAIAPHAS ON SCREEN

Popular as mystery and Passion plays were in their day, their reach has long been surpassed by the movies. Since the birth of cinema in the late nineteenth century, Jesus' Passion has been portrayed in hundreds of films in Hollywood and around the world.[1]

The first Jesus movies were dramatizations of Passion plays. The first known example of a Jesus movie was *The Passion Play at Oberammergau* (1898). While it claimed to be an authentic film of the Oberammergau Passion play, this nineteen-minute movie was actually staged and filmed on the roof of the Grand Central Palace in New York, using props and costumes that had been created for an aborted New York stage production. Even after the public learned that this movie was a "faked re-creation" of the Oberammergau production, the film remained immensely popular.[2] Although most Jesus movies from the silent period to the present retell Jesus' life story from his birth, the Passion play has continued to influence the Jesus film genre, including films that set Jesus' story in ancient Judaea and Galilee (*The King of Kings*, 1927; *The Passion of the Christ*, 2004) and those that frame the Passion story in a more contemporary context (*Jesus Christ Superstar*, 1973; *Jesus of Montreal*, 1989).

Jesus movies are almost always set in early-first-century Galilee, Samaria, and Judaea; most—including epics such as *The Greatest Story Ever Told* (1965) and *Jesus of Nazareth* (1979)—tell Jesus' entire life story from the nativity through to the resurrection appearances. Others, such as Mel Gibson's *The Passion of the Christ*, focus on specific parts of that story, most often the events leading to his death. With the exception of Pier Paolo Pasolini's *The Gospel According to Saint Matthew* (1964) and Philip Saville's *The Gospel of John* (2003), filmmakers make use of the events and dialogue from all four canonical Gospels and also invent scenes, dialogue, and even characters that fill in the Gospels' gaps in order to create a coherent and compelling story.

Most Jesus movies belong to the biographical film genre, commonly known as the "biopic."[3] Biopics are feature films that are set in a specific historical time and place and whose subjects are historical figures. They combine historical narrative with fictionalized elements; while they generally adhere to the known biographical facts of their subjects, they also invent narrative, characters, and dialogue freely.[4] As a genre biopics shape their narratives according to a fixed template that, interestingly enough, almost always includes a trial scene.[5] In biopics the trial scenes provide the opportunity for the protagonists to explain their philosophy and to force the characters in the film as well as the audience to take sides for or against them. The trial scenes serve either to solidify the opposition against the protagonists or, alternatively, to disarm them, by persuading the viewer that the protagonist is righteous.

Filmmakers draw on numerous sources to flesh out their portrait of Jesus. The writings of Josephus provide details of the social and political contexts of Jesus' life, and the fanciful narratives of apocryphal gospels such as the *Infancy Gospel of Thomas* can be drawn upon to develop Jesus' early life, about which the canonical Gospels are almost entirely silent. Filmmakers often also create fictional frames within which to situate their portraits of Jesus, as in *Ben-Hur* (1959) or *Jesus of Montreal* (1989); similarly they may use the Passion play tradition to explore the events surrounding his death and other Jesus movies to pay homage to certain iconic images and scenes.[6] Nicholas Ray's *King of Kings* (1961) links Judas and Barabbas and places them among the leadership of a militant Jewish group that seeks to exploit Jesus' charisma for the good of the revolution. Robert Young adds romantic interest to his 1999 television movie, *Jesus*, but avoids controversy by having the youthful savior fall in love with Mary of Bethany and then renounce marriage in order to pursue his messianic destiny.

Most obviously filmmakers create the visual and aural elements that no written text can convey fully, including the physical appearance of the characters, the tone and quality of their voices, the sounds and images of their contexts, and their body movements and gestures. Some of these elements come from the art tradition. For example many films include a brief scene in which Jesus' mother, Mary, cradles her dead son in her lap, in homage to Michelangelo's *Pietà*, and many also arrange their scene of the last supper to imitate Leonardo's famous fresco. Most cinematic Jesuses are slight of build, with light brown hair and blue eyes, reflecting the stereotypical Jesus image made popular by Warner Sallman's iconic image of 1940.[7]

Perhaps the most salient and interesting characteristic of this genre is the fact that it simultaneously makes a claim to historical accuracy and undermines that claim. Claims to historicity range from explicit comments, as found for example in the 1912 silent movie *From the Manger to the Cross*, which introduces itself as "a review of the saviour's life according to the gospel-narrative," or more subtly, to references to dates and events in voice-over narrated in a deep and authoritative-sounding voice, as in the introduction to the 1961 *King of Kings*, impressively narrated by Orson Welles.

Related to this ambivalence and ambiguity about history is the tension between "faithfulness"—to the Gospels and/or to Christian theology—and relevance to the present day. The Jesus movies are not only a medium through which viewers can "see" Jesus, but they are also a vehicle for considering Jesus' ongoing relevance for society. For this reason they address the concerns and anxieties of their own time. For example as overt anti-Semitism became less acceptable, the Jesus movies began to shift focus away from the role of the Jewish people in Jesus' death to lay blame on Caiaphas (*The King of Kings*), a fictional character (the scribe Zerah in *Jesus of Nazareth*), or Rome (*The Miracle Maker*, 2000). Similarly the changing role of women in society and in some streams of Christianity is reflected in the roles given to Jesus' mother, Mary (*Il Messias*, 1975); Martha of Bethany (*The Last Temptation of Christ*, 1988); and Mary Magdalene (*Jesus of Montreal*, *The Passion of the Christ*) in more recent films.

The Jesus movies not only interpret the Gospels, but also bow to the conventions of their era and genre. Cecil B. DeMille's magnificent *The King of Kings* features the spectacle, near-nudity, romance, and circus animals that were de rigueur in the late silent era. Ray's *King of Kings* and George Stevens's *The Greatest Story Ever Told* feature the majestic scenery, symphonic music, and large casts of famous actors that characterized the epic genre in the period after World War II. David Greene's *Godspell* (1973) and Norman Jewison's *Jesus Christ Superstar* are rock operas that share many features with other musical productions, such as *Hair* (dir. Milos Forman, 1979) and *Tommy* (dir. Ken Russell, 1975). *The Passion of the Christ* owes much, to be sure, to the spiritual memoirs of Anne Catherine Emmerich (1833) but even more to the contemporary action movie genre, to which Gibson himself has contributed.[8]

Not all films portray Caiaphas as the one who bears the weight of responsibility for Jesus' death. Martin Scorsese's *Last Temptation of Christ* portrays an outburst by Jesus against Caiaphas, whom he encounters in the Temple precincts. "God doesn't need a palace, he doesn't need shekels.... You think God belongs only to you? God's an immortal spirit who belongs to everybody, to the whole world. You think you're special? God is not an Israelite!"[9] This outburst, which occurs during a ruckus in the Temple area, expresses the film's main theme, which is the struggle, and eventual triumph, of the spirit over the flesh. In the film this is a struggle that takes place first and foremost within Jesus himself, but here it is expressed as the contrast between the universal and omnipresent spirit of God and the particularism of the "Israelites," for whom the Temple was both a cultic and a financial center. Scorsese, however, does not portray Caiaphas as reacting to Jesus' outburst or to his activities in the Temple area. Nor does *Last Temptation* assign to Caiaphas a major role in Jesus' death, focusing instead on the trial before Pilate, who is shown as indifferent to Jesus, considering him no more than one Jewish troublemaker among many.

Last Temptation is an exception, however. Most Jesus movies make much of Jesus' trial before the high priest and, at the same time, accentuate Caiaphas's role in the story by portraying him as an active participant in the trial before Pilate. In doing so they insert the high priest in the places that the "chief priests" occupy in the canonical accounts and attribute Caiaphas's actions against Jesus to various factors from the personal to the religious and political.

WHY CAIAPHAS PLOTTED AGAINST JESUS

Greed

The New Testament and Josephus do not expound upon Caiaphas's vices and virtues, but in many films the high priest is a character flawed by excessive greed. The anti-Semitic cliché that associates Jews and money is abundantly expressed in the German film *Der Galiläer* (*The Galilean*; 1921), in which Caiaphas asks: "Why should we forgo the money that temple commerce brings?"[10] When he turns the thirty pieces of silver over to Judas, Caiaphas says: "Happiness is here, before you, in your hand. You will be rich and a respected man, among the people and before the Sanhedren [sic]." As he hands the money over, the Jews all laugh at Judas.[11]

In DeMille's *The King of Kings*, Caiaphas is the prime example of the money-grubbing Jew for whom the pursuit of profit overrides all other considerations. DeMille introduces the high priest as "the Roman appointee Caiaphas, the High Priest—who cared more for Revenue than for Religion—and saw in Jesus a menace to his rich profits from the Temple." Caiaphas sits in a richly appointed office. Lest we mistake him for a Roman or some "oriental" ruler, Hebrew letters are visible on the wall behind him. DeMille's high priest pays only lip service to his spiritual heritage and religious responsibilities. Whereas to the "Faithful of Israel" the Temple is "the dwelling place of Jehovah," to Caiaphas it is "a corrupt and profitable market-place." As Stern, Jefford, and DeBona note, DeMille has drawn Caiaphas "with the bold strokes of a medieval and Reformation caricature of the greedy Jews." Caiaphas "represents all things evil about the unwavering hardness of first-century Judaism as it was portrayed by the later church" and "finds an unyielding, corrupt beacon of legalism against which the faithful (and religiously pure) Jesus offers the flexible mercy of the loving Father God."[12] Many years later the theme of greed was revived in *The Passion of the Christ,* in which the camera lingers with intensity on the image of Caiaphas handing the money over to Judas through the camera work and the use of slow motion.

Satan

The imputation of greed places the blame on Caiaphas as a flawed human being. *The Passion of the Christ* portrays Caiaphas in more cosmic terms, as one of Satan's agents in the world. Satan is a character in numerous Jesus movies because of the scene in the synoptic Gospels in which Jesus resists three temptations that Satan poses to him in the wilderness (Mark 1:12–13; Matt. 4:1–11; Luke 4:1–13). The Gospels of Luke and John also link Judas's betrayal of Jesus to the work of Satan (Luke 22:3; John 13:27). But Gibson's film takes this notion further by implying that Caiaphas too is an agent of Satan. Although Gibson's film associates Satan, an androgynous figure, with all of Jesus' opponents, including the Romans, the camera work calls most attention to the Jews. In this film the Jews are always portrayed in dark clothing, in surroundings lit by red flames, evoking images of hellfire. Satan moves smoothly and stealthily among the Jews as they condemn Jesus to death, as they watch the sadistic Roman soldiers scourge and torture Jesus within an inch of his life, and as they watch Jesus carry his cross toward Golgotha. At the moment of Jesus' death, Caiaphas holds on to his head and screams. Moments later the camera cuts away to Satan, now banished below the earth, who screams in pain as his or her hair lifts up off her head and the earth closes over her. The synchronic nature of the screams—priest's and Satan's—associates them even more directly.

Political Considerations

In most films, as in some novels and plays, Caiaphas has political concerns about Jesus (see John 11:49–52). Caiaphas's actions against Jesus are most often attributed to the political realities of Roman Judaea and the assumption that the high priest had no choice but to kowtow to Rome by maintaining order among his own people. This interpretation, prominent in the epics of the 1960s and 1970s, serves at least two important purposes: it lends coherence by creating a causal link between the events, and it allows for a more sympathetic portrayal of Caiaphas in the post-Holocaust era when public anti-Semitism was no longer acceptable.

Caiaphas's unenviable political position is a major focus of Ray's *King of Kings*. This film prepares viewers for Caiaphas's role in Jesus' death by having Pilate attempt to make him responsible for handling John the Baptist, whom viewers, if not Ray's Pilate and Caiaphas, know is Jesus' precursor (for example Matt. 3:11). "Punish such conduct," Pilate orders the high priest, who protests: "Punishment does not dampen their ardor. Better to ignore the ravings of these people rather than to prosecute. In my opinion this man seeks martyrdom." Caiaphas, though clearly an underling, also has enough power and status to object, thereby showing his own distaste for taking the life of a fellow Jew.

Young's made-for-television *Jesus* is sympathetic to the difficult situation in which Caiaphas and the other Jewish leaders found themselves. As Pilate and his troops enter Jerusalem for the first time, the Jews watch the Romans stream in. The camera shows a panoramic shot from above, then returns to street level. Pilate enters the scene and surveys his surroundings with curiosity. Livio, his aide and the self-proclaimed historian to Caesar, is by his side. Livio draws Pilate's attention to Caiaphas and identifies him to Pilate as the high priest appointed by Rome. "On the one hand he has to appear to be a presider over his own people, on the other hand he owes his position to Rome. Narrow path to tread."

CAIAPHAS: Welcome, Pontius Pilate. I am Caiaphas the High Priest of this temple. We come to wish you well, as you undertake the post of governor of Judea.

PILATE: I thank you, priest. Allow me to get right to the point. Rome is displeased with the number of legions it has to keep in this barren land in order to maintain peace. Your taxes don't begin to pay back the cost.

CAIAPHAS: You speak of the past.

PILATE: This disorder derives directly from your current religion which derives directly from this temple. This ends today. My soldiers will be posted here every minute of every day from now on.

CAIAPHAS: This order defiles the Temple.

ANOTHER JEW: Our religion forbids graven images in the Temple. Your soldiers are an abomination to the Temple. Even their flags break our laws. We allow no graven images and your images carry . . .

PILATE: These shields are symbols of Roman dominion. No building in Judea, not even the Temple is exempt from the display of these symbols. What your religion forbids Rome demands.

(Caiaphas looks on grimly, hanging on to his staff as a potent symbol. They are all quiet. The music is ominous.)

CAIAPHAS: We submit . . . to your swords. *(Kneels down.)* Here is my bare neck. Let Rome cut it.
(Pilate looks on; all other followers do the same.)
CAIAPHAS: We will die before we allow the Temple to be defiled.
(The Jews all kneel down. Pilate is flabbergasted, and Livio approaches him.)
LIVIO: Governor, an awful lot of blood for your first day. I am not sure Rome would be happy if you were to murder every priest in the Temple.
(Pilate stands down—this time.)[13]

Later Pilate watches Jesus' triumphal entry into Jerusalem with great concern and says, "This man must be arrested." Livio concurs: "He will bring ruin down on us all. He must be stopped; dead. I could kill this messiah tomorrow, there would be another one right behind him. Or, we could see that he becomes a problem for some of his own people. They would solve the problem for us."

This film reverses the narrative of the Gospels, in which the Jewish leadership puts Pilate up to crucifying Jesus by having him concoct the plot that he will manipulate the Jewish leadership into carrying out.

(Caiaphas approaches Pilate slowly.)
PILATE: There are rumors in the streets, priest.
CAIAPHAS: Rumors?
PILATE: Don't be coy with me! This man Jesus rides an ass into town and is welcomed like a king. Herod wants to kill him but does nothing and you promised me you can keep peace in the temple but I had to use swords! I will not be silent forever! *(Pilate works himself into a highly theatrical temper.)*
CAIAPHAS: These false messiahs . . .
PILATE *(shouting):* I don't care about your religion, I care about peace.
CAIAPHAS: Peace, yes, I too care about peace . . .
PILATE: Well then get control of this man!
CAIAPHAS: I fear my power is . . . limited.
PILATE: So you want me to do your dirty work for you.
CAIAPHAS: I have no choice. I cannot endanger Israel for one man.
PILATE: Bring him to me. I will eliminate him.

Caiaphas nods in reluctant agreement and leaves Pilate's presence like an old and worried man. Livio claps bravo to Pilate, making it clear that this entire conversation was a setup. They laugh hysterically. Through this exchange Young casts the burden of responsibility upon the Romans, specifically Pilate, and shows the Jewish authorities caught between Rome and the people.

In some films politics and self-interest go hand in hand. The 1973 production of *Jesus Christ Superstar* has Caiaphas debate with others over the degree of danger that Jesus poses to the population. Caiaphas warns: "We've been sitting on the fence for far too long . . . while he starts a major war we theorize." Others are less concerned—"He's just another scripture-thumping hack from Galilee" but Caiaphas is frightened by the fact that "they call him king": "What about the Romans? When they see King Jesus crowned do you think they will stand around?" Again someone takes a calmer view: "Why take their toy away? He's a craze." But Caiaphas will not be deterred. "Put yourself in my place. I cannot step aside, let my hands be tied, I am law and order. The priesthood could fall. If we are to last at all, we cannot be divided. . . . Then we are decided?" The others respond: "Then we are decided."

HOW CAIAPHAS CARRIED OUT HIS PLAN

In order to put his plan in motion, Caiaphas required reliable intelligence as to Jesus' activities and whereabouts. The Gospels briefly suggest that the chief priests had spies who provided them with the necessary information. In John 11:57 "the chief priests and the Pharisees had given orders that anyone who knew where Jesus was should let them know, so that they might arrest him." Similarly in Luke 20:19–20: "When the scribes and chief priests realized that he had told this parable against them, they wanted to lay hands on him at that very hour, but they feared the people. So they watched him and sent spies who pretended to be honest, in order to trap him by what he said, so as to hand him over to the jurisdiction and authority of the governor."

The biopics exploit these spies for their full dramatic possibilities and turn Caiaphas into their employer. In addition to explaining how the high priest got his information about Jesus' activities, the spies' reports inform the viewing audience about Jesus' miracles, which are familiar to readers of the Gospels but difficult to portray convincingly on screen.

The silent movie *INRI* (1923) shows Caiaphas consulting with spies. The intertitle states: "The people say the Nazarene shall come unto Jerusalem as king. Go ye and spy him out." There follows a lengthy interrogation in which the spies question Jesus about the Temple ("Didst thou say that thou art able to destroy the temple of God and build it again in three days?") and then ask outright: "Art thou the promised messiah?" Jesus holds up his arms and responds, "For God so loved the world . . . John 3.16." The camera then cuts to the Temple. In the background there is a large Star of David. In the middle of the star, there is a large ark in the shape of the two tablets of the law, with the Ten Commandments inscribed on them. Other decorations include a stylized menorah.

These Jewish symbols leave no doubt as to the priest's jurisdiction over the Temple. Yet Jesus claims that the Temple is his. He strides into this area and demands: "What have ye made of my father's house?" and proceeds to create a major stir. Caiaphas does not allow the others to seize him just yet—"Nay, the people yet acclaim him, it would be dangerous"—and then wonders whether he can find a traitor among the disciples. The spies enter and presumably provide Caiaphas with the possibility that Judas may be his man.

DeMille's *The King of Kings* describes the high priest's spies as being "driven by the fury of religious hatred." The spies declare to Caiaphas: "Before our own eyes he broke the Sabbath! And he said, also, that God was His Father—making Himself equal with God! . . . We would have laid hands on Him, but we feared the multitude—because they take Him for a prophet!" Caiaphas castigates them angrily: "Are ye also deceived?" He sends them off and ponders. Now he has an idea. He has his soldiers bring in the woman caught in adultery. "This woman hath been convicted of adultery. Wouldst thou that we stone her to death?" Caiaphas looks at her in disgust. "Make him judge her. If he frees her, he breaketh the law of Moses, and may be stoned in her stead." He sends out his men and rubs his hands in glee.

Later the spies report to Caiaphas: "He is driving the money-changers from the Temple and those who buy and sell." Caiaphas is alarmed and goes to see for himself. He confronts Jesus: "By what authority doest thou these things?" Jesus responds, "It is written: My house shall be called the house of prayer but ye have made it a den of thieves." Caiaphas calls out "Seize him!" He grabs a spear, his eyes burning with rage. The epics also pick up this theme. In *The Greatest Story Ever Told,* Caiaphas sends a spy to Galilee to investigate the rumors that have been circulating about Jesus' miraculous deeds. "Only a child would believe such a story." Nicodemus invites himself along: "I have always been fond of children's stories. Children's stories always have a central truth." In *Jesus of Nazareth* (1979), Zeffirelli too uses this device though he sees Zerah, not Caiaphas as the mastermind. As Zerah tells Judas, "Your master has very little political sense, but he is an extraordinary man and we shall continue to watch his mission with great interest."

CAIAPHAS THE CHRIST-KILLER?
JESUS' TRIAL BEFORE THE HIGH PRIEST

A handful of films follow the Gospels of John and Luke in omitting a trial before Caiaphas. DeMille's film, for example, has Jesus enter the room where Caiaphas and the council await but does not show the trial. Rather it cuts immediately to Jesus' delivery to Pilate. Most films, however, portray the Jewish trial scene at some length. In *Der Galiläer* the trial before Caiaphas is hardly an objective, dignified process but a hate rally in which Caiaphas vigorously incites his council to condemn Jesus to death. The high priest is enthroned in his chambers, laughing and carrying on with his associates, as a bound Jesus stands there in front of them. The contrast in the appearance and behavior between the judge and the accused could not be greater, and whereas the former and his supporters are vocal, Jesus says not a word.

> CAIAPHAS: Was trifft den, der verachtet Gottes Priester? (What does he deserve, then, the one who scorns God's priests?)
> THE COUNCIL: Tod! (Death!)
> CAIAPHAS: Was trifft den Sabbathschander?! Den, der Sünder schützt! (What does he deserve, the one who desecrates the Sabbath? The one who defends sinners!)
> THE COUNCIL: Tod! (Death!)
> CAIAPHAS: Und den, der Gott selbst frech gelästert? (And the one who has slandered God himself?)
> THE COUNCIL: Der Tod und abermals der Tod! (Death and death again!)
> CAIAPHAS: So hor'dein Ürtail, Ketzer, Lästerer! Und sei des Todes! (So hear your fate, you heretic and blasphemer! And be sentenced to death!)

Zeffirelli, by contrast, deflects blame from Caiaphas onto the fictional Zerah. It is Zerah who orchestrates a "meeting" between Jesus and the high priest that in fact is his trial before the Sanhedrin on charges of blasphemy. The council hears lengthy testimony both for and against Jesus, and Caiaphas, far from being a greedy schemer, is portrayed as a wise leader seeking to do what is right in God's eyes. Then Caiaphas asks Jesus formally: "I ask you now, in the name of the Eternal: Are you the Messiah, the Son of God?" Jesus pauses at length, as the camera focuses on his face in extreme close-up: "I am... and you shall see the Son of Man sitting at the right hand of the power of God." Caiaphas closes his eyes, and the camera scans the room to show the stunned reaction of the Sanhedrin. The high priest then recites, slowly and solemnly, yet with great emotion, "Hear O Israel the Lord Our God the Lord is One!" He rips his garment, in the ritual sign of mourning. Zerah steps in: "We have heard enough. Let him be taken before the Procurator Pontius Pilate in whose hands lies the final authority for trial and judgment."

CAIAPHAS AT THE TRIAL BEFORE PILATE

Most dramatic, however, are the cinematic depictions of the trial before the Roman governor and the role that Caiaphas plays in those scenes. All four Gospels state that it was the "chief priests" who incited the crowds against Jesus and thus forced Pilate to have him crucified (Mark 15:11; Matt. 27:20; Luke

22:1–5; John 19:15). None, however, identifies Caiaphas specifically as being present at the Roman trial and its aftermath.

Ray's *King of Kings*

Closest to the Gospels are those films that do not put Caiaphas himself at the trial before Pilate. Ray's *King of Kings* departs from the image of the reluctant Pilate. Pilate conducts a legal proceeding that owes more to other films and television shows from the 1960s than to what is known about Roman legal proceedings. Pilate explains to Jesus (and the movie audience):

> You have just been interrogated by Caiaphas. They have judged you guilty on two counts: blasphemy and sedition. This court takes no cognizance of your blasphemy, but the charge of sedition is a major offense. The rules of Roman law will prevail. I Pontius Pilate, Governor of Judea, by grace of the Emperor the divine Tiberius of Rome will judge your case. No matter what you've done up to this moment, no matter what others have accused you of doing, I and I alone have authority to sentence you to be crucified or flogged or to set you free. How you conduct yourself here and now will determine your fate. Do you understand?

He gives Jesus two opportunities to state his defense, but as in the synoptic Gospels, Jesus remains silent. Pilate then calls on his aide, the fictitious Lucius, to advocate for Jesus, rather like the public defender in an American legal television series. Lucius begins: "For the benefit of the accused, so that he comprehends the gravity of his case, I request that the charge against him be repeated." Lucius does a convincing job of defending Jesus. He argues that Jesus was not guilty of sedition; the kingdom of God of which Jesus speaks poses no challenge to Rome's authority.

When Pilate proposes to send Jesus to Herod Antipas, Lucius counters that Herod Antipas is prejudiced against him. Pilate's will prevails. As in the Gospel of Luke (23:11), Herod soon tires of Jesus and sends him back to Pilate. Pilate orders Lucius to make him confess. Here, as in Matthew, Pilate's wife is favorably disposed toward Jesus, a development that backfires, as Pilate concludes that Jesus must truly be dangerous if he can influence even the daughter of Caesar.

In this movie there is no portrayal of the trial before the Jewish authorities, though references to it come up in the trial before Pilate. The story emphasizes Pilate's attempts to ensure that this trial is fair but also implies that he is suspicious of Jesus and not at all opposed to sentencing him to death. In contrast to earlier films, there are no angry Jewish crowds here. The focus is entirely on Pilate. He does not wash his hands of the affair, nor does he proclaim his innocence in the matter.

Stevens's The Greatest Story Ever Told

A similar approach is taken in George Stevens's *The Greatest Story Ever Told*. In this film Pilate washes his hands but does not declare himself "innocent of this man's blood." Nor does the crowd declare responsibility. Instead the film offers a voice-over that recites from the Apostles' Creed: "suffered under Pontius Pilate, was crucified, dead and buried." The omissions and the voice-over point to Pilate as the major culprit in causing Jesus' suffering and death. Similarly Scorsese's *The Last Temptation of Christ* does not include any trial before Caiaphas, and no Jews are present at Jesus' trial before Pilate, which in this film is more a private interview than a public trial.

Zeffirelli's Jesus of Nazareth

Zeffirelli's *Jesus of Nazareth* goes to great lengths to avoid blaming Caiaphas or the Jews more generally by creating an entirely fictional character, the scribe Zerah, and holding him responsible for the plot against Jesus and ultimately his death. When Pilate moves to acquit Jesus, Zerah intervenes:

> ZERAH: Procurator, we, the leaders of the Sanhedrin, have always had the same aim as you, peaceful administration of our country for the good of our people.
>
> PILATE: Please, please, please, please, don't talk to me about the people. As long as they obey, we care as much about your children of Israel as we do the mob in Rome. Let us speak directly. Why does the Sanhedrin consider this man so dangerous that they send you yourself here to make sure that he is condemned?
>
> ZERAH: . . . If you knew him as well as we do, you would also find him dangerous.

After the crowd chooses Barabbas over Jesus, Pilate pronounces the death sentence. The camera zooms in on Jesus, cuts to Pilate as he walks away, then turns slightly to watch Jesus being taken away for crucifixion. Zeffirelli reproduces the stereotypical portrait of Pilate as mildly sympathetic and the Jewish authorities as overtly hostile. But the role normally played by Caiaphas is here assumed by the fictional Zerah. Zeffirelli's Pilate does not wash his hands, nor do his Jews take collective responsibility. By these means Zeffirelli aims not only to portray a Jewish Jesus but strongly to refute the deicide charge, which he views as a tragedy.[14]

Dimitri Buchowetzki's Der Galiläer

Several films, however, not only place Caiaphas at this climactic trial scene but also emphasize his role. The 1921 silent movie *Der Galiläer* lingers on Caiaphas as he whips a huge Jewish crowd into a bloodthirsty frenzy. The crowd rushes to Pilate's palace screaming for Jesus' death. Pilate, filled with compassion, offers to release him, but the crowd demands Barabbas alive and Jesus dead. Pilate does not wash his hands but puts the blood curse on the Jews: "On you comes his blood" (Auf euch komme sein blut). The huge crowd takes Jesus' blood upon themselves and their children, not once, as in Matthew, but twice: "On us and on our children comes his blood. We take it upon ourselves" (Auf uns und unsere kinder komm' sein Blut. Wir nehmen es auf uns). In this film the blood curse is repeated three times. The film is not merely faithful to Matthew 27:24–26; it magnifies the elements upon which the deicide charge is based. Also noteworthy is the visual appearance of Caiaphas and the other Jewish leaders, who wear headgear that looks suspiciously like horns, another prevalent anti-Semitic image.[15]

DeMille's The King of Kings

Cecil B. DeMille's *The King of Kings* presents the most complex and no doubt the most influential silent version of the trial before Pilate. This film consistently portrays Caiaphas as a money-hungry power monger, but it clears the Jewish crowds of major moral responsibility. When Pilate asks "Shall I crucify your king?" it is Caiaphas, not the crowd (as it is in John 19:15), who declares, "We have no King but Caesar." After Pilate washes his hands of the affair, it is the high priest and not the crowd who proclaims a version of Matthew 27:25: "If thou, imperial Pilate, wouldst wash thy hands of this Man's death, let it be upon me and me alone!"

The contrast between Pilate and Caiaphas is nowhere more apparent than in their behavior in the final frames of the scene. Pilate pronounces himself "innocent of the blood of this just Man" and then stalks off to sob alone in his throne room. Self-satisfied, Caiaphas smirks, arms folded, savoring his victory. By reassigning to Caiaphas the lines that the Gospels attribute to the Jewish crowd as a whole, DeMille reconfigures the trial scene to place blame squarely—and solely—upon the high priest. Babington and Evans describe DeMille's Caiaphas as "the Romans' Jew," an "anti-Semite's dream caricature of wickedness: obese, cynical, rubbing his plump fingers together in gleeful anticipation of his plots, appearing like a well-fed devil at Pilate's side to whisper 'Crucify him!' The scapegoat . . . is the living epitome of ethnic guilt." DeMille's portrait is at home in 1920s America, in which anti-Semitism was an almost respectable response to waves of Eastern European Jewish immigration and Jewish connections to labor unrest, all fed by well-established anti-Semitic caricature.[16]

Pasolini's The Gospel According to Saint Matthew

The skillful camera work in Pasolini's *The Gospel According to Saint Matthew* offers a more subtle approach than do most other Jesus biopics. In the trial scene, the camera places the viewer among the crowd that has gathered at the Temple compound to witness the trials before the high priest and Pilate, which take place one after the other in the courtyard in front of the Temple. We crane our necks to see above the heads of the bystanders; we can distinguish the main players but we are too far away to see them clearly. The effect of the camera work is to erase any differentiation between the Jewish and Roman authorities and simultaneously to create a gap between the governing elites and the crowd of commoners. This visual gap symbolizes the social, political, economic, and ideological chasm between these two groups.

By situating his viewers among the crowd on the screen, Pasolini engages their support in opposition to social hierarchy and political authority. We watch helplessly as a gross injustice is committed. We hear Pilate declare himself innocent of Jesus' blood, and we hear a lone disembodied voice cry out: "His blood be on us and on our children!" The speaker, whom we can neither locate nor identify, does not represent either the watching crowd as a whole or any faction among them. Pasolini would have us view this scene not as a faithful rendition of history or scripture but as an allegory of contemporary Italian society. The opposition between political and religious authorities on the one hand and the people on the other reflects Pasolini's own Marxist worldview and his critique of the social and political institutions in Italy at this time.[17]

Rossellini's Il Messias

In contrast to *The Gospel According to Saint Matthew*, Roberto Rossellini's *Il Messias* (*The Messiah*, 1975) takes the conventional route of some of the silents and epics.[18] Pilate is sympathetic to Jesus; Caiaphas is accusatory and manipulative. When Caiaphas brings Jesus to him, Pilate is highly annoyed.

> PILATE: I want a concrete accusation against this man.... Don't think it is enough for me that he has insulted your religion.... Rome is not interested if someone breaks the laws of your fathers!
>
> CAIAPHAS *(anxious not to make Pilate too angry):* It is not only this that makes him guilty. We brought him here as token of our friendship. We found him inciting our people to revolt against your government.... He was telling people not to pay the tribute to Caesar and proclaiming himself king and messiah.

Pilate finds no case against him and informs the Jewish authorities that if they bring this man for judgment, they must provide proof and motives. He concludes: "As far as I am concerned, as far as my authority and legal power are concerned, you have brought this man before me under the accusation of subverting the people. As you saw, I have interrogated him in your presence and could not find him guilty of any of the charges you have brought against him. Therefore according to the law of Rome, he has done nothing to merit being put to death." Still the priests persist, and Pilate gives in; he washes his hands and dries them with a white towel. Rossellini shows a reluctant Pilate and emphasizes Jewish responsibility, especially that of Caiaphas. This interpretation is rather surprising given the film's overall positive representation of Jews and Judaism.

Arcand's Jesus of Montreal

Denys Arcand's *Jesus of Montreal*, which features a group of actors as they create and perform a Passion play on the grounds of St. Joseph's Oratory on the top of Mount Royal, has a complex view of the trial scene. The Passion play that is at the core of this film places both Caiaphas and Pilate at Jesus' trial, but Pilate is clearly the key player. Caiaphas hovers at his side, prayer shawl draped over his head.

Pilate interviews Jesus—is he a member of a sect, or perhaps a prophet?—and mocks Jesus' emphasis on love: "Isn't that a bit optimistic? You wouldn't last a week in Rome." He declares Jesus harmless and hands the file back to Caiaphas. Pilate expresses his disdain for priests, who, he says, are either idiots or profiteers.

CAIAPHAS: The priests support Rome. You wouldn't want rumors to spread. Tiberius is a suspicious ruler. We want to help you govern, but one must set an example. He attracts crowds. He has disciples.
PILATE: Who are unarmed.
CAIAPHAS: He performs miracles. He's caused riots in the temple. Crucify him. *(Smiling superciliously as he walks away.)* "It's better to sacrifice one man . . ." [cf. John 11:50].

Pilate returns to Jesus. Apparently the priest's words have convinced him, for he now informs the prisoner of what will now transpire:

My soldiers will take you. They're brutes, of course. We don't get the elite. You'll be whipped, then crucified. It won't be pleasant. You're not Roman, but try to be brave. Who knows, I may be doing you a favor. A philosopher said the freedom to kill oneself during hardship is the greatest gift man has. In a few hours you'll cross the Styx, the River of Death, whence no one has returned, except Orpheus, it is said. Perhaps your kingdom lies on the far shore. Or maybe Jupiter Capitolinus awaits you, or Athena, or the god of the Germans or the Franks. There are so many gods. Perhaps the river has no other shore and vanishes into darkness. You at least will know. Courage.

He then orders the soldiers to take Jesus away.

On the face of it, the figure of Pilate in the Montreal Passion play does not particularly desire Jesus' death, but he gives in to Caiaphas's demands for political reasons. The Caiaphas figure resembles DeMille's high priest; he has a similarly stocky build, wears the same arrogant expression on his smiling face, and oozes the same ostentatious piety. But if we view this scene in the context of the film as a whole, a different interpretation emerges. Like all other aspects of the film's Passion play, the trial is allegorical, pointing beyond the details of the Passion narratives to a devastating critique of contemporary Quebecois society. Pilate's invective against the priests is not directed at the high priesthood in first-century Judaea but at what the movie consistently portrays as the corrupt and hypocritical Catholic priesthood in late-twentieth-century Quebec.

Also relevant is one of the final scenes of the frame narrative. Daniel has sustained a terrible injury when the cross on which he is suspended falls and crushes his head during the final performance of the Passion play. He is first taken to St. Mark's Hospital, where he is met with indifference and left to wait in a crowded emergency room. His treatment is contrasted with that at Montreal Jewish General, where he and the friends who accompanied him, Constance and Mireille, are treated with compassion and genuine concern. Once it is clear that Daniel is going to die, the Jewish doctor gently suggests to the women that some good might come from transplanting his corneas and heart. This scene implies, then, that it is not the Jews who killed this Jesus but the callous Roman Catholic establishment, through the hypocrisy of the church and the indifference of its hospital. The Jewish doctors and nurses, on the other hand, allow him to die with dignity and, more than this, to be resurrected to renewed life through the enhanced lives of those who receive his donated organs. Contributing to this point is the visual detail of the Star of David on the uniforms of the hospital workers, which subtly evokes the Jewish badge worn by Jewish residents of the ghettos and concentration camps of the Nazi regime. This scene powerfully asserts that the Christians at St. Mark's have rejected the dying Jesus, whereas the Jews, who have suffered so much, have taken him in.

Saville's The Gospel of John

The 2003 film *The Gospel of John* demonstrates a sincere attempt to diminish the Jews' role in the trial, a difficult task given its commitment to reproducing every word of the Johannine text. Any modification to the portrayal of the Jews in the trial scene must therefore come, as in the Pasolini film, from elements other than the dialogue. In this regard the film makes some attempts to deflect attention from the Jews.

Caiaphas is present, but he is not singled out as the sole or principal culprit, nor does he confer directly with Pilate as do his counterparts in the films of

DeMille and Arcand. Still there is palpable antagonism between the two leaders, and the crowd is unmistakably Jewish, as the men's fringed garments make obvious. The dark garments worn by some members of the Jewish crowd convey a rather sinister impression, as does the zeal with which some clamor for Jesus' death. At least the crowd is relatively small in size, suggesting that it was not all or even the majority of Jews in Jerusalem who pressed for Jesus' death.

The film's production team and the academic advisory committee recognized that using the entire Gospel of John as the script for the movie created serious problems, particularly in the Passion scenes. Because this film undertook to reproduce faithfully virtually every word in the Good News Bible translation of the Gospel of John, it was not possible to omit dialogue or to reassign it to other characters, as other filmmakers have done. Under this constraint the academic advisory committee composed a brief text to scroll at the beginning of the film. This text emphasizes that Jesus was tried and executed under Roman auspices and that the way in which the Fourth Gospel tells its story reflects Jewish/proto-Christian hostility at the time it was written, not necessarily the realities of Jesus' own lifetime: "Although crucifixion was the preferred Roman method of punishment, it was not one sanctioned by Jewish law. Jesus and all his early followers were Jewish. The Gospel reflects a period of unprecedented polemic and antagonism between the emerging church and the religious establishment of the Jewish people."

Gibson's The Passion of the Christ

By contrast not only does Gibson's *The Passion of the Christ* include all of the problematic elements of the Gospel sources, but much like the 1921 film *Der Galiläer,* it also exaggerates the Jews' role far beyond the Gospel accounts. In Gibson's version of the trial before Pilate, the Roman governor attempts to please the crowd, as in Mark. He washes his hands of Jesus' blood, as in Matthew. He sends Jesus off to Herod Antipas, as in Luke. And he dithers at length before finally ordering Jesus' execution, as in John. Compared to other post-Holocaust Jesus movies, *The Passion* accentuates the role of Caiaphas, his fellow Jewish leaders, and the Jewish crowds. Caiaphas is a bloodthirsty, scheming, vicious villain who will do everything in his power to persuade the suave, compassionate Pilate to order Jesus' crucifixion. Richly clothed, Caiaphas is not only physically ugly, but also morally repugnant as well in his hate for Jesus and in his disdain for truth, justice, or God. The Jewish crowds are huge, as in almost all of the Jesus movies. The occasional voices that speak in Jesus' favor all belong to his disciples; the crowd easily overwhelms them. Like his counterparts in DeMille's *The King of Kings* and *The Greatest Story Ever Told,* Gibson's Pilate is a compassionate man who does his utmost to exonerate Jesus. It is the Jewish crowds and, above all, Caiaphas and his fellow priests who are responsible for Jesus' extreme suffering and his death, even if it is the Romans who inflict the most savage blows, extract the most blood, and nail him to the cross.

ANTI-SEMITISM

Gibson defended himself against the charge of anti-Semitism numerous times in the media. Here is how he explained himself to Diane Sawyer in an ABC interview aired on February 18, 2004: "He [Jesus] was born into Judaea, into the House of David. He was a child of Israel among other children of Israel. The Jewish Sanhedrin and those who they held sway over and the Romans were the material agents of his demise. Critics who have a problem with me don't really have a problem with *me*, they have a problem with the four Gospels."

In his defense against charges of anti-Semitism, Gibson points to his removal of the English subtitle for Matthew 27:25 ("Let his blood be on us and on our children"). With or without this line, however, the villainy of the Jews is made abundantly clear. And the line is still present in Aramaic on the soundtrack, hence comprehensible to any viewer who knows this Semitic language. Given the worldwide distribution of the film and the diversity of its global audience, the absence of this line from the subtitles may or may not have the desired effect.[19]

As the debate around Gibson's film made clear, any film about Jesus must reckon with the delicate question of anti-Semitism. As a prominent character, Caiaphas the Jewish high priest can become a flashpoint for this question. In *Jesus Christ Superstar,* for example, all the dramatis personae of the trial scenes are equally despicable. Caiaphas and the other Jewish leaders are predatory and powerful, Herod is a foppish fool, and Pilate has no patience for Jesus whatsoever. The crowd does play a part in inciting Pilate to pronounce the death sentence, but Pilate for his part shows no reluctance to do so. When Jesus refuses to speak, Pilate declares, in song: "Die, if you want to, you misguided martyr." He washes his hands in red water and continues, "I wash my hands of your demolition, you innocent puppet." Even as he declares Jesus' innocence, Pilate displays his contempt for this "superstar." Yet despite the negative depiction of all those involved, the portrayal of the Pharisees, Caiaphas, and others is disturbing.

As Baugh notes:

> If *Jesus Christ Superstar* can be defended against the charges of racism [referring to the controversy created by having a black actor play Judas], it is much more difficult to dismiss the repeated charges of anti-Semitism leveled at the film. Clearly, the film places the blame for the death of Jesus on

the Jews. Shifting the account of the Gospel, neither Webber and Rice nor Jewison attempt to attenuate the responsibility of the Sanhedrin for the death of Jesus. They make Pilate a weak and fearful man and Herod a spoiled child and a comic figure. Their responsibility for Jesus' death is diminished by these characterizations. On the other hand, the Sanhedrin, first appearing in black cloaks on the scaffolding above the ruin, "like giant vultures roosting on the branches of a tree," are portrayed as strong, determined, politically astute and sadistically evil.[20]

Nevertheless we must remember that Jewison's Jesus is also not a particularly appealing figure. The overall unrealistic nature of this film—its studied absence of authenticity despite its setting in Israel's Negev desert—does attenuate its anti-Semitism.

Less problematic are those films, such as the epics of the 1960s, that portray Caiaphas as an underling caught in the middle between his people and the Roman overlords. In these films Caiaphas is portrayed in a not-unsympathetic light as someone who is himself unhappy about the role that he is forced to play in the events leading to Jesus' death. In *Jesus of Nazareth,* for example, the high priest is portrayed as a man of integrity and spiritual depth, who is duped by his own scribe and experiences genuine pain at Jesus' blasphemy in the course of the trial.

The films that are the most successful at avoiding the charge of anti-Semitism, however, are those that directly and explicitly allegorize the high priest. At the same time as it plays with the stereotypes and conventions of the Jesus film genre, *Jesus of Montreal* makes it abundantly clear that Caiaphas does not represent the Jewish people, in the past or in the present, but the Catholic priests of present-day Montreal, whose actions in the film result in the death of the Jesus figure, Daniel Coulombe. The question of anti-Semitism is entirely irrelevant to a more recent allegorical treatment, Mark Dornford-May's 2006 film, *Son of Man,* which situates the story in modern Africa and has an entirely black cast. In this powerful film, all players in the story of Jesus, from Jesus to Caiaphas and Pilate, are African, and the conflict does not involve distinctions of race, ethnicity, or religious belief.[21]

CONCLUSION

It would not be realistic to expect feature films to be more precise than the Gospels themselves about Caiaphas or his role in Jesus' death, for films tend to simplify rather than complicate the story lines of their textual sources. It suits the movie medium to have the conflict as simple and as stark as possible, so that viewers can easily identify the adversaries.

In the case of the Jesus biopic, it is obvious that the "good guy" is Jesus. For most films, as in the New Testament Apocrypha, patristic commentary, and medieval drama, the role of the "bad guy" is shared by the Romans and the Jews and, among the Jews, Caiaphas the high priest in particular. The portioning out of relative blame varied over time. But here too, as in the history of the Oberammergau play, a shift occurs in the mid–twentieth century. The films made prior to World War II cheerfully saw the Jewish leaders as Jesus' main opponents, even if some of them tried to avoid blaming the Jews as a whole for Jesus' death. In addition to cohering well with the Gospel accounts, this approach made for a better story, as it is more dramatic to have Jesus' own people turn against him than to have him face off directly with the large and anonymous Roman imperial machinery. Films from the second half of the twentieth century present a more nuanced scenario, no doubt under influence of the post-Holocaust sensibilities that lessened the acceptability of public anti-Semitism. These films tend to portray Caiaphas and other Jewish authorities as being caught between their people and the Romans, and as motivated in the case of Jesus by the strong and not unreasonable fear that disorder or disobedience will lead to harsh reprisals. There may be an echo here of the role of the Judenrat, or Jewish council, in the ghettos of the Nazi period, though there is no direct evidence that filmmakers had such detailed knowledge about the Nazi regime.[22] In this context the displacement of anti-Semitic stereotypes onto Caiaphas the high priest in some films from both before and after the Holocaust era does not eliminate the anti-Semitic impact. Surely it is not lost on the viewers of either DeMille or Gibson that Caiaphas was Jewish; blaming Caiaphas does not therefore mitigate the deicide charge.

CAIAPHAS IN HISTORIOGRAPHY

At the outset of this study, I commented on the striking similarities between the portraits of Caiaphas in New Testament scholarship and those in art, fiction, drama, and film. Having examined many of those artistic and literary portraits, it is time to return to New Testament historiography to examine the ways in which scholars have embedded Caiaphas in their narratives.

As we have seen, Caiaphas plays a number of different roles in nonhistoriographical genres of literature and artistic expression. A number of general trends can be observed, however. For most Caiaphas is of interest not for his own sake but for his role in the Jesus story, and specifically the Passion narrative. To be sure, his portraits take the sources—primarily Josephus and the canonical Gospels—into account and often draw on biblical and postbiblical descriptions of high priests and the high priesthood as well. But the overall paucity of detail allows Caiaphas to be molded into whatever sort of personage is required for the particular Jesus narrative being told.

The narrative imperative, therefore, is a major force in the depiction of Caiaphas. Narratives are shaped by the need for coherence, that is, a cause-and-effect relationship between events, but also by the perspectives, values, beliefs, and ideas of the artist or author. A Jesus story told from a political perspective will place Caiaphas within the fraught relationship between Rome and Judaea and speculate as to how the colonial situation would have affected the high priest's relationships with Pilate on the one hand and Jesus on the other. A story told from a cosmological perspective will assign Caiaphas a role within the struggle between God and Satan.

Stories also express values. The portrayals of Caiaphas are powerfully shaped by the artist or author's stance toward the deicide charge, as well as toward Jews, anti-Semitism, and even the ecclesiastical authorities of their own eras. This chapter will argue that in New Testament historiography and exegesis, as in non-historical genres, Caiaphas is a malleable figure whom scholars shape to serve different, even contradictory agendas.

Collingwood and Hayden White draw attention to the similarities between fictional and historical narrative. Historians, however, work under a set of constraints from which novelists may be free if they so choose. According to Collingwood, a historical account must work within the following conditions: the picture must be localized in time and space; it must be consistent with itself (that is, with the broader context); and it must take into account "something called evidence."[1] Evidence, however, cannot be taken at face value. Indeed historians routinely "tamper" with the evidence, in three ways: by selecting what they think is important and omitting the rest; by interpolating things they do not explicitly say (that is, filling in the gaps); and by criticizing, rejecting, or amending aspects of the evidence that they judge as being "due to misinformation or mendacity."[2] As we shall see, the process of selecting, critiquing, and assembling the "evidence" is at the core of the portraits of Caiaphas in historiography.

WHO CARES ABOUT CAIAPHAS?

As a Jewish high priest in the late Second Temple period, Caiaphas naturally belongs to the history of Second Temple Judaism. Yet with the exception of James VanderKam's excellent study of the high priests from Joshua to the first revolt, few historians of Second Temple Judaism consider him at any length. To be sure, studies of Jewish religious practice, such as Schürer's *The History of the Jewish People in the Age of Jesus Christ* and Sanders's *Judaism: Practice and Belief 63 BCE–66 CE*, discuss the roles of the priests in general and the high priest in particular.[3] These works, however, pay little or no attention to Caiaphas himself.

If Caiaphas tends to be ignored in the studies of Second Temple Judaism, however, he is a significant player in historical Jesus research. Scholars discuss his name, his role vis-à-vis the Roman governor on the one hand and the people of Judaea on the other, and his motivation for acting against Jesus. The distribution of references to Caiaphas in textual sources provides one obvious reason for why New Testament scholars care about Caiaphas while scholars of Second Temple Judaism apparently do not. Josephus mentions him only twice; rabbinic sources, which some historians use to fill out their understanding of the Temple and its personnel, do not mention this particular high priest at all.[4] By contrast the Gospels give him a narrative role in the most important event of Jesus' life: his Passion.

The fact that New Testament scholars care more about Caiaphas than do their Second Temple colleagues thus reflects quite directly the concerns and interests of their primary sources. But there is a more important, and more interesting, reason for the discrepancies. Certainly historical Jesus researchers draw upon Josephus and other extrabiblical sources, both textual and material, and they generally consider Caiaphas's role and responsibilities in the relationship between Judaea and Rome. But the question that drives their interest in Caiaphas is his role in the violent manner of Jesus' death, which became an integral part of the Christian message and mission. Caiaphas is a central figure in this narrative, and his degree of responsibility is a question that cries out for resolution. Historians of Second Temple Judaism, on the other hand, do not entirely overlook Jesus' story, but the drama that matters most to them is the Jewish revolt against Rome and its climax, the destruction of the Temple, which occurred some four decades after Jesus' death on the cross. The high priests play a varied role in the various constructions of these events, but in the view of most, Caiaphas lived too early in the century to have had a direct impact on the revolt and its consequences.

It is evident, then, that from the vantage point of modern scholarship, there are two distinct stories that take place on the soil of first-century Judaea—the story of Jesus and the story of the Jewish revolt—and for many these two stories barely intersect. To put it differently, the question of who cares about Caiaphas may well come down to the question of who cares about Jesus, historically, religiously, or both.

Given these considerations, it is primarily to historical Jesus scholarship that we must look for attempts to insert Caiaphas into a coherent historical narrative. When it comes to their treatment of the high priest, these narratives address two main questions: what did Caiaphas do, and why did he do it? The literature on this subject is vast, encompassing not only the hundreds of "lives of Jesus" that have been attempted over the course of at least three "quests,"[5] but also the massive library of commentaries on the Gospels in general and the trials of Jesus in particular.[6] The present treatment will not even attempt to be comprehensive, but it will illustrate a range of answers to both of these questions.

WHAT DID CAIAPHAS DO?

Maximalist Views

The portraits of Caiaphas that are painted by historians and exegetes can be classified as maximalist, minimalist, or somewhere in between. Maximalists are the least selective and also the least critical; they tend to view all the Gospel accounts of Caiaphas as historical and arrive at a coherent narrative by harmonizing them, interpolating as necessary. Maximalist accounts affirm the following points: that Caiaphas articulated a rationale for Jesus' death (John 11:49–52); that his father-in-law, Annas, conducted an interrogation (John 18:13, 19–24); that Caiaphas presided over a more or less formal meeting of the Sanhedrin or council at which false testimony was heard; and that the high priest charged Jesus with blasphemy, after which the council pronounced him guilty and deserving of death (Matt. 26:59–68).

A prominent proponent of this view is Josef Blinzler, who vigorously defended the historicity of the Gospel accounts against all critics[7] and freely filled in the gaps by resorting to extracanonical traditions and his own imagination. Among his more imaginative ideas are that Annas lived in a wing of Caiaphas's palace, on the basis of a fourth-century tradition attributed to the pilgrim of Bordeaux,[8] and that Caiaphas had an honorable, if personal, reason for allowing Annas to interrogate Jesus: "In handing Jesus over to Annas for a time, Caiaphas doubtless wished to publicly show his high regard for his father-in-law, and probably also really counted on the latter's experience and cunning to find material which would serve later in the trial before the Sanhedrin. In this way, the time until the formal meeting of the court was usefully filled in."[9]

Blinzler rejects any notion that "Annas did not wish to take part in the sitting of the Sanhedrin as an ordinary member and could not act as president, or that the intention was to save the old gentleman from having to go out of doors in the cold night air."[10] The Johannine omission of the actual account of the formal trial is explained by the nature of the audience:

> The Fourth Evangelist's readers, converts from paganism, would have been very little interested in a Jewish court trial, especially as they already knew from St. John's Gospel all about the messianic claim of Jesus, which formed the climax of that trial. Now, John knows, besides, of a short proceeding before the ex-high priest Annas which none of his predecessors had taken notice of. Despite its slightness of content, he includes it because it provides him with the framework, so to speak, for the story of Peter's denial which, in the absence of the account of the trial before Caiaphas, would have had no place otherwise.[11]

As there is no reason to doubt that "Mark and Matthew have described the course of the trial correctly in its essentials,"[12] Blinzler asserts that the high priest himself conducted the interrogation as president of the court.[13] Caiaphas's aim was to force a decision and thereby to ensure Jesus' conviction.[14] After exhaustive examination Blinzler concludes that the principal responsibility for the death of Jesus rests with the contemporary Jewish authorities.[15] Blinzler's account is fundamentally a harmonization of the four Gospel accounts that smooths over their contradictions and places Caiaphas at the center of the chain of events that resulted in Jesus' execution.

Minimalist Views

Minimalists, by contrast, are the most selective and the most critical. They too interpolate, however, in order to create a coherent account of how these stories came to be, what needs they served for the earliest communities, or what traditions they used. A prominent example is found in the work of Hans Leitzmann, who in 1931 concluded that Mark 14:55–56, the basis for the other Gospel accounts of the trial, is a complete fabrication or even a fantasy. In his view the Jewish authorities did not try or sentence Jesus but only arrested him and delivered him to the Romans.

Leitzmann offers several reasons for this minimalist view. In the first place, there were no material witnesses to the trial. It is therefore difficult to ascertain how an Evangelist would have known what went on at the proceedings.[16] Furthermore there is considerable evidence from Acts, Josephus, and rabbinic literature to show that the Jewish authorities did indeed have power over life and death. Had Jesus been condemned for blasphemy, he would have been stoned, not handed over to Pilate for trial, conviction, and execution.[17] Finally it is unlikely that a Jewish high priest would have viewed the "Son of God" title as blasphemous, given that this was not a Jewish messianic title but rather a Christian title that likely postdated the time of Jesus.[18] Leitzmann thus criticizes the historicity of the Marcan account and suggests that the trial story is a Marcan interpolation into the Second Evangelist's own account of Peter's denial, which is the main focus of the first part of the Passion narrative.[19]

Minimalist accounts are also offered by Paul Winter and, more recently, Michael Cook, both of whom argue that Mark invented the account of the trial for apologetic and literary purposes.[20] Variations of this theory are presented by John Dominic Crossan and Bernard Jackson, who argue that Mark's account is an example of "prophecy historicized."[21] In their view the high priest's role may have been created to show that Jesus' manner of death fulfilled Psalm 2: "The kings of the earth set themselves and the rulers take counsel together against the Lord and his anointed."[22] The role of Annas, however, would have been read back from later Christian experience, given that the first three martyrs mentioned in Acts were all executed during the tenure of high priests from Annas's family: Stephen (under Caiaphas; Acts 6–7); James brother of John (under Matthias; see Acts 12 and *Ant.* 19:316); and James brother of Jesus (under Annas II; *Ant.* 20:197–203).[23]

Perhaps the most passionate, if least convincing, of the minimalist accounts is that offered by Haim Cohn, who was attorney general of Israel in 1949, minister of justice in 1952, and a member of Israel's Supreme Court from 1960 to 1981. Cohn conducted a thorough examination of the trial sequences against the background of rabbinic law and came to the conclusion that far from wanting to indict Jesus, the high priest aimed to protect him. Indeed it was at the high priest's insistence that Jesus had been detained, in order to forestall the likelihood that he would imminently be taken into Roman custody. He knew of Jesus' arrest by Roman forces and had sent his own officers to negotiate for Jesus' release.[24] The council that assembled in Caiaphas's house did not hold a trial or conduct any sort of investigation, which would have been forbidden during the Passover season.[25] Cohn states: "There can, I submit, be only one thing in which the whole Jewish leadership of the day can have been, and indeed was, vitally interested: and that was to prevent the crucifixion of a Jew by the Romans, and more particularly, of a Jew who enjoyed the love and affection of the people."[26] Why, he asks rhetorically, would the Jews have cared? The irony of his response leaps off the page:

> I do not allow myself to speculate that the Jewish leaders might have been prompted by ethico-religious considerations, such as the prohibition of standing by quietly when the blood of a neighbor is shed (Lev. 19:16), or the prescript to save the persecuted from the hands of his persecutor. The great importance of the matter inhered not in its moral and religious aspects, but in wholly realistic, political factors. We saw that the high priest found himself in a very precarious situation vis-à-vis the people: unless he did something about it, his standing and prestige in their eyes would steadily decline. He must have been desperately anxious to raise the esteem in which the public held him, and especially to demonstrate that he was a good and loyal Jew, admirably qualified for Jewish leadership, and not merely an instrument in Roman hands. . . . For it [the Sanhedrin] to deliver Jesus into the hands of the Roman governor would, then, in the governor's eyes, have been tantamount to admission of sanhedrial failure and incapacity to preserve law and order; and, in the eyes of the people, to a contemptible infringement of national solidarity and treasonable collaboration with the enemy.[27]

When Caiaphas tore his garments, it was not because of shock or rage at Jesus' blasphemy but "his anguish that Jesus ostensibly refused to cooperate and was moving stubbornly toward his disastrous fate, and not least, that Roman oppression would claim another Jewish victim, with all the consequences that might flow from the Roman killing of a man of Jesus' standing and popularity."[28]

The Middle Road

Despite their patent differences, the maximalist and the minimalist views are made equally possible by the nature of the Gospel sources themselves: their omissions, their contradictions, and their vagueness. Most scholars, however, hold to a middle position, accepting some aspects of the Gospels as historical and dismissing others. Perhaps the most convincing discussion is that of Raymond Edward Brown, who, more explicitly than most, addresses the anti-Jewish implications of the story. It is "lucidly clear," says Brown, that Jesus was "sentenced by a Roman prefect to be crucified on the political charge that he claimed to be 'the King of the Jews.'... The real problem concerns whether and to what degree the Sanhedrin or the Jewish authorities of Jerusalem played a role in bringing about the crucifixion of Jesus." He continues:

> True, there is another problem raised by the New Testament itself as to whether responsibility for the crucifixion of Jesus is to be placed on the whole Jewish nation of his time and even on subsequent generations of Jews. Embarrassing as this second problem is to many Christians today, one must honestly recognize that it has its origins in New Testament generalizations about the Jews.... This problem is not solved either by pretending that the respective New Testament authors did not mean what they said or by excising the offending passages.... the solution lies in acknowledgment that the books of both Testaments can serve as meaningful guides only when allowance is made for the spirit of the times in which they were written. Nevertheless, this is obviously more a theological problem than a historical problem.[29]

Brown insists that the only problem that offers hope of historical solution is the involvement of the Jewish authorities. He distinguishes four views: that the Jewish authorities bear the main responsibility and the Romans were little more than executioners (held, for example, by Schürer and Blinzler); that the authorities were involved but the legal formalities were carried out by the Romans (held by many Christian scholars);[30] that the Romans were the primary movers (held by many Jewish scholars); or that the Jewish leaders were not involved at all. Brown rules out options one and four (those that we have called the maximalist and minimalist options).[31]

While we cannot be sure to what extent the Gospel accounts are historical, Brown notes that they all consist of religious questions that have a political overtone (cf. John 18:19; Matt. 26:61)[32] and concludes that the Sanhedrin—like all councils, including those of all later Christian churches—had "a mixture of ecclesiastical politicals, righteous men of burning zeal and pious men of mercy and justice. In turning Jesus over to the Romans with the recommendation that he be tried as a potential revolutionary with monarchical claims, some were undoubtedly acting selfishly ... others out of political motivation. There is scarcely a Christian church that cannot find in its history condemnations of good men leveled by religious assemblies with a similar variety of motives."[33]

WHY DID HE DO IT?

Aside from minimalists who attach no credence whatsoever to the Gospel accounts, most historians accept that Caiaphas did something, even if they do not agree on exactly what. The question that seems to interest them most, however, is why. Theories in this regard can be broadly classified into three categories: personal, political, and religious/ideological, though these are not mutually exclusive.

Personal Reasons

Like some filmmakers and novelists, some historians suggest that Caiaphas was motivated at least in part by personal reasons. Blinzler is one of the most explicit proponents of this view. He describes Caiaphas as an able diplomat, as evidenced by the fact that he was able to remain in power for nineteen years, far longer than any other first-century high priest.[34] Although elsewhere Blinzler insists that "it is useless to indulge in idle conjecture" with regard to issues upon which the sources are silent,[35] he states that Caiaphas must have bribed his way into office under Gratus and, he implies, provided financial incentives to Pilate for the privilege of serving under him as well:

> Valerius Gratus, governor of Judea from 15 to 26 A.D., through whom Caiaphas came into office, must also have been susceptible to bribery, for he left none of the three immediate predecessors of Caiphas in office longer than a year.... Doubtless Caiaphas must have spared him the trouble of this roundabout method of obtaining money by making changes. He definitely did not lack the necessary means to do so.... It is no less remarkable that Caiphas succeeded in remaining in office also during the whole governorship of Pontius Pilate (26–36 A.D.), an official who—be it noted—is reproached by his contemporaries not only with brutality but also with venality.[36]

In support of this view, Blinzler cites the Babylonian Talmud, Tractate Yoma 8b, which states that the high priests paid for the privilege, and for that reason the position changed hands every twelve months. The Talmud, though compiled in the sixth century C.E., does contain some earlier traditions. The cited section from Yoma 8b, however, is not corroborated by any first-century source, and in any case this statement refers not to the Roman high priests but to Hasmonean ones.[37]

For Blinzler, Caiaphas was motivated entirely by his desire for power and would go to any lengths to preserve it. Thus his role as the head of the council that condemned Jesus "showed how unscrupulously he was wont to act against anyone who could possibly endanger his position of power.... Precisely because [Jesus] threatened to draw the masses away from the ruling caste, He had to be sacrificed to reasons of state as a Caiaphas would understand these."[38] Like Dante, Blinzler views Caiaphas as a hypocrite. It misses the point entirely to argue that the high priest's angry reaction was proof of the sincerity of his conviction. "Caiaphas dared not, on any account, omit that gesture of sorrow and indignation, whether his excitement was spontaneous and sincere or simulated and hypocritical. Besides, it is not to be assumed that he was wearing his gorgeous high-priestly robes at that session of the Sanhedrin."[39] There is little to differentiate Blinzler's account from many of the imaginative narratives in fiction, drama, and film.

Bruce Chilton has articulated the sensible response to this line of interpretation: "No judgment of Caiaphas's character or motivation can make any serious claim on our attention, except as an imaginative exercise. Historically speaking, the available evidence will not permit conclusions of that sort."[40]

Political Reasons

Blinzler's explanation of Caiaphas's motivation blends the personal with the political. Most recent studies of the historical Jesus focus more directly on the political, without, however, impugning Caiaphas's character to the same degree as Blinzler does. Rather they situate Caiaphas's actions in the particular political, social, and economic structures of the Roman Empire. As high priest Caiaphas was the one who mediated between Israel and God. In the Roman period, however, the high priest was also charged with the important if unenviable task of mediating between Israel and Rome. E. P. Sanders argues that in contriving to eliminate Jesus, Caiaphas was simply carrying out his duties as prescribed: to preserve the peace and to prevent riots and bloodshed. Jesus was dangerous because his self-declarations as well as his behavior in the Temple could all too easily cause a riot, which Roman troops would put down with great loss of life.[41] Similarly Paula Fredriksen views Caiaphas's actions in the specific context of the need for order. She attributes no role whatsoever to Jesus' teaching or his "temple tantrum" but rather argues that it was the crowd's enthusiastic if ill-informed acclamation of Jesus as Messiah that led Caiaphas to act.[42] Fredriksen does not place sole or even primary responsibility for Jesus' death upon

Caiaphas, but like the novelist Norman Mailer, she argues that Caiaphas and Pilate would have arranged things together, moving swiftly, effectively, and in secret in order to avoid a public riot.[43]

According to the position represented by Sanders and Fredriksen, Caiaphas responded not to any particular element in Jesus' teaching but only to the potential for havoc that his presence and activities in Jerusalem created. A number of recent studies provide another perspective on Caiaphas's actions by placing them explicitly within the context of the relationship between Rome as colonizer and the Jews as colonized. Marcus Borg states that "the society of which Jesus was a part had been promised universal sovereignty [by God] and yet found itself in a colonial situation under a mighty and often ruthless world power with its own claims to universal sovereignty."[44] In contrast to Fredriksen, who argues that Jesus did not intend a revolt against Rome when he came to Jerusalem for the Passover festival, John Dominic Crossan believes that Jesus had a personal and corporate social program for the kingdom of God there and then in the Lower Galilee and, later, in Jerusalem as well. "That program opposed the systemic injustice and structural violence of colonial oppression by Roman imperialism."[45] Many contemporary historical Jesus scholars connect this political program to apocalypticism, an ideology of resistance that in their view fueled Jesus' actions both in Galilee and in Jerusalem on the eve of his last Passover, and which directly prompted Caiaphas's strong opposition to him.[46]

Some scholars emphasize other kinds of tensions in addition to or instead of the political issues mentioned above. John Meier summarizes the various aspects of Jesus' background that converged to put him on a collision course with Caiaphas and the Jerusalem priesthood: "he was a no-account Galilean in conflict with Jerusalem aristocrats; he was (relative to his opponents) a poor peasant in conflict with the urban rich; he was a charismatic wonderworker in conflict with priests very much concerned about preserving the central institutions of their religion and their smooth operation; he was an eschatological prophet promising the coming of God's kingdom in conflict with Sadducean politicians having a vested interest in the status quo." Meier argues that these tensions stemmed from a more fundamental conflict, that between laity and clergy. In his view Jesus "was a religiously committed layman who seemed to be threatening the power of an entrenched group of priests."[47]

Borg, Crossan, and Meier view Caiaphas's actions as motivated not only by a desire to maintain order, but also by Jesus' direct challenge to the various hierarchies in which the high priest was involved. Jesus' challenge incorporated the essence of his social message, namely, a concern for the poor, the rural, and the colonized. For this reason Jesus inevitably and indeed intentionally came into conflict with the high priest, who represented the rich, urban Jewish leadership in collaboration with the Roman oppressor.

Religious/Cultural Interpretations

According to some scholars, Caiaphas's condemnation of Jesus is to be situated not only in the hierarchies and power politics of Roman occupation but in a much broader, explicitly religious, framework: the opposition between Judaism and Hellenism. In this scenario the crucifixion is the tragic outcome of a far-reaching conflict between pure untainted Judaism, represented by Jesus, and corrupt and materialistic Hellenism, represented by Caiaphas.

That the opposition between Judaism and Hellenism was an important factor in the experience of Palestinian Jewry in the time of Jesus is emphasized by Chilton. He argues that Jesus is to be placed firmly in the company of Jewish peasants who "were a beleaguered people under the thumb of Rome who cherished their rich Judaic customs and traditions" and "vigilantly shielded themselves from the incursions of Hellenistic culture."[48] Caiaphas mediated the relationship between the Jewish populace and the Roman prefect Pilate, occupying an uncomfortably liminal position with respect to each.[49]

David Flusser, on the other hand, couples the opposition between Judaism and Hellenism tightly to the opposition between the Pharisees and the Sadducees in the post-Maccabean period. Flusser views the Sadducees as the prime representatives of Hellenism in its Palestinian Jewish mode. This much is implied by the evidence concerning a certain Jerusalemite named Jason, a Sadducee who bears a Greek name and whose tomb boasts a Greek inscription inviting men to enjoy life.[50] By the time of Jesus, the Sadducees had made a pact with Rome and ensconced themselves in the Jerusalem Temple through the high priest and his priestly council.[51] By contrast the Pharisees fought against Hellenism and defended Jewish law and custom in the civil war of the late Maccabean period. By Jesus' time they were recognized as the teachers of the masses and consciously identified themselves with popular faith in line with a non-sectarian universal Judaism.[52] Although Jesus criticized the hypocrisy of the Pharisees, this critique was not instrumental in his death. The Pharisees would never have handed a fellow Jew over to the Romans, since they considered this to be a "repulsive act of sacerdotal despotism."[53] Flusser suggests that "Caiaphas decided to act because he feared that Jesus' movement and its possible success among the people would trigger violent Roman intervention. His anxiety was exaggerated but not unfounded. This way of reasoning and acting was and is without doubt contrary to the Jewish faith's humane approach—but a Sadducean High Priest could disagree."[54] By virtue of his official role and Sadducean affiliations, Caiaphas, the Sadducean and, by implication, highly Hellenized high priest, becomes the antithesis of a humane Jewish faith that is represented both by Jesus and by the Pharisees, who, though not identical with the later rabbis, should be seen as their spiritual predecessors.[55]

The notion that the conflict between Jesus and Caiaphas is propelled by the fundamental opposition between Judaism and Hellenism comes to detailed and explicit expression in the work of N. T. Wright. Wright argues that "if Jesus is to be vindicated as the true representative of YHWH's people; and if he, Caiaphas, is presently sitting in judgment on him; then Caiaphas himself, and the regime he represents, are cast in a singularly unflattering light. His court has become part of the evil force which is oppressing the true Israel, and which will be overthrown when YHWH vindicates his people. Caiaphas, the High Priest, has become the new Antiochus Epiphanes, the great tyrant oppressing YHWH's people."[56]

Wright's description of Caiaphas as the new Antiochus is not merely a colorful and provocative rhetorical flourish. It is part and parcel of an elaborate theory regarding Jesus' messianic and martyrological consciousness that can be pieced together rather easily from his massive study, *Jesus and the Victory of God*.

The basic premise of Wright's theory is that Jesus, like all first-century Jews living in Palestine, would have been very familiar with the story of Hanukkah in which the underdog Maccabean warriors succeeded in resisting the imposition of Hellenistic religion engineered by Antiochus IV and his Jewish collaborators. Jesus and his compatriots would have seen this story not only as an important element of their people's history but also as a paradigm of or analogy to their own situation under Roman rule. Jesus saw himself as the one who would deliver the faithful Jews from this current incarnation of the Hellenistic menace to their ancestral religion and way of life.[57] Indeed Jesus modeled his teachings and actions on the words and deeds of the Maccabean martyrs, often taking them a step or two further.[58] For example his aphorism regarding money rendered to Caesar should be read as a coded statement in which he deliberately echoes and subverts the meaning of Mattathias's last words as recorded in 1 Maccabees 2:66–68: "Pay back the Gentiles in full, and obey the commands of the law."[59] Where Mattathias called for retribution, however, Jesus called for prompt filing of one's tax return.[60]

Similarly Jesus' so-called cleansing of the Temple can be seen as a new and improved version of the Maccabean rededication of the Temple. For Jesus, says Wright, the activities of the present Temple authorities, led by Caiaphas, polluted the Temple, much as the Seleucids did under Antiochus IV. Jesus fought not so much to restore the Temple to its pristine state, as did Judas Maccabeus before him, but to bring God's rule into the world once and for all.[61] In doing so Jesus had in view the scene painted in 2 Maccabees 8:16–17, according to which "Maccabeus gathered his forces together ... and exhorted them not to be frightened by the enemy and not to fear the great multitude of Gentiles who were wickedly coming against them, but to fight nobly, keeping before their eyes the lawless outrage that the Gentiles had committed against the holy place, and the torture of the derided city, and besides, the overthrow of their ancestral way of life."

It was Jesus' disruptive scene at the Temple, above all, that set the high priest against him, for he too understood Jesus' actions in light of the sequence of events enshrined in the celebration of Hanukkah. The Hanukkah plot line included victory over the pagans, cleansing of the Temple, fulfillment of the promises, and establishment of the new dynasty.[62] So too, Caiaphas feared, might Jesus' audacious victory in the Temple overthrow his own rule and disrupt the current order of things forever.

For Wright not only Jesus' words and deeds but also his suffering death brought him into a direct line with the Maccabean martyrs. These martyrs experienced a suffering death that can be seen as redemptive, in the sense that their suffering was intended to spare the nation as a whole.[63] Jesus' expectation of a suffering death was grounded in the story of the seven martyred sons in 2 Maccabees 7. This passage recounts how one son after another chose to die rather than transgress the laws of his ancestors by eating forbidden meat. Before each son finally succumbed to the horrendous torture prepared under the king's orders, he spoke passionately about atonement for sin, the hope for future resurrection, and God's eventual punishment of the king for having fought against God (2 Macc. 7:19).[64] These declarations help to explain Jesus' mindset as he approached his own martyrdom in Jerusalem.

Thus, according to Wright, "Jesus's story sets him firmly within major narratives of Jewish tradition: Daniel would face the lions and be exalted, Judith would go into the tent of the enemy commander and emerge victorious. Maccabean martyrs would die horribly and a new dynasty would be set up within an independent Israel. The son of man would suffer at the hands of the beasts and then be lifted up to the right hand of the Ancient of Days."[65] Jesus reenacted the suffering of the Maccabean martyrs and also completed the story that they had begun. He was not simply "enabling the nation of Israel to escape from her exile while the rest of the world lurched towards its doom. His symbolic actions had pointed towards a renewal of Israel which broke the boundaries, the wineskins, the taboos, and which incorporated a new set of symbols. His last symbolic action, we may assume, was intended to continue and complete this process."[66]

Wright portrays Jesus as the representative of "true" and pure Judaism in holy conflict with the corrupting powers of Hellenism. These powers were embodied not only in Rome but also in the Jewish authorities, and in Caiaphas in particular. Wright expresses Jesus' assessment of Caiaphas in the harshest possible terms: "The satan had taken up residence in Jerusalem, not merely in Rome, and was seeking to pervert the chosen nation and the holy place into becoming a parody of themselves, a pseudo-chosen people intent on defeating the world with the world's methods, a pseudo-holy place seeking to defend itself against the world rather than to be the city set on a hill, shining its light on the world."

Jesus had no choice but to fight this evil power with every means at his disposal: "He would go, then, to the place where the satan had made his dwelling. He would defeat the cunning plan which would otherwise place the whole divine purpose in jeopardy.... He would stand, like Mattathias or Judas, against not only the pagans but also the compromisers within the chosen people, more particularly those who wielded power, those who ran the holy place, the shepherds who had been leading the people astray. Jesus, once more, was a first-century Jew, not a twentieth-century liberal."[67] In taking this bold stand against the high priest, the "new Antiochus Epiphanes," Jesus was not at all rejecting Judaism and the fundamental principles of election and Temple. On the contrary he constituted the full embracing and indeed fulfillment of these quintessentially Jewish concepts.[68]

Wright's grand theory about Jesus' Maccabean consciousness has the drama and pathos befitting his weighty tome. Of course the analogies he draws between the players in the Hanukkah story and those in the Jesus story do not quite fit. One would think, for example, that the Roman emperor, or even Pilate, and not the Jewish high priest would take on the role of Antiochus IV. Leaving such problems aside, the sharp opposition between Judaism and Hellenism that emerges in the work of Wright and others is surprising in the context of contemporary New Testament scholarship, for these studies reintroduce through the back door a distinction that was evicted from the standard narratives of Second Temple Judaism some thirty years ago.

In works prior to the late 1960s, it is not uncommon to encounter the assertion that Judaism remained untainted by Hellenism. Typical is Günther Bornkamm's *Jesus of Nazareth*, which asserts that "through the power of ... faith, not only ancient Israel but no less post-exilic Judaism did its best to hold aloof from the changing foreign powers, although the land lay in the magnetic field of their aspirations. Again and again it repelled the influences of their cultures and religions, and never produced anything like Babylonian or Egyptian science, not to mention anything of the type of Greek philosophy and science."[69]

Although there were significant studies from the 1930s through the 1960s that undermined the sharp distinction between Judaism and Hellenism,[70] arguably the most influential for New Testament scholarship was the work of Martin Hengel, *Judaism and Hellenism*, first published in German in 1969. Speaking of

New Testament scholarship at the time of his study, Hengel notes that "one fundamental presupposition of historical work on the New Testament which seems to be taken for granted is the differentiation, in terms of tradition, between 'Judaism' on the one hand and 'Hellenism' on the other."[71] Hengel's detailed study of the literary and other evidence for the complex relationship between Judaism and Hellenism in the period between Alexander's conquest in 332 B.C.E. and the Maccabean revolt in circa 165–66 B.C.E. concludes that all of the major groups of Second Temple Judaism that emerged from that conflict, that is, the Pharisees, Sadducees, and Essenes, were strongly influenced by Hellenism. "For this reason," says Hengel, "the distinction between 'Palestinian' Judaism and the 'Hellenistic' Judaism of the Greek-speaking Diaspora, which has been customary for so long, now becomes very questionable. Strictly speaking, for the Hellenistic Roman period the Judaism of the mother country must just as much be included under the heading 'Hellenistic Judaism' as that of the western Diaspora."[72]

Not all New Testament scholars accept Hengel's last statement, at least in its absolute form. Géza Vermès disagrees with Hengel rather categorically, declaring that he is firmly convinced of the "untenability" of the declaration that all Judaism from the middle of the third century B.C.E. must be designated "Hellenistic Judaism."[73] Sanders offers a more tempered view. He argues that while "Simon and his successors acted very much like other Hellenistic kings, and various aspects of Hellenistic culture continued to percolate through Palestine," the Maccabean victory ensured that distinctive Jewish practices such as circumcision, as well as the normative role of Jewish law, would be maintained, and that "there would be no further effort to break down the barriers between Judaism and the rest of the Graeco-Roman world."[74]

Yet the maintenance of distinctive practices and beliefs does not in itself argue against Hellenistic influence, nor does it necessarily place barriers between Judaism and Hellenism. Martin Goodman argues that in fact "the oddities of the Jews in the Graeco-Roman world were no greater than that of the many other distinctive ethnic groups, such as Idumaeans, Celts, or Numidians, who between them created the varied tapestry of society in this region and period."[75] Indeed if we were to base our view of the Jews solely on what others said about them, "Jews would not seem anything like as marginal in the Graeco-Roman world as they do when their own, often jaundiced, views of the outside provide the basis for understanding them."[76]

Virtually every recent historical Jesus study includes a survey of the Jewish background of Jesus that acknowledges the pervasive impact of Hellenism upon the diverse groups within Second Temple Palestinian Judaism. But when it comes time to account for the timing and manner of Jesus' death, this nuanced view often falls away. Even scholars who view Palestinian Judaism as thoroughly Hellenized can find a way to incorporate the sharp opposition between Judaism and Hellenism into their analysis. Crossan, for example, places Jesus within a broad Mediterranean context in which the central philosophical trends and schools of the Hellenistic world have become firmly entrenched among all levels of society. Crossan's Jesus is an itinerant Cynic Jewish philosopher who traveled the hills and dales of Galilee with his followers, teaching "free healing and common eating, religious and economic egalitarianism" to rural Galilean peasants.[77] Yet Crossan too must finally account for the fact that one Hellenized Jew, Caiaphas, plotted against the life of another Hellenized Jew, Jesus. He does so by positing a distinction between exclusivism and inclusivism within Hellenistic Judaism itself. Crossan defines this difference on the basis of exclusive and inclusive reactions to Hellenism. While he explicitly disavows value judgments according to which exclusivity is wrong and inclusivity is right,[78] his distinctions between exclusive and inclusive Judaism correspond rather neatly to the distinctions between Judaism and Hellenism as drawn by both Flusser and Wright. Exclusive Judaism means a Judaism seeking to preserve its ancient traditions as conservatively as possible with minimal conjunction with Hellenism; inclusive Judaism is that form of Judaism that sought to adapt its ancestral customs as liberally as possible with maximal association, combination, or collaboration with Hellenism.[79]

Crossan's interpretive move subsumes the Judaism/Hellenism dichotomy into his framework of a Hellenized Jewish Palestine. In doing so he can have it both ways: he can accept the evidence for Hellenization in first-century Palestine and still retain the crucial opposition of elements within Judaism as an explanation for the conflict between Jesus and the Jewish authorities headed by Caiaphas.

Interestingly even Hengel himself backs away from the implications of his own theory. Despite the bold way in which he collapses the dichotomy between pure Palestinian Judaism and Hellenized Diaspora Judaism, he limits the most powerful effects of Hellenization to those he refers to as the Jewish upper classes. He argues that the "process of Hellenization did not affect all the Jewish population in the same way. Following the character of the new civilization in the conquered areas of the East as being a civilization for the aristocrats and more well-to-do citizens, it had an open and direct influence only on the relatively narrow, but normative stratum of the priestly and lay nobility and the prosperous city population."[80] Thus Hengel's work provides both a basis upon which to critique the Judaism/Hellenism dichotomy of historical Jesus narratives and also a foundation upon which to support the polarity as well.

Not only does the Judaism versus Hellenism framework fly in the face of what is now known to have been the profound penetration of Hellenism into all types and aspects of Judaism in Jesus' time, but it also places an insupportable burden upon Caiaphas himself. If Caiaphas were indeed a second Antiochus Epiphanes, as Wright calls him, one might have expected him to do all he could to insinuate Greek language and Hellenistic culture into the "pure" Judaism of first-century Palestine. One might have expected him to establish a gymnasium right under the citadel; to induce Jewish young men to wear the Greek hat, as did the high priest Jason according to 2 Maccabees 4:12; to advocate the removing of the marks of circumcision; and to abandon the holy covenant, as did the Hellenizers described in 1 Maccabees 1:13–15, or raid the Temple sanctuary for his own enrichment, plunder the city, persecute its Jewish inhabitants, install Gentile cults, and burn the books of the law, as Antiochus IV is described as doing in 1 Maccabees 1:20–56. But the primary sources provide no support for the notion that Caiaphas either imposed or promoted Hellenization in any form.[81] Just as Caiaphas in effect crucifies Jesus on the basis of false testimony, so do these scholars, colloquially speaking, "crucify" Caiaphas, on the basis of no evidence whatsoever.

The identification of Caiaphas as the supreme Hellenizing villain out to destroy Jesus, the champion of pure, uncorrupted Judaism, is difficult to square with the cultic role of the high priest as the one who preserves the covenantal relationship between God and Israel through the administration of the sacrificial cultus and, especially, his entry into the Holy of Holies on the Day of Atonement. At least two factors are at work here. One is a tendency, in at least some New Testament scholarship, to view Hellenism as the force that corrupted the pure Judaism of the Second Temple period. Although, as Tessa Rajak points out, Greek culture was often valued above Hebraic culture throughout the history of ideas, this evaluation was often reversed by Christian scholars, for whom "rampant polytheism" was a major obstacle.[82] This point is well illustrated in a passage in the entry on Hellenism in the *Anchor Bible Dictionary*, written by Hans Dieter Betz. Betz repeatedly asserts the opposition between Jesus the Jew and Hellenism at the same time that he acknowledges the lack of evidence for at least some elements of his argument. According to him, "The movement initiated by Jesus of Nazareth was anti-Hellenistic. So much at least seems to be clear in spite of the dearth of reliable data.... In the eyes of Jesus, Hellenism was represented in Palestine by the Roman occupation and by the Jewish authorities imposed on the Jews by Rome. Although the Christian gospel writers who were Hellenists themselves have done their best to tone down these anti-Hellenistic sentiments, Jesus's rejectionist attitudes are clearly stated in the tradition.... The fact that Jesus was crucified as a messianic revolutionary is a sure indication of his anti-Roman and thus anti-Hellenistic attitude."[83] Although Caiaphas is not mentioned here, Betz maintains the fundamental opposition between the

Jewish Jesus and the Hellenized Roman and Jewish authorities, without, however, providing any evidence or even argument for Hellenism as a corrupting force.

The second factor at work in the persistence of the Judaism/Hellenism opposition is more subtle and, I admit, more speculative on my part. It seems to me that the opposition between Judaism and Hellenism around which some of the recent historical Jesus accounts are built functions as a substitute for an older and now discredited opposition, namely, that between Jesus and Judaism. Until the middle of the twentieth century, and in some cases beyond, scholars posited a sharp opposition between Jesus, the unique Messiah and son of God, and the Jews, including the chief priests, scribes, and those misguided, legalistic Pharisees, who blindly rejected him, called for his death, and took responsibility for his blood upon themselves and their children. So, for example, although Günther Bornkamm states categorically that "only a criticism blinded by racial ideologies could deny the Jewish origin of Jesus,"[84] his own analysis of Jesus' relationship to Judaism consistently sets Jesus apart from his Jewish compatriots. Bornkamm declares that "Jesus's attitude to the law . . . his concern about the people and his behaviour towards tax collectors and sinners, which was offensive to all pious Jews, prove that he stands in a complete contrast to these separate circles of the 'righteous,' as well as to the representatives of official Judaism."[85] Jesus is also completely unlike the various messianic rebel movements to which Josephus attests.[86]

The absolute isolation of Jesus from his Jewish contemporaries is no longer possible. The best of current scholarship fully acknowledges his Jewish identity. One of the tasks of current historical Jesus research is to situate Jesus within the sphere of Second Temple Judaism rather than in contrast to it. Furthermore negative representation of all of Judaism, or even of the Jews of Jesus' time, has become unacceptable, due to increased sensitivity to the anti-Jewish potential of such representations. This sensitivity is apparent, for example, in the heated debate over the meaning and intention of Matthew 23, in which the Matthean Jesus repeatedly calls the Pharisees hypocrites. To many post-Holocaust scholars, both Matthew 23 and also much of the history of its interpretation sound unacceptably anti-Semitic in light of the fact that traditional Judaism posits a continuity between the Pharisees and the later rabbis of the Mishnah and Talmud, the foundational texts of traditional Judaism to this day. Nevertheless the element of conflict between Jesus the Jew and at least some other Jews cannot be eliminated, because the Gospels themselves include many controversy narratives, refer repeatedly to the Jews' or Jewish leaders' murderous intent toward Jesus, and explicitly implicate Jews in Jesus' death. Transforming the opposition between Jesus and Judaism into a conflict between Jesus, the representative and champion of pure Judaism, and Caiaphas the Hellenized Sadducean high priest of Roman Palestine, not only takes care of the problems of the Jewish Jesus and apparently avoids anti-Semitism, but also maintains the traditional warm image of Jesus as the watchdog of the poor and oppressed rural peasants.

For the proponents of this construction, however, one problem remains: the obvious fact that the rural, poor, and pure Jews for whom Jesus battled the Hellenistic enemy apparently did not appreciate his sacrifice on their behalf. Accounts of the historical Jesus must have at least one eye on the history of the early church, which eventually became a separate and to some extent antagonistic entity with respect to the majority of Jews.

It is Hengel himself who allows us to see how the pattern is worked into the story of Christian origins both within and beyond the life span of the earthly Jesus. In Hengel's view the lower, nonaristocratic strata of the population reacted against the Hellenization of the upper classes by fixating rigidly on the law. This fixation, according to Hengel, "meant that any fundamental theological criticism of the cult and the law could no longer develop freely within Judaism."[87] Unfortunately every critique of law was misinterpreted by the rank-and-file Jews, in analogy to the attempt of the Hellenistic reformers in the time of Antiochus, as an attack on the Israelite faith or apostasy to polytheism. "Here," says Hengel, "is the profound tragedy of the reaction of Judaism to the primitive Christian movement which developed from its midst. Jesus of Nazareth, Stephen, Paul came to grief among their own people because the Jews were no longer in a position to bring about a creative, self-critical transformation of the piety of the law with its strongly national and political colouring."[88] As a community rigidly fixated on the law, first-century Judaism could not recognize, let alone appreciate, the prophetic spirit that emerged within it through Jesus' good offices. Hengel concludes his study as follows: "That it [the Jesus movement] was misunderstood from the Jewish side at that time as a new sect urging apostasy from the law and assimilation is indirectly the last and most grievous legacy of those Jewish renegades who, between 175 and 164 BC, attempted to do away with the law and 'make a covenant with the people round about.' The zeal for the law aroused at that time made impossible all attempts at an internal reform of the Jewish religion undertaken in a prophetic spirit, as soon as the nerve centre, the law, was attacked."[89] Thus Hengel resorts to the familiar portrayal of postexilic Judaism as a narrow and indeed petrified version of ancient Israelite religion.[90]

CONCLUSION

Most historical Jesus narratives assign to Caiaphas a crucial and instrumental role in the events leading to Jesus' death, and their only interest in the high priest is in what he did and why he did it. For most what Caiaphas did was to articulate and orchestrate a plot leading to Jesus' arrest, trial, and execution by the Romans; whether the high priest was motivated by personal, political, or religious factors or some combination thereof remains a matter of debate. The reconstructions of Caiaphas are shaped at least to some degree by matters quite separate from the high priest per se. Some imply an attempt to walk the fine line between historical criticism and Christian faith; others the conviction that despite their canonical status, the Gospels' historicity must be evaluated according to the same criteria as noncanonical sources.

Views of Caiaphas's role reflect not only belief (or nonbelief) in the spiritual and historical authority of the canonical Gospels, but also particular perceptions of how religion, power, and politics work. This is especially clear in narratives that treat Caiaphas as a pragmatic politician trapped between his Jewish constituency and his Roman masters. This type of portrait, which humanizes Caiaphas by viewing him as a complex figure, resonates with contemporary readers and makes his behavior more comprehensible, if still reprehensible. In general, however, the portrait of Caiaphas and the interpretation of his motivations are directly dependent on, and even a function of, the portrait of Jesus. Those who see Jesus primarily as the son of God sent to redeem humankind view Caiaphas as a near-demonic figure who carries out Satan's determined but ultimately unsuccessful plan to undermine God's saving activity in and for the world. Those who see Jesus as the champion of the poor and oppressed lower classes perceive Caiaphas as the wealthy and powerful Sadducee who was as much an instrument of oppression as the Roman Empire itself.

But the most important and powerful factor in these reconstructions is the narrative imperative: the need to create a coherent narrative in which the events are tied together by the principle of cause and effect. There is a certain narrative logic in the assertion that Caiaphas had a decisive role in the events that resulted in Jesus' death. The one certain fact of Jesus' Passion is his crucifixion; it is almost impossible to conceive of a reason why the Evangelists would have made this up. Crucifixion was a Roman form of execution, a punishment for treason. The question, then, is how would Rome (that is, the Roman governor Pilate) have known about Jesus and become suspicious of him on political grounds? Given that Jesus' main activity was among the Jews, it must have been the Jews who brought him to Pilate's attention. But ordinary Jews would not have had the ear of the Roman governor. Therefore it must have been the Jewish authorities who did so. Narrative logic necessarily writes the Jewish high priest into the story.

But why would Caiaphas have acted? Here logic and reason draw attention to Caiaphas's political role as the mediator between Rome, represented by the governor Pilate, and the Jews. It is logical to assume that Caiaphas, as the local authority, would have been charged with the role of maintaining order on behalf of Rome. Doing so would keep life as bearable as possible for the residents of Judaea and make it possible for the sacrificial cult to continue without disruption. As the one who had jurisdiction over the Temple, it is reasonable to think that Caiaphas would have been aware of Jesus' disruptive activities in the vicinity of the Temple, whether this was the "cleansing of the Temple," as most scholars argue, or the triumphal entry into Jerusalem.

This picture is both plausible and coherent; it also governed by the three constraints that Collingwood has described: it is localized in time and space (early-first-century Judaea); it is consistent with itself and the broader context (Judaea as a small slice of the Roman Empire); and it takes the evidence (Josephus, Gospels) into account. Although narrative accounts of the life of Jesus differ considerably, they all flesh out the high priest as the highest Jewish leader under the governor Pilate, with responsibility for maintaining order. Whether or not he felt a personal animosity toward Jesus or perceived Jesus' activities as a threat to his own power and jurisdiction, Caiaphas's concern for the potentially disruptive consequences of Jesus' activities and his popularity led him to act against him, with the support of other members of the Jewish leadership. But this picture is independent of the narratives told by first-century sources. Indeed, as the next chapter will show, it exists only through the imaginative gap-filling activity undertaken under pressure of the narrative imperative itself.

8

CAIAPHAS IN HISTORY

For historical Jesus research, Caiaphas provides the crucial link between the Jewish man who had gathered a following of disciples and the Roman governor who pronounced the death sentence. These scholarly narratives construct Caiaphas in different ways, but there is general, though not universal, agreement about what the high priest did (formulate and help carry out a plot to have Jesus eliminated by the Roman authorities) and why (to keep order in the empire for fear of Roman reprisal, a fear that was raised by Jesus' actions in the Temple or vicinity prior to the Passover festival).

The notion that Caiaphas was involved in the plan against Jesus privileges the Gospel of John, in which the high priest warns of the need to eliminate Jesus in order to avoid Roman reprisals, and downplays the synoptic Gospels, which do not explicitly include the high priest in the planning of Jesus' demise. But the ideas that Caiaphas was responsible for keeping order and that it was Jesus' "temple tantrum" that put the plot against him into motion are not stated anywhere; rather they are inferences that are necessary in order to fill in the gap between Jesus' ministry and his execution.

THE HIGH PRIEST AND ORDER

There is general though not complete consensus on what Caiaphas did: plot against Jesus, accuse him of blasphemy, and send him to Pilate for trial, sentencing, and execution. Caiaphas's actions are plausibly explained by the claim that as a high priest he was charged with keeping order on behalf of Rome. The need to keep order is seen as the primary motivation for his intervention with regard to Jesus, even for those scholars who also impute to Caiaphas a personal animosity toward Jesus or a fear of what the Galilean might represent. The evidential "hook" for this view is John 11:49–52, in which Caiaphas formulates a political and national rationale for plotting Jesus' death.

The need for order in any society, ancient or modern, is self-evident. Goodman notes that "riots in the cities of the empire threatened the good order of the society as it was perceived by the Romans themselves, and they believed that urban unrest could only be properly controlled through such representation by a trusted elite."[1] This local aristocracy provided an existing administrative structure on which Rome could build.[2] Carter argues that by appointing the high priests, Rome was able to secure the cooperation of the local elite and thereby to control priestly loyalties.[3]

In Goodman's view it was this practice that, after decades of unrest, caused the Jews to revolt against Rome. He suggests that while there was certainly a broad range of complex factors that led to the revolt, most important was the power struggle within the Jewish "ruling class" that Rome put in place when it took over direct rule of Judaea in 6 C.E.[4] The first Roman governor of Judaea had only a small staff, few troops, and no civil service. Only with the cooperation of local leaders could stable government be assured.[5] What Rome found in Judaea was the high-priestly class created by Herod the Great. Herod's high priests did not have their roots in Judaea and therefore had little or no connection with Judaean politics and little allegiance from the Judaean population. Herod had excluded them from secular and political matters, confining them to the management of the Temple. This made them unfit for political responsibility and also meant that they did not have the prestige in the eyes of the population that earlier high priests had enjoyed. Their status was further diminished by the fact that Herod deposed and appointed high priests on a whim and for his own political motives. It was to this unprepared and unpopular priestly elite that Rome handed over the local administration of Judaea.[6] Goodman observes that "It was just unfortunate, for Rome and for themselves, that the high priests thus entrusted with power were, because of Herod's deliberate tactics, weak men who lacked the local prestige which might have enabled them to carry the people with them on behalf of Rome."[7]

If Goodman is correct, the high priests would indeed have been charged with the task of keeping order, even if they did not have the ability to be effective in doing so. Sanders finds evidence in the writings of Josephus to support this construction of the high-priestly role in maintaining the public good. He points to an extended and complicated (dare I say confusing) narrative in *Ant.* 17, paralleled in *War* 2, that spans the period of change from Herodian to direct Roman rule of Judaea. After the death of Herod the Great, his successor, Archelaus, kept Joazar on as high priest. When he returned from Rome after being confirmed as ethnarch, he deposed Joazar for having supported those who objected to him (*Ant.* 17.339), but then reappointed him in 6 C.E. Archelaus himself was deposed, and Quirinius, the legate of Syria, was dispatched to take a census of Judaea. There was opposition to registration of property for tax purposes, but in an effort to maintain order, Joazar persuaded many of the people to comply with Roman wishes (*Ant.* 18:3). Despite his efforts, there were uprisings, and Quirinius deposed Joazar because he had been overpowered by a popular faction (*Ant.* 18:26), that is, he had failed to keep order. From this Sanders concludes that the secular authorities—whether the ethnarch or Rome—expected the high priest to be in control. A high priest who failed in this regard would find himself out of office. The fact that Caiaphas remained high priest for so long therefore implies that he was adept at maintaining order.[8]

If the high priest needed to keep order, he must have had a staff with which to do so. And indeed the Gospels refer to the Temple police, who were presumably under the control of the Jewish leadership if not the high priest directly. John depicts the chief priests and Pharisees as dispatching the Temple police (*hoi hypēretai*) to arrest Jesus at the Feast of Tabernacles when they heard the people muttering about him; Luke and John both include the Temple police (*hoi stratēgoi* in Luke 22:4; *hoi hypēretai* in John 18:3) in the force that arrests Jesus during the night after the final supper.

Exactly who these police were and what their responsibilities were, however, is by no means clear. Philo (*Spec. Leg.* 1:156) mentions Levites who watched over the Temple gates, courts, and porticoes.[9] Jeremias asserts that these Levites constituted a police force that was at the disposal of the Sanhedrin and made arrests and executed punishments at the direction of the high priest, who was the leader of this judicial body.[10] The sources that he cites to support this view, however, are much less specific than his discussion would suggest. Neither *Antiquities* 20.131 nor *War* 6.294 describes a police force as such. The former passage simply states that Quadratus ordered a group of priests, among them possibly the high priest's second in command, to be put to death but does not describe the role, if any, of the Temple police in carrying out this action. The latter passage describes a bizarre and either fantastic or miraculous event (depending on one's perspective)—a cow giving birth to a lamb behind a massive gate that had opened of its own accord—observed by the Temple watchmen and reported to their superior, who came by and shut the gate with enormous difficulty. Philo mentions the priests who stood at the entrance and in the vestibule of the Temple area to ensure that unauthorized people did not enter, and others who acted as day or night watchmen, took charge of the porticoes and open-air courts, and took out the rubbish and maintained general cleanliness (*Spec. Leg.* 1:156). They were not responsible, however, for overall enforcement of law and order in Judaea. Rather their role sounds much like that of the security guards at art galleries and museums: they control the crowds, admonish individuals who venture too close to forbidden areas, and maintain cleanliness. The sources therefore do not describe a police force that would have been used by the high priest in the enforcement of law and order on Rome's behalf.

Aside from the incident involving Joazar, Josephus's writings do not describe the high priests as the ones who kept order but rather assign this role to the Roman prefects and, later, the procurators. In *Antiquities* 18.261–72 Gaius dispatches Petronius as his legate to Syria to succeed Vitellius. His orders are to lead a large force in Judaea and, if the Jews consent to receive him, to set up an image of Gaius in the Temple of God. If, however, they are obstinate, he is to subdue them by force of arms. In the event a multitude did indeed come to Petronius with petitions, and Petronius petitioned Gaius on their behalf, with satisfactory results. Josephus says that Petronius requested "those in authority" to conciliate the people with optimistic propaganda (18:284). "Those in authority" may have included the high priest, but he is not mentioned specifically.

The high priest is absent from similar incidents recounted in the *Antiquities*. In *Antiquities* 18.88 it is Pilate who quells a Samaritan uprising; the high priest is not mentioned. In *Antiquities* 20.97–98 Fadus intervenes directly to quell the unrest caused by Theudas and his following. In *Antiquities* 20.105–20 Josephus describes the fear of the governor Cumanus that the presence of many Jews in Jerusalem would spark an uprising; the Roman governor ordered a company of soldiers to take up arms and stand guard at the porticoes of the Temple so as to quell any unrest that might occur. Josephus notes that "this had been in fact the usual practice of previous procurators of Judaea at the festivals." When a Roman soldier exposed himself, onlookers said it was blasphemy. Cumanus sent soldiers to deal with the unrest and, later, again in the hope of preventing a melee, executed a soldier for destroying a copy of the Torah (20.115). In an ongoing quarrel between Jews and Samaritans, Quadratus crucified those among the two groups who had taken part in the unrest and whom Cumanus had taken prisoner (*Ant.* 20.118). These examples suggest that while order was crucial, Rome did not rely on the high priest to keep it.

Caiaphas, Pilate, and Order in Judaea

John 11:49–52 attributes to Caiaphas the strategic principle "that it is better . . . to have one man die for the people than to have the whole nation destroyed." Caiaphas's comment suggests that the high priest saw the potential for disorder or unrest as a consequence of Jesus' activities in Judaea and that he had a plan, indeed a plot, for tackling the situation. Among the components of the plan, so implies the Fourth Evangelist, were Jesus' arrest and prosecution and his delivery to Pilate for execution.

If John 11 suggests that Caiaphas was concerned about protecting the people by defusing the potential for unrest, the Gospel accounts of Jesus' trial before Pilate create a rather different impression. In Matthew, Mark, and John, Jesus is handed over to Pilate after his interview with the high priest. Caiaphas then drops out of the narrative completely; from this point on, Jesus' accusers are described as the "chief priests and elders" (for example Matt. 27:12). When Pilate shows himself reluctant to crucify Jesus, they incite the crowds, who in turn clamour so vigorously for Jesus' death that Pilate, fearing a riot, gives in and orders Jesus to be crucified.

In this part of the story, then, Caiaphas plays no role directly at all, nor do the chief priests and elders take on the task of keeping order that scholars attribute to the high priest. Rather these groups pit themselves against Pilate, who desires only to release Jesus. The stories suggest that the main motivation of the chief priests and elders is to ensure Jesus' death, not to maintain order. On the contrary, to get their way, they incite the people against Jesus, and it is at this point, fearing a riot against his own clemency, that Pilate—unaided by any Jewish authorities—relents and orders Jesus to be crucified. What might have begun as a conflict between two factions within the Judaean people—those who favored Jesus and those who feared him—has turned into a riot against Roman rule. Where is Caiaphas when his mediating services are so sorely needed? The New Testament evidence suggests that Rome did not after all rely on the high priest to maintain order at this particular Passover celebration; Pilate alone decided that he had better give in to the restless crowd rather than release Jesus.

This scenario is not the exception; rather the absence of the high priest from the Gospel picture is consistent with other accounts of Temple-related incidents during Pilate's governorship. In *Antiquities* 18.55–62 (paralleled in *War* 2.169–74), Josephus describes the following episode:

> Now Pilate, the procurator of Judea, when he brought his army from Caesarea and removed it to winter quarters in Jerusalem, took a bold step in subversion of the Jewish practices, by introducing into the city the busts of the emperor that were attached to the military standards, for our law forbids the making of images. . . . Pilate was the first to bring the images into Jerusalem and set them up, doing it without the knowledge of the people, for he entered at night. But when the people discovered it, they went in a throng to Caesarea and for many days entreated him to take away the images. He refused to yield, since to do so would be an outrage to the

emperor; however, since they did not cease entreating him, on the sixth day he secretly armed and placed his troops in position, while he himself came to the speaker's stand ... surrounded them with his soldiers and threatened to punish them at once with death if they did not put an end to their tumult and return to their own places. But they, casting themselves prostrate and baring their throats, declared that they had gladly welcomed death rather than make bold to transgress the wise provisions of the laws. Pilate, astonished at the strength of their devotion to the laws, straightway removed the images from Jerusalem and brought them back to Caesarea.

Philo also has an account of this incident, in *De Legatione ad Gaium* (*On the Embassy to Gaius*) 299–305:

To Gaius: the lieutenant of Tiberius Caesar was Pilate, who was appointed to govern Judaea. He, not so much to honour Tiberius as to annoy the multitude, dedicated in Herod's palace in the holy city some shields coated with gold. They had no image work traced on them nor anything else forbidden by the law apart from the barest inscription stating two facts, the name of the person who made the dedication and of him in whose honour it was made. But when the multitude understood the matter which had by now become a subject of common talk, having put at their head the king's four sons, who in dignity and good fortune were not inferior to a king, and his other descendants and the persons of authority in their own body, they appealed to Pilate to redress the infringement of their tradition caused by the shields and not to disturb the customs which throughout all the preceding ages had been safeguarded without disturbance by kings and by emperors. ... he refused, and they clamoured ...... "Do not take Tiberius as your pretext for outraging the nation; he does not wish any of our customs to be overthrown. If you say that he does, produce yourself an order or a letter or something of the kind so that we may cease to pester you and having chosen our envoys may petition our lord." It was this final point which particularly exasperated him, for he feared that if they actually sent an embassy they would also expose the rest of his conduct as governor by stating in full the briberies, the insults, the robberies, the outrages and wanton injuries, the executions without trial constantly repeated, the ceaseless and supremely grievous cruelty. So with all his vindictiveness and furious temper, he was in a difficult position. He had not the courage to take down what had been dedicated nor did he wish to do anything which would please his subjects. ... Tiberius was furious with Pilate.

Antiquities (18.60–62) recounts yet another incident:

He [Pilate] spent money from the sacred treasury in the construction of an aqueduct to bring water into Jerusalem, intercepting the source of the stream at a distance of 200 furlongs. The Jews did not acquiesce in the operations that this involved, and tens of thousands of men assembled and cried out against him, bidding him relinquish his promotion of such designs.... When the Jews were in full torrent of abuse he gave his soldiers the prearranged signal. They, however, inflicted much harder blows than Pilate had ordered, punishing alike both those who were rioting and those who were not. But the Jews showed no faintheartedness; and so, caught unarmed, as they were, by men delivering a prepared attack, many of them actually were slain on the spot, while some withdrew disabled by blows. Thus ended the uprising.

The parallel is in *War* 2.175–77:

On a later occasion he provoked a fresh uproar by expending upon the construction of an aqueduct the sacred treasure known as Corbonas.... Indignant at this proceeding, the populace formed a ring round the tribunal of Pilate, then on a visit to Jerusalem, and besieged him with angry clamour. He, foreseeing the tumult, had interspersed among the crowd a troop of his soldiers, armed but disguised in civilian dress, with orders not to use their swords, but to beat any rioters with cudgels. He now from his tribunal gave the agreed signal. Large numbers of the Jews perished, some from the blows which they received, others trodden to death by their companions in the ensuing flight. Cowed by the fate of the victims, the multitude was reduced to silence.

These incidents are directly related to order and disorder in Judaea, yet neither Josephus nor Philo makes any reference whatsoever to the high priest as having the responsibility to intervene. It is the Roman governor Pilate, not the Jewish high priest Caiaphas, who assesses the situation and quells the disturbances. It is possible, of course, that Caiaphas did indeed play a role in these events and that Josephus simply chose not to report it. After all Josephus is not particularly interested in Caiaphas. But we cannot rule out the possibility that Caiaphas was simply not involved in the major events that Josephus chooses to recount.[11]

The New Testament evidence and the narratives of Josephus and Philo describe three major incidents in which Pilate apparently handled matters of law and order without Caiaphas's assistance. The length of Caiaphas's tenure is usually interpreted as evidence that he worked well with Pilate and, in particular, that he was instrumental in keeping order in Judaea on Pilate's behalf. While the silence of both the Gospels and Josephus in this regard does not necessarily mean that this interpretation is incorrect, it may also suggest the opposite: that Caiaphas managed to stay in his position for so long precisely because he kept his head down and did not rock the boat or interfere in the relationship between Pilate and the local population. If Goodman is correct with regard to the weakness of the high-priestly class, Caiaphas may well be a prime example.

THE HIGH PRIEST AND THE TEMPLE

Most investigations into the historical circumstances of Jesus' death link the high priest's plot against Jesus to a concern for the Temple, the Temple cult, and his own role in Judaean religion and society. The general consensus is that it was Jesus' dramatic "cleansing" of the Temple that led the high priest and the other Jewish leaders to act against Jesus.

Michael Grant declares that "the manner of Jesus' entry into Jerusalem, and above all his Cleansing of the Temple, had imperatively invited Jewish retaliation."[12] According to Chilton, Jesus' actions in the Temple were aimed directly at measures that Caiaphas himself had instituted not long before. Chilton argues that it was Caiaphas who had permitted the installation of vendors in the Temple; Jesus reacted to this new measure with force, and the collision of the two was finally adjudicated by Pilate, Caiaphas's protector.[13] Borg and Crossan see Jesus' act as symbolic and therefore highly offensive: it proclaimed the already present kingdom of God against both the already present Roman imperial power and the already present Jewish high-priestly collaboration. Temple ritual had to empower justice rather than excuse one from it.[14] Sanders views the act as in keeping with Jesus' self-understanding as an eschatological prophet who expected God to interrupt human history. He expected the Temple to be destroyed so that when the kingdom of God arrived a new one would be built.[15]

Given the Temple's centrality to Jewish ritual, spiritual, and economic life, it is certainly plausible that it would be the locus of conflict between Jesus and Caiaphas. Yet, as we shall see, the Gospels stop short of saying so. The Gospels link Jesus closely with the Temple, and they also know that the high priest and other priests have jurisdiction over the Temple, but at no point do they connect the dots between Jesus, the Temple, the high priest, and the Passion.

Jesus and the Temple

The Temple is mentioned eighty-six times in the Gospels and Acts. In addition to describing the setting of many of Jesus' activities, these passages establish a strong association between Jesus and the Temple. In Matthew 4:5 (Luke 4:9) the devil tests Jesus by taking him to the Holy City and placing him on the pinnacle of the Temple. Jesus performs many of his miraculous healings in the Temple area (for example Matt. 21:14; John 5:14) and spends considerable time walking in the vicinity of the Temple (for example Mark 11:27) and teaching there (Mark 12:35; John 7:14, 10:23). According to the Gospels, Jesus both had a special interest in the Temple and claimed some degree of spiritual authority over it. The tearing of the Temple curtain at the moment of his death implies the same (Matt. 27:51). Yet there is nothing in the Gospel narratives to suggest that Jesus' sense of authority with regard to the Temple was a primary cause of the high priest's animosity toward him. Jesus himself points out during his arrest: "Have you come out with swords and clubs to arrest me as though I were a bandit? Day after day I sat in the temple teaching, and you did not arrest me" (Matt. 26:55; Mark 14:49; Luke 22:53; cf. John 18:20).

In all four versions of this scene, Jesus enters the Temple, drives out the merchants, and quotes a verse from scripture. To discern whether or how this event precipitated the Passion plot, however, it is necessary to look closely at each account, with particular focus on the response of the Jews or the Jewish authorities to the episode.

In the synoptic Gospels, the cleansing scene takes place in the period immediately preceding the Passover. While it is not the last act that Jesus does before his last supper, it is by far the most dramatic. Mark's version of the story is as follows:

> 15 Then they came to Jerusalem. And he entered the temple and began to drive out those who were selling and those who were buying in the temple, and he overturned the tables of the money changers and the seats of those who sold doves; 16 and he would not allow anyone to carry anything through the temple. 17 He was teaching and saying, "Is it not written, 'My house shall be called a house of prayer for all the nations'? [Isa. 56:7]. But you have made it a den of robbers [Jer 7:11]." 18 And when the chief priests and the scribes heard it, they kept looking for a way to kill him; for they were afraid of him, because the whole crowd was spellbound by his teaching. (11:15–18)

Implicit in Jesus' actions is his right to enter the Temple and pass judgment on the types of activities that are permitted there. He is not protesting the authority of the priests, the preparations for the feast, or even the sacrificial cult as such, but rather the presence and activity of money changers and merchants. He uses scripture to criticize the presence of commerce in the Temple area but also to suggest that the central activity in the Temple is prayer.[16] Most important for our purposes is the comment that the chief priests and scribes sought to kill him when they heard "it." It is not clear here whether the *it* refers to the action in the Temple, his teachings, or both. The second part of the verse, however, suggests that the Jewish authorities' plan was not based on a threat to the Temple but was due to their fear of Jesus on account of the spell that his teaching cast on the crowd.[17]

Luke's version is similar to Mark's account: "Then he entered the temple and began to drive out those who were selling things there; and he said, 'It is written, "My house shall be a house of prayer"; but you have made it a den of robbers.' Every day he was teaching in the temple. The chief priests, the scribes, and the leaders of the people kept looking for a way to kill him; but they did not find anything they could do, for all the people were spellbound by what they heard" (Luke 19:45–48).

The difference between Luke's and Mark's versions is small but important. Whereas Mark portrays the prophetic quotations as the content of Jesus' teaching, Luke stresses that Jesus' teaching was a regular occurrence in the Temple. His version therefore provides a more explicit rationale for the leaders' desire to kill Jesus; in contrast to Mark, who attributes the leaders' anger to the spell cast over the crowd, Luke sees the crowd's fascination as a deterrent to the leaders' ability to act on their wishes to kill Jesus. In neither case, however, is this desire to kill Jesus traced back to the cleansing of the Temple as such.

Matthew's version too is similar to Mark's account; his additional details, however, imply a different rationale for the Jewish leaders' response.

> [12] Then Jesus entered the temple and drove out all who were selling and buying in the temple, and he overturned the tables of the money changers and the seats of those who sold doves. [13] He said to them, "It is written, 'My house shall be called a house of prayer'; but you are making it a den of robbers." [14] The blind and the lame came to him in the temple, and he cured them. [15] But when the chief priests and the scribes saw the amazing things that he did, and heard the children crying out in the temple, "Hosanna to the Son of David," they became angry [16] and said to him, "Do you hear what these are saying?" Jesus said to them, "Yes; have you never read, 'Out of the mouths of infants and nursing babies you have prepared praise for yourself'?" [Psalm 8:2]. (Matt. 21:12–16)

The act of cleansing the Temple and the accompanying scriptural passage are followed here by Jesus' healing of the blind and lame in the Temple area. This detail, however, suggests a broad antecedent for the authoritites' response. The "amazing things" that Jesus did include not only the Temple cleansing and the teaching but also, and more immediately, the healing of the blind and lame as well as the triumphant outcry of the children. For this reason the authorities' anger seems not to be aimed specifically at the cleansing but at this entire series of events. By the end of the passage, however, the focus is specifically on the children's outcry. This is the subject of the Jewish authorities' outraged question to Jesus, and of the scriptural quotation with which he responds; by this point Jesus' Temple act has receded in importance.

John's account appears early in Jesus' mission, not at the end, and while it corresponds to the same general outline noted earlier, it differs from the synoptic account in many of its details.

> [13] The Passover of the Jews was near, and Jesus went up to Jerusalem. [14] In the temple he found people selling cattle, sheep, and doves, and the money changers seated at their tables. [15] Making a whip of cords, he drove all of them out of the temple, both the sheep and the cattle. He also poured out the coins of the money changers and overturned their tables. [16] He told those who were selling the doves, "Take these things out of here! Stop making my Father's house a marketplace!" [17] His disciples remembered that it was written, "Zeal for your house will consume me" [Ps. 69:9; cf. Zech. 14:21; Mal. 3:1]. [18] The Jews then said to him, "What sign can you show us for doing this?" [19] Jesus answered them, "Destroy this temple, and in three days I will raise it up." [20] The Jews then said, "This temple has been under construction for forty-six years, and will you raise it up in three days?" [21] But he was speaking of the temple of his body. [22] After he was raised from the dead, his disciples remembered that he had said this; and they believed the scripture and the word that Jesus had spoken. (John 2:13–22)

The Johannine version of this event is much more detailed than its synoptic parallels, in that it describes precisely how Jesus chased the undesirable elements from the Temple area. These details have the effect of drawing the reader's attention to the act itself. In John, Jesus' words are not a quotation from scripture but his own outcry. Like the verses quoted in the synoptic Gospels, Jesus' exclamation provides the reason for his act and labels commercial activity as inappropriate to the Temple area. Even more, however, it states unequivocally Jesus' authoritative and exclusive claim to the Temple area. It is his father's house and therefore his own as well.

The passage then describes the responses of two sets of witnesses. The first are the disciples, who recall a scriptural verse that perfectly sums up Jesus' behavior as an expression of zeal for his father's house. The second are "the Jews," possibly the authorities, but they are not described more specifically in terms of their roles or functions. The narrator does not note any intention on their part to arrest or kill him, though their question is confrontational: "What sign can you show us for doing this?" Here finally there seems to be some direct engagement with the act of cleansing as such. Jesus' response, however, shifts the topic from his own actions to the fate of the Temple as such. "Destroy this temple and in three days I will raise it up." Whereas we might see his behavior as a portent of the Temple's future destruction, his bold words dare his interlocutors to destroy the Temple and predict that he, not they, will see to its rebuilding, and in a miraculously short period of time at that. The Jews' response leaves the notion of destruction behind, expressing incredulity at Jesus' prediction: "Will you raise it up in three days?" The narrator comes to the rescue, explaining that Jesus was speaking not of the Jerusalem Temple but of his body, a point that the disciples would understand only after Jesus' resurrection.

Although in John's Gospel the cleansing scene takes place at the outset of Jesus' ministry, its conclusion foreshadows the Passion narrative and its exultant resolution. Even so, the Temple cleansing is not positioned as the impetus for the Passion story; indeed neither the high priest nor any high-priestly authorities are singled out as being present at the scene or among those who interrogated Jesus afterward. Rather for John it is Jesus' resurrection of the dead and buried Lazarus of Bethany that prompts the council to meet and Caiaphas to declare "that it is better for you to have one man die for the people than to have the whole nation destroyed" (John 11:50).

Caiaphas, Jesus, and the Temple

The Gospels of Matthew and John involve Caiaphas in their Passion narratives. Neither, however, describes the high priest as having a particularly strong concern for the Temple or his own Temple-related authority. In Matthew, Caiaphas presides over the council that hears false testimony that Jesus said "I am able to destroy the temple of God and to build it in three days" (Matt. 26:61). This testimony conveys the notion that Jesus is a threat to the Temple and therefore may imply that he is also a threat to the high priest's authority. In response the high priest stands up and demands an answer from Jesus: "Have you no answer? What is it that they testify against you?" (26:62). But when the high priest puts Jesus under oath, the issue is not Jesus' putative threat to the Temple but his self-identification as the Messiah, the son of God. It is Jesus' response to this question, not his response—or lack thereof—to the Temple accusation that causes Caiaphas to rend his clothes and ask the council to give its verdict.

A similar shift in focus away from the Temple occurs in the Fourth Gospel. Unlike Matthew, John does not explicitly depict Caiaphas as the one who presides over the council; he is merely described as "one of them" (John 11:49). But his authority is clear. Interesting here are the subtle differences in the nature and purview of Jesus' perceived threat as the discussion proceeds. In John 11:47–48 the chief priests and the Pharisees are concerned about Jesus' signs, especially his resurrection of Lazarus. If Jesus goes unchecked, they fear, "everyone will believe in him, and the Romans will come and destroy both our holy place and our nation." Caiaphas's response, however, omits all reference to the holy place—the Temple. Rather in verse 50 he expresses concern for the nation as a whole. The narrator's explanation initially repeats Caiaphas's reported speech, which he describes as prophecy: "He did not say this on his own, but being high priest that year he prophesied that Jesus was about to die for the nation" (John 11:51). The narrator, however, also adds a new element: "and not for the nation only, but to gather into one the dispersed children of God" (11:52). If the holy place was included in the concerns of some council members, it is ignored both by the narrator and by the high priest himself.

The same tendency to overlook Caiaphas's connection to the Temple is apparent in Acts. According to Acts 4:1–15, Peter and John were arrested by the priests, the captain of the Temple, and the Sadducees after healing a man from illness in the name of the resurrected Jesus. The next day, Annas, Caiaphas, and others of the high-priestly family interrogated the prisoners, but when they "saw the man who had been cured standing beside them, they had nothing to say in opposition. So they ordered them to leave the council while they discussed the matter with one another" (4:14–15). Here too, however, the high priest is not specifically concerned about the Temple and the sacrificial activities that take place therein.

Neither is a strong concern for the Temple manifested in the passages that refer to the high priest without mentioning him by name. Some of these references occur in the Marcan and Lucan parallels to Matthew's trial scene; they do not add any information whatsoever with regard to Caiaphas and the Temple.[18] One passage that does connect the Temple and the high priest is Acts 5:16–6:1, in which the high priest—presumably Caiaphas, though this is not certain—and others arrest the apostles, who were curing the sick and those tormented by evil spirits, and put them in public prison. Mysteriously these prisoners are later released in the night by an angel of the Lord (5:19). The discovery of their escape from prison causes great consternation among the captain of the Temple police and the chief priests (5:24), which only increases when they learn that the men whom they had imprisoned were at that moment in the Temple and teaching the people (5:25).

Here too, however, the high priest's concern has little to do with the Temple as such. Rather it is focused on the apostles' teaching activity. According to Acts 5:27–28, "The high priest questioned them, saying, 'We gave you strict orders not to teach in his name, yet here you have filled Jerusalem with your teaching and you are determined to bring this man's blood on us.'" The Pharisee Gamaliel intervened on the apostles' behalf, and the story concludes in triumph: "And every day in the temple and at home they did not cease to teach and proclaim Jesus as the Messiah" (5:42).

According to Acts 6:7–7:2, Stephen faced a similar interrogation at the hands of the high priest. Here it is the "synagogue of the Freedmen" that seeks false witnesses, who oblige them by testifying: "This man never stops saying things against this holy place and the law; for we have heard him say that this Jesus of Nazareth will destroy this place and will change the customs that Moses handed on to us" (6:13–14). Again, however, the high priest does not react specifically to the accusations against the Temple but rather asks in a general way: "Are these things so?" (7:1). Later on in Acts (9:1–2), Paul asks the high priest to write letters to the synagogues in Damascus authorizing him to arrest any Christ-believers and bring them to Jerusalem. This request implies that the high priest was regularly involved in disciplinary actions against Jesus' followers, though it is likely that Caiaphas was not the high priest in question.

On the basis of this survey of passages about Caiaphas, the high priest, and the Temple, as well as the four accounts of the Temple cleansing scenes, it is clear that the Gospels do not either implicitly or explicitly present the cleansing scene as the provocation for the plot that ends in Jesus' death. As portrayed in the Gospels, the high priest Caiaphas and other authorities among the Jews are indeed disturbed by Jesus, but their anger and distrust do not stem from any threat to their authority. Rather they are focused on his popularity with the crowds and the behaviors that led to that popularity, principally teaching and healing.

The Gospel writers know three things. They know that Jesus engaged in some dramatic behavior in the area of the Temple, perhaps during the Passover pilgrimage festival (though which year is uncertain);[19] they know that Jesus came into conflict with the Jewish authorities; and they know that Jesus was crucified. The Gospels connect the second and third points, positing that the process that led to Jesus' crucifixion was due to a conflict with Jewish authorities. But they do not connect the first point to that process.

The synoptic Gospels remain entirely silent on which event specifically provoked the high priest and his associates. Perhaps it was Jesus' teaching, his healing, the fascination that he held for the children, or the Jewish crowds more generally. John, on the other hand, does provide an answer: it was the resurrection of Lazarus that prompted the concern of the Jewish authorities for Roman reprisal, which in turn led to Caiaphas's pronouncement that one man should die for the sake of the nation. This is not to say, however, that John's narrative is any more historical than that of the synoptic Gospels. For John the raising of Lazarus is the most spectacular of Jesus' signs; the dramatic nature of Jesus' miracles increases from chapter 2 to chapter 11 in tandem with the Jews' hostility toward him. Lazarus's resurrection foreshadows Jesus' own, and hence from both a narrative and a theological perspective it is the appropriate point at which a formal plot against Jesus should be announced. One may speculate that the Fourth Evangelist recognized the gap in the narrative tradition that finds expression in the synoptic Gospels and therefore took pains to supply a catalyst for the Jewish plot against Jesus.[20]

CONCLUSION

The portrait of Caiaphas that emerges so clearly from New Testament scholarship fragments and recedes when we look at the primary sources. In the end there is no clear evidence for his direct or even indirect involvement in the events leading to Jesus' death. The sources do not portray him, or even most of his successors or his predecessors, as being instrumental in the efforts of Rome to keep order in Judaea, nor do they support the claim that he was disturbed or threatened by Jesus' behavior at the Temple or in Jerusalem. In other words the sources resist coherence. In acceding to the narrative imperative—the need to create a plausible story line in which events are linked by cause and effect—we can impose coherence by selecting some passages and ignoring others and then filling in the gaps in a way that satisfies the need for coherence. We should just be aware that we are doing so. This is not to say that the usual construction of Caiaphas as the mastermind and prime mover of the plot against Jesus is false. It is simply that the inconsistencies and silences of the sources do not permit us to say for certain.

Of course the deconstruction of these gap-fillers presented in these pages is also a symptom of the narrative imperative at work, only in reverse. It is both a claim that the narrative constructed in many of these historiographical works, while presented as evidence-based and coherent, is in fact neither and it is a refusal to fill in the gaps that allow the story to be told in the first place.

FACE TO FACE WITH CAIAPHAS

In a small village in the Bavarian alps, on a rainy and cold May afternoon, I joined five thousand other spectators in a large, unheated theater auditorium. Anticipation was in the air as we settled into our seats, thumbed through textbooks, and waited for the curtain to rise on the premiere of the 2010 production of the Oberammergau Passion play.

This was a moment that I had been looking forward to for years. Soon I would see Caiaphas face to face! It would not be Caiaphas himself, of course, but a thirty-nine-year-old forester named Anton Burkhart.[1] Nevertheless for this afternoon and evening, Burkhart would play the high priest of Oberammergau, don the sacred vestments, and do his part to elevate Jesus from an itinerant Galilean Jew to the crucified son of God. How would he look? How would he act? And what would it feel like to watch him play his part in this Passion drama? In just a few minutes I would know.

By the time I arrived in Oberammergau, I had already come to know the high priest as well as one can know this shadowy figure from the past. To be precise, I knew next to nothing about the man himself, beyond the fact of his existence and his tenure as high priest in Jerusalem for two decades in the early part of the first century. What I did know were his numerous guises: as the wicked deicide, political strategist, ruthless statesman, and quavering underling. I had even worked my way through his successive Oberammergau incarnations, observing with interest as his medieval hatred for Jesus, still evident in 1960, softened, if only slightly, by 2010. Our relationship, however, was purely textual. Seeing Caiaphas would complete the picture of the high priest that had already begun to take shape in my mind.

The directors, costume designers, and actors[2] at Oberammergau did not have to invent their Caiaphas de novo, for there exists a long tradition of representing the physical Caiaphas, first in art, later in drama, and, most recently, in cinema, upon which they could draw. For the most part, this tradition encodes in visual form the assessment of Caiaphas expressed in most of the textual materials: he is a wicked deicide worthy only of contempt. But there are glimpses here and there of another set of impressions: Caiaphas as the awe-inspiring high priest who tends to the spiritual relationship between his people and the divine and for that reason is worthy of respect, perhaps even reverence.

IMAGES OF CONTEMPT

Visual Art

Caiaphas as wicked deicide is portrayed most vividly in visual art, beginning in the thirteenth century. Although it is the trial before Pilate that leads directly to Jesus' demise, medieval and Renaissance art is far more interested in the trial before the high priest.[3] Typically paintings, illuminations, or engravings will include not only Caiaphas and Jesus, but also Annas, other members of the Sanhedrin, and soldiers, usually in or in front of Caiaphas's palace. The scene is dynamic; Caiaphas is usually caught in the act of tearing his garment, as a member of the crowd, perhaps Annas's servant (see John 18:22), raises his hand to strike Jesus.[4]

Neither Josephus nor the New Testament provides any hints as to Caiaphas's appearance. This did not deter artists from depicting the high priest in ways that resonated with their audiences within their own contexts. Three elements of these paintings stand out: Caiaphas's costume, his body type, and his position vis-à-vis Jesus.

Paintings from the medieval and Renaissance periods generally do not relate in any way to the biblical descriptions of the high priest, either in his dress or his physical appearance. Instead of clothing him in his high-priestly vestments, they garb Caiaphas in a simple robe. While he is occasionally bareheaded, most often he wears one variation or another of the "Jew hat" that was forced upon the Jews in medieval European towns and villages from the thirteenth century onward.[5] As art historian Ruth Mellinkoff suggests, artists did not have a clear idea of what headgear was actually worn by the ancient high priests, and in the medieval period these confused ideas were confounded even more by the requirement in certain locales that Jews wear special hats. Mellinkoff notes that while Jews depicted in northern European art most often wear pointed hats, other types of head coverings—conical, dome-shaped, terminating in a knob or in a spoke—are also in evidence.[6]

Most surprising is the fact that in many paintings Caiaphas does not wear a "Jew hat" but rather a bishop's miter.[7] For Mellinkoff these paintings show that "whether or not something is true is often less important than whether or not

Giotto di Bondone (1266–1336). *Christ before Caiaphas.* Scrovegni Chapel, Padua, Italy © Scala / Art Resource, N.Y.

it is believed to be true. The fictitious Jewish miter stands as a vivid reminder of life's ironic twists. The use of the Christian bishop's miter as a Jewish miter represents one of those blazing paradoxes that move firmly and steadily through history until imagination becomes solid reality."[8] The satirical role of Caiaphas in the critique of ecclesiastical authority, as seen in the mystery plays and Sayers's radio plays, may also be a factor in the portrayal of the mitered high priest.

In contradiction to the biblical sources, which emphasize that the high priest had to be free of blemishes of any sort (Lev. 21:17–20), artists most often depict Caiaphas as physically grotesque and severely blemished.[9] This depiction is not unique to Caiaphas but is characteristic of the depiction of the wicked, especially the persecutors of Christ, that is, Jews, who are portrayed with ill-proportioned bodies, contorted postures, and unappealing facial features such as bulging or crossed eyes, bulbous noses, fleshy lips, dark skin, warts, and blemishes.[10] Thus for medieval audiences, these paintings immediately identify Caiaphas as a despicable deicide.

This identification is also emphasized by the positioning of the figures within these paintings. The relative positioning of Jesus and Caiaphas conveys not only the negative evaluation of Caiaphas but also his role in the Jesus narrative and his degraded spiritual status that contrasts so sharply with the exalted nature of his victim. A few examples will illustrate how these three aspects work together to evoke the Passion narrative, its spiritual significance for Christians, and Caiaphas's villainous nature.

The famous Florentine artist Giotto portrayed Caiaphas sitting down on his throne at the right-hand margin, tearing his green gown wide open, and showing his bare chest. He is looking at Christ, but Christ, who is center left, looks away.[11] Although Caiaphas is seated on a platform two steps up from the floor, Jesus takes up much more space, his head in the center of the image or just above it, while Caiaphas's head is just below. Caiaphas, ostensibly the spiritual leader of the people Israel, has his eyes fully on Jesus; Jesus, by contrast, has eyes for no one but God. These postures point up the contrast between the crassness of Caiaphas and the divinity of Jesus. This disjunction with regard to focus is significant as it falls precisely at the moment when Caiaphas has proclaimed Jesus guilty of blasphemy, that is, of claiming divinity. Caiaphas's garment is plain, far less remarkable than Jesus' red and blue robes; his bare head, unusual in comparison to other depictions of this same scene, contrasts with Jesus' haloed head.

In the *Green Passion* (1504)[12] by the German painter Albrecht Dürer, Caiaphas is grotesque in appearance, with a big round belly and a Jew's hat. His arm is outstretched, as he presumably asks Jesus, "Are you the Christ?" The *Small Passion* (1511) portrays Caiaphas one moment later, as the high priest tears his robe in response to Jesus' answer. He sits elevated, on a throne, and he is again grotesque in appearance but this time wearing an elaborate bishop's miter. As in Giotto's rendition, Jesus seems very tall, as he is eye to eye with Caiaphas although the latter is elevated on his throne.[13] In this painting, however, Caiaphas and Jesus are looking at one another, suggesting that the battle between them is of central importance to the moment being depicted and to the larger narrative in which it is embedded.

In the *Maiesta* (1308–11) by Duccio, on the other hand, it is Christ who looks at Caiaphas as the high priest looks away. Here Caiaphas's failure to meet Jesus' eyes does not bespeak spirituality and superiority, as in Giotto's work, but fear and perhaps even shame. Jesus is taller than Caiaphas, as in the work of Giotto

Duccio di Buoninsegna (c. 1260–1319). *Christ before Caiaphas*. Panel from the back of the Maesta altarpiece. Mueso dell'Opera Metropolitana, Siena, Italy. © Scala / Art Resource, N.Y.

and Dürer. He is wearing a shawl over his head, as are the other Jews; he has a long curly grey beard but is not grotesque.[14]

Such depictions are not limited to Italian art. The Salvin Hours, a late-thirteenth-century book of hours made in Oxford, includes an image of Christ standing before Caiaphas.[15] Christ is a "serene, pale, dignified and well-proportioned figure, whose physical form contrasts sharply with that of both Caiaphas and the arresting soldier, whose dark skins and grotesque physiognomy reveal their moral degeneracy."[16] This representation of Caiaphas is consistent with the overall visual code of medieval art in which Jews are identified by unattractive physical features.

One exception, and one of the most evocative paintings of Caiaphas, is *Christ before the High Priest* by the Dutch painter Gerrit van Honthorst. This painting shows Christ standing peacefully at the right-hand part of the painting. His head is inclined toward Caiaphas, who is sitting on the left, a large book, presumably of the scriptures, open before him. He is questioning Jesus, with his left elbow on the table, hand in the air, index finger pointing. The light in which Jesus is bathed presumably comes from candle that sits on the table between him and Caiaphas. It is curious, however, that no light shines upon the high priest. This suggests that the light may be symbolic of Christ's own inner light, and a play upon the imagery of light and darkness in the Gospel of John, in which Jesus is the light of the world (9:5) and the Jewish high priests, like all unbelievers, walk in darkness (9:46). In contrast to many other paintings of the trial, however, Caiaphas is not portrayed in a grotesque way, nor does he wear a vicious facial expression. He wears a fur-lined robe and hat rather than the "Jew hats" worn by the men on the periphery of the painting, who are presumably the other priests and elders at the trial. The mood is contemplative rather than excited or violent. Nevertheless Jesus is higher in the frame than Caiaphas, much higher, in fact, than in the paintings that use overtly anti-Jewish imagery to portray the high priest. Finally the serenity of Jesus' countenance creates a sense of peace and stillness around him, in contrast to the interrogative expression on the face of his interlocutor, whose emphatic expression is accentuated by the raised index finger of his left hand.[17]

The Salvin Hours. © The British Library Board

Gerrit van Honthorst (1590–1656). *Christ before the High Priest*, about 1617. National Gallery, London, Great Britain. © National Gallery, London / Art Resource, NY

Clothing Caiaphas in the garb of their era permitted artists to make a number of points. Caiaphas's clothing and, especially, his headgear often associated him directly with the Jews of the artist's own time and place and thereby conveyed the deicide message by alluding to the Jews' role in calling for Jesus' death and taking his blood upon themselves for future generations, as stated in Matthew and restated in numerous retellings thereafter. The postures of the figures declared that Caiaphas was responsible for Jesus' death, an event that served to honor and exalt Jesus as it shamed and diminished his high-priestly opponent. Caiaphas's posture and his positioning on a platform inside or in front of a palatial building also hinted at a critique of ecclesiastical authority, as in the mystery plays and Sayers's *Man Born to Be King*. Most of all these depictions would have evoked a sense of revulsion or disgust at the sight of Jesus' archenemy.

Mystery Plays

While there are no photos of the early mystery and Passion plays, the costume lists and instructions that have survived for some of these plays suggest that Caiaphas was often made to be physically grotesque, as in European art, and dressed in clothing similar to bishop's robes. Speaking of Caiaphas and Annas in the York mystery cycle, Pamela King notes:

> What they wore seems critical to the effect of their presentation. It seems unlikely, however that they appeared as exotic eastern figures in the early life of the cycle, only to turn into "bishops" when the, probably later, alliterative-verse pageant was written. On the other hand, there are numerous visual representations of them in headgear which would have singled them out as exotic. Whatever the precise visual codes, the confrontation between the by now adult artisan Christ and two representatives of ecclesiastical authority, that leaves the latter bemused, again contains potential for anti-clerical humour. The cycle, therefore, may in performance have situated the institutionalised Church as the butt of parody, as churchmen are wrong-footed by the people's Christ and his followers.[18]

According to the instructions accompanying the Ludus Coventriae play, Annas was to "show himself dressed as a bishop of the Old Law."[19] In the Wakefield play, Caiaphas wore a belted gown and a large episcopal ring, which would have looked strange except that he and Annas also wore miters and held crosiers. Robinson suggests that, as with well-dressed medieval English bishops, the robes worn by Caiaphas and Annas were probably dalmatics (long-sleeved tunics such as those still worn for liturgical purposes in the Catholic and some Protestant churches) under heavy cloaks with fur collars. Caiaphas was likely to have been corpulent, not only to conform to the conventional manner of

At Oberammergau, pre-2000. © Shoshana Walfish [original drawing]

depicting Jewish leaders but to fulfill the words of Job 15:25–27, in which those who "stretched out their hands against God, and bid defiance to the Almighty" have "covered their faces with their fat, and gathered fat upon their loins." As Robinson notes, "This fatness was sometimes taken literally and so the actors were dressed in ample padding."[20] By dressing the high priests in this way, the producers of the Wakefield play not only drew the analogy between the ancient ecclesiastical authorities and those of their own time, but also associated the corpulent Caiaphas with the fat "wicked one," that is, Satan.

Oberammergau Passion Play

In contrast to the mystery plays, the costuming for the Oberammergau Passion play in many productions did not imitate bishop's clothing but included a tunic and breastplate that resembled the descriptions of the high-priestly vestments in Exodus 28 and 39. Most distinctive, however, was the headgear, documented from the mid–eighteenth century until 1990.[21] This headgear was a cap with two hornlike protrusions at the very top. The effect unmistakably recalls the anti-Semitic stereotype of the horned Jew and thereby associates Caiaphas with the devil.

In giving visual expression to the deicide charge and contempt for Caiaphas and his fellows Jews, the Passion plays also acted as a vehicle for anti-Semitic views in their audiences. James Carroll recounts his own experience as a teenager in the 1950s, and the impression that Passion plays left upon him:

> For a long time I carried vivid images of Passion plays I associated with Germany, and I took them for renditions of a sacred truth. . . . As much as I remembered the Pharisees and the Sadducees, who trailed along behind, the High Priest with his turban, and the Rabbis with their robes and hooked noses, I remembered the Jews with their conical hats and unsubtle horns, which made them like devils. . . . I remembered those "Jews" waiving their knotted leather cords above their heads, to whip down on Jesus. As the tableaux passed before us, in my memory, the Passion was being read over loudspeakers. . . . When the chorus of "Jews" cried out their "Crucify him!" I understood. Jews. Jews all. Jews forever with blood on upon them and upon their children.[22]

The visual elements of the play, from props to costumes to the physical stature and appearance of the actors themselves, may well override the script in terms of the impact on the audiences, including their views on who is responsible for Jesus' death. For the 2000 production, the horned turban was eliminated, and Pharisees no longer so clearly differentiated from the other Jewish leader. Yet despite the best efforts of Christian Stückl and Otto Huber to eliminate the anti-Jewish elements of the script and costuming, the notion of Jewish blame did not disappear. As we have already seen, Franklin Sherman and James Shapiro both expressed some dismay at the scenes of Jesus' trial and crucifixion.[23]

Movies

Whereas Passion plays have an impact only on those who attend their performances, movies are able to reach huge, worldwide audiences, and they continue to do to an even greater extent through the global availability of DVDs and the Internet. The influence of Oberammergau on the early silent movies is evident in the costume of the high priest in the explicitly anti-Semitic German film *Der Galiläer*, in which Caiaphas wears a horned turban and flowing robes. The Caiaphas figure in DeMille's silent blockbuster, *The King of Kings*, is dressed in a similar manner, and in his physical appearance closely resembles the stereotype of medieval art. DeMille's Caiaphas is an obese and rather short man with a

The King of Kings (1927), dir. Cecil B. DeMille

The Miracle Maker (2000), dir. Derek W. Hayes

straggly beard and beady, intelligent, but crafty eyes. He wears a turban with horns, though these are less prominent in their appearance than in *Der Galiläer*. There is no doubt that he is the villain of the piece, as far as DeMille is concerned.

Later films, such as the 1961 epic *King of Kings* and Franco Zeffirelli's television miniseries *Jesus of Nazareth*, substitute a simple prayer shawl held in place by a small hat, and some attempt to re-create the priestly garb as described in the Hebrew scriptures. The Caiaphas of the 1988 film *The Last Temptation of Christ*, for example, wears breastplates adorned with the twelve stones symbolizing the twelve tribes and a turbanlike headdress (see Exod. 28:28–30, 39). In *Jesus Christ Superstar*, the high priest also wears a huge black hat, shaped like a dome. He wears the breastplate with the twelve stones but otherwise is barechested, in what appears to be a deliberate inversion of the elaborate robes of the high priest as described in the Hebrew Bible. This high priest, and the other priests and Pharisees of his entourage, are sinister vultures who apparently reside in the scaffolding above Jesus and his followers, just waiting to swoop down upon them. The anti-Jewish potential is clear.[24]

Perhaps the most authentic-looking Caiaphas, that is, the Caiaphas whose outfit corresponds most directly to the biblical description, is that of the 2000 animated film *The Miracle Maker*. In this film the high priest is dressed in his full regalia, in vivid color, including the bright stones on the breastplate and the brilliant blue of his robe. He looks rather fierce but certainly awe-inspiring.

In a number of other films, however, the high priest is characterized by unusual and disproportionately large headgear that is based not on scripture but on art. In Pasolini's *The Gospel According to Saint Matthew*, Caiaphas wears a large and tall black headcovering that looks like an inverted cone. These hats, as well as the distinctive headgear of the Pharisees and Sadducees, are modeled, quite precisely and rather ironically, after Christian figures in Piero della Francesca's painting *The Legend of the True Cross* (1452–66).[25]

As with the Passion plays, the high priest's appearance in film has the potential to convey anti-Semitism to the audience. In previews of the 2003 film *The Gospel of John*, Jewish audiences were dismayed at the dark color of the priestly robes.[26] While the costume designer did a significant amount of research in order to reproduce the costumes as accurately as possible, the color was darkened by the camera. Similar concerns were raised by the visual appearance of Caiaphas in Mel Gibson's *The Passion of the Christ*. Gibson's Caiaphas is dressed in elaborate robes; while he is by no means obese, his face is sinister and grows uglier and more disfigured as the film proceeds, thus conveying his guilt in visual form.[27]

The Gospel According to Saint Matthew (1964), dir. Pier Paolo Pasolini

Caiaphas is not a major presence in all Jesus films, however. Scorsese's *The Last Temptation of Christ*, like most films, has Jesus "cleanse" the Temple and challenge the authority of the high priest, but Caiaphas himself is not singled out visually. In this regard Scorsese's film differs significantly from the book upon which it is based. Kazantzakis's novel describes the high priest graphically, and with derision: "Beautiful, nimble adolescents were conveying a litter decorated in gold; and lying inside stroking his beard was a blubbery notable complete with clothes of silk, golden rings and a face greasy with easy living. 'Caiaphas, the high goat priest!' said the innkeeper. 'Hold your noses, lads. The first part of the fish to stink is the head.' He squeezed his nostrils and spat. 'He's on his way again to his garden to eat, drink and play with his women and pretty boys.'"[28] Later the narrator describes Caiaphas as "a fat bow-legged pygmy whose immense behind nearly scraped the ground."[29] These words cohere well with the impressions left by the visual representations discussed above. These images mock and debase Caiaphas, which after all are fitting treatment of the man who orchestrated Jesus' death on the cross and thereby epitomizes wickedness.

IMAGES OF RESPECT

Art and Literature

The painting by Honthorst hints at a different perspective on the high priest. While clearly depicting Christ's superiority over Caiaphas, this painting maintains a level of respect for the high priest; at least it not does not portray the latter as grotesque, satanic, and relentlessly hostile. Images of respect are more prevalent, however, in literary descriptions of the high priest than in visual art. Norman Mailer, for example, portrays Caiaphas as "a tall man, and his white beard was worthy of a prophet. He stood in the midst of the others and asked gently: 'Will you reply to my questions?'"[30] Sholem Asch describes the high priest as "a man of lofty stature, like his father-in-law; again like his father-in-law he wore his beard in the double-pointed style, but in his case the beard was more curled. On his head he carried a crown-like tiara, and on his forehead flashed a diadem. But most striking in his appearance were the heavy curls which flowed from under the tiara. They had been woven with such extraordinary art, so delicately and minutely, that the headdress resembled the product of an unimaginably fine loom."[31]

The narrator in Morley Callaghan's *A Time for Judas* is awestruck by the high priest:

> I stared and stared, full of wonder, dazzled by the majesty and power of this apparition from another, barbaric world. On his head was a tiara and under it a beautiful turban with the god's name inscribed on it. Golden bells encircled his ankle-length robe and when he moved the tinkling bells seemed to be calling. . . . I saw now in him the secret of his people. It was hidden in some of them, yet in them all just the same. They were all from this other world—Mary, Judas, the Galilean locked in that house, and Simon too—and in their secret security they didn't really care what I thought or felt, how anyone judged them.[32]

These descriptions pertain just as much to the high-priestly vestments as to the high priest himself. Even in the biblical period, these vestments inspired awe and reverence; otherwise it would be hard to understand why the book of Exodus devotes two full chapters to describing them (Exod. 28:2–29:1; 39:1–31).

Postbiblical Descriptions

The grotesque portrayal of the high priest also contrasts with the dazzling descriptions in ancient Jewish literature. The Letter of Aristeas (second century B.C.E.) describes the high priest Eleazar as follows:

> It was an occasion of great amazement to us when we saw Eleazar engaged on his ministry, and all the glorious vestments, including the wearing of the "garment" with precious stones upon it in which he is vested; golden bells surround the hem (at his feet) and make a very special sound. Alongside each of them are "teasels" adorned with "flowers," and of marvelous colors. He was clad in an outstandingly magnificent "girdle," woven in the most

beautiful colors. On his breast he wears what is called the "oracle," to which are attached "twelve stones" of different kinds, set in gold, giving the name of the patriarchs in what was the original order, each stone flashing its own natural distinctive color—quite indescribable. Upon his head he has what is called the "tiara," and upon this the inimitable "mitre," the hallowed diadem having in relief on the front in the middle in holy letters on a gold leaf the name of God, ineffable in glory. The wearer is considered worthy of such vestments at the services. (96–98)

After this enthusiastic description, the author describes the impact of the vested high priest on all who see him: "Their [the vestments] appearance makes one awe-struck and dumbfounded: A man would think he had come out of this world into another one. I emphatically assert that every man who comes near the spectacle of what I have described will experience astonishment and amazement beyond words, his very being transformed by the hallowed arrangement on every single detail" (Letter of Aristeas 99).[33]

From the same era, Ben Sira describes the high priest Simon, son of Onias, "who in his life repaired the house, and in his time fortified the temple" (Sirach 50:1) . The appearance of Simon was breathtaking:

[5] How glorious he was, surrounded by the people, as he came out of the house of the curtain. [6] Like the morning star among the clouds, like the full moon at the festal season; [7] like the sun shining on the temple of the Most High, like the rainbow gleaming in splendid clouds; [8] like roses in the days of first fruits, like lilies by a spring of water, like a green shoot on Lebanon on a summer day; [9] like fire and incense in the censer, like a vessel of hammered gold studded with all kinds of precious stones; [10] like an olive tree laden with fruit, and like a cypress towering in the clouds. [11] When he put on his glorious robe and clothed himself in perfect splendor, when he went up to the holy altar, he made the court of the sanctuary glorious. (Sirach 50:5–11)[34]

Enthusiasm for the vestments continued into the Roman period, at least according to the writings of Philo of Alexandria and Josephus. Philo described the vestments of the high priest in some detail (*Life of Moses* 2.109–16). But mere description was not enough; as he states, "I must not leave untold its meaning and that of its parts." For Philo the robe, colored violet, is an image of the air. The fact that it is floor-length symbolizes that the air "stretches down from the region below the moon to the ends of the earth, and spreads out everywhere" (2.118). The trimming of pomegranates, flowers, and bells is also significant. The flowers represent the earth and the pomegranates water, while the bells "represent the harmonious alliance of these two." The ephod is a symbol of heaven

(2.122). The twelve stones at the breast signify the zodiac (2.124). The fact that a turban, rather than a diadem, is set on the high priest's head expresses the judgment "that he who is consecrated to God is superior when he acts as a priest to all others, not only the ordinary laymen, but even kings" (2.131). The name of God on the gold plate above the turban means "that it is impossible for anything that is to subsist without invocation of Him; for it is His goodness and gracious power which join and compact all things" (2.132).[35]

In *War* 5.230–37 Josephus describes the appearance of the high priest at length, from his underclothing to his magnificent outer cloak, the bejewelled ephod, and the mitre. In *Jewish Antiquities* 3.179 he declares that "the hatred which men have for us and which they have so persistently maintained" would fall away if only others understood the vestments, along with the construction of the Tabernacle and the high-priestly vessels, as what they truly are—imitations and representations of the universe:

> The high priest's tunic . . . signifies the earth, being of linen, and its blue the arch of heaven, while it recalls the lightnings by its pomegranates, the thunder by the sound of its bells. His upper garment, too, denotes universal nature, which it pleased God to make of four elements; being further interwoven with gold in token, I imagine, of the all-pervading sunlight. . . . Furthermore, the head-dress appears to me to symbolize heaven, being blue; else it would not have borne upon it the name of God, blazoned upon the crown—a crown, moreover, of gold by reason of that sheen in which the Deity most delights. (*Ant.* 3:184–87).

These descriptions show the intermingling of the spiritual, the aesthetic, the symbolic, and the affective. At the same time as the high priest's appearance is integrally related to his spiritual role, it also creates powerful emotions of awe and wonder in the viewer. It is also interesting to note that for Josephus, the appearance of the high priest should create a positive rather than a negative view of Jews and Judaism.

Jewish Liturgy

Although written down centuries after the first Jewish revolt, Jewish sources such as the Mishnah and Talmud devoted considerable attention to the Temple, the sacrifices, and the high priesthood. Whereas rabbinic sources did not glorify or exalt the high priesthood (for example Mishnah Yoma 1:6), they continued to view the institution as relevant to Jewish spiritual life. Liturgical descriptions of the required sacrifices kept the memory of the Temple alive, and anticipation of the restoration of the Temple in the messianic days to come remain a part of traditional Jewish belief.

The most elaborate and moving example of the ongoing role of the high priesthood in Jewish liturgy is the Avodah service recited on the Day of Atonement, which describes the appearance, postures, and confession of the high priest on that day. The Avodah service originated in the early centuries after the destruction of the Temple and demonstrates the ongoing influence of the Temple and its ritual in the liturgical and spiritual life of the people. The recollection and poetic reenactment of the service may have served as strategies for coping with the loss of the sanctuary in an age when most Greco-Roman communities practiced some form of sacrifice.[36]

The Avodah service glorifies the priesthood, placing the high priest at the center not only of Judaism but of the cosmos. It also, however, creates a sense of identification with the high priest.[37] Congregants follow his preparation, including the donning and removing of the special vestments, and prostrate themselves at the moment that the high priest would have made his most exalted confessions. This ritual and liturgy not only keep the memory of the Temple and high priesthood alive, but also allow us, for a brief moment, to experience the glory and majesty of this solemn service and focus on the central role that the high priest played in the cosmic drama of human repentance and divine forgiveness that was central to the covenantal relationship between God and Israel.

Like the writers of the Second Temple period, the liturgist provides a vivid sense of the extraordinary power and beauty of the high priest's appearance:

> And so, how radiant was the Kohen Gadol [high priest] when he came out from the Holy of Holies in peace. Like the resplendent canopy spread over the vaults of heaven—was the appearance of the Kohen. Like the lightning that flashes from the effulgence of the angels—was the appearance of the Kohen.... Like the iridescent appearance of the rainbow in the midst of the cloud—was the appearance of the Kohen.... Like the splendor with which the Creator clothed the [first] beings—was the appearance of the Kohen. Like a rose set in a delightful garden was the appearance of the Kohen. Like a diadem placed upon the forehead of a king was the appearance of the Kohen. Like the grace that shines on the face of a bridegroom—was the appearance of the Kohen. Like the brightness reflecting from the [Kohen's] headdress—was the appearance of the Kohen. Like [Moses] in concealment imploring the King [for forgiveness]—was the appearance of the Kohen. Like the bright morning star shining in the eastern horizon—was the appearance of the Kohen.[38]

The liturgy also acknowledges the destruction of the Temple, which renders the congregants unable to view these splendid rituals for themselves: "Fortunate is the eye that saw all these; indeed, when the ear hears of it our soul grieves. Fortunate is the eye that saw our Temple amidst the rejoicing of our congregation, indeed, when the ear hears of it our soul grieves. . . . Fortunate is the eye that saw the *Kohen Gadol* clearly pronounce the Divine Name and cry out 'O God; indeed, when the ear hears of it our soul grieves.'"[39]

In addition to the Avodah service itself, there arose a sizeable corpus of liturgical poetry that can be dated to as early as the fourth century C.E. One of the striking features of these poems (*piyyutim* in Hebrew) is their elaborate and detailed glorification of the high priest; not only is he virtuous and heroic, pious and wise, but he also has tremendous physical stature and strength, all of which are needed in order to perform the sacrifices properly. One poem describes the great strength of the high priest, who was "wrapped in a blue robe, / as bright as the firmament, His rounded arms filled the sleeves. . . . His strong body / filled his tunic, / doubled and woven / as far as the sleeves."[40] Another likens the high priest to an angel;[41] the poet marvels how "his stature / rose to the height of a cedar / when he was fit with embroidered garments / to ornament his body"[42] and suggests that the vestments not only represent Israel to God but also arouse God's compassion for his people on the Day of Judgment so that God will dispel the forces of evil.[43] This literature testifies to the persistence of the prestige of the priesthood despite the ambivalence toward the priesthood expressed in rabbinic sources.[44]

Who would the Caiaphas of Oberammergau be, the contempt-worthy deicide or the awe-inspiring spiritual leader?

FACE TO FACE WITH CAIAPHAS

At 2:30 P.M. sharp, the dignified narrator led the choir out onto the stage and introduced the first tableau vivant: the expulsion of Adam and Eve from Paradise. As the tableau disappeared, a crowd gathered on the stage, and a young man riding a live donkey was led to the front of the stage, to the shouts of "Hosanna!" "Praised be the anointed one!" Amid the hubbub a group of elaborately dressed men strode on from stage left, led by a tall man dressed in a long white robe and wearing a very tall, white, conical hat.[45] Caiaphas at last!

I was relieved to see that neither Caiaphas's costuming nor his headgear reproduced the anti-Jewish stereotypes of European art and earlier plays and movies. The color of his garments even recalled the white linen vestments worn by the high priest during the most solemn moment of the liturgical calendar, the entry into the Holy of Holies on the Day of Atonement. If one tried hard, one could see this costuming as an allusion to the atoning death of Jesus, the "great high priest" (Heb. 4:14), on the cross; it is unlikely, however, that many in the audience would have made this connection.

At Oberammergau 2010. © Shoshana Walfish [original drawing]

Caiaphas's behavior in the opening scenes also steered clear of anti-Jewish stereotypes. Indeed it was evident that the high priest, for all of his power, was in an unenviable situation, caught between the loud demands of most of his council members and the forceful command of his Roman overlord, to whom he bowed with exaggerated obsequiousness (holding lightly onto his tall hat so that it would not fall off his head). That Jesus was a problem for Caiaphas was not in doubt; not only did the Galilean's activities threaten the status quo, but his behavior and the claims made by his followers thoroughly irritated Caiaphas and his fellow priests. But it was a problem that the high priest preferred to handle internally. So far so good, I thought, as the first part ended, and the theater emptied out for the dinner break.

The second half began at 8 P.M. It was dusk. The rainy, cold weather outside complemented the somber mood on stage as the drama moved inexorably toward its dramatic conclusion.[46] My optimism about a new Caiaphas, free of anti-Semitic stereotypes and with a more nuanced stance toward Jesus, waned along with the daylight.

Three moments stand out. The first is Caiaphas's dramatic entry onto the stage to preside over Jesus' trial. Rather than stride in with his fellow council members, as he did at other points in the play, Caiaphas is carried in ceremoniously on a litter (act 6, scene 2). This has the effect of elevating him from Pilate's lackey to a powerful authority who will bend the Roman governor's will to his own. The second is his incitement of the crowd. By this activity he demeans himself, for how can someone who is the supreme religious authority of his people stoop so low as to persuade them to call for the death of a fellow Jew at the hands of the despised Roman overlord? The third, and by far the most powerful, moment did not involve Caiaphas alone, but the entire crowd, now persuaded to cry out for the release of Barabbas and the crucifixion of Jesus. Hearing and seeing a crowd of nine hundred people shout "crucify him, crucify him," repeatedly, in unison, and in German no less, was both shocking and frightening, as it suddenly and unexpectedly evoked my parents' stories of their Holocaust experiences that had been part of my consciousness as long as I can remember. I felt, absurdly, that it was me the crowd was after, and that I had better run or disappear through the floor before I was caught. My rational self quickly overcame this visceral reaction, and I derived some ironic amusement from the fact that in momentarily seeing myself as the object of the crowd's fury, I could finally identify with Jesus himself. Despite the directors' best intentions, the attempt to place primary blame on Pilate foundered, eclipsed by the visual and aural elements of the production as the tragedy moved forward to its climax. By the time the curtain fell, I was anxious to leave the theater and go out into the cold, rainy night.[47]

Yet in retrospect the harsh moments have faded, and I am left with the sense of having enjoyed the play for what it was: a spectacle that meant different things to its many different viewers. What redeemed the experience for me was being in Oberammergau in person. Oberammergau makes a deep impression not only because of its history and its earnestness, but because of the integration of the play into the everyday life of the village and therefore into the experience of the visitor as well. To run into "Jesus" and his girlfriend (who wore an "I love Jesus" button) at a local restaurant, or to stand in the supermarket checkout line behind "Pilate" and his young son, humanized the Passion play itself. "Caiaphas," or rather, Anton Burkhart, proved to be an engaging young man who had clearly given much thought to the role and to its contribution to a visually compelling production that could be acceptable to the traditionalists within the village as well as to the critics from outside. Christian Stückl and Otto Huber are passionate about the play and thoughtful and articulate about their struggle to achieve their vision, which includes the portrayal of a fully Jewish Jesus and a drama that is free of anti-Semitic stereotypes. I could see that

Author, with Anton Burkhart. © Barry Walfish

walking the fine line between tradition and reform, strength and subservience is not an easy matter. The easy access to the actors and directors and the charm and friendliness of the villagers provided a positive context within which to consider the Passion play as such. While my personal experiences in Oberammergau did not neutralize the negative emotions that were at various points aroused by the production, they made me optimistic that at least some in this Bavarian village were working hard toward a situation in which maintaining the tradition of the Passion play did not also entail perpetuating the deicide charge. If that goal has not yet been reached, there is hope that the future productions will continue the significant moves in that direction that were begun in 1990.

Coming face to face with the actor playing Caiaphas is of course not the same as facing the high priest himself. But given the elusive nature of the man, and the numerous layers of tradition, image, and narrative that have surrounded him, an encounter with the man who inhabits Caiaphas's consciousness for six hours a day, through a year of rehearsals and five months of performances, is as close as one can get.

CONCLUSION

The attempts to visualize the high priest Caiaphas, whether in words, in still images, on stage, or on film, lead in two different directions. A few focus on his cultic role, the magnificence of his vestments, the grandeur of his presence, and the profound spiritual role that his activities played in mediating the important processes of communal repentance and divine forgiveness that allowed Israel to remain in its covenantal relationship with God. These representations not only depict this role but also express the awe and amazement experienced by those who witnessed the high priest or imagined themselves doing so.

Most images of Caiaphas, however, like most of the histories, novels, plays, and movies that we have surveyed, depict an overbearing and often grotesque or buffoonish character, so threatened by and obsessed with Jesus that he will go to any length to have him killed. While many of these images, such as those that portray Caiaphas tearing his garments, are based on scripture, they imply a narrative that goes far beyond any scriptural evidence and a negative evaluation of Caiaphas's character that does not emerge from the primary sources. For the most part, despite some differences, the narrative and visual traditions about Caiaphas are consistent and show little fundamental variation. One can only conclude that this imaginary Caiaphas has served, and perhaps continues to serve, an important and even essential role in the imagination: as the implacable foe defeated by the son of God even as he celebrates the success of his evil plans.

AFTERWORD

> The evil that men do lives after them,
> The good is oft interred with their bones.
> *Julius Caesar,* act 3, scene 2

The search for Caiaphas has two opposing trajectories. One, the quest for the Caiaphas of history, is a journey from flesh to bones. The historical narratives about the death of Jesus, the fruits of historical Jesus research, present a Caiaphas who acts out of a range of political, religious, and personal motivations and persuades his colleagues and his superior, Pilate, to play their parts. Investigating the sources of these narratives, however, is akin to throwing water on the Wicked Witch of the West and watching her melt away until nothing is left but her hat and shoes. Peeling away the layers of narrative and tradition takes us to the core first-century sources, which, however, reveal almost nothing about Caiaphas except the facts of his existence, his service as high priest, and perhaps the ossuary in which his bones may have rested.[1]

The other, the quest for Caiaphas's *Nachleben,* is a journey from bones to flesh, a resurrection or, perhaps, an incarnation story that tells of Caiaphas's adventures in literature, art, drama, and film from the early centuries of Christianity's development to the present day. It is in this story that Caiaphas truly comes alive, in both body and soul. A stroll through any major art gallery, a visit to Oberammergau, or an evening spent watching a Jesus movie will let us see the high priest, often—but not always—as a corpulent, even grotesque old man with a straggly beard, hook nose, blotchy complexion, and a sly, even devilish grin, wearing robes and an elaborate head covering with hornlike protrusions. If we want to know what Caiaphas thought of Jesus, Pilate, or his father-in-law, we have only to open the pages of *The Nazarene, King Jesus,* or any other of the hundreds of Jesus novels in which the high priest, whether gleefully or unhappily, sets in motion the chain of events that leads Jesus to the cross.

The historical Caiaphas and the Caiaphas of imagination can be discussed apart from one another, but in reality they are inseparable. All attempts, from the Gospels to the most recent life-of-Jesus research, to determine what the "real" Caiaphas thought, said, and did about Jesus require the same imaginative activity as the representations of Caiaphas in art, fiction, drama, and film. That includes the attempts made, or resisted, within the pages of this book too. As we have seen, Gospel writers and modern historians alike must fill in the gaps and connect the dots in order to arrive at a coherent and plausible narrative in which events are causally linked with one another and make sense in the larger context of first-century Judaea. The resulting narratives have much in common with the fictional stories that are guided by the same narrative imperative.

There is a narrative logic to assigning Caiaphas a prominent place in the story of Jesus' Passion. Stories need villains, without whom there would be no heroes. In the Jesus story, the hero, Jesus, dies, and the villain, Caiaphas, is the agent of his death. The hero is the son of God, and the villain is associated with the devil. There is also a certain theological logic to this scenario: according to the Gospels and subsequent Christian theology, the crucifixion was a necessary part of the divine plan for salvation. For if Jesus were not crucified, he would not, according to Christian faith and the Gospels, have been resurrected, in which case there would be no Christianity. From this point of view, to the extent that Caiaphas helped to move this plot along, he is a crucial player without whom Christianity as such would not exist. Mark and Matthew say as much, as it is the fulfillment of prophecy, and John too, as an interpretation of what Caiaphas is reported to have said to the Pharisees and elders in John 11.

Although Caiaphas is the focus of attention in these pages, he is a secondary character in almost all other works in which he appears. For most Caiaphas is important not for his own sake but because he can be drafted to fill in an important causal gap in *Jesus'* story: how and why did it come to pass that a Roman governor ordered the crucifixion of a Galilean itinerant? Those who see Jesus primarily as the son of God sent to redeem the world may view Caiaphas as a near-demonic figure who carries out Satan's determined but ultimately unsuccessful plan to undermine God's will for humankind. Those who see Jesus as the champion of the poor and oppressed lower classes may consider Caiaphas the wealthy and powerful Sadducee who was as much an instrument of oppression as the Roman Empire itself. Indeed, perhaps because of the scarcity of historical evidence, Caiaphas is a plastic figure who can be shaped in many different ways, for satire, for tragedy, and to suit many variations on the basic Jesus story. Yet he remains problematic, at best the pawn of Pilate and at worst the devil incarnate.

There are a number of threads that run through all of these depictions, from the historical to the fictional. The most basic is the role of Caiaphas as Christ-killer, a role that defines him as the villain of the piece, whether he is motivated by Satan, stuck between a rock (his fellow Jews) and a hard place (the Roman governor), or caught up in machinations among the high-priestly family into which he married. Caiaphas can conveniently stand in for the targets of satire, criticism, and ridicule of later times and other places, in particular, ecclesiastical authorities such as the clerics of wartime Britain or the Catholic priests of late-twentieth-century Quebec. The imagined Caiaphas becomes a fact of history when he is used as a vehicle for anti-Jewish sentiment that under certain conditions can be used as justification for anti-Semitic attitudes and behaviors, as was indeed the case with regard to the medieval Passion play.

CAIAPHAS AND ANTI-SEMITISM

Whereas my interest in Caiaphas began as a purely historical one, it soon became infused with concern for the way in which this figure has been constructed and used as an expression of anti-Jewish theologies. Piecing together the study of his resurrection has been a fascinating exercise that has taken me into many places where I would not have thought to find this first-century high priest. At the same time, it has been a sobering exercise that has forced me to confront the persistence of a negative stereotype and of hatred of Jews as it was intertwined with Christian theology, exegesis, and imagination over so many centuries. One detects it, even if only faintly and, I would like to believe, inadvertently, in some of the contemporary fictional and historical narratives as well.

Of course Caiaphas should not bear the full burden of responsibility for anti-Semitic ideologies. Even if he were omitted from all narratives about Jesus, anti-Semitism would still exist. Nevertheless his depictions not only express but also perpetuate anti-Semitic stereotypes such as the deicide charge and the inordinate love of money and power. Obvious as this seems, it has not always been easy to make the case. In discussions with colleagues, I have often been told that Caiaphas should not be identified with the Jews, nor they with him. As a collaborator with Rome, Caiaphas stood apart from his people. For this reason negative portraits of Caiaphas as a wicked deicide are not anti-Semitic and should not be read as such. This point is sometimes bolstered with historical arguments: ordinary Jews of Jesus' own time disliked, distrusted, or repudiated the high priesthood; as a member of the ruling class, Caiaphas did not represent the views of the populace; as a Sadducee he was more Hellenized and therefore more sympathetic to Greco-Roman culture than the rest of the population.

These are not unreasonable points; first-century Jewish society was characterized by considerable religious, economic, and social diversity, in which tensions and factionalism were inevitable. Nevertheless for better or for worse, the high priest was seen by Jews—not only residents of Judaea but elsewhere, including the Diaspora—as well as by non-Jews as the head and therefore representative of the people Israel. Ultimately, however, what matters is not how Caiaphas would have appeared to the Jews of his time, but how he has been construed by Christian audiences who are the primary consumers of the high priest's depictions in all historical periods and in all media. As a Jew I wince at nearly every portrayal of Caiaphas; where the high priest is, the charge of deicide is not very far behind.

If, as Collingwood believes, the creation of historical knowledge is the perpetuation of past acts in the present, each narrative in which Caiaphas plots Jesus' death in some way recrucifies Jesus—and victimizes those who believe in him—all over again. At the same time, the use of anti-Semitic images in the construction of Caiaphas also serves to reinforce, reinscribe, and perpetuate those same images in the present, even when that is not the intention.

In the absence of truly compelling and unequivocal evidence to the contrary, let us remember Caiaphas kindly. Let us acknowledge that neither the Evangelists nor Josephus knew exactly what he did or did not do during his long tenure as high priest. The only thing that we know for certain is that every year on Yom Kippur he would don his vestments and enter the Holy of Holies to atone for his sins and the sins of the entire people, thereby renewing Israel's covenantal relationship with God. Let us allow him to complete his prayers, emerge unharmed from the Holy of Holies, and remove and fold his vestments. Then let us rebury him in his shroud, replace his bones in his ossuary. From here on in, may he rest in peace.

NOTES

PREFACE

1. Bond, *Caiaphas*, vii. The full-length study by Rainer Metzner, *Caiphas: Der Hohepriester jenes Jahres Hosepriester*, appeared in 2010 after I had submitted the final draft of the present manuscript.

INTRODUCTION

1. Cf. Matthew 26:33–34; Mark 14:29–30; John 13:37–38. All translations of biblical passages are from the New Revised Standard Version (1989) unless otherwise noted.
2. Cf. Matthew 26:69–72; Mark 14:66–72; Luke 22:54–62; John 18:25–27.
3. The image has Jesus in the center, his hands tied in front of him, as he is being mocked by three men, none of whom is the high priest (see Matthew 26:27).
4. Whether the historical Caiaphas ever lived at this spot, however, is not known. Contrary to the company that created my Jerusalem map, the archaeologists by and large are unconvinced by this attribution, as they are by many of the other sites associated with New Testament personalities. Indeed there is a nearby site, beneath a fifteenth-century Armenian monastery, for which the same claim is made. Broshi, "Excavations in the House of Caiaphas," 57. For a description of this site, though not its association with Caiaphas, see Broshi, "Excavations on Mount Zion." For detailed discussion and bibliography, see Bond, *Caiaphas*, 154–59. The earliest traditions, which associate Caiaphas's palace with Mount Zion, stem from the fourth century. Given the compact size of the Old City, however, this uncertainty is not overly consequential; whether or not we can identify Caiaphas's abode, we know that he, like other high priests of his era, served in Herod's Temple, the one major site whose location is not in question. Surely he would have lived in the vicinity of, even if not precisely at, a site nearby.
5. The bones have been buried in the cemetery on the Mount of Olives, and the ossuary itself is housed at the Israel Museum. Charlesworth, *Jesus and Archaeology*, 327.
6. In favor of the identification of the ossuary with the high priest are Reich, "Ossuary Inscriptions of the Caiaphas Family"; Reich, "Ossuary Inscriptions from the Caiaphas Tomb"; Reich, "Ossuary Inscriptions from the 'Caiaphas' Tomb"; Flusser, "To Bury Caiaphas." More skeptical is Horbury, "'Caiaphas' Ossuaries."
7. References to, citations of, and quotations from the works of Josephus are from the Loeb Classical Library edition unless otherwise noted. Another excellent resource for translations and commentary can be found at http://pace.mcmaster.ca/york/york/index.htm (accessed June 21, 2010). This site is closely connected to the Brill Josephus Project, edited by Steve Mason, which has published twelve volumes to date. The volume that includes the Caiaphas material (*Ant.* 18) has not yet been published.
8. Critical discussion and analysis of the "state of the question" is the subject of Munslow, *Narrative and History*.

9. Collingwood, *Idea of History*, 233.
10. Ibid., 247.
11. Ibid., 218.
12. Ibid., 248.
13. Ibid., 218.
14. Ibid., 282.
15. Ibid., 245–46.
16. Ibid., 246.
17. See also White, *Metahistory*.
18. White, "Value of Narrativity," 9.
19. Ibid., 13.
20. Piovanelli, personal communication, June 3, 2010.
21. Reinhartz, *Jesus of Hollywood*, 25–29.
22. Ibid., 236–37, 248–50.
23. Collingwood, *Idea of History*, 218.

24. For those who are unfamiliar with the field, useful discussions of the authorship and dating of the Gospels and other New Testament books can be found in any standard New Testament introduction. See, for example, Brown, *Introduction*.

25. Anti-Judaism is often distinguished from anti-Semitism, on the grounds that anti-Judaism refers to negative attitudes or behavior toward the beliefs and practices associated with Jews, and those who practice them, whereas *anti-Semitism* is a racial term, coined in the nineteenth century, that refers to negative attitudes or behavior toward those who are identified by others as belonging to the Jewish people. This is a useful distinction to a point; it is clear, for example, that the diatribes in the Gospels against Jews or Jewish groups who refused to believe in Jesus (e.g., Matt. 23; John 8:44) are anti-Jewish rather than anti-Semitic, but in numerous expressions of the deicide charge the difference is not particularly meaningful.

26. One example is the annual production that takes place in Jaffna, Sri Lanka. See "Actors Draw on War Experience for Passion Play," *CathNews India*, March 26, 2010, http://www.cathnewsindia.com/2010/03/26/actors-draw-on-war-experience-for-passion-play/.

CHAPTER 1: CAIAPHAS IN CONTEXT

1. Mason, *Josephus*, 180.
2. Ibid., 188.
3. Ibid., 185.
4. Ibid., 186.
5. Ibid.
6. For a detailed discussion of each high priest, see VanderKam, *From Joshua to Caiaphas*.
7. On Josephus and history, see Mason, "Contradiction or Counterpoint?"; Price, "Provincial Historian"; Villalba i Varneda, *Historical Method*; Bilde, *Flavius Josephus*.
8. VanderKam, *From Joshua to Caiaphas*, 426.
9. Bond, *Pontius Pilate*, 19.
10. Catchpole, *Trial of Jesus*, 249.
11. Schwartz, *Studies in the Jewish Background*, 198–99.
12. Smallwood, "High Priests," 22.
13. Bond, *Pontius Pilate*, 19; see also Smallwood, "High Priests," 22.
14. Borg and Crossan, *Last Week*, 41.
15. Smallwood, "Date of the Dismissal." See the useful summary of this issue in VanderKam, *High Priests*, 432–34.

16. Bond, *Caiaphas*, ekes as much information as is humanly possible from the meager hints in the primary sources, but as she admits, any information about his family, the source of their wealth, and other personal matters is highly speculative.

17. See the *Narrative of Joseph of Arimathea*, chapter 1. For discussion see chapter 3.

18. Bond, *Caiaphas*, 5.

19. Reich, "Ossuary Inscriptions of the Caiaphas Family." See also Price, "Burial Cave." For discussion of the name, see Brody and Schwartz, "Caiaphas and Cantheras."

20. VanderKam, *High Priests*, 447; Kokkinos, *Herodian Dynasty*, 219–21.

21. Abusch, "Sacrifice in Mesopotamia"; Petropoulou, *Animal Sacrifice*.

22. See Exodus 25–31; 33:7–10; 35–40. Discussions of the Tabernacle can be found in commentaries on Exodus, such as Propp, *Exodus 19–40*, and Sarna, *Exodus*, as well as in numerous monographs: see, for example, Myung Soo Suh, *Tabernacle*.

23. There is a vast literature on the Temple and sacrificial system in ancient Israel. See, for example, Anderson, *Sacrifices and Offerings*. For a recent critical reconsideration, see Klawans, *Purity, Sacrifice*.

24. In *Antiquities* 13.288 Josephus recounts that John Hyrcanus, a Hasmonean king and high priest, was criticized by the Pharisee Eleazer because of an apparently false rumor that his mother, wife of the high priest Simon, had been taken captive in war under Antiochus Epiphanes IV and therefore could not have been the legitimate wife of a high priest. Rabbinic literature also records the behavior of a deviant high priest, Joshua b. Gamaliel (63–65 C.E.), who, contrary to the law, was betrothed to a widow of the house of Boethus (Mishnah Yevamot 6.4).

25. For the portrayal of Caiaphas as grotesque in appearance, see chapter 9.

26. For detailed exposition see Milgrom, *Leviticus 1–16*.

27. For further details see Jeremias, *Jerusalem*, 148–52.

28. Bond, *Pontius Pilate*, 17.

29. Sloyan, *Jesus on Trial*, 12.

30. See Mantel, *Studies in the History*, and Rocca, *Herod's Judaea*, 270–71. Rocca suggests that the Synedrion/Sanhedrin was created in the Herodian period as a religious court and continued that way until 70. Nevertheless it evolved after the death of King Herod, when the Sadducees came to dominate what had previous been a Pharisaic institution.

31. Schürer, *History of the Jewish People*, 218–23; Winter, *On the Trial*, 74–90.

32. Bartlett, "Zadok and His Successors."

33. Ezra 6 implies that sacrifices were resumed when the Persian conquerors of the Babylonian Empire permitted the exiles to return to Jerusalem and to rebuild the Temple. The transition from the First Temple to the Second Temple period so briefly summarized here is the subject of numerous scholarly studies. For discussion of the Persian period, see Carter, *Emergence of Yehud*; Kaufmann, *History of the Religion*.

34. Himmelfarb, *Kingdom of Priests*, 6.

35. Goodman, *Ruling Class of Judaea*, 31.

36. Although Tacitus and Josephus refer to the equestrian governors who administered Judaea from 6 until 66 as procurators, this title is incorrect for the period 6–41, as shown by a Latin inscription found in Caesarea that refers to Pilate as a prefect. This evidence is congruent with other epigraphic sources that similarly use the title prefect for governors in this period. The term *procurator* is correct for governors after 44. Smallwood, *Jews under Roman Rule*, 144. The first physical proof linking to Pilate was found in 1961, when a hunk of limestone was found in the Roman theater at Caesarea Maritima, the capital of the prefecture of Judaea, bearing a dented commitment by Pilate of a Tiberieum. This commitment

mentions that he was "ECTVS IUDA" (typically read as *praefectus iudaeae*), that is, prefect/superintendent of Judaea. See Vardaman, "New Inscription"; Bond, *Pontius Pilate*.

37. Smallwood, "High Priests," 15–16.
38. VanderKam, *High Priests*, 487–90.
39. Schwartz, "On Two Aspects"; Kugler, "Priesthood at Qumran."
40. See Exodus 39:1–31 for a detailed description of the vestments. Numerous attempts have been made to depict the vestments; one example can be found at Martyn Barrow, "The High Priest and His Garments," http://www.domini.org/tabern/highprst.htm (accessed July 2, 2009). Nevertheless there are numerous issues that are unclear, such as the precise color of the linen garments and the number of times that the high priest was to change his garments on the Day of Atonement. For detailed discussion see Sanders, *Judaism*, 92–102.
41. Ibid., 326.
42. Winter, *On the Trial*, 24.
43. For discussion see chapter 3.

CHAPTER 2: CAIAPHAS IN THE NEW TESTAMENT

1. *Pace* Bauckham, *Gospels for All Christians*, it is reasonable to assume that the Gospels were written for specific communities and reflected, at least in an indirect way, the concerns and theologies of those groups. For detailed critique of Bauckham's view, see Reinhartz, "Gospel Audiences."
2. Collingwood, *Idea of History*, 247, 218.
3. Matthew 26:3, 57; Luke 3:2; John 11:49, 18:13, 14, 24, 28.
4. Matthew 26:3, 51, 57–58, 62–63, 65; Mark 2:26, 14:47, 53–54, 60–61, 63, 66; Luke 22:50; John 11:49, 51; 18:13, 15–16, 19, 22, 24, 26.
5. The most detailed discussion of the Passion narrative is Brown, *Death of the Messiah*.
6. Marcus, *Mark 1–8*, 40–45.
7. Numerous theories have been put forward with regard to the identity of this young man. He is variously seen as a disciple, an angel, a symbol of Jesus, the Christian undergoing initiation, or even those who desert Jesus in time of need. See, for example, Donahue, *Gospel of Mark*, 417.
8. For a range of views, see Collins, "Charge of Blasphemy"; Bock, *Blasphemy and Exaltation*.
9. Marcus notes that "Son of the Blessed One" is a circumlocution for God; rabbinic traditions refer to God as the Holy One Blessed Be He. Marcus, *Mark 8–16*, 1004.
10. Collins, "Charge of Blasphemy."
11. Note that Joseph was not really dead, though Jacob thought he was. See Genesis 37:31–36.
12. Winter, *On the Trial*, 38–39.
13. Marcus, *Mark 8–16*, 1017.
14. Winter, *On the Trial*, 38–39.
15. Schrenk, "Archiereus"; Brown, *Death of the Messiah*, 1425–27.
16. Winter, *On the Trial*, 50. Others suggest that the reason for Mark's ignorance is his use of an early Passion source in which the high priest was not named. See Theissen, *Gospels in Context*, 172–73.
17. Fitzmyer, *Gospel According to Luke*, 1456.
18. Brown, *Gospel According to John*, 1:821.
19. Bond, *Caiaphas*, 103–8; the quotation is on p. 108.
20. Ibid., 105.
21. In the parallel section, Mark has chief priests, scribes, and elders (for example, Mark 14:53, 15:1).

22. Brown, *Death of the Messiah*, 119n3.

23. Bond says that the contrast is developed further in the continuation of the trial sequence, "which continues to name the high priest as Caiaphas." It must be noted, however, that there is in fact no further reference to the high priest by name in the continuation of the story. The only two Matthean references, as discussed above, are 26:3 and 57. Bond, *Caiaphas*, 126.

24. Ibid.

25. Ibid., 193n23.

26. Ibid., 126.

27. A similar argument has been made with regard to Qumran. The question as to whether the Qumran community saw themselves in fact as a new temple replacing the old one is a matter of debate, but at least the association is made explicit in the scrolls. For discussion see Haber, "Metaphor and Meaning."

28. Bond, *Caiaphas*, 124.

29. Fitzmyer, *Gospel According to Luke*, 2:1456.

30. On the complex question of the inclusion of Annas, see Brown, *Death of the Messiah*, 411–17.

31. Bond, *Caiaphas*, 112.

32. Fitzmyer, *Gospel According to Luke*, 1:458.

33. Winter, *On the Trial*, 44–45.

34. Bond, *Caiaphas*, 111–12.

35. Brown, *Death of the Messiah*, 463.

36. Bond, *Caiaphas*, 116.

37. Ibid., 118.

38. Brown, *Gospel According to John*, 1:439. Winter suggests that "our holy place" refers to the official status, position, or rank that Caiaphas and other members of the Sanhedrin held under the constitution granted by Rome to the representatives of the Jewish nation. This interpretation seems unlikely, however. Winter, *On the Trial*, 54.

39. Winter, *On the Trial*, 55.

40. See Schwartz, *Studies in the Jewish Background*, 31–34; Gray, *Prophetic Figures*, 112–44; Miller, "Whom Do You Follow?"

41. Warren Carter sees in 11:49–52 a comment about the imperial context in which the action takes place. He notes that this passage stresses the "oft-missed" antithesis between believing in Jesus and a putative Roman response. "Caiaphas is concerned with loyalty to Jesus because it threatens the imperial status quo. Just how Caiaphas perceives this threat is not at this point made clear: the only reason Caiaphas gives is the hypothetical declaration 'Everyone will believe in him.' We might guess that this means that loyalty to one who as God's agent has demonstrated life-giving practices and declared them to be sanctioned by God is more 'attractive' or life-giving than the death-bringing, destructive ways of empire that Caiaphas, Rome's ally, names." Carter, *John and Empire*, 272. This explanation is opaque, but in any case it is worth noticing that it is not Caiaphas but the other leaders who express this fear and make the connection between belief and the Roman response.

42. Brant, *Dialogue and Drama*, 45. On the scapegoat see chapter 2.

43. Hakola, "Counsel of Caiaphas." A sacrificial interpretation coheres with John 1:29, which refers to Jesus as "the Lamb of God who takes away the sin of the world" (see also John 1:36), which may be an allusion to the Passover sacrifice. This interpretation is supported by the fact that Jesus is condemned to death and crucified on the day that the Passover lambs are slaughtered (19:14) and is offered a sponge of sour wine on a hyssop branch (19:29), recalling the hyssop that saved the Israelites in Egypt from the tenth plague, the slaughter of the

firstborn (Exod. 12:22). Jesus' legs are left unbroken, as a fulfillment of Exodus 12:46; cf. John 19:32–36.

44. Cf. Leviticus 16:5; Wick, *Urchristlichen Gottesdienste*, 329.
45. Bond, *Caiaphas*, 132.
46. Ibid., 133.
47. Ibid.
48. On the "I am" sayings, see Ball, "*I Am*."
49. Culpepper, *Anatomy of the Fourth Gospel*, 145.
50. Reinhartz, "Jesus as Prophet."
51. Bond, *Caiaphas*, 138. Caiaphas and Annas are presumably part of the group of chief priests and officers that brings Jesus before Pilate (18:35; 19:6, 15). Neither man, however, is mentioned by name; they have once again taken their place among Jesus' enemies.
52. Note that in the synoptic Gospels, the arrest and interrogation take place on the first night of Passover, that is, after the festival has begun, whereas in John these events take place on the day before Passover begins.
53. Bond, *Caiaphas*, 136.
54. Ibid., 138.
55. Brant, *Dialogue and Drama*, 193.
56. See the introduction to Fitzmyer, *Acts of the Apostles*, 49.
57. The question of whether Johannine Christians experienced an expulsion from the synagogue remains highly debated in Johannine studies. The case in favor of this view is best put by Martyn, *History and Theology*. For counterarguments see Reinhartz, "Johannine Community."
58. Others in John do accuse Jesus of blasphemy. See John 10:33, in which "the Jews" clarify that "it is not for a good work that we are going to stone you, but for blasphemy, because you, though only a human being, are making yourself God."
59. Schürer, *History of the Jewish People*, vol. 2, 232.
60. Bond, *Caiaphas*, 141–43.
61. Winter, *On the Trial*, 33–35.
62. Borg and Crossan, *Last Week*, 39.
63. Bond, "Discarding," 193. See also Köstenberger, "Destruction," 215.
64. Bond, "Discarding," 183.
65. An opinion shared by Sanders, *Jesus and Judaism*, 298.
66. See Sanders, *Jesus and Judaism*, 310, who argues that the primary role that the Gospels attribute to the chief priests likely reflects historical reality.

CHAPTER 3: CAIAPHAS IN EARLY CHRISTIAN IMAGINATION

1. The category "Christianity" is now being reconsidered, for example, by Boyarin, "Rethinking Jewish Christianity." I will refer to these writings as Christian without taking a stand on when it becomes appropriate to use this term, on the assumption that at some point in time, those responsible for reading and preserving these texts would have identified themselves as Christians.
2. Ramsey, *Beginning to Read*, 8.
3. Ibid. For an introduction see Ramsey, *Beginning to Read*; Chadwick, *Early Church*; Chadwick, *East and West*; Chadwick, *Heresy and Orthodoxy*; Chadwick, *History and Thought*; and the online collection of the works of early church fathers at Christian Classics Ethereal Library, http://www.ccel.org/fathers.html (accessed October 9, 2010).
4. Roberts and Donaldson, *Ante-Nicene Fathers*, 3:559. Tertullian's dates are approximately 160–220 C.E.

5. Ibid., 5:170.
6. Ibid., 7:438.
7. Schaff, *Nicene and Post-Nicene Fathers. Second Series*, 4:177.
8. Ibid., 4:94.
9. Ibid., 4:409.
10. Ibid., 4:577.
11. Cf. Breck, *Scripture in Tradition*, 2. For an introduction to the church fathers on scripture, see Hall, *Reading Scripture*.
12. Schaff, *Nicene and Post-Nicene Fathers. First Series*, 1:96–97.
13. Ibid., 10:477.
14. Ibid., 6:278.
15. Ibid., 6:420.
16. See Bond, *Caiaphas*, 137, who argues that the trial before Annas is the Evangelist's own construction.
17. Roberts and Donaldson, *Ante-Nicene Fathers*, 7:444.
18. Schaff, *Nicene and Post-Nicene Fathers. First Series*, 6:186.
19. Ibid., 6:187.
20. Ibid., 6:190–91.
21. See the similar wording in *The Harmony of the Gospels* 3.7.27; Schaff, *Nicene and Post-Nicene Fathers. First Series*, 6:190.
22. Schaff, *Nicene and Post-Nicene Fathers. First Series*, 7:421.
23. Ibid., 7:278.
24. Ibid., 4:228.
25. Ibid., 3:81. Cf. John 11:51.
26. All citations to Origen are to the edition of *Commentary on the Gospel According to John* edited by Ronald E. Heine and published by the Catholic University of America Press. Origen's concern about prophecy also emerged in his treatment of 1 Samuel 28 and the medium of Endor. For discussion in the context of patristic rhetoric, see Mitchell, "Patristic Rhetoric." Origen lived in Alexandria from 185 to approximately 254. He considered the Fourth Gospel to be the high point of scripture, and his lengthy, though incomplete, commentary on John is a masterpiece of patristic exegesis. The commentary was addressed to Ambrose and may have been written at his instigation.
27. In a note Heine explains that Origen's statement here is reflecting the vocabulary and concerns of a polemic against the late-second-century Montanist prophets and prophetesses of Phrygia, who uttered their prophecies while in a trance. Origen, *Commentary*, 327n201.
28. Heine notes that the Greek literally means "and the fact that he has been moved under the feet of the Spirit." Origen, *Commentary*, 332n222.
29. On dates see Piovanelli, "Reception of Early Christian Texts"; Piovanelli, "What Is a Christian Apocryphal Text?"
30. Norris, "Apocryphal Writings," 28. For a good general introduction to this literature, see Lapham, *Introduction*, especially the general bibliography on viii–ix; Schneemelcher and Wilson, *New Testament Apocrypha*, 1:9–75; Klauck, *Apocryphal Gospels*; Klauck, *Apocryphal Acts*; Foster, *Non-Canonical Gospels*; Foster, *Apocryphal Gospels*.
31. Elliott, "Relevance," 119. For the impact of the Apocrypha on art, see Cartlidge, *Art*. One fascinating example of the use of the Christian Apocrypha in Byzantine churches can be found in the Church of St. Savior in Cora, in Istanbul, Turkey. The mosaics in the first three bays of the inner narthex give an account of the life of Mary and her parents based directly on the Protoevangelium of James. For discussion and the history of this book's influence on the visual representations of the life of Mary, see Cartlidge, *Art*, 21–46.

32. A glance at the table of contents in Schneemelcher and Wilson, *New Testament Apocrypha*, provides a good summary of the genres within this category.

33. Elliott, "Relevance," 118.

34. See Thilo, *Codex Apocryphus*, xxixn21. Many thanks to Pierluigi Piovanelli for this reference.

35. Roberts and Donaldson, *Ante-Nicene Fathers*, 8:405. English translations of the New Testament Apocrypha and patristic literature can be found online at http://www.newadvent.org/fathers/ and http://www.earlychristianwritings.com/. Precise dating is not possible with many of the apocryphal texts and in any case not germane to the present discussion. The dates included here are based on the introductions in Roberts and Donaldson, *Ante-Nicene Fathers*, and Schaff, *Nicene and Post-Nicene Fathers*.

36. Piovanelli, "Rewritten Bible."

37. Piovanelli, "What Is a Christian Apocryphal Text?"; Uro, *Thomas*.

38. For discussion of the date and provenance of this text, see pages 66–67 below.

39. See also Scheidwiler, "Gospel of Nicodemus," 450.

40. Quotations are from the First Greek Form, Roberts and Donaldson, *Ante-Nicene Fathers*, 8:416–38.

41. Piovanelli, "Livre du coq." See also the Anaphora Pilati and the Paradosis Pilati; in both of which Jesus is delivered to his death by Herod, Archelaus, Philip, Annas and Caiaphas, and all the multitude of the Jews. Elliott and James, *Apocryphal New Testament*, 209, 212.

42. This is a late text, likely from the fourteenth or fifteenth century, and is cited from Klijn, *Jewish-Christian Gospel Tradition*, 114.

43. On the tradition surrounding the identification of the Fourth Evangelist as John son of Zebedee, see Culpepper, *John*.

44. Elliott and James, *Apocryphal New Testament*, 225.

45. All quotations are from Elliott and James, *Apocryphal New Testament*, 217–22. On the *Acts of Pilate* and the *Gospel of Nicodemus*, see Gounelle and Izydorczyk, "Thematic Bibliography"; Gounelle and Izydorczyk, "Addenda et Corrigenda."

46. Bond, *Caiaphas*, 5.

47. See Scheidwiler, "Gospel of Nicodemus," and the versions found online at New Advent, http://www.newadvent.org/fathers/0807.htm (accessed October 9, 2010), and at Early Christian Writings, http://www.earlychristianwritings.com/text/gospelnicodemus.html (accessed October 9, 2010). The discussion here will be based on the First Greek Form. For an excellent bibliography, see Gounelle and Izydorczyk, "Thematic Bibliography" and "Addenda et Corrigenda."

48. For a detailed catalog of the manuscripts, see Izydorczyk, *Manuscripts*.

49. The quartodecimans were Christians who celebrated Easter on the fourteenth day of Nissan to coincide with the Jewish celebration of Passover. See Steel, *Marking Time*, 96–97.

50. Scheidwiler, "Gospel of Nicodemus," 501.

51. Quasten, *Patrology*, 1:116.

52. Schaff, *Nicene and Post-Nicene Fathers. Second Series*, 2:359.

53. This story is similar to Acts 4:5–6, which recounts the miraculous escape from prison of a number of Jesus' followers who were arrested by the Jewish authorities, including Caiaphas and Annas.

54. See also Solomon, *Book of the Bee*.

55. Roberts and Donaldson, *Ante-Nicene Fathers*, 8:89–96.

56. Ibid., 8:1115.

57. Elliott, "Relevance," 123.

CHAPTER 4: CAIAPHAS IN LITERATURE

1. This translation is that of Henry F. Cary (1888), quoted from http://www.sacredtexts.com/chr/dante/in23.htm (accessed January 10, 2010). A more modern translation by Robert M. Durling can be found in Dante Alighieri, *Divine Comedy*, 353.
2. Durling, *Divine Comedy*, 360
3. Carroll, *Exiles of Eternity*, 337–38.
4. Many thanks to Simcha Walfish for drawing this reference to my attention.
5. Graves, *King Jesus*, 318.
6. Kazantzakis, *Last Temptation*, 446.
7. Ibid., 447.
8. Callaghan, *Time for Judas*, 153.
9. Mailer, *Gospel According to the Son*, 214–15. For discussion of this novel, see Partridge, "*Gospel According to the Son*"; McDonald, "Post-Holocaust Theodicy."
10. Graves, *King Jesus*, 318.
11. Ibid., 329.
12. Saramago, *Gospel According to Jesus Christ*, 375.
13. Bulgakov, *Master and Margarita*, 36–37. The portrayal of both Caiaphas and Pilate and the role of the Master's work within the novel as a whole is both fascinating and extremely complicated. See Fiene, "'Pilatism'"; Jones, "Gospel According to Woland." For a defense of Bulgakov as not anti-Semitic, see Milne, "Nationalism."
14. Graves, *King Jesus*, 280.
15. Ibid., 282.
16. Ibid., 282–83.
17. Ibid., 323.
18. Mailer, *Gospel According to the Son*, 186.
19. Ibid., 212–13.
20. Martin, *Letters of Caiaphas*, author's preface.
21. Ibid., 9–11.
22. This is implied by Mark 12:18–23, in which the Sadducees mock this belief.
23. Martin, *Letters of Caiaphas*, 44.
24. Ibid., 72–75.
25. Ibid., 81.
26. Ibid., 86.
27. Ibid., 93.
28. For biographical information see Durkin, *Dorothy L. Sayers*; Hone, *Dorothy L. Sayers*.
29. Hone, *Dorothy L. Sayers*, 103.
30. Sayers draws from all four Gospels but has a special affinity for the Fourth Gospel, making extensive use also of commentaries and other secondary sources. Sayers, *Man Born to Be King*, 33–36.
31. Dale, "*Man Born to Be King*." On Sayers's treatment of Judas, see Curran, "Word Made Flesh."
32. Sayers, *Man Born to Be King*, 116.
33. Ibid., 160.
34. The usual term for the council is *Sanhedrin*. Sayers uses the term *Sanhedrim* to refer to council members, as indicated by the use of the Hebrew masculine plural ending *im* and the plural verb.
35. Sayers, *Man Born to Be King*, 175.
36. Ibid.

37. Cf. also Josephus' own sentiments, according to *War* 5.362–419. See Price, "Provincial Historian," 115.
38. Sayers, *Man Born to Be King*, 23.
39. For detailed description and analysis of Neville Chamberlain and the policy of appeasement, see Caputi, *Neville Chamberlain*; McDonough, *Neville Chamberlain*.
40. Hone, *Dorothy L. Sayers*, 95. Curran, however, sees in Sayers's Caiaphas the echo of a different war-era personality: "Caiaphas, a conservative Jewish leader, was no less politically motivated in convicting Christ than Marshal Pétain in donating France to the Nazis." Curran, "Word Made Flesh," 73.
41. Sayers, *Man Born to Be King*, 203.
42. Ibid., 262.
43. Ibid., 289.
44. Ibid., 301–2.
45. Ibid., 334.
46. Robertson, *British Board*, 74–76, 180.
47. See the foreword by Dr. J. W. Welch, who commissioned the plays as director of religious broadcasting for the BBC, in Sayers, *Man Born to Be King*, 9–16.
48. Heilbrun, "Dorothy L. Sayers," 11–12. Heilbrun laments Barbazon's assessment of Sayers's anti-Semitism, although she acknowledges that Sayers continued to help her own Nazi governess even after the war.
49. For an exhaustive and fascinating study of British anti-Semitism, see Julius, *Trials of the Diaspora*. For his discussion of *The Man Born to Be King*, see 175–76.
50. Orwell, "Anti-Semitism," 322. The essay was written in 1945.
51. On Sayers's portrayal of Jewish characters in her novels, see McGregor and Lewis, *Conundrums*, 30–31; Patterson, "Images of Judaism"; Turnbull, *Victims or Villains*, 87–94.
52. Brabazon, *Dorothy L. Sayers*, 217.
53. Ibid.
54. Ibid., 218.
55. Sayers, *Man Born to Be King*, 252.
56. Ibid., 23.
57. Asch's "Gospel of Judas" is not to be identified with the Gnostic text known by the same name. On the latter see Cockburn, "Judas Gospel"; De Conick, *Thirteenth Apostle*; Ehrman, *Lost Gospel*; Kasser, Meyer, and Wurst, *Gospel of Judas*.
58. Asch, *Nazarene*, 70.
59. Ibid., 65–66.
60. Ibid., 68.
61. Ibid., 46.
62. Ibid., 51.
63. Ibid., 92.
64. Ibid., 614–15.
65. Ibid., 616.
66. Ibid., 619.
67. Ibid., 619–20.
68. Ibid., 620.
69. Ibid., 643.
70. Sarna, *American Judaism*.
71. Asch, *Nazarene*, 436.
72. Ibid., 440.
73. On the impact of the Enlightenment and the emancipation on Jewish religious life, see Ellenson, *After Emancipation*; Rudavsky, *Modern Jewish Religious Movements*.

74. This concern is hinted at in the novel, in the repeated references to the German soldiers that Rome had at its disposal and who were fiercely hated by the Jews. Asch, *Nazarene*, 56.
75. Fischthal, "Reactions of the Yiddish Press," 266.
76. Norich, "Sholem Asch," 251.
77. Fischthal, "Reactions of the Yiddish Press," 275.
78. Norich, "Sholem Asch," 255.
79. Asch's earlier Christian works include the story "In a Karnival Nacht," perhaps written as early as 1907. See Hoffman, "Sholem Asch's True Christians," 281.
80. McNulty, "Three Artists."
81. Norich, "Sholem Asch," 264.
82. Hoffman, "Sholem Asch's True Christians," 279–80.
83. Norich, "Sholem Asch," 264.
84. According to Josephus, the younger Annas did eventually become high priest (in 62 C.E.) and is best known for his actions against James, the brother of Jesus (*Ant.* 20:198–203). VanderKam, *From Joshua*, 476–82.
85. For an analysis of Asch's views of Christianity and Judaism, see Morgentaler, "Foreskin of the Heart."
86. Hoffman, "Sholem Asch's True Christians," 281.
87. Norich, "Sholem Asch," 253.

CHAPTER 5: CAIAPHAS ON STAGE

1. For discussion see White, *Scripting Jesus*; Brant, *Dialogue and Drama*.
2. On the Isango Portobello productions, see Mark Dornford-May, "Exclusive: Mark Dornford-May on Why the Chester Mystery Plays Are So Important to Him," Official LondonTheatre.co.uk, September 7, 2009, http://www.officiallondontheatre.co.uk/news/the-feature/view/item107332/Exclusive:-Mark-Dornford-May-on-why-the-Chester-Mystery-Plays-are-so-important-to-him/. In addition to the four play cycles mentioned, there are also two long composite and late mystery plays that have survived from Coventry and fragments of others. On the mystery plays, see King, *York Mystery Cycle*, 1–2. Generally the York Cycle is taken to refer to the series of forty-seven pageants that survive in British Library Additional MS 35290. This is the York Register, a record of the pageants as performed, which was commissioned and established by the civic authorities in the 1460s–70s and maintained from year to year by a succession of civic officials, the Common Clerks, until the mid–sixteenth century. Other records of the York Cycle are found in Johnston and Rogerson, *Records*. For details of these and other manuscript evidence, see Records of Early English Drama (REED), Centre for Research in Early English Drama, http://www.reed.utoronto.ca/ (accessed July 15, 2009).
3. The Corpus Christi festival appeared in the late twelfth century as a reflection of the belief that the Eucharistic host actually contains the living body of Christ and entailed the veneration of the sacramental wafer. The feast gave the opportunity for the development of a variety of art forms around this belief. See Travis, *Dramatic Design*, 2.
4. Beckwith, *Signifying God*, xv.
5. King, *York Mystery Cycle*, 182.
6. Laut, "Drama Illustrating Dogma," 145–46.
7. King, *York Mystery Cycle*, 192.
8. For a detailed discussion, see Woolf, *English Mystery Plays*, 250–53; Robinson, *Studies in Fifteenth-Century Stagecraft*, 176–200.
9. All quotations are taken from Records of Early English Drama (REED), Centre for Research in Early English Drama, http://www.reed.utoronto.ca/. For Pageant 29 see http://www.reed.utoronto.ca/yorkplays/York29.html. Another very important pageant is Pageant

38, *The Resurrection*, sponsored by the Winedrawers' Guild, in which Pilate, Annas, and Caiaphas react to the finding of the empty tomb. See http://www.reed.utoronto.ca/yorkplays/York38.html (all sites accessed July 15, 2009). For discussion see Beckwith, *Signifying God*, 81–83.

10. Here the soldier, presumably a member of the Temple police (he answers to Caiaphas), swears by the name of Mohammed. For analysis and other examples of this usage in medieval English drama, see Chemers, "Anti-Semitism."

11. For a discussion of buffeting, see Robinson, *Studies in Fifteenth-Century Stagecraft*, 176–77.

12. It should be noted, however, that the Sabbath, like all Jewish festivals, begins at sundown.

13. On dancing with the devil, see Laut, "Drama Illustrating Dogma," 231–37.

14. Robinson, *Studies in Fifteenth-Century Stagecraft*, 189.

15. Ibid., 178.

16. Ibid., 188–89.

17. Ibid., 188.

18. For a detailed consideration of the deicide motif throughout history and in different media, see Cohen, *Christ Killers*.

19. Robinson, *Studies in Fifteenth-Century Stagecraft*, 192.

20. Beckwith, *Signifying God*, 108–9.

21. West, *Saint Gall Passion Play*, 11–14.

22. Sticca, *Latin Passion Play*, xvii.

23. Ibid., 19–22. Also important was the art of illumination. One of the earliest Passion plays still extant was written in Montecassino, which was also an important center for the production of South Italian manuscripts, especially the Exultet Roll, which in the liturgy of the Roman Church was used in the ceremony of the Blessing of the Paschal Candle on Easter Eve. The text of the Exultet Roll was inscribed on a long strip of parchment or velum and illustrated with illuminated pictures. The pictures are in reverse to the text, which means that as the deacon chanted and unrolled the scroll, the illustrations of the unrolled portion he had just read would fall over the back of the lectern, thereby displaying them right side up in front of the congregation. In that way the congregation was able to visualize the action as well as to hear the words themselves. Sticca, *Latin Passion Play*, 45.

24. Sticca, *Latin Passion Play*, 51. For a survey of the extant Passion plays, see West, *Saint Gall Passion Play*, 23–28.

25. Sticca, *Latin Passion Play*, 87–88.

26. Ibid., 105–6.

27. West, *Saint Gall Passion Play*, 38.

28. Ibid., 38–39.

29. Ibid., 46. On the association of Jews with red hair and the negative meaning of red hair, see Mellinkoff, "Judas's Red Hair."

30. West, *Saint Gall Passion Play*, 70–71.

31. Ibid., 79–80.

32. Ibid., 94–96.

33. Ibid., 106.

34. Bentley, *Oberammergau*, 13.

35. Shapiro, *Oberammergau*, 59.

36. Ibid., 67.

37. Mork, "Christ's Passion on Stage." For detailed discussion of the history of the play, see Shapiro, *Oberammergau*, 58–100.

38. *Oberammergau: The Passion Play 2010*, title page. The play has always been performed in German. Spectators can buy translations in several languages, which they can follow during the performances. These were referred to as playbooks until 2000 and thereafter as textbooks.

39. Christian Stückl, personal communication, May 13, 2010.

40. Daisenberger, *Passion Play in Oberammergau* (1922); Daisenberger, *Passion Play at Oberammergau* (1930); Daisenberger, *Passion Play at Oberammergau* (1960).

41. Potter, *Movement for Actors*, 28.

42. Daisenberger, *Passion Play at Oberammergau* (1960), 27.

43. Ibid., 103.

44. Ibid., 57.

45. Ibid., 82.

46. Ibid., 104.

47. Ibid., 105.

48. Ibid., 113.

49. Ibid., 113–14.

50. Ibid., 128–29.

51. Krauskopf, *Rabbi's Impressions*, 31–32.

52. Ibid., 32–33.

53. Ibid., 91–92.

54. Ibid., 95.

55. Ibid., 125.

56. Ibid., 137.

57. These comments by Rabbi Krauskopf also read ironically today, when in the wake of a smattering of violent incidents in the past two decades, synagogues around the world do have security guards especially on the major festivals. In the fall of 2009 I attended religious services at the main synagogue in Düsseldorf, which was guarded by several police officers and half a dozen security guards who interrogated worshippers as they entered the grounds of the synagogue.

58. Bentley, *Oberammergau*, 38. For further discussion of Oberammergau and Nazism, see Shapiro, *Oberammergau*, 149–73.

59. Hitler, *Hitler's Table Talk*, 424–25.

60. For the text of *Nostra Aetate*, see http://www.vatican.va/archive/hist_councils/ii_vatican_council/documents/vat-ii_decl_19651028_nostra-aetate_en.html (accessed May 20, 2010).

61. Shapiro, *Oberammergau*, 12–13. For more detailed discussion, see pp. 77–80.

62. *Oberammergau Passion Play, 1634–1984*, 52–55.

63. Ibid., 73.

64. Ibid., 100.

65. Ibid., 100–101.

66. Ibid., introduction.

67. Friedman, *Oberammergau Passion Play*, 52.

68. For detailed discussion see Shapiro, *Oberammergau*, 188–223.

69. Christian Stückl, personal communication, May 13, 2010.

70. Daisenberger, *Oberammergau Play* (1990), 88.

71. Ibid., 89.

72. There is no scene number. Daisenberger, *Oberammergau Passion Play 2000*, 17.

73. Ibid., 32.

74. Ibid., 33.

75. Ibid., 69.

76. This is an error, for if Josephus is correct, Caiaphas was appointed by Gratus in 18 C.E. and therefore was in place for a full decade before Pilate arrived in Judaea. See *Antiquities* 18.35.

77. Daisenberger, *Oberammergau Passion Play 2000*, 83.

78. Ibid., 96.

79. Ibid.

80. In addition to changes in the script, attempts to neutralize the anti-Jewish potential of the play included serious education of the cast. In preparation for both the 2000 and 2010 productions, the actors playing the principal roles toured the Holy Land to visit Christian sites and become acquainted with the landscape. For a description see Schmidt, "Ausflug Nach Israel."

81. Sherman, "Oberammergau 2000."

82. Shapiro, *Oberammergau*, 218–19.

83. These have since been published, in Kratz and Mödl, *Freunde und Feinde-Vertraute*.

84. A selection of responses to the 2010 production can be found on the Web site of the American Jewish Committee, http://www.ajc.org/site/c.ijITI2PHK0G/b.6082199/k.686D/Oberammergau_Passion_Play.htm (accessed June 20, 2010).

85. Otto Huber, personal communication, May 14, 2010.

86. Oberammergau 2010, 35–36

87. Ibid., 81.

88. Ibid., 36.

89. Ibid., 83.

90. Ibid., 104.

91. Ibid., 104.

92. Ibid., 17.

93. Oberammergau 2010, 32. This same move is made in Denys Arcand's 1989 film *Jesus of Montreal*.

94. Ibid., 43

95. Ibid., 71.

96. Ibid.

97. Ibid., 36–37.

98. Bentley, *Oberammergau*, 35.

99. Martin, *Representations of Jews*, 33.

100. Council of Centers on Christian-Jewish Relations, "Ad Hoc Committee Report."

101. Quality Christian Tours to Europe, http://www.reformationtours.com/site/490868/page/927720 (accessed May 20, 2010).

102. Otto Huber, personal communication, May 13, 2010.

CHAPTER 6: CAIAPHAS ON SCREEN

1. For a comprehensive listing of Jesus films to 1990, see Kinnard and Davis, *Divine Images*. For discussion of the genre, see Reinhartz, *Jesus of Hollywood*.

2. Kinnard and Davis, *Divine Images*, 19–20.

3. Custen, *Bio/Pics*, 144.

4. The discussion in this chapter focuses primarily on English-language films or foreign films that received wide distribution in North America. Numerous Jesus films have been made in other languages, primarily for local distribution. One example among many is the Indian film *Karunamayudu* (Telugu for "Man of Compassion"), released in 1978. For discussion see Friesen, "Showing Compassion."

5. Custen, *Bio/Pics*, 144.

6. The 2000 film *The Miracle Maker*, for example, reproduces a number of scenes from Zeffirelli's 1979 epic *Jesus of Nazareth*, and Gibson's Pilate character is similar in appearance to the Pilate of Stevens's *The Greatest Story Ever Told*.

7. See the Warner Sallman Collection, http://www.warnersallman.com/collection/images/head-of-christ/ (accessed June 9, 2010).

8. On the indebtedness of this film to other genres, including Gibson's previous films, see Thistlethwaite, "Mel Makes a War Movie."

9. All trancriptions of motion picture and televised media are by the author unless otherwise noted.

10. Although this film was not widely released, it is one of the most blatantly anti-Semitic portrayals of Caiaphas. Translations of the German intertitles are my own.

11. For a detailed analysis of this film, particularly with regard to its anti-Semitism, see Zwick, "Antijüdische Tendenzen."

12. Stern, Jefford, and DeBona, *Savior*, 39.

13. The filmmaker here has inserted Caiaphas into Josephus's account of Pilate's confrontation with the population of Jerusalem in *Antiquities* 18.55–62; cf. *War* 2.169–74. For discussion see chapter 8.

14. Zeffirelli testifies to having been deeply moved by *Nostra Aetate*, the declaration of the Second Vatican Council absolving the Jews as a people of collective guilt in the death of Jesus. Zeffirelli, *Franco Zeffirelli's Jesus*, 6.

15. On the persistent association of Jews with the devil in Western culture, to which the vague hornlike appearance of Caiaphas's headgear in *Der Galiläer* alludes, see Trachtenberg, *Devil and the Jews*. On anti-Semitism in *Der Galiläer*, see Zwick, "Antijüdische Tendenzen."

16. Babington and Evans, *Biblical Epics*, 122.

17. Walsh, *Reading the Gospels*, 107.

18. This film was not widely released in North America due to distribution issues. See Gallagher, *Adventures of Rossellini*, 670.

19. On the reception of the film in Muslim countries, see Fredriksen, "No Pain"; Charles Levinson, "Arab Censors Giving 'Passion' Wide Latitude: Gibson Film Packs Mideast Movie Houses," SFGate.com, http://articles.sfgate.com/2004-4-1/news/17420888_1_controversial-film-united-arab-emirates-movie (accessed June 6, 2010).

20. Baugh, *Imaging the Divine*, 37–38.

21. Dornford-May's *Son of Man* is based on the part 2 of the mystery play performed by the Isango Portobello theater group. See chapter 5.

22. On the role of the Judenrat, see Eichengreen and Fromer, *Rumkowski*.

CHAPTER 7: CAIAPHAS IN HISTORIOGRAPHY

1. Collingwood, *Idea of History*, 246.

2. Ibid., 235.

3. Schürer, *History of the Jewish People*, 2:227.

4. Caiaphas is not mentioned in rabbinic literature except in Tosefta Yevamot 1:10, which refers obliquely to his family: "But I hereby give testimony concerning the family of the house of 'Aluba'i of Bet Seba'alefim and concerning the family of the house of Qipa'alefi of Bet Meqoshesh, 'that they are children of co-wives, and from them have been chosen high priests, and they did offer up sacrifices on the Temple altar.'" Neusner and Sarason, *Tosefta*, 3:3. As we shall see later, the historiography of Second Temple Judaism (as opposed to early Christianity) is indifferent to Caiaphas, as he plays no role whatsoever in the grand drama of the

Jewish revolt against Rome. There are some notable exceptions with regard to the New Testament Apocrypha and patristic literature, notably the *Acts of Pilate*, *Gospel of Nicodemus* and Origen's *Commentary on the Gospel of John*. These are discussed in chapter 3.

5. The landmark early study is Schweitzer, *Quest of the Historical Jesus*. Among the numerous accounts of the history of the quest are Dunn and McKnight, *Historical Jesus*; Powell, *Jesus as a Figure*.

6. A few of the many works that refer to the trial of its title are Bammel, *Trial of Jesus*; Blinzler, *Trial of Jesus*; Bowe, "Trial of Jesus"; Brandon, *Trial of Jesus of Nazareth*; Catchpole, *Trial of Jesus*; Cohn, *Trial and Death*; Donahue, *Are You the Christ?*; Jackson, "Trials of Jesus"; Sloyan, *Jesus on Trial*; Winter, *On the Trial*.

7. Blinzler, *Trial of Jesus*, 117–21.
8. Ibid., 81.
9. Ibid., 84.
10. Ibid.
11. Ibid., 88.
12. Ibid., 104.
13. Ibid., 101.
14. Ibid., 104–5.

15. Blinzler emphasizes that finding the Jewish authorities responsible in Jesus' death can be neither an excuse nor a cause for anti-Semitism. Nevertheless the tone of his writing is somewhat disturbing. "Others, again, make departures from legal procedure an excuse for casting suspicion on the evangelists as reporters. Convinced that no Jewish court could possibly have disregarded so flagrantly the rules of its own legal code, they hold all the gospel accounts to be anti-Jewish inventions—Jewish authors [note 53 lists Hyason, von Hauss, Goldin, van Paassen, Lippe, Drews, Lipsius] especially so. In refutation of this petty view, the English Jew Montefiore has aptly remarked that there have been illegal trials in every age, yet it does not occur to anyone simply to reject the reports of such trials as inventions. Moreover, what the gospels tell of the rejected witnesses definitely does not look like an anti-Jewish invention." See Blinzler, *Trial of Jesus*, 139–40.

16. Lietzmann, "Prozess Jesu," 254. Against this Blinzler points out that present at the trial were Nicodemus and Joseph of Arimathea, both members of the Sanhedrin who were favorably disposed toward Jesus and therefore could have reported on the proceedings to Jesus' followers. Blinzler, *Trial of Jesus*, 118.

17. Lietzmann, "Prozess Jesu," 258–60.
18. Ibid., 255.
19. Ibid., 253–54.
20. Winter, *On the Trial*; Cook, "Problem of Jewish Jurisprudence."
21. Crossan, *Who Killed Jesus?* 4. A similar argument is made by Jackson, "Trials of Jesus."
22. Crossan, *Who Killed Jesus?* 82. Some of the church fathers also read the trial scene in conjunction with Psalm 2, as we saw in chapter 3.
23. Ibid., 116.
24. Cohn, *Trial and Death*, 96.
25. Ibid., 112.
26. Ibid., 114.
27. Ibid., 116–17.
28. Ibid., 113.
29. Brown, *Gospel According to John*, 1:792–93.
30. Fitzmyer places himself in this camp. Fitzmyer, *Gospel According to Luke*, 2:1456. Another example is Sloyan, *Jesus on Trial*.

31. Brown, *Gospel According to John*, 1:792–93.
32. Ibid., 1:799.
33. Ibid., 1:802.
34. Blinzler, *Trial of Jesus*, 91.
35. Ibid., 99.
36. Ibid., 92.
37. To be fair, Blinzler is not the only scholar to mention this point. See Catchpole, *Trial of Jesus*, 249. Catchpole is cited in this regard also by Bond, who adds that Annas may have offered Pilate financial inducements to keep his son-in-law in office until his own son was old enough to take over. Bond, *Pontius Pilate*, 19n109. The speculative nature of these theories must be stressed.
38. Blinzler, *Trial of Jesus*, 92–93.
39. Ibid., 110.
40. Chilton, "Caiaphas," 805.
41. Sanders, *Historical Figure*, 272–73.
42. Fredriksen, *Jesus of Nazareth*, 265.
43. Ibid., 258.
44. Borg, *Conflict, Holiness and Politics*, 2.
45. Crossan, "Itinerants and Householders," 9–10.
46. Ehrman, *Jesus*, 107.
47. Meier, *Marginal Jew*, 347.
48. Chilton, *Rabbi Jesus*, xx.
49. Ibid., 232–33.
50. Flusser, *Jesus*, 67.
51. Ibid., 137–38.
52. Ibid., 67–68.
53. Ibid., 74.
54. Ibid., 204–5.
55. Ibid., 68.
56. Wright, *Jesus*, 525–26.
57. Ibid., 351.
58. Ibid., 595.
59. Ibid., 503–4.
60. Goldstein, *I Maccabees*, 239.
61. Wright, *Jesus*, 491–92, 525.
62. Ibid., 493.
63. Ibid., 583.
64. Ibid., 582.
65. Ibid., 465.
66. Ibid., 596.
67. Ibid., 609.
68. Ibid., 608.
69. Bornkamm, *Jesus of Nazareth*, 29.
70. See the excellent survey by Levine, *Judaism and Hellenism*, 6–15.
71. Hengel, *Judaism and Hellenism*, vol. 1, 1.
72. Ibid., 311–12.
73. Vermès, *Jesus*, 26.
74. Sanders, *Judaism*, 22.
75. Goodman, "Jews, Greeks," 14.

76. Ibid., 13.
77. Crossan, *Historical Jesus*, 422.
78. Ibid., 418.
79. Ibid.
80. Hengel, *Judaism and Hellenism*, 310.
81. Nor is there evidence that he himself was comfortable with the Greek language; indeed his ossuary is inscribed in Aramaic, not in Greek. See Reich, "Ossuary Inscriptions of the Caiaphas Family."
82. Rajak, "Jews and Greeks," 57.
83. Betz, "Hellenism," 130.
84. Bornkamm, *Jesus of Nazareth*, 53. Bornkamm is here referring to the theory of the "Aryan Jesus." See p. 199n2. For a detailed and fascinating discussion of the "rehabilitation" of Jesus by theologians in Nazi Germany, see Heschel, *Aryan Jesus*.
85. Bornkamm, *Jesus of Nazareth*, 43.
86. Ibid., 44.
87. Hengel, *Judaism and Hellenism*, 306.
88. Ibid.
89. Ibid., 314.
90. Cf. Bornkamm, *Jesus of Nazareth*, 37.

CHAPTER 8: CAIAPHAS IN HISTORY

1. Goodman, *Ruling Class*, 33.
2. Ibid., 29.
3. Carter, *Matthew and Empire*, 149.
4. Goodman, *Ruling Class*, 19.
5. Ibid., 33.
6. Ibid., 41.
7. Ibid., 43. That the high-priestly classes bear considerable, if not total, responsibility for the process leading to the revolt has been accepted by many scholars. For a reevaluation of his views and discussion of the state of the question, see Goodman, "Current Scholarship," 16–21.
8. Sanders, *Judaism*, 322–28.
9. All quotations from the works of Philo are taken from the Loeb Classical Library edition.
10. Jeremias, *Jerusalem*, 209–10.
11. Bond, *Caiaphas*, 51–55. Bond notes these incidents and explains that they occurred at locations (Caesarea) or at times (during festivals) that prevented Caiaphas's involvement. This response is speculative but allows her to maintain the majority position of Caiaphas as the one responsible for maintaining order.
12. Grant, *Jesus*, 153.
13. Chilton, "Caiaphas," 805–6. Chilton is following Eppstein here; see Eppstein, "Historicity."
14. Borg and Crossan, *Last Week*, 53.
15. Sanders, "Jerusalem and Its Temple," 93.
16. The Gospels and Acts refer frequently to the Temple. The activities that they depict going on there involving people other than Jesus are not sacrifices but praying (Luke 2:37, 18:10), fasting (Luke 2:37), and teaching (Luke 2:46).
17. Chilton speculates that it may have been Caiaphas who was behind the installation of the vendors in the Temple. Chilton, "Caiaphas," 803–6.

18. Mark 14:43–15:1 and Luke 22:66–71. Helen Bond suggests that Mark knows that Caiaphas was high priest but chooses to refer to him only by his title in an attempt to broaden Jewish responsibility for Jesus' death. Bond, *Caiaphas*,103–8.

19. According to the synoptic Gospels, the "cleansing" occurred on the Passover during which Jesus was crucified. According to John, the event occurred during the first recorded Passover of Jesus' ministry, two years prior to his crucifixion.

20. Whether John knew one or more of the synoptic Gospels continues to be a much-debated point in Johannine scholarship. For discussion see Smith, *John among the Gospels*.

CHAPTER 9: FACE TO FACE WITH CAIAPHAS

1. For a brief biography, see the Oberammergau newsletter at http://www.oberammergau-passion.com/en-us/html-newsletter/newsletter-newsletter-customers-march_82b41c06f6.html (accessed June 10, 2010). Although this was Burkhart's first season as Caiaphas, he has played major roles in the past, including Judas (1990) and Jesus (2000).

2. Burkhart was one of two actors playing Caiaphas during the 2010 season. The other one was Anton Preisinger. For photographs see http://www.passionplay-oberammergau.com/index.php?id=240 (accessed June 21, 2010).

3. Derbes, *Picturing the Passion*, 72.

4. Ibid., 74.

5. Strickland, *Saracens*, 105. Schreckenberg and Schubert, *Jewish Historiography*, 94. Josephus is portrayed this way as well.

6. Mellinkoff, *Outcasts*, 59–60.

7. Ibid., 88.

8. Ibid., 86–87.

9. Ibid., 128, 165

10. Ibid., 167.

11. Giotto di Bondone, *Christ before Caiaphas*, in the Cappella Scrovegni a Padova, http://de.wikipedia.org/wiki/Datei:Giotto_-_Scrovegni_-_-32-_-_Christ_before_Caiaphas.jpg.

12. This is an ink drawing on green primed paper. It is part of a set of twelve, which may have been preliminary sketches for stained glass windows. Thausing and Eaton, *Albert Dürer*, 326–28; Koerner, *Moment of Self-Portraiture*, 242–44. This work is in the Graphische Sammlung Albertina, Vienna, http://www.wga.hu/html/d/durer/2/11/2/07greenp.html.

13. British Museum, http://www.lib-art.com/artgallery/9729-small-passion-13-christ-before-ca-albrecht-d-rer.html.

14. The image of Caiaphas in on the back central panel. The work is in the Museo dell'Opera del Duomo, Siena, Italy.

15. Books of hours are the most common type of illuminated manuscript in the Middle Ages, usually containing Latin texts of Psalms and prayers with illustrations. For a detailed study, see Harthan, *Book of Hours*.

16. Hassig, "Iconography of Rejection," 29. See also the discussion in the superb book by Mellinkoff, *Outcasts*, 128 and plate VI.26.

17. Mellinkoff, *Outcasts*, 41. Mellinkoff's book contains provides numerous other examples, beautifully reproduced.

18. King, *York Mystery Cycle*, 192–93.

19. Mellinkoff, *Outcasts*, 87. Costume lists in the Lucerne Passion play exhibit the same concepts.

20. Robinson, *Studies in Fifteenth-Century Stagecraft*, 179–80.

21. See the photos in Shapiro, *Oberammergau*.

22. Carroll, *Constantine's Sword*, 32–33.

23. Sherman, "Oberammergau 2000."
24. Stover, "Anti-Semitism."
25. Piero's painting can be seen at http://projects.ias.edu/pierotruecross/zoomify/esaltazione.html (accessed July 3, 2009).
26. 26. Paul Shaviv, "Drabinsky's Gospel," *Canadian Jewish News*, November 6, 2003.
27. For the anti-Semitic potential in this portrayal, see http://www.adl.org/interfaith/gibson_qa.asp (accessed November 28, 2010).
28. Kazantzakis, *Last Temptation*, 299.
29. Ibid., 394.
30. Mailer, *Gospel According to the Son*, 212.
31. Asch, *Nazarene*, 45.
32. Callaghan, *Time of Judas*, 74–75.
33. This translation is by Shutt, "Letter of Aristeas."
34. For detailed study of this passage, including the precise identification of the high priest, see Mulder, *Simon the High Priest*.
35. The entire costume is summarized in *Life of Moses* 2:133. The costume is described again in Special Laws 1:84–97, and its symbolism also is explained again, as well as in Questions and Answers on Exodus, 2:107–24.
36. Swartz and Yahalom, *Avodah*, 1–3.
37. Ibid., 38–39.
38. Mangel, *Machzor for Yom Kippur*, 257–58.
39. Ibid.
40. Swartz and Yahalom, *Avodah*, 34–35.
41. Ibid., 37.
42. Ibid., 34; *Az be-'En Kol* (fourth or fifth century C.E.), lines 551–52.
43. Swartz and Yahalom, *Avodah*, 36.
44. Ibid., 371.
45. The hats and caps of the other members of the Jewish leadership also resemble the figures from Pasolini's film. This association was somewhat disorienting, since when all the authorities were on stage the visual references were quite overwhelming, making me feel that I had somehow landed in the middle of the 1964 black and white classic.
46. The Passion Play Theatre is a large unheated space that holds approximately five thousand seats. There is a roof over the audience, but the stage is open to the air. If the audience had to huddle under heavy coats and blankets, the cast fared much more poorly. During the crucifixion I was completely distracted by the thought of how cold and damp Jesus and the two crucified on either side of him must have been, dressed only in loincloths on a stage almost completely open to the elements.
47. It is possible that the comments made by myself and other Jewish viewers after the preview on May 13 had some effect, as in later performances the voices of Jesus' supporters were clearly heard in the "Crucify him!" mass scene. Personal communication (email), Rabbi Noam Marans, associate director for interreligious and intergroup relations and contemporary Jewish life for the American Jewish Committee, August 12, 2010.

AFTERWORD

1. In 2008 another Caiaphas family ossuary was found, bearing the inscription "Miriam, daughter of Yeshua, son of Kipa, priest of Ma'azyah from the house of Imri." The inscription was first published with critical discussion in 2011, by Zissu and Goren, in "The Ossuary of Miriam."

BIBLIOGRAPHY

Abusch, Tzvi. "Sacrifice in Mesopotamia." In *Sacrifice in Religious Experience*, ed. by Albert I. Baumgarten, 39–48. Leiden & Boston: Brill, 2002.
Anderson, Gary A. *Sacrifices and Offerings in Ancient Israel: Studies in Their Social and Political Importance*. Harvard Semitic Monographs 41. Atlanta: Scholars, 1987.
Asch, Sholem. *The Nazarene*. Translated by Maurice Samuel. New York: Putnam, 1939.
Babington, Bruce, and Peter William Evans. *Biblical Epics: Sacred Narrative in the Hollywood Cinema*. Manchester: Manchester University Press, 1993.
Ball, David Mark. *"I Am" in John's Gospel: Literary Function, Background, and Theological Implications*. Journal for the Study of the New Testament. Supplement Series 124. Sheffield: Sheffield Academic Press, 1996.
Bammel, Ernst, ed. *The Trial of Jesus: Cambridge Studies in Honour of C. F. D. Moule*. Studies in Biblical Theology. Naperville, Ill.: Allenson, 1970.
Barker, Margaret. "John 11:50." In Bammel, *The Trial of Jesus*, 41–46.
Bartlett, John R. "Zadok and His Successors at Jerusalem." *Journal of Theological Studies* 19 (1968): 1–18.
Bauckham, Richard. *The Gospels for All Christians: Rethinking the Gospel Audiences*. Grand Rapids, Mich.: Eerdmans, 1998.
Baugh, Lloyd. *Imaging the Divine: Jesus and Christ-Figures in Film*. Communication, Culture and Theology. Kansas City, Mo.: Sheed & Ward, 1997.
Beckwith, Sarah. *Signifying God: Social Relation and Symbolic Act in the York Corpus Christi Plays*. Chicago: University of Chicago Press, 2001.
Bentley, James. *Oberammergau and the Passion Play: A Guide and a History to Mark the 350th Anniversary*. New York: Penguin, 1984.
Betz, Hans Dieter. "Hellenism." In *The Anchor Bible Dictionary*, ed. David Noel Freedman, 127–35. New York: Doubleday, 1992.
Bilde, Per. *Flavius Josephus, between Jerusalem and Rome: His Life, His Works and Their Importance*. Journal for the Study of the Pseudepigrapha. Supplement Series. Sheffield: JSOT, 1988.
Blackman, Philip. *Mishnayoth: Pointed Hebrew Text, English Translation, Introduction, Notes, Supplement, Appendix, Indexes, Addenda, Corrigenda*. 7 vols. New York: Judaica, 1963.
Blinzler, Josef. *The Trial of Jesus; the Jewish and Roman Proceedings against Jesus Christ Described and Assessed from the Oldest Accounts*. Westminster, Md.: Newman, 1959.
Bock, Darrell L. *Blasphemy and Exaltation in Judaism and the Final Examination of Jesus: A Philological-Historical Study of the Key Jewish Themes Impacting Mark 14:61–64*, Wissenschaftliche Untersuchungen zum Neuen Testament. 2. Series. Tübingen: Mohr Siebeck, 1998.
Bond, Helen K. *Caiaphas: Friend of Rome and Judge of Jesus?* Louisville, Ky.: Westminster John Knox, 2004.

———. "Discarding the Seamless Robe: The High Priesthood of Jesus in John's Gospel." In *Israel's God and Rebecca's Children: Christology and Community in Early Judaism and Christianity: Essays in Honor of Larry W. Hurtado and Alan F. Segal*, ed. David B. Capes, Larry W. Hurtado, and Alan F. Segal, 183–94. Waco, Tex.: Baylor University Press, 2007.

———. *Pontius Pilate in History and Interpretation*. Monograph Series, Society for New Testament Studies. New York: Cambridge University Press, 2004.

Borg, Marcus J. *Conflict, Holiness and Politics in the Teachings of Jesus*. Studies in the Bible and Early Christianity. New York: Mellen, 1984.

Borg, Marcus J., and John Dominic Crossan. *The Last Week: The Day-by-Day Account of Jesus's Final Week in Jerusalem*. San Francisco: HarperSanFrancisco, 2006.

Bornkamm, Günther. *Jesus of Nazareth*. New York: Harper, 1960.

Bowe, Barbara E. "Trial of Jesus." In *A Dictionary of Jewish-Christian Relations*, ed. Edward Kessler and Neil Wenborn, 428–29. Cambridge: Cambridge University Press, 2005.

Boyarin, Daniel. "Rethinking Jewish Christianity: An Argument for Dismantling a Dubious Category (to Which Is Appended a Correction of My Border Lines)." *Jewish Quarterly Review* 99 (2009): 7–36.

Brabazon, James. *Dorothy L. Sayers: A Biography*. New York: Scribner, 1981.

Brandon, S. G. F. *The Trial of Jesus of Nazareth*. Historic Trials Series. New York: Stein & Day, 1968.

Brant, Jo-Ann A. *Dialogue and Drama: Elements of Greek Tragedy in the Fourth Gospel*. Peabody, Mass.: Hendrickson, 2004.

Breck, John. *Scripture in Tradition: The Bible and Its Interpretation in the Orthodox Church*. Crestwood, N.Y.: St. Vladimir's Seminary Press, 2001.

Brody, Robert, and Daniel R. Schwartz. "Caiaphas and Cantheras." In *Agrippa I: The Last King of Judaea*, 190–95. Tübingen: Mohr, 1990.

Broshi, Magen. "Excavations in the House of Caiaphas, Mount Zion." In *Jerusalem Revealed: Archaeology in the Holy City 1968–74*, ed. Yigal Yadin, 57–60. Jerusalem: Israel Exploration Society, 1975.

———. "Excavations on Mount Zion, 1971–72: Preliminary Report." *Israel Exploration Journal* 26 (1976): 81–88.

Brown, Raymond Edward. *The Death of the Messiah: From Gethsemane to the Grave: A Commentary on the Passion Narratives in the Four Gospels*. 2 vols. The Anchor Bible Reference Library. New York: Doubleday, 1994.

———. *The Gospel According to John*. The Anchor Bible. 2 vols. Garden City, N.Y.: Doubleday, 1966, 1970.

———. *An Introduction to the New Testament*. The Anchor Bible Reference Library. New York: Doubleday, 1997.

Bulgakov, Mikhail. *The Master and Margarita*. Translated by Richard Pevear and Larissa Volokhonsky. Penguin Twentieth-Century Classics. London: Penguin, 1997.

Callaghan, Morley. *A Time for Judas*. New York: St. Martin's, 1984.

Caputi, Robert J. *Neville Chamberlain and Appeasement*. Selinsgrove, Penn.: Susquehanna University Press, 2000.

Carroll, James. *Constantine's Sword: The Church and the Jews: A History*. Boston: Houghton Mifflin, 2001.

Carroll, John S. *Exiles of Eternity: An Exposition of Dante's "Inferno."* Port Washington, N.Y.: Kennikat, 1971.

Carter, Charles E. *The Emergence of Yehud in the Persian Period: A Social and Demographic Study*. Journal for the Study of the Old Testament, Supplement Series 294. Sheffield: Sheffield Academic Press, 1999.

Carter, Warren. *John and Empire: Initial Explorations*. New York: Clark, 2008.

———. *Matthew and Empire: Initial Explorations*. Harrisburg, Pa.: Trinity Press International, 2001.

Cartlidge, David R. *Art and the Christian Apocrypha*. London: Routledge, 2001.

Catchpole, David R. *The Trial of Jesus: A Study in the Gospels and Jewish Historiography from 1770 to the Present Day*. Studia Post-Biblica 18. Leiden: Brill, 1971.

Chadwick, Henry. *The Early Church*. Rev. ed. Penguin History of the Church. New York: Penguin, 1993.

———. *East and West: The Making of a Rift in the Church: From Apostolic Times until the Council of Florence*. Oxford History of the Christian Church. New York: Oxford University Press, 2003.

———. *Heresy and Orthodoxy in the Early Church*. Brookfield, Vt.: Variorum, 1991.

———. *History and Thought of the Early Church*. London: Variorum, 1982.

Charlesworth, James H. *Jesus and Archaeology*. Grand Rapids, Mich.: Eerdmans, 2006.

Chemers, Michael Mark. "Anti-Semitism, Surrogacy, and the Invocation of Mohammed in the Play of the Sacrament." *Comparative Drama* 41 (2007): 25–55.

Chilton, Bruce. "Caiaphas." In *The Anchor Bible Dictionary*, vol. 1, ed. David Noel Freedman, 803–6. New York: Doubleday, 1992.

———. *Rabbi Jesus: An Intimate Biography*. New York: Doubleday, 2000.

Cockburn, Andrew. "The Judas Gospel." *National Geographic Magazine*, May 2006, 78–95.

Cohen, Jeremy. *Christ Killers: The Jews and the Passion from the Bible to the Big Screen*. New York: Oxford University Press, 2007.

Cohen, Shaye J. D. *The Beginnings of Jewishness: Boundaries, Varieties, Uncertainties*. Hellenistic Culture and Society 31. Berkeley: University of California Press, 1999.

Cohn, Haim Hermann. *The Trial and Death of Jesus*. New York: Harper & Row, 1971.

Collingwood, R. G. *The Idea of History*. Oxford: Clarendon, 1946.

Collins, Adela Yarbro. "The Charge of Blasphemy in Mark 14:64." In *The Trial and Death of Jesus: Essays on the Passion Narrative in Mark*, ed. Geert van Oyen and Tom Shepherd, 149–70. Leuven & Dudley, Mass.: Peeters, 2006.

Cook, Michael J. "The Problem of Jewish Jurisprudence and the Trial of Jesus." In *Pondering the Passion: What's at Stake for Christians and Jews?* ed. Philip A. Cunningham, 13–25. Lanham, Md.: Rowman & Littlefield, 2004.

Council of Centers on Christian-Jewish Relations. "Ad Hoc Committee Report on the 2010 Oberammergau Passion Play Script." May 14, 2010. http://www.ccjr.us/news/813-ccjr2010may14.

Crossan, John Dominic. *The Historical Jesus: The Life of a Mediterranean Jewish Peasant*. San Francisco: HarperSanFrancisco, 1991.

———. "Itinerants and Householders in the Earliest Jesus Movement." In *Whose Historical Jesus?* ed. William E. Arnal and Michel Robert Desjardins, 7–24. Waterloo, Ont.: Published for the Canadian Corporation for Studies in Religion by Wilfrid Laurier University Press, 1997.

———. *Who Killed Jesus? Exposing the Roots of Anti-Semitism in the Gospel Story of the Death of Jesus*. San Francisco: HarperSanFrancisco, 1995.

Culpepper, R. Alan. *Anatomy of the Fourth Gospel: A Study in Literary Design*. Foundations and Facets: New Testament. Philadelphia: Fortress, 1983.

———. *John, the Son of Zebedee: The Life of a Legend*. Studies on Personalities of the New Testament. Columbia: University of South Carolina Press, 1994.

Curran, Terrie. "The Word Made Flesh: The Christian Aesthetic in Dorothy L. Sayers's *the Man Born to Be King*." In *As Her Whimsey Took Her: Critical Essays on the Work of*

Dorothy L. Sayers, ed. Margaret P. Hannay, 67–77. Kent, Ohio: Kent State University Press, 1979.

Custen, George Frederick. *Bio/Pics: How Hollywood Constructed Public History*. New Brunswick, N.J.: Rutgers University Press, 1992.

Daisenberger, J. A. *The Oberammergau Passion Play 1970: A Religious Festival Play in Three Sections with Eighteen Tableaux Vivants*. [Oberammergau:] Parish of Oberammergau, 1970.

———. *Oberammergau Passion Play 2000: Textbook English*. Revised by Otto Huber and Christian Stuckl. Translated by Ingrid Shafer. Oberammergau: Gemeinde Oberammergau, 2000.

———. *The Oberammergau Play of the Suffering, Death, and Resurrection of Our Lord Jesus Christ*. Revised by the Village of Oberammergau. Oberammergau: Village of Oberammergau, 1990.

———. *The Passion Play at Oberammergau: A Religious Festival in Three Sections with 20 Tableaux Vivants*. [Oberammergau:] Community of Oberammergau, 1960.

———. *The Passion Play at Oberammergau: A Religious Festival in Three Sections with 24 Tableaux Vivants*. Munich: Huber, 1930.

———. *The Passion Play in Oberammergau: A Religious Play*. Munich: Huber, 1922.

Dale, Aliza Stone. "*The Man Born to Be King*: Dorothy L. Sayers's Best Mystery Plot." In *As Her Whimsey Took Her: Critical Essays on the Work of Dorothy L. Sayers*, ed. Margaret P. Hannay, 78–90. Kent, Ohio: Kent State University Press, 1979.

Dante Alighieri. *The Divine Comedy of Dante Alighieri*. Edited and translated by Robert M. Durling. New York: Oxford University Press, 1996.

De Conick, April D. *The Original Gospel of Thomas in Translation: With a Commentary and New English Translation of the Complete Gospel*. New York: Clark, 2007.

———. *Recovering the Original Gospel of Thomas: A History of the Gospel and Its Growth*, Library of New Testament Studies. New York: Clark International, 2005.

———. *The Thirteenth Apostle: What the Gospel of Judas Really Says*. New York: Continuum, 2007.

DeMille, Cecil B., and Donald Hayne. *The Autobiography of Cecil B. Demille*. Englewood Cliffs, N.J.: Prentice-Hall, 1959.

Derbes, Anne. *Picturing the Passion in Late Medieval Italy: Narrative Painting, Franciscan Ideologies, and the Levant*. Cambridge: Cambridge University Press, 1996.

Donahue, John R. *Are You the Christ? The Trial Narrative in the Gospel of Mark*. Facsimile ed. Society of Biblical Literature. Dissertation Series. [Missoula, Mont.]: [Society of Biblical Literature for the Seminar on Mark], 2008.

———. *The Gospel of Mark*. Sacra Pagina Series 2. Collegeville, Minn.: Liturgical Press, 2005.

Dunn, James D. G., and Scot McKnight. *The Historical Jesus in Recent Research*. Winona Lake, Ind.: Eisenbrauns, 2005.

Durkin, Mary Brian. *Dorothy L. Sayers*. Boston: Twayne, 1980.

Ehrman, Bart D. *Jesus, Apocalyptic Prophet of the New Millennium*. New York: Oxford University Press, 1999.

———. *The Lost Gospel of Judas Iscariot: A New Look at Betrayer and Betrayed*. New York: Oxford University Press, 2006.

Eichengreen, Lucille, and Rebecca Fromer. *Rumkowski and the Orphans of Lodz*. San Francisco: Mercury House, 2000.

Ellenson, David Harry. *After Emancipation: Jewish Religious Responses to Modernity*. Cincinnati: Hebrew Union College Press, 2004.

Elliott, J. K. "The Relevance of the Christian Apocrypha." *Union Seminary Quarterly Review* 57 (2003): 118–30.

Elliott, J. K., and M. R. James. *The Apocryphal New Testament: A Collection of Apocryphal Christian Literature in an English Translation*. Oxford: Clarendon, 1993.
Eppstein, Victor. "The Historicity of the Gospel Account of the Cleansing of the Temple." *Zeitschrift für die Neutestamentliche Wissenschaft* 55 (1964): 42–58.
Esmeijer, Anna C. *Divina Quaternitas: A Preliminary Study in the Method and Application of Visual Exegesis*. Assen, Netherlands: Van Gorcum, 1978.
Fiene, Donald. "'Pilatism' in Mikhail Bulgakov's *The Master and Margarita*," in *Bulgakov: The Novelist-Playwright*, ed. Lesley Milne, 125–41. Luxembourg: Harwood, 1995.
Fischthal, Hannah Berliner. "Reactions of the Yiddish Press to *The Nazarene* by Sholem Asch." In *Sholem Asch Reconsidered*, ed. Nanette Stahl, 266–78. New Haven, Conn.: Beinecke Rare Book and Manuscript Library, 2004.
Fitzmyer, Joseph A. *The Acts of the Apostles: A New Translation with Introduction and Commentary*. New York: Doubleday, 1998.
———. *The Gospel According to Luke: Introduction, Translation, and Notes*. 2 vols. The Anchor Bible. Garden City, N.Y.: Doubleday, 1981.
Flusser, David. "To Bury Caiaphas, Not to Praise Him." *Jerusalem Perspective* 4 (1991): 23–28.
Flusser, David, and R. Steven Notley. *Jesus*. Jerusalem: Magnes, 1997.
Foster, Paul. *The Apocryphal Gospels: A Very Short Introduction*. New York: Oxford University Press, 2009.
———, ed. *The Non-Canonical Gospels*. London & New York: Clark, 2008.
Fredriksen, Paula. *Jesus of Nazareth, King of the Jews: A Jewish Life and the Emergence of Christianity*. New York: Knopf, 1999.
———. "No Pain, No Gain." In *Mel Gibson's Bible: Religion, Popular Culture, and the Passion of the Christ*, ed. Timothy K. Beal and Tod Linafelt, 91–108. Chicago: University of Chicago Press, 2006.
Friedman, Saul S. *The Oberammergau Passion Play: A Lance against Civilization*. Carbondale: Southern Illinois University Press, 1984.
Friesen, Dwight. "Showing Compassion and Suggesting Peace in *Karunamayudu*, an Indian Jesus Film." *Studies in World Christianity* 14 (2008): 125–41.
Gallagher, Tag. *The Adventures of Roberto Rossellini*. New York: Da Capo, 1998.
Goldstein, Jonathan A. *I Maccabees: A New Translation, with Introduction and Commentary*. The Anchor Bible. Garden City, N.Y.: Doubleday, 1976.
Goodman, Martin. "Current Scholarship on the First Revolt." In *The First Jewish Revolt: Archaeology, History, and Ideology*, ed. Andrea Berlin and J. Andrew Overman, 15–26. New York: Routledge, 2002.
———. "Jews, Greeks, and Romans," in *Jews in the Graeco-Roman World*, ed. Martin Goodman, 3–14. Oxford: Clarendon.
———. *The Ruling Class of Judaea: The Origins of the Jewish Revolt against Rome, A.D. 66–70*. New York: Cambridge University Press, 1987.
Gounelle, Rémi, and Zbigniew Izydorczyk. "Thematic Bibliography of the Acts of Pilate," in *The Medieval Gospel of Nicodemus: Texts, Intertexts, and Contexts in Western Europe*, ed. Zbigniew Izydorczyk, 419–519. Tempe, Ariz.: Medieval and Renaissance Texts and Studies, 1997.
———. "Thematic Bibliography of the Acts of Pilate: Addenda and Correginda." *Apocrypha* 11 (2001): 259–92.
Grant, Michael. *Jesus: An Historian's Review of the Gospels*. New York: Scribner, 1977.
Graves, Robert. *King Jesus*. London: Cassell, 1966.
Gray, Rebecca. *Prophetic Figures in Late Second Temple Jewish Palestine: The Evidence from Josephus*. New York: Oxford University Press, 1993.

Haber, Susan. "Metaphor and Meaning in the Dead Sea Scrolls." In *"They Shall Purify Themselves": Essays on Purity in Early Judaism*, edited by Adele Reinhartz, 93–124. Atlanta: Society of Biblical Literature, 2008.

Haber, Susan. *"They Shall Purify Themselves": Essays on Purity in Early Judaism*, ed. Adele Reinhartz. Early Judaism and Its Literature. Atlanta: Society of Biblical Literature, 2008.

Hakola, Raimo. "The Counsel of Caiaphas and the Social Identity of the Johannine Community (John 11:47–53)." In *Lux Humana, Lux Aeterna: Essays on Biblical and Related Themes in Honour of Lars Aejmelaeus*, ed. Antti Mustakallio et al., 140–63. Helsinki: Finnish Exegetical Society / Göttingen: Vandenhoeck & Ruprecht, 2005.

Hall, Christopher A. *Reading Scripture with the Church Fathers*. Downers Grove, Ill.: InterVarsity Press, 1998.

Harthan, John P. *The Book of Hours: With a Historical Survey and Commentary*. New York: Park Lane, 1982.

Hass, Angela. "Two Devotional Manuals by Albrecht Dürer: The *Small Passion* and the *Engraved Passion*. Iconography, Context and Spirituality." *Zeitschrift für Kunstgeschichte* 63 (2000): 169–230.

Hassig, Debra. "The Iconography of Rejection: Jews and Other Monstrous Races." In *Image and Belief: Studies in Celebration of the Eightieth Anniversary of the Index of Christian Art*, ed. Colum Hourihane, 25–46. Princeton, N.J.: Index of Christian Art, Department of Art and Archaeology, Princeton University, in association with Princeton University Press, 1999.

Heaton, Vernon. *The Oberammergau Passion Play*. 3er. ed. London: R. Hale, 1983.

Heilbrun, Carolyn G. "Dorothy L. Sayers: Biography between the Lines." In *Dorothy L. Sayers: The Centenary Celebration*, ed. Alzina Stone Dale, 1–13. New York: Walker, 1993.

Hengel, Martin. *Judaism and Hellenism: Studies in Their Encounter in Palestine during the Early Hellenistic Period*. 2 vols. London: SCM, 1974.

Heschel, Susannah. *The Aryan Jesus: Christian Theologians and the Bible in Nazi Germany*. Princeton, N.J.: Princeton University Press, 2008.

Himmelfarb, Martha. *A Kingdom of Priests: Ancestry and Merit in Ancient Judaism*. Jewish Culture and Contexts. Philadelphia: University of Pennsylvania Press, 2006.

Hitchman, Janet. *Such a Strange Lady: An Introduction to Dorothy L. Sayers (1893–1957)*. London: New English Library, 1975.

Hitler, Adolf. *Hitler's Table Talk, 1941–1944: His Private Conversations*. Updated ed. New York City: Enigma, 2008.

Hoffman, Matthew. "Sholem Asch's True Christians: The Jews as a People of Christs." In *Sholem Asch Reconsidered*, ed. Nanette Stahl, 279–88. New Haven, Conn.: Beinecke Rare Book and Manuscript Library, 2004.

Hone, Ralph E. *Dorothy L. Sayers: A Literary Biography*. Kent, Ohio: Kent State University Press, 1981.

Horbury, William. "The 'Caiaphas' Ossuaries and Joseph Caiaphas." *Israel Exploration Quarterly* 126 (1994): 33–48.

Izydorczyk, Zbigniew. *Manuscripts of the Evangelium Nicodemi: A Census*. Subsidia Mediaevalia. Toronto: Pontifical Institute of Mediaeval Studies, 1993.

Jackson, Bernard S. "The Trials of Jesus and Jeremiah." In *Essays on Halakhah in the New Testament*, 33–57. Leiden & Boston: Brill, 2008.

James, M. R. *The Apocryphal New Testament*. Oxford: Clarendon, 1924.

Jeremias, Joachim. *Jerusalem in the Time of Jesus: An Investigation into Economic and Social Conditions during the New Testament Period*. London: SCM, 1969.

Johnston, Alexandra F., and Margaret Rogerson, eds. *Records of Early English Drama: York.* 2 vols. Toronto & Buffalo: University of Toronto Press, 1979.

Jones, Malcolm V. "The Gospel According to Woland and the Tradition of the Wandering Jew," in *Bulgakov: The Novelist-Playwright,* ed. Lesley Milne, 115–24. Luxembourg: Harwood, 1995.

Julius, Anthony. *Trials of the Diaspora: A History of Anti-Semitism in England.* Oxford & New York: Oxford University Press, 2010.

Kasser, Rodolphe, Marvin Meyer, and Gregor Wurst. *The Gospel of Judas: From Codex Tchacos.* Washington, D.C.: National Geographic, 2006.

Kaufmann, Yehezkel. *History of the Religion of Israel, Volume IV: From the Babylonian Captivity to the End of Prophecy.* New York: Ktav, 1977.

Kazantzakis, Nikos. *The Last Temptation of Christ.* Translated by P. A. Bien. New York: Simon & Schuster, 1960.

King, Pamela M. *The York Mystery Cycle and the Worship of the City.* Westfield Medieval Studies. New York: Brewer, 2006.

Kinnard, Roy, and Tim Davis. *Divine Images: A History of Jesus on the Screen.* New York: Carol, 1992.

Klauck, Hans-Josef. *The Apocryphal Acts of the Apostles: An Introduction.* Translated by Brian McNeil. Waco, Tex.: Baylor University Press, 2008.

———. *Apocryphal Gospels: An Introduction.* Translated by Brian McNeil. London & New York: Clark, 2003.

Klausner, Joseph. *Jesus of Nazareth: His Life, Times, and Teaching.* Translated by Herbert Danby. New York: Macmillan, 1925.

Klawans, Jonathan. *Impurity and Sin in Ancient Judaism.* New York: Oxford University Press, 2000.

———. *Purity, Sacrifice, and the Temple: Symbolism and Supersessionism in the Study of Ancient Judaism.* New York: Oxford University Press, 2006.

Klijn, Albertus Frederik Johannes. *Jewish-Christian Gospel Tradition.* Supplements to Vigiliae Christianae 17. Leiden & New York: Brill, 1992.

Koerner, Joseph Leo. *The Moment of Self-Portraiture in German Renaissance Art.* Chicago: University of Chicago Press, 1993.

Kokkinos, Nikos. *The Herodian Dynasty: Origins, Role in Society and Eclipse.* Journal for the Study of the Pseudepigrapha. Supplement Series. Sheffield: Sheffield Academic Press, 1998.

Köstenberger, Andreas J. "The Destruction of the Second Temple and the Composition of the Fourth Gospel." *Trinity Journal* 26 (2005): 205–42.

Kratz, Matthias, and Ludwig Mödl. *Freunde und Feinde-Vertraute und Verräter: Sieben Biografische Zugänge Zu Biblischen Personen Im Passionsgeschehen.* Munich: Sankt Michaelsbund, 2009.

Krauskopf, Joseph. *A Rabbi's Impressions of the Oberammergau Passion Play: Being a Series of Six Lectures, with Three Supplemental Chapters Bearing on the Subject.* Philadelphia: Stern, 1901.

Kugler, Robert A. "Priesthood at Qumran." In *The Dead Sea Scrolls after Fifty Years: A Comprehensive Assessment,* ed. Peter W. Flint and James C. VanderKam, 93–116. Leiden & Boston: Brill, 1998.

Lapham, F. *An Introduction to the New Testament Apocrypha.* Understanding the Bible and Its World. New York: Clark International, 2003.

Laut, Stephen J. "Drama Illustrating Dogma: A Study of the York Cycle." Ph.D. diss., University of North Carolina, 1959.

Levine, Lee I. *Judaism and Hellenism in Antiquity: Conflict or Confluence?* Peabody, Mass.: Hendrickson, 1998.

Lietzmann, Hans. "Der Prozess Jesu." In *Kleine Schriften II*, ed. Kurt Aland, 251–63. Berlin: Akademie-Verlag, 1958.

Macgregor, G. H. C. *The Gospel of John.* Moffatt New Testament Commentary 4. Garden City, N.Y.: Doubleday, Doran, 1929.

Maier, Paul L. "Oberammergau Overhaul." *Christianity Today*, August 7, 2000, 74–75.

Mailer, Norman. *The Gospel According to the Son.* New York: Random House, 1997.

Mantel, Hugo. *Studies in the History of the Sanhedrin.* Cambridge, Mass.: Harvard University Press, 1961.

Marcus, Joel. *Mark 1–8: A New Translation with Introduction and Commentary.* 2 vols. The Anchor Bible. New York: Doubleday, 2000.

———. *Mark 8–16: A New Translation with Introduction and Commentary.* The Anchor Bible. New York: Doubleday, 2009.

Martin, James. *Letters of Caiaphas, the High Priest.* New York: Harper, 1960.

Martin, John D. *Representations of Jews in Late Medieval and Early Modern German Literature.* Studies in German Jewish History 5. Oxford: Lang, 2004.

Martyn, J. Louis. *History and Theology in the Fourth Gospel.* 3rd ed. The New Testament Library. Louisville, Ky.: Westminster John Knox, 2003.

Mason, Steve. "Contradiction or Counterpoint? Josephus and Historical Method." *Review of Rabbinic Judaism* 6 (2003): 145–88.

———. *Josephus and the New Testament.* 2nd ed. Peabody, Mass.: Hendrickson, 2003.

McDonald, Brian. "Post-Holocaust Theodicy, American Imperialism, and the 'Very Jewish Jesus' of Norman Mailer's *The Gospel According to the Son.*" *Journal of Modern Literature* 30 (2007): 78–90.

McDonough, Frank. *Neville Chamberlain, Appeasement, and the British Road to War.* New Frontiers in History. Manchester: Manchester University Press, 1998.

McGregor, Robert Kuhn, and Ethan Lewis. *Conundrums for the Long Week-End: England, Dorothy L. Sayers, and Lord Peter Wimsey.* Kent, Ohio: Kent State University Press, 2000.

McNulty, Edward N. "Three Artists View Christ: Marc Chagall, Abraham Rattner, and Robert Lentz." *Christianity and the Arts* 6 (1999): 10–16.

Meier, John P. *A Marginal Jew: Rethinking the Historical Jesus.* Anchor Bible Reference Library. New York: Doubleday, 1991.

Mellinkoff, Ruth. "Judas's Red Hair and the Jews." *Journal of Jewish Art* 9 (1982): 31–46.

———. *Outcasts: Signs of Otherness in Northern European Art of the Late Middle Ages.* 2 vols. California Studies in the History of Art 32. Berkeley: University of California Press, 1993.

Metzner, R. *Kaiphas Der Hohepriester Jenes Jahres: Geschichte Und Deutung*: Brill Academic Publishers, 2010.

Milgrom, Jacob. *Leviticus 1–16: A New Translation with Introduction and Commentary.* The Anchor Bible. New York: Doubleday, 1991.

Miller, David M. "Whom Do You Follow? The Jewish Politeia and the Maccabean Background of Josephus's Sign Prophets." In *Common Judaism: Explorations in Second-Temple Judaism*, ed. Wayne O. McCready and Adele Reinhartz, 173–83. Minneapolis: Fortress, 2008.

Milne, Lesley. "Nationalism, Anti-Semitism, and Bulgakov," in *Bulgakov: The Novelist-Playwright*, ed. Lesley Milne. Luxembourg: Harwood, 1995.

Mitchell, Alan C., and Daniel J. Harrington. *Hebrews.* Sacra Pagina Series. Collegeville, Minn.: Liturgical Press, 2007.

Mitchell, Margaret M. "Patristic Rhetoric on Allegory: Origen and Eustathius Put 1 Samuel 28 on Trial." *Journal of Religion* 85 (2005): 414–45.
Morgentaler, Goldie. "The Foreskin of the Heart: Ecumenism in Sholem Asch's Christian Trilogy." *Prooftexts* 8 (1988): 219–44.
Mork, Gordon R. "Christ's Passion on Stage: The Traditional Melodrama of Deicide." *Journal of Religion and Film* 8, no. 1 (2004): 1–11.
Mulder, Otto. *Simon the High Priest in Sirach 50: An Exegetical Study of the Significance of Simon the High Priest as Climax to the Praise of the Fathers in Ben Sira's Concept of the History of Israel.* Supplements to the *Journal for the Study of Judaism* 78. Leiden & Boston: Brill, 2003.
Munslow, Alun. *Narrative and History.* Theory and History. New York: Palgrave Macmillan, 2007.
Neusner, Jacob, and Richard S. Sarason, eds. *The Tosefta.* 6 vols. Translated by Jacob Neusner et al. New York: Ktav, 1977–1986.
Norich, Anita. "Sholem Asch and the Christian Question." In *Sholem Asch Reconsidered,* ed. Nanette Stahl, 251–65. New Haven, Conn.: Beinecke Rare Book and Manuscript Library, 2004.
Norris, Richard A., Jr. "Apocryphal Writings and Acts of the Martyrs." In *The Cambridge History of Early Christian Literature,* ed. Frances M. Young, Lewis Ayres, and Andrew Louth, 28–35. New York: Cambridge University Press, 2004.
The Oberammergau Passion Play, 1634–1984. Revised by the Parish of Oberammergau. Oberammergau: Weixler, 1984.
Oberammergau: The Passion Play 2010. Munich: Pastel, 2010.
Origen. *Commentary on the Gospel According to John.* Edited by Ronald E. Heine. 2 vols. The Fathers of the Church. Washington, D.C.: Catholic University of America Press, 1989.
Orwell, George. "Anti-Semitism in Britain." In *The Collected Essays, Journalism and Letters of George Orwell: As I Please, 1943–1945,* ed. Sonia Orwell and Ian Angus, 332–33. London: Secker & Warburg, 1968.
Partridge, Jeffrey F. L. "*The Gospel According to the Son* and Christian Belief." *Journal of Modern Literature* 30 (2007): 64–77.
Patterson, Nancy-Lou. "Images of Judaism and Anti-Semitism in the Novels of Dorothy L. Sayers." *Sayers Review* 2 (1978): 17–24.
Petropoulou, M. Z. *Animal Sacrifice in Ancient Greek Religion, Judaism, and Christianity, 100 BC–AD 200.* Oxford Classical Monographs. New York: Oxford University Press, 2008.
Piovanelli, Pierluigi. "Exploring the Ethiopic Book of the Cock, an Apocryphal Passion Gospel from Late Antiquity." *Harvard Theological Review* 96 (2003): 427–54.
———. "Le livre du coq." In *Ecrits Apocryphes Chrétiens,* ed. François Bovon and Pierre Geoltrain, 137–203. Paris: Gallimard, 2005.
———. "The Reception of Early Christian Texts and Traditions in Late Antique Apocryphal Literature." In *The Reception and Interpretation of the Bible in Late Antiquity: Proceedings of the Montréal Colloquium in Honour of Charles Kannengiesser, 11–13 October 2006,* ed. Charles Kannengiesser, Lorenzo DiTommaso, and Lucian Turcescu, 429–39. Leiden & Boston: Brill, 2008.
———. "Rewritten Bible ou Bible in progress? La réécriture des traditions mémoriales bibliques dans le judaïsme et le christianisme anciens." *Revue de théologie et de philosophie* 139 (2007): 295–310.
———. "What Is a Christian Apocryphal Text and How Does It Work? Some Observations on Apocryphal Hermeneutics." *Nederlands Theologisch Tijdschrift* 59 (2005): 31–40.

Potter, Nicole. *Movement for Actors*. New York: Allworth, 2002.
Powell, Mark Allan. *Jesus as a Figure in History: How Modern Historians View the Man from Galilee*. Louisville, Ky.: Westminster John Knox Press, 1998.
Power, Edmond. "The Church of St. Peter at Jerusalem: Its Relation to the House of Caiphas and Sancta Sion." *Biblica* 9 (1928): 167–86.
———. "The House of Caiphas and the Church of St. Peter. II, Archaeological Proof of the Authenticity of the Site." *Biblica* 10 (1929): 394–416.
———. "St. Peter in Gallicantu." *Biblica* 12 (1931): 411–46.
Price, Jonathan J. "461–465. Burial Cave in the Peace Forest ("Caiaphas Cave")." In *Corpus Inscriptionum Iudaeae/Palestinae : A Multi-Lingual Corpus of the Inscriptions from Alexander to Muhammad*, edited by Hannah Cotton et al., 651–58. Berlin and New York: De Gruyter, 2010.
——— "The Provincial Historian in Rome." In *Josephus and Jewish History in Flavian Rome and Beyond*, ed. Joseph Sievers and Gaia Lembi, 100–118. Leiden & Boston: Brill, 2005.
Propp, William Henry. *Exodus 19–40: A New Translation with Introduction and Commentary*. The Anchor Bible. New York: Doubleday, 2006.
Quasten, Johannes. *Patrology*. 2 vols. Utrecht: Spectrum; Westminster, Md.: Newman, 1950, 1953.
Rajak, Tessa. "Jews and Greeks: The Invention and Exploitation of Polarities in the Nineteenth Century." In *The Uses and Abuses of Antiquity*, ed. Michael Denis Biddiss and Maria Wyke, 57–77. Bern & New York: Lang, 1999.
Ramsey, Boniface. *Beginning to Read the Fathers*. New York: Paulist, 1985.
Reich, Ronny. "Ossuary Inscriptions from the 'Caiaphas' Tomb." *Atiqot* 21 (1992): 72–77.
———. "Ossuary Inscriptions from the Caiaphas Tomb." *Jerusalem Perspective* 4, no. 4 (1991): 13–22.
———"Ossuary Inscriptions of the Caiaphas Family from Jerusalem." In *Ancient Jerusalem Revealed. Expanded Edition*, ed. Hillel Geva, 223–25. Jerusalem: Israel Exploration Society, 2000.
Reinhartz, Adele. "Gospel Audiences: Variations on a Theme." In *The Audience of the Gospels: Further Conversation about the Origin and Function of the Gospels in Early Christianity*, ed. Edward W. Klink III. Winona Lake, Ind.: Eisenbrauns, 2009.
———. "Jesus as Prophet: Predictive Prolepses in the Fourth Gospel." *Journal for the Study of the New Testament* 36 (1989): 3–16.
———. *Jesus of Hollywood*. New York: Oxford University Press, 2007.
———. "The Johannine Community and Its Jewish Neighbors: A Reappraisal." In *What Is John? Literary and Social Readings of the Fourth Gospel*, ed. Fernando F. Segovia, 111–38. Atlanta: Scholars, 1998.
Ricci, Nino. *Testament*. Toronto: Doubleday Canada, 2002.
Roberts, Alexander, and James Donaldson. *The Ante-Nicene Fathers: The Writings of the Fathers Down to A.D. 325*. 10 vols. Rev. and chronologically arranged, with brief prefaces and occasional notes, by A. Cleveland Coxe. Peabody, Mass.: Hendrickson, 1994.
Robertson, James C. *The British Board of Film Censors: Film Censorship in Britain, 1896–1950*. Dover, N.H.: Croom Helm, 1985.
Robinson, J. W. *Studies in Fifteenth-Century Stagecraft*. Early Art, Drama, and Music Monograph Series. Kalamazoo: Medieval Institute Publications, Western Michigan University, 1991.
Rocca, Samuel. *Herod's Judaea: A Mediterranean State in the Classical World*. Tübingen: Mohr Siebeck, 2008.
Rudavsky, David. *Modern Jewish Religious Movements: A History of Emancipation and Adjustment*. 3rd rev. ed. New York: Behrman House, 1979.

Sanders, E. P. *The Historical Figure of Jesus*. New York: Penguin, 1996.

———. "Jerusalem and Its Temple in Early Christian Thought and Practice." In *Jerusalem: Its Sanctity and Centrality to Judaism, Christianity, and Islam*, ed. Lee I. Levine, 90–103. New York: Continuum, 1999.

———. *Judaism: Practice and Belief, 63 BCE–66 CE*. Philadelphia: Trinity Press International, 1992.

Saramago, José. *The Gospel According to Jesus Christ*. Translated by Giovanni Pontiero. San Diego: Harcourt Brace, 1994.

Sarna, Jonathan D. *American Judaism: A History*. New Haven, Conn.: Yale University Press, 2004.

Sarna, Nahum M. *Exodus = [Shemot]: The Traditional Hebrew Text with the New JPS Translation*. The JPS Torah Commentary. Philadelphia: Jewish Publication Society, 1991.

Sayers, Dorothy L. *The Man Born to Be King: A Play-Cycle on the Life of Our Lord and Saviour, Jesus Christ*. London: Gollancz, 1943.

Scheidwiler, Felix. "The Gospel of Nicodemus: Acts of Pilate and Christ's Descent into Hell." In Schneemelcher and Wilson, *New Testament Apocrypha*, 2:501–36.

Schmidt, Friedrich. "Ausflug Nach Israel: Jesus und Petrus in Badeshorts." *Frankfurter Allgemeine Zeitung*, September 19, 2009.

Schaff, Philip. *A Select Library of the Christian Church: Nicene and Post-Nicene Fathers*. First Series. 14 vols. Peabody, Mass.: Hendrickson, 1994.

Schaff, Philip, and Henry Wace. *A Select Library of the Christian Church: Nicene and Post-Nicene Fathers*. Second Series. 14 vols. Peabody, Mass.: Hendrickson, 1994.

Schneemelcher, Wilhelm, and R. McL. Wilson. *New Testament Apocrypha*. Rev. ed. 2 vols. Cambridge: Clarke; Louisville, Ky.: Westminster/John Knox Press, 1991.

Schreckenberg, Heinz, and Kurt Schubert. *Jewish Historiography and Iconography in Early and Medieval Christianity*. Compendia Rerum Iudaicarum Ad Novum Testamentum. Section 3, Jewish Traditions in Early Christian Literature 2. Assen, Netherlands: Van Gorcum / Minneapolis: Fortress, 1992.

Schrenk, Gottlob. "Archiereus." In *Theological Dictionary of the New Testament*, vol. 3, ed. Gerhard Kittel, Gerhard Friedrich, and Geoffrey William Bromiley. 265–83. Grand Rapids, Mich.: Eerdmans, 1964.

Schürer, Emil. *A History of the Jewish People in the Age of Jesus Christ (175 B.C.–A.D. 135)*. 3 vols. Translated by T. A. Burkill et al. Revised and edited by Géza Vermès, Fergus Millar, and Martin Goodman. Edinburgh: Clark, 1973.

Schwartz, Daniel R. "On Two Aspects of a Priestly View of Descent at Qumran." In *Archaeology and History in the Dead Sea Scrolls: The New York University Conference in Memory of Yigael Yadin*, ed. Lawrence H Schiffman, 157–79. Sheffield: JSOT, 1990.

———. *Studies in the Jewish Background of Christianity*, Wissenschaftliche Untersuchungen Zum Neuen Testament. Tübingen: Mohr, 1992.

Schweitzer, Albert. *The Quest of the Historical Jesus: A Critical Study of Its Progress from Reimarus to Wrede*. Translated by William Montgomery. New York: Macmillan, 1910.

Shapiro, James S. *Oberammergau: The Troubling Story of the World's Most Famous Passion Play*. New York: Pantheon, 2000.

Shaviv, Paul. "Drabinsky's Gospel." *Canadian Jewish News*, November 6, 2003.

Sherman, Franklin. "Oberammergau 2000." *Christian Century*, August 16–23, 2000, 822–23.

Shutt, R. J. H. "Letter of Aristeas." In *The Old Testament Pseudepigrapha and the New Testament: Prolegomena for the Study of Christian Origins*, ed. James H. Charlesworth, 7–34. New York: Cambridge University Press, 1985.

Sloyan, Gerard Stephen. *Jesus on Trial: A Study of the Gospels*. 2nd ed. Minneapolis: Fortress, 2006.

Smallwood, E. Mary. "The Date of the Dismissal of Pontius Pilate from Judaea." *Journal of Jewish Studies* 5 (1954): 12–21.

———. "High Priests and Politics in Roman Palestine." *Journal of Theological Studies* n.s. 13 (1962): 14–34.

———. *The Jews under Roman Rule: From Pompey to Diocletian*. Studies in Judaism in Late Antiquity. Leiden: Brill, 1976.

Smith, D. Moody. *John among the Gospels*. 2nd ed. Columbia: University of South Carolina Press, 2001.

Solomon. *The Book of the Bee, the Syriac Text Ed. from the Manuscripts in London, Oxford, and Munich*. Anecdota Oxoniensia. Semitic Series, vol. 1, pt. 2. Edited by E. A. Wallis Budge. Oxford: Clarendon, 1886.

Steel, Duncan. *Marking Time: The Epic Quest to Invent the Perfect Calendar*. New York: Wiley, 2000.

Stern, Richard C., Clayton N. Jefford, and Guerric DeBona. *Savior on the Silver Screen*. New York: Paulist, 1999.

Sticca, Sandro. *The Latin Passion Play: Its Origins and Development*. Albany: State University of New York Press, 1970.

Stover, Dale. "Anti-Semitism: Boundary of Jewish-Christian Understanding." *Christian Century*, June 26, 1974, 668–71.

Strickland, Debra Higgs. *Saracens, Demons, and Jews: Making Monsters in Medieval Art*. Princeton, N.J.: Princeton University Press, 2003.

Suh, Myung Soo. *The Tabernacle in the Narrative History of Israel from the Exodus to the Conquest*. Studies in Biblical Literature. New York: Lang, 2003.

Swartz, Michael D., and Joseph Yahalom. *Avodah: An Anthology of Ancient Poetry for Yom Kippur*. Penn State Library of Jewish Literature. University Park: Pennsylvania State University Press, 2005.

Thausing, Moritz, and Frederick Alexis Eaton. *Albert Dürer: His Life and Works*. London: Murray, 1882.

Theissen, Gerd. *The Gospels in Context: Social and Political History in the Synoptic Tradition*. Translated by Linda M. Maloney. Minneapolis: Fortress, 1991.

Thilo, Johannes C. *Codex Apocryphus Novi Testamenti*. Leipzig: Vogel, 1832.

Thistlethwaite, Susan. "Mel Makes a War Movie." In *Perspectives on "The Passion of the Christ,"* 127–45. New York: Miramax, 2004.

Trachtenberg, Joshua. *The Devil and the Jews: The Medieval Conception of the Jew and Its Relation to Modern Antisemitism*. New Haven, Conn.: Yale University Press, 1943.

Travis, Peter W. *Dramatic Design in the Chester Cycle*. Chicago: University of Chicago Press, 1982.

Turnbull, Malcolm J. *Victims or Villains: Jewish Images in Classic English Detective Fiction*. Bowling Green, Ohio: Bowling Green State University Popular Press, 1998.

Uro, Risto. *Thomas: Seeking the Historical Context of the Gospel of Thomas*. New York: Clark, 2003.

VanderKam, James C. *From Joshua to Caiaphas: High Priests after the Exile*. Minneapolis: Fortress / Assen, Netherlands: Van Gorcum, 2004.

Vardaman, Jerry. "New Inscription Which Mentions Pilate as 'Prefect.'" *Journal of Biblical Literature* 81 (1962): 70–71.

Vermès, Géza. *Jesus and the World of Judaism*. London: SCM, 1983.

Villalba i Varneda, Pere. *The Historical Method of Flavius Josephus*. Arbeiten zur Literatur und Geschichte des hellenistischen Judentums 19. Leiden: Brill, 1986.

Walsh, Richard G. *Reading the Gospels in the Dark: Portrayals of Jesus in Film.* Harrisburg, Pa.: Trinity Press International, 2003.
West, Larry E. *The Saint Gall Passion Play.* Brookline, Mass.: Classical Folia, 1976.
Westcott, Brooke Foss, and Arthur Westcott. *The Gospel According to St. John: The Greek Text with Introduction and Notes.* London: Murray, 1908.
White, Hayden V. *Metahistory: The Historical Imagination in Nineteenth-Century Europe.* Baltimore: Johns Hopkins University Press, 1973.
———. "The Value of Narrativity in the Representation of Reality." *Critical Inquiry* 7 (1980): 5–27.
Wick, Peter. *Die Urchristlichen Gottesdienste: Entstehung und Entwicklung im Rahmen der Früjüdischen Tempel-, Synagogen- und Hausfrömmigkeit.* Beiträge zur Wissenschaft vom Alten und Neuen Testament. Stuttgart: Kohlhammer, 2002.
Wilde, Oscar. *The Ballad of Reading Gaol.* London: Smithers, 1898.
White, L. Michael. *Scripting Jesus: The Gospel Authors as Storytellers and Their Images of Jesus.* New York: HarperOne, 2010.
Winter, Paul. *On the Trial of Jesus.* 2d ed. Rev. and ed. T. Alec Burkill and Géza Vermès. Berlin & New York: De Gruyter, 1974.
Woolf, Rosemary. *The English Mystery Plays.* Berkeley: University of California Press, 1972.
Wright, N. T. *Jesus and the Victory of God.* Christian Origins and the Question of God 2. Minneapolis: Fortress, 1996.
Zeffirelli, Franco. *Franco Zeffirelli's Jesus: A Spiritual Diary.* San Francisco: Harper & Row, 1984.
Zissu, B. and Goren Y, "The Ossuary of 'Miriam Daughter of Yeshua Son of Caiaphas, Priests [of] Ma'aziah from Beth 'Imri.'" *Israel Exploration Journal* 61 (2011): 74–95.
Zwick, Reinhold. "Antijüdische Tendenzen im Jesusfilm." *Communicatio Socialis* 30 (1997): 227–46.

INDEX OF ANCIENT SOURCES

BIBLE

Hebrew Bible/Old Testament

Genesis
12:1–3	15
17:5	15
37:34	28

Exodus
12:22	211–12n43
12:46	212n43
19:5–6	15
28	188
28:1–43	20
28:2–29:1	193
28:28–30	191
28:28–39	191
28:40–42	20
39	188
39:1–31	20, 193, 210n40

Leviticus
9	17
6:14–15	17
16:1–30	16
16:4	20
16:10	17
16:13–14	17
16:20–22	17
16:23–24	17
19:16	149
21:10–20	16
21:17	16
21:17–20	182
21:18–20	16

Numbers
19:1–20	17

Joshua
13:22	59

1 Samuel
22:20	25

2 Samuel
1:11–12	28

1 Kings
2:35	18
21:12–15	41
22:20	60

2 Kings
18:30–19:1	28

Psalms
2	53, 148
8:2	174
21:17	99
110:1	27

Job
5:12	99
15:25–27	188

Daniel
7:13	27

Ezra
6	209n33

1 Chronicles
6:3–15	18
6:50–53	18

INDEX OF ANCIENT SOURCES

Deuterocanonical and Pseudepigraphal Works

Letter of Aristeas 193–94

1 Maccabees
1:13–15	160
1:20–56	160
2:66–68	155

2 Maccabees
4:12	160
5:15–20	41
5:19–20	40–41
7	156
7:19	156
8:16–17	155–56

Sirach
50:1	194
50:5–11	194

Wisdom
1:5	60

New Testament

Matthew
1:21	34
1:23	34
3:11	129
4:1–11	128
4:5	172
6:2	60
16:21	35–36
18:20	34
20:18	36
21:12–16	174
21:14	173
21:15	36
21:23	36
22:7	50
23	119–20, 161
23:27–28	74
23:38	50
26	98
26:1–5	31–32, 33
26:3–5	3
26:14	36
26:14–15	50
26:47	60
26:47–56	32–33
26:55	173
26:57	2, 56
26:57–58	32
26:57–67	33–35
26:59–68	147
26:61	150, 176
26:62	176
26:64	3
26:65	4
26:69–75	35
26:70	2
27:1	56
27:1–2	35
27:12	36, 50, 169
27:20	36, 133
27:24–26	119, 136
27:25	113, 115, 136, 141
27:27–31	38
27:41	36
27:51	173
27:59–60	64
27:62	36
28:13–15	81
28:18–20	68
28:20	34

Mark
1:12–13	128
2:26	24–25
8:31	26, 30
10:33	30
11:15–18	173–74
11:18	30
11:27	173
12:35	173
14:1	29, 30
14:1–2	25–26
14:10	30
14:43–52	25, 26
14:43–15:1	3
14:49	173
14:53	39
14:53–65	25, 26–29
14:55–56	148
14:62	30, 34
14:63	4

INDEX OF ANCIENT SOURCES

14:64b	28	11:47–48	176–77
14:66–72	25, 29	11:47–53	40–43
15:1	17, 25, 29, 56	11:49	50, 54, 176
15:3	31	11:49–50	1
15:10	31	11:49–52	3, 41, 44, 58, 61, 101, 128,
15:11	31, 133		147, 166, 168, 211n41
15:16–20	38	11:50	176
15:31	31	11:51	54, 61, 177
15:46	64	11:52	177
		11:57	131
Luke		12:10	42
1:1–4	24	12:10–11	41
3:1–2	3, 36–37, 39, 47, 54, 67	12:19	41
3:1–5	39, 46	12:42–43	70
3:2	3, 25, 55–56	13:16	46
4:1–13	128	13:27	128
4:9	172	13:38	46
19:45–48	174	14:2–3	46
20:19–20	131	16:2	48
22:1–5	133–34	16:22	46
22:3	128	16:23–24	46
22:33–34	1	17	46
22:4	167	18:1–11	43–44
22:47–54	37	18:3	167
22:53	173	18:12–14	44
22:54–62	37–38	18:13	16, 54, 56, 147
22:63–65	38	18:15–18	44–45
22:66–23:1	38–40	18:16	64
23:11	134	18:19	3, 150
23:53	64	18:19–24	45, 56, 147
		18:20	173
John		18:22	181
1:19–28	46	18:25–27	45–46
1:29	42, 211n43	18:28	2, 46–47
2:13–22	175	18:31	18
5:14	173	19:6	50
7:14	173	19:14	211n43
7:32	43	19:15	134, 136
7:39	60	19:29	211n43
7:45	43	19:38–42	64
9	101	21:24	24
9:41	41		
9:46	185	Acts	
9:5	185	4–5	39
10:23	173	4:1–15	47, 177
10:33	212n58	4:5–6	63, 214n53
11	84, 203	4:14–15	3, 177
11:47	50	5:16–6:1	177

5:17–42	47–48	18.120–24	14
5:19	177	18.261–72	168
5:24	177	18:284	168
5:25	177	19:316	148
5:27–28	177	20.97–98	168
5:42	177	20:97–99	42
6–7	49, 148	20:118	168
6:7–7:2	48, 178	20.131	167
6:9–7:60	39	20:169–72	42
6:13–14	178	20:188	42
7:1	178	20.197	11, 148
7:54–8:2	18	20.197–203	49
9:1–2	178	20.200	18
12	148	20.203	11, 23, 148
12:2	49	20.205	44
21:38	41–42	20.213	23

Hebrews
4:14	197

OTHER ANCIENT WRITINGS
Jewish Authors

Josephus

Antiquitates judaicae
(Antiquities of the Jews)
3.151–92	11
3.179	195
3:184–87	195
12.158	11
13.288	209n24
14.167	18
15.173	18
15.405–9	34
15.408	17
17	166–67
17.339	167
18:26	167
18:3	167
18.33–3	12
18.34	23
18.34–35	13
18.55–62	169–70, 221n13
18.60–62	170–71
18:88	168
18.90–95	13–14, 34
18.91–95	20–21
18.95	21

Bellum judaicum (Jewish War)
2	166
2.169–74	169, 221n13
2.175–77	171
2.243	48
2.258–63	42
2.379	84
2.389	84
2.401	84
2.441	44
2.563	11
2.648–53	11
4.15–17	11
5.230–37	195
6.294	167

Vita (The Life)
62	18
193	44

Philo

De Legatione ad Gaium
(On the Embassy to Gaius)
299–305	170

De Vita Mosis
(On the Life of Moses)
2.109–16	194
2.118	194
2.122	194–95
2.124	195

2.131	195	Athanasius	
2.132	195	*Epistle to the Bishops*	54
2:133	226n35	*Four Discourses*	54
		Dionysius	54
De Specialibus Legibus		*To Adelphius*	54
(On the Special Laws)			
1:156	167	Augustine of Hippo	
		Harmony of the Gospels	

RABBINIC SOURCES

Mishnah

		3.6.19	56, 57
		3.6.24	56–57
Gittin		*Lectures or Tractates on the Gospel*	
6:7	18	*According to St. John*	
		49	55
Horayot		49:27	58
1:518		113	55–56
		114	57–58
Parah		*On the Holy Trinity*	59
3:5	14	*Reply to Faustus the*	
		Manichaean	59
Sanhedrin			
4	18	Eusebius	
11:2	18	*Church History*	54–55, 67
Sotah		Hippolytus	
1:4	18	*Exposition of Psalm 2*	53
9:1	18		
		John Chrysostom	
Yevamot		*Homily 79*	55
6.4	209n24		
		Justin Martyr	
Yoma		*First Apology*	66
1:6	195		
		Origen	
Tosefta		*Commentary on the Gospel*	
Yevamot		*According to John*	59–62
1:10	221n4		
		Tertullian	
BABYLONIAN TALMUD		*Apologeticum*	66
Yoma		*On the Resurrection*	
8b	151–52	*of the Flesh*	53

EARLY CHRISTIAN LITERATURE

Church Fathers

Anon.
*Apostolic
  Constitutions*   53–54, 56

NEW TESTAMENT APOCRYPHA

Acts of John	63
Acts of Paul	63
Acts of Peter	63
Acts of Pilate	63–64, 66–69, 221–22n4

Arabic Gospel of the
  Infancy of the Saviour   63
Gospel of the Nazaraeans   64
Gospel of Nicodemus   66–69, 71,
                           221–22n4
Infancy Gospel of Thomas   63, 125
Narrative of Joseph
  of Arimathea   64–66
Recognitions of Clement   69–70

OTHER

*Didache: the Teaching
  of the Apostles*   70–71

CLASSICAL AUTHORS

Tacitus
Annales
2.42.5   13

INDEX OF MODERN AUTHORS

Asch, Sholem, 9, 73, 82, 89–95, 193, 217n79

Babington, Bruce, 136
Bauckham, Richard, 210n1
Baugh, Lloyd, 141–42
Beckwith, Sarah, 99–100
Betz, Hans Dieter, 160–61
Blinzler, Josef, 147–48, 150, 151–52, 222n15–16
Bond, Helen, 31, 34–35, 37, 39, 43, 46–47, 49–50, 209n16, 211n23, 223n37, 224n11, 225n18
Borg, Marcus J., 13, 49, 153, 172
Bornkamm, Günther, 157, 161
Brant, Jo-Ann A., 46
Brown, Raymond E., 31, 39, 150
Bulgakov, Mikhail, 77–78

Callaghan, Morley, 76, 193
Carroll, John, 75, 189
Carter, Warren, 166, 211n41
Chilton, Bruce, 152, 154, 172
Cohn, Haim, 149
Collingwood, Robin G., 4–5, 6, 7, 24, 145, 164, 205
Cook, Michael, 148
Crossan, John Dominic, 13, 49, 148, 153, 159, 172

Durling, Robert M., 74–75

Elliott, James Keith, 63, 71
Evans, Peter William, 136

Fadiman, Clifton, 93
Fitzmyer, Joseph A., 31, 34
Flusser, David, 154–55, 159
Fredriksen, Paula, 152–53
Friedman, Saul, 113

Grant, Michael, 172
Graves, Robert, 76–77, 78–79, 95
Goodman, Martin, 158, 166, 172
Goren, Yuval, 226

Heilbrun, Carolyn G., 216n48
Hengel, Martin, 157–58, 159, 162

Jackson, Bernard, 148

Kazantzakis, Nikos, 76, 192
Kazin, Alfred, 93
King, Pamela, 187
Klausner, Joseph, 93
Krauskopf, Joseph, 107–10, 219n57

Laut, Stephen J., 97
Leitzmann, Hans, 148

Marcus, Joel, 28, 210n9
Martin, James, 80–82
Martin, John D., 121
Mailer, Norman, 76, 79–80, 95, 153, 193
Meier, John, 153
Mellinkoff, Ruth, 181–82

Orwell, George, 87

Price, Jonathan J., 208n7, 209n19, 216n37

Quasten, John, 67

Rajak, Tessa, 160
Ramsey, Boniface, 52–53
Ricci, Nino, 76
Robinson, John W., 99, 187, 188
Rocca, Samuel, 209n30

Sanders, Ed P., 145, 152, 153, 158, 166–67, 172, 212n66
Saramago, Jose, 77
Sayers, Dorothy, 9, 73, 82–89, 94–95, 117, 182, 187, 215n30
Schürer, Emil, 48–49, 145, 150
Schwartz, Daniel, 12–13
Shapiro, James, 102, 116–17, 189
Sherman, Franklin, 116, 189
Smallwood, E. Mary, 14

VanderKam, James, 145
Vermès, Géza, 158

White, Hayden, 5–6, 145
Wilde, Oscar, 75
Winter, Paul, 21, 28, 31, 37, 40, 49, 148, 211n38
Wright, N. Thomas, 155–57, 159, 160

Zissu, Boaz, 226

SUBJECT INDEX

Aaron, 11, 16, 18
Acts of the Apostles: Caiaphas in, 3, 8, 47–48, 53, 63, 215n53; reference to the Temple in, 172, 177–78, 224n16; trial and execution of Stephen in, 18, 39, 48, 49, 148
Agrippa I, 19, 21, 84
American Jewish Committee, 103, 111, 220n84
Annas (Ananus): death of, 64; family of, 19, 22; in historiography, 147; interrogation of Jesus, 44, 45, 46–47, 48, 50, 53, 56–58, 65, 67, 68–69, 147; in literature, 73–75, 76, 79, 80, 81, 84, 90, 94–95; opposition to Jesus, 52, 53, 63, 65, 66, 69, 71, 76, 107; paired with Caiaphas, 3, 8, 47, 52, 55–56, 63–64, 65, 67, 72, 76, 79, 84, 94, 101, 121, 122; and Pilate, 12; reference in Luke to Caiaphas and, 36–37, 39, 47, 54–56; on stage, 97–100, 101, 104, 105, 107, 108, 111, 113, 115, 116, 120–1, 122, 187; vagueness in Gospels concerning role of, 48–49, 94
Annas II (Ananus II), 11, 22, 49, 95, 148, 217n84
anti-Semitism: anti-Jewish tone of apocryphal literature, 71; vs. anti-Judaism, 208n25; 'Anti-Semitism in Britain' (Orwell), 87; and Asch, 93, 94, 95; church fathers as anti-Jewish, 52–53, 208n25; and portrayal of Caiaphas, 6, 7, 8, 9, 10, 87–89, 100, 107, 121, 128, 136, 141–42, 143, 144–45, 184, 185, 189, 197, 204–5; and Jesus films, 126, 136, 141–42, 143, 189, 191, 197; Jesus used to describe experience of, 94; and Matthew 23 and its interpretations, 161; and Oberammergau Passion play, 9, 10, 107–11, 112–13, 116–17, 121, 122–23, 189, 197, 198–99, 220n8; and Sayers, 87–89, 95, 216n48

Apocrypha. *See* New Testament Apocrypha
Arcand, Denys. *See Jesus of Montreal*
Archelaus, 19, 20, 64, 76, 166–67, 214n41
Asch, Sholem. See *The Nazarene*
Avodah service, 196–97

The Ballad of Reading Gaol (Wilde), 75
Barabbas, 31, 36, 50, 77, 105, 106, 119, 122, 125, 135, 136, 199
B'nai B'rith: Anti-Defamation League, 103, 111
Buchowetzki, Dimitri. See *Der Galiläer* (film)
Burkhart, Anton, 180, 199, 200 (image), 225n1

Caiaphas: in Acts, 3, 8, 47–48, 53, 63, 215n53; appearance of, 16, 181; appointment as high priest, 12, 22, 54–55, 220n76; career and personal life, 14–21; in context, 11–23; covenantal and cultic role of, 1, 7–8, 14–15, 16–17, 201; daughter of, 14, 64–65, 66; death of, 21–22, 64; in early Christian imagination, 52–72; elusiveness of, 2–3, 6, 10, 180, 200; exploited for comic and satirical potential, 96, 97, 99, 100, 182, 204; in the Gospels, 2, 3, 7, 8, 24–51, 57, 58, 72, 82, 94, 147, 150, 151, 172, 178, 203; and greed, 127–28; guises of, 2, 144, 180; in historiography, 4, 5, 6, 9–10, 144–64, 179; in history, 10, 165–79; house of, 1–2, 57–58, 207n4; images of contempt, 181–92; images of respect, 192–97; and Jewish-Roman relations, 2, 6, 19, 42, 84, 90, 94, 95, 114, 115, 117, 119, 122, 128–31, 144, 146, 152–54, 163–64, 165, 169, 171, 204; in 'life of Jesus' narratives, 2, 8, 9, 73, 78, 203; in literature, 4, 5, 8, 9, 73–95; long tenure of, 12–13, 22, 151, 167, 171–72; and

Caiaphas (*continued*)
  need to keep order on behalf of Rome, 2, 9, 10, 76, 128, 152, 153, 164, 165–72, 179; in New Testament Apocrypha, 6, 8, 14, 21–22, 62–72; and opposition between Judaism and Hellenism, 154–62; ossuary of, 2, 3, 14, 22, 23, 64, 202, 205, 207n5, 207n6; 224n81; 226; and Pilate, 1, 2, 4, 9, 12–13, 22, 55, 58, 62, 76–78, 106, 115, 119, 120, 136, 139–40, 144, 151, 153, 154, 168–72, 199, 202, 204; plasticity of, 72, 145, 203–4; and plot to kill Jesus, 2, 3, 4, 8, 9–10, 31, 32, 40, 42, 47, 50–1, 53, 59, 61, 63–64, 65–66, 72, 83, 91, 104, 121, 127–32, 159, 163, 165, 168–69, 179, 205; prophecy of, 8, 42, 43, 58–62, 72, 84, 94; removal from office, 13–14; reputation as deicide, 6, 7–10, 22, 51, 52, 53–54, 59, 62, 71, 73, 74, 76, 78, 82, 95, 99, 100, 110–11, 121, 122, 135, 136, 143, 144, 180, 181, 183, 189, 197, 200, 204, 205, 208n25; and Satan, 43, 128, 136, 144, 157, 163, 188, 203, 204, 221n15; on screen, 4, 5, 9, 124–43, 189–92; as secret believer in Jesus, 70–71, 71–72; and spies, 131–32; as stand-in for the unbeliever, 72; on stage, 4, 5, 9, 96–123, 187–89; as symbol of 'heretical' groups, 8, 62, 72; and tearing of garments, 3, 4, 21, 34, 38, 48, 133, 149, 176, 181, 183, 201; and the Temple, 172–79; as villain, 8, 34, 51, 78, 122, 140, 143, 160, 183, 191, 203, 204; visual representation of, 4, 10, 180–201; in writings of Josephus, 2, 3, 6, 7, 11–23, 145, 205; in writings of the church fathers, 8, 52–62, 72, 75
Chagall, Marc: *White Crucifixion*, 93
Christ before Caiaphas (Duccio), 183–84
Christ before Caiaphas (Giotto), 182 (image), 183
Christ before the High Priest (van Honthorst), 184–85, 186 (image), 192–93
church fathers: as anti-Jewish, 52–53, 208n25; Athanasius, 54; Augustine of Hippo, 52, 55–59; Caiaphas in patristic literature, 8, 52–62, 72, 75; diversity among, 52–3; Eusebius, 54–55, 67; harmonization of Gospel accounts, 57, 58, 62, 72; Hippolytus, 53; Jerome, 52; and Johannine references to Caiaphas as high priest 'that year,' 54–56; John Chrysostom, 52, 55; Justin Martyr, 52, 66; Origen, 8, 52, 59–62, 213n26–27; overview of patristic literature, 52–53; Tertullian, 52, 53, 66, 212n4; on the trial(s) of Jesus, 56–57

Daisenberger, Joseph Alois. *See* Oberammergau Passion play: Daisenberger version
Dante. *See The Divine Comedy*
DeMille, Cecil B. *See The King of Kings* (1927 film)
The Divine Comedy (Dante), 73–75, 83, 152
Dornford-May, Mark: *Son of Man*, 142
Duccio di Buoninsegna: *Christ before Caiaphas*, 183–84
Dürer, Albrecht: *Green Passion*, 183; *Small Passion*, 183

Eleazar, 12, 18, 22, 193–94, 209n24
Epiphanius, 66
Exultet Roll, 218n23

Fadus, 21, 168
films. *See* Jesus films

Der Galiläer, 127, 132–33, 135–36, 140, 189, 191, 221n15
Gamaliel, 47–48, 63, 67, 70, 71, 81, 177, 209n24
Gibson, Mel. *See The Passion of the Christ*
Giotto di Bondone: *Christ before Caiaphas*, 182 (image), 183
The Gospel According to Jesus Christ (Saramago), 77
The Gospel According to Saint Matthew (film), 124, 136–37, 191, 192 (image), 226n45
The Gospel According to the Son (Mailer), 76, 79–80, 95, 153, 193
The Gospel of John (film), 124, 139–40, 191
Gospels: anonymous high priest in Passion account in Mark, 3, 25–31, 34–35, 56, 210n16, 225n18; appearance of title high priest in, 24–25; Caiaphas in, 2, 3, 7, 8, 24–51, 57, 58, 72, 82, 94, 147, 150, 151, 172, 178, 203; Caiaphas in John, 3, 24, 40–47, 48, 50, 56, 57, 58, 59–60, 61, 70, 76, 84, 94, 101, 112, 128, 138, 147, 165, 166, 168–69, 176,

203; Caiaphas in Luke, 3, 24, 36–40, 48, 54–55, 57, 67; Caiaphas in Matthew, 3, 24, 31–36, 48, 50, 56, 176; 'chief priests' in, 25–26, 27, 30–31, 32, 33, 35–36, 39–40, 43, 49, 50, 51, 52, 133–34, 169; differences among (concerning Caiaphas), 24, 25, 32, 33–34, 35, 36, 38–39, 40, 44, 45, 46, 48, 50, 57, 62, 176; historical value of, 8, 24, 62, 146–47, 148, 150, 151, 163; 'I am' (*ego eimi*) formula in John, 44; influence on Jesus films, 124–25, 126, 128, 130, 132, 133–34, 136, 139, 140, 142, 143; influence on Passion plays, 100, 101, 103, 104, 107, 109, 117, 119, 122; Johannine references to Caiaphas as high priest 'that year,' 40, 42, 54–56; and narrative imperative, 50; Passion accounts in, 3, 8, 21, 23, 25–51, 101; Peter's denial of Jesus in, 2, 25, 29–30, 35, 37–38, 44–46; reference in Luke to Caiaphas and Annas, 36–37, 39, 47, 54–56; reference to *synedrion* in, 17; reference to the Temple in, 172–76; as retrospective works, 24; vagueness concerning role of Annas, 48–49, 94
Gratus, Valerius, 12, 13, 22, 151, 220n76
Green Passion (Dürer), 183
Greene, David: *Godspell*, 126
The Greatest Story Ever Told (film), 124, 126, 132, 135, 140, 221n6

Hayes, Derek W. See *The Miracle Maker*
Herod Antipas, 104–5, 134, 140
Herod the Great, 19, 20, 21, 36, 52, 53, 54, 63, 67, 86, 91, 130, 141, 142, 166, 209n30, 214n41
high priests: anonymous high priest in Passion account in Mark, 3, 25–31, 34–35, 56, 210n16, 225n18; and Covenant, 14–15; cultic responsibilities of, 16–17; hereditary basis of high priesthood, 18–19; Herod's, 166; Jewish liturgical descriptions of, 195–97; Josephus on, 11–22, 166–68, 194, 195; lifestyle of, 16; political responsibilities of, 17–18; role in maintaining the public good, 166–68; vestments of, 19–21, 181, 187, 188, 191, 193–95, 210n40. *See also* Aaron; Annas; Annas II; Caiaphas; Eleazar; Hyrcanus; Joazar; Jonathan
Historia passionis Domini, 64

historiography: Caiaphas in, 4, 5, 6, 9–10, 144–64, 179; Caiaphas in historical Jesus research, 145–46, 165; Caiaphas in studies of Second Temple Judaism, 145–46, 221–22n4; and historical imagination, 4, 5, 7, 8; maximalist, minimalist, and in-between accounts of Caiaphas in, 146–51; and narrative imperative, 5, 7, 10, 50, 64, 144, 163, 164, 179; similarities between history and fiction, 4–7, 10, 144–45; theories concerning Caiaphas's motivations in, 151–62, 163–64, 165
Hitler, Adolf, 9, 84–85, 88, 93, 110
Holocaust, 6, 73, 94, 110, 128, 140, 143, 161, 199
Huber, Otto, 103, 113–22, 189, 199
Hyrcanus, 19, 20, 86, 209n24

Jesus: arrest of, 25, 26, 37, 43–44, 66, 148, 167, 173, 212n52; baptism (dating of), 54; brother James, 49, 148, 217n84; Caiaphas's role in plot to kill, 2, 3, 4, 8, 9–10, 31, 32, 40, 42, 47, 50–1, 53, 59, 61, 63–64, 65–66, 72, 83, 91, 104, 121, 127–32, 163, 165–66, 179, 205; Caiaphas in 'life of Jesus' narratives, 2, 8, 9, 73, 78, 203; and council's jurisdiction in capital offenses, 18; crucifixion of, 3, 4, 25, 31, 32, 36, 50, 74, 92, 95, 140, 150, 163, 211n43; death of, 61, 147, 156, 158–59; historical Jesus narratives, 144–64; interrogation of, 3, 21, 25, 26–29, 33–35, 38–40, 44, 45, 46–47, 48, 50, 53, 56–58, 67, 132–34; Jesus novels, 76–82, 89–94, 95, 203; Judas' betrayal of, 25, 26, 31, 32, 36, 37, 43–44, 50, 53, 60, 63, 65–66, 83, 104, 120, 128; mocking of, 31, 36, 38, 207n3; Peter's denial of, 2, 25, 29–30, 35, 37–38, 44–46, 57, 58, 147, 148; portrayal by Asch, 93–94; portrayal by Sayers, 87; prohibition against portraying, 87; resurrection of, 66, 74, 81, 82, 178; Sallman's iconic image of, 125; and the Temple, 172–79; and Temple 'cleansing,' 10, 91, 104, 155, 156, 164, 172, 173, 174, 175, 176, 178, 192, 225n19; 'temple tantrum' of, 152, 165; used to describe experience of anti-Semitism, 94 *See also* Jesus films; mystery cycles; Passion plays
Jesus (television movie), 125, 129

Jesus Christ Superstar (film), 124, 131, 141–42, 191; compared with *Hair* and *Tommy*, 126

Jesus films, 9, 124–43, 189–92; and anti-Semitism, 126, 136, 141–42, 143, 189, 191, 197; *Ben-Hur*, 125; as biopics, 125; and claims to historicity, 126; *From the Manger to the Cross*, 126; *Der Galiläer*, 127, 132–33, 135–36, 140, 189, 191, 221n15; *Godspell*, 126; *The Gospel According to Saint Matthew*, 124, 136–37, 191, 192 (image), 226n45; *The Gospel of John*, 124, 139–40, 191; *The Greatest Story Ever Told*, 124, 126, 132, 135, 140, 221n6; Indian film *Karunamayudu*, 220n4; influence of the Gospels on, 124–25, 126, 128, 130, 132, 133–34, 136, 139, 140, 142, 143; *INRI*, 131; *Jesus* (television movie), 125, 129; *Jesus Christ Superstar*, 124, 126, 131, 141–42, 191; *Jesus of Montreal*, 124, 125, 126, 138–39, 142; *Jesus of Nazareth*, 124, 126, 133, 135, 142, 191, 221n6; *The King of Kings* (1927), 124, 126, 127–28, 132, 136, 140, 189–91; *The King of Kings* (1961), 125, 126, 129, 134, 191; *The Last Temptation of Christ*, 126–27, 135, 191, 192; *Il Messias* (*The Messiah*), 126, 137–38; *The Miracle Maker*, 126, 190 (image), 191, 221n6; *The Passion of the Christ*, 124, 126, 128, 140–1, 191, 221n6; *The Passion Play at Oberammergau*, 124; and Passion plays, 124, 125, 138, 139; portrayals of Caiaphas in, 126–43; portrayals of Caiaphas at Jesus' trial in, 127, 132–41; portrayals of Caiaphas plotting against Jesus in, 127–32; *Son of Man*, 142; visual representation of Caiaphas in, 189–92

Jesus of Montreal (film), 124, 125, 126, 138–39, 142

Jesus of Nazareth (Klausner), 93

Jesus of Nazareth (miniseries), 124, 126, 132, 133, 135, 142, 191, 221n6

Jewish revolt against Rome, 11, 12, 19, 49, 84, 94, 146, 166, 221–22n4

Jewison, Norman. See *Jesus Christ Superstar*

Jonathan, 13–14, 22

Joseph of Arimathea, 63, 64–66, 67–68, 68–69, 78, 81, 85–86, 92–93, 105, 120

Josephus Flavius: and *Arabic Gospel of the Infancy of the Saviour*, 63; on Caiaphas, 2, 3, 6, 7, 11–23, 145, 171, 205; on the high priesthood, 11–22, 166–68, 194, 195; on Roman force used against Jewish followers of would-be messiahs, 42; on the stoning of Jesus' brother James, 49; use of high-priestly title in reference to former priests, 44, 48; use of term *stol*, 34; writings as retrospective works, 24; writings as sources for Asch and Sayers, 94; writings as sources for Jesus films, 125; writings as sources for modern scholarship, 146, 164

Joazar, 166–67, 168

Judas: betrayal of Jesus, 25, 26, 31, 32, 36, 37, 43–44, 50, 53, 60, 63, 65–66, 83, 104, 120, 128; described as Caiaphas's nephew, 65, 66; in literature, 75, 83–85, 89; on screen, 125, 127, 128, 132, 141; on stage, 101, 104, 120

King Jesus (Graves), 76–77, 78–79, 95, 203

The King of Kings (1927 film), 124, 126, 127–28, 132, 136, 140, 189–91

The King of Kings (1961 film), 125, 126, 129, 134, 191

The Last Temptation of Christ (Kazantzakis), 76, 192

Last Temptation of Christ (film), 126–27, 135, 191, 192

The Legend of the True Cross, 191

The Letters of Caiaphas, the High Priest (James Martin), 80–82

literature (featuring Caiaphas): 4, 5, 8, 9, 73–95; *The Ballad of Reading Gaol* (Wilde), 75; *The Divine Comedy* (Dante), 73–75, 83, 152; fiction, 76–95; *The Gospel According to Jesus Christ* (Saramago), 77; *The Gospel According to the Son* (Mailer), 76, 79–80, 95, 153; *King Jesus* (Graves), 76–77, 78–79, 95, 203; *The Last Temptation of Christ* (Kazantzakis), 76, 192; *The Letters of Caiaphas, the High Priest* (Martin), 80–82; *The Man Born to Be King* (Sayers), 9, 73, 82–89, 94–95, 117, 187; *The Master and Margarita* (Bulgakov), 77–78; *The Nazarene* (Asch), 9, 73, 82, 89–95, 193, 203; poetry, 73–75; relationship between Caiaphas and Pilate in, 76–78;

SUBJECT INDEX

Testament (Ricci), 76; *A Time for Judas* (Callaghan), 76, 193

The Man Born to Be King (Sayers), 9, 73, 82–89, 94–95, 117, 187; and anti-Semitism, 87–89, 95, 216n48; reception of, 87
Mary (mother of Jesus), 63, 104, 105, 125, 126; *planctus*, 100
Mary Magdalene, 104, 105, 126
The Master and Margarita (Bulgakov), 77–78
Il Messias (*The Messiah*), 126, 137–38
Michelangelo: *Pietà*, 125
The Miracle Maker (film), 126, 190 (image), 191, 221n6
Moses, 11, 15, 16, 55, 59, 101, 106, 107, 114, 116, 132, 178
mystery cycles, 96–100; Chester cycle, 96, 97; Lichfield Mysteries, 96; Ludus Coventriae play, 187; N Town cycle (Lincoln mystery plays), 96; and 'pageant waggons,' 97; staging of, 99; Towneley/Wakefield plays, 96, 99, 187, 188; York cycle, 96, 97–99, 187, 217n2; visual representation of Caiaphas in, 187–88

narrative imperative, 5, 7, 10, 50, 66, 144, 163, 164, 179, 203
Narrative of Joseph of Arimathea, 64–66
The Nazarene (Asch), 73, 82, 89–95, 193, 203; reception of, 93–94; sympathetic use of Christian subject matter in, 93–94
New Testament. *See* Gospels; New Testament Apocrypha
New Testament Apocrypha: *Acts of John*, 63; *Acts of Paul*, 63; *Acts of Peter*, 63; *Acts of Pilate*, 63, 65–69; anti-Jewish tone of, 71; *Arabic Gospel of the Infancy of the Saviour*, 63; Caiaphas in, 6, 8, 14, 21–22, 62–72; *Didache: the Teaching of the Apostles*, 70–71; *Gospel of Nicodemus*, 66–69; *Gospel of the Nazaraeans*, 64; impact on art, 213n31; *Infancy Gospel of Thomas*, 63, 125; and narrative imperative, 66; *Narrative of Joseph of Arimathea*, 64–66; overview of, 62–63; Pseudo-Clementines, 69–72; as rewritten Bible, 63

Nicodemus, 63, 65, 67, 68–69, 71, 81, 83, 85–86, 105, 120, 132, 222n16
Nostra Aetate, 110–11, 221n14

Oberammergau Passion play, 9, 10, 96, 102–23, 180; and anti-Semitism, 9, 10, 107–11, 112–13, 116–17, 121, 122–23, 189, 197, 198–99, 220n8; Caiaphas's hatred of Jesus in, 105–7, 111, 112, 114, 180; Daisenberger version, 103–13; film adaptation of, 124; and Hitler, 110; legend concerning, 102–3; and *The Passion and Resurrection of Christ*, 102; Stückl-Huber versions, 103, 113–22, 189, 199; transitional period, 103, 110–13; visual representation of Caiaphas at Oberammergau pre-2000, 188–89; visual representation of Caiaphas at Oberammergau 2010, 197–200; Weis version, 103. *See also* Passion plays

Pasolini, Pier Paolo. *See The Gospel According to Saint Matthew*
The Passion of the Christ (film), 124, 126, 128, 140–1, 191, 221n6; and spiritual memoirs of Anne Catherine Emmerich, 126
Passion plays, 9, 96, 100–123; and art of illumination, 218n23; banning of, 103; early, 101–2; influence of the Gospels on, 100, 101, 103, 104, 107, 109, 117, 119, 122; and Jesus films, 124, 125, 138, 139; Montecassino text, 101; origins of, 100–101; Saint Gall play, 101–2. *See also* Oberammergau Passion play
patristic literature. *See* church fathers
Pesch, Rudolph, 113
Peter: denial of Jesus, 2, 25, 29–30, 35, 37–38, 44–46, 57, 58, 147, 148
Pharisees, 40, 41, 43, 46, 50, 60, 61, 70, 74, 79, 81, 94, 119, 131, 141, 154, 155, 158, 161, 167, 176, 189, 191, 203. *See also* Eleazar; Gamaliel; Nicodemus
Philo, 93, 167, 171, 194–95
Piero della Francesca: *The Legend of the True Cross*, 191
Pietà (Michelangelo), 125
Pilate: and Caiaphas, 1, 2, 4, 9, 12–13, 22, 55, 58, 62, 76–78, 106, 115, 119, 120, 136, 139–40, 144, 151, 153, 154, 168–72, 199, 202, 204; death of, 64; in historiography, 151; Hitler

Pilate (*continued*)
on, 110; Jesus' trial before, 3, 25, 29, 31, 32–33, 35, 36, 38–40, 46, 50, 67, 109, 127, 133–41, 148, 165, 181; Latin inscription referring to Pilate as a prefect, 209–10n36; in literature, 76–78, 79, 81, 83, 85, 88, 90–91; opposition to Jesus, 52, 53, 63, 64; portrayed as a Goebbels-like figure, 117; on screen, 127, 129–30, 132, 133–42, 144, 221n6; on stage, 97, 98–100, 101, 102, 104–6, 107, 112, 113–14, 115, 116, 117–19, 120, 122, 199

plays. *See* mystery cycles; Oberammergau Passion play; Passion plays

Pseudo-Clementines, 69–72

Ray, Nicholas. *See The King of Kings* (1961 film)

Rossellini, Roberto. *See Il Messias*

Sadducees, 19, 47, 81, 92, 153, 154–55, 158, 163, 177, 189, 191, 203, 205, 209n30, 215n22. *See also* Annas; Annas II; Caiaphas

Saint Gall play, 101–2

Sallman, Warner, 125

The Salvin Hours, 184, 185 (image)

Satan, 43, 128, 136, 144, 157, 163, 188, 203, 204, 221n15

Saville, Philip. *See The Gospel of John*

Sayers, Dorothy. *See The Man Born to Be King*

Scorsese, Martin. *See Last Temptation of Christ* (film)

Small Passion (Dürer), 183

Solomon, 18, 64

Son of Man (film), 142

Stephen (trial and execution of), 18, 39, 48, 49, 80, 148, 178

Stevens, George. *See The Greatest Story Ever Told*

Stückl, Christian, 103, 113–22, 189, 199

tearing of garments: and Annas, 101; and anonymous high priest in Mark, 27, 30, 48; and Caiaphas, 3, 4, 21, 34, 38, 48, 133, 149, 176, 181, 183, 201; and regulations concerning high priests, 16; as symbolic act, 28

Testament (Ricci), 76

Theudas, 47, 168

Tiberius, 12, 13, 36, 54, 64, 66, 67, 107, 114, 115, 134, 138, 170

A Time for Judas (Callaghan), 76, 193

van Honthorst, Gerrit: *Christ before the High Priest*, 184–85, 186 (image), 192–93

Vitellius Germanicus, 12, 13, 14, 21, 168

White Crucifixion (Chagall), 93

Wilde, Oscar: *The Ballad of Reading Gaol*, 75

York cycle. *See under* mystery cycles

Young, Robert. *See Jesus* (television movie)

Zeffirelli, Franco. *See Jesus of Nazareth* (miniseries)

www.ingramcontent.com/pod-product-compliance
Lightning Source LLC
Chambersburg PA
CBHW051939290426
44110CB00015B/2040